JONATHAN EDWARDS

Jonathan Edwards
A PROFILE

EDITED BY
DAVID LEVIN

AMERICAN PROFILES

General Editor: Aïda DiPace Donald

American Century Series

HILL AND WANG : NEW YORK

Contents

His general manner of life
His dismission from Northampton, with the occasion
and circumstances of it
His mission to the Indians at Stockbridge, etc.
His being made President of New Jersey College;
his sickness and death

Contents

Contents

Introduction

Despite his vigorous leadership in one of the most powerful mass movements of the eighteenth century, biographers have consistently argued that "the real story of the life of Jonathan Edwards is to be found in the life of the mind." Edwards holds the attention of admirers and critics with the strength of his intellect and the intensity of his piety. Freethinking critics from Vernon L. Parrington to Peter Gay lament that this mind, which might have liberated men, worked instead to revive a cramping Calvinism. Perry Miller declares that Edwards surpassed Isaac Newton in divining the philosophical significance of atomic physics. Alan Heimert places Edwards' ideas among the chief influences on the American Revolution.

Scholar and poet, moreover, choose the same phenomena to suggest the intellectual and pious force of the man. Before he was twelve, they remind us, Edwards wrote a remarkable essay on the spiders he had observed about his father's Connecticut farm; and at Yale, in his early teens, he wrote his brilliant "Notes on the Mind," which reveal a profound comprehension of Locke's *Essay concerning Human Understanding*. To represent his piety scholars invariably cite one of the religious experiences of his youth that are recounted in his own "Personal Narrative":

The first instance that I remember of that sort of inward, sweet delight in God and divine things that I have lived much in since, was on reading those words, I Tim. 1. 17. *Now unto the King eternal, immortal, invisible, the only wise God, be honor and glory for ever and ever, Amen.* As I read the words, there came into my soul, and was as it were diffused through it, a sense of the glory of the Divine Being; a new sense, quite different from any thing I ever experienced before.

Jonathan Edwards would be a memorable historical figure if only because his religious experience typified the piety of revivalism, or if only because he achieved some of the best theological and philosophical exposition of his century. What makes him especially valuable is his consistent devotion to both rigorous thought and uncompromising piety. He stands before us as the exemplary Puritan, striving to think clearly in the world for the glory of God.

We must therefore recognize in Edwards not only the lad who, while reading Timothy and again later while walking in his father's pasture, was suddenly illuminated with "a divine and supernatural light" that gave him a new apprehension of all the things he perceived. We must also study the meticulous psychologist of religion who in his late thirties reconstructed these experiences in his "Personal Narrative." It is only through the narrative that we know Edwards' experiences of rapture, and in that context the boy's experiences are no more important than the man's precise observation and narrative. By lifting the boy's rapture out of the man's analytical narrative, we risk overlooking Edwards' conscientious effort to trace the distinguishing marks of a work of the Spirit of God.

For these reasons a modern biographical Profile will avoid the excesses of caricature if it takes some of its outlines from pious writers of the eighteenth century. The best descriptive commentary on Jonathan Edwards' religious experience is his own "Personal Narrative," and the best biographical account of his entire religious activity is the book by his disciple Samuel Hopkins, in which the "Personal Narrative" was first published a few years after Edwards' death. Hopkins takes care to distinguish the boy's experience from the man's narrative.

Hopkins' little biography has not been reprinted for more than a century, and it has never been reprinted without editorial improprieties that made substantive changes in both Edwards' and Hopkins' texts.[1] By presenting it to modern readers in a version that makes no changes except for normalizing spelling and capitalization, I hope to re-establish the best text of Edwards' famous narrative and also to suggest the value of considering piety in its own terms. Hopkins takes seriously Edwards' entire set of beliefs. He therefore gives us a chance to form a conception of the pious life without the mediation of a modern skeptic's explanatory comment, and according to the custom of early biographers he relies heavily on Edwards' own words. Readers should notice that the large space I have allotted to Hopkins in this Profile belongs almost equally to Edwards himself, for Hopkins gives Edwards' Resolutions, diary, and letters as much space as the "Personal Narrative."

In this representation we see Edwards' whole life under the rule of faith. From the time he wrote a solemn covenant a few months after his nineteenth birthday, he strove to dedicate all his effort to the service of God. His account of this action implies a control, a disciplined capacity to will, that seems to us far from the rapturous desire he has experienced at other times, far from the desire to be annihilated and swallowed up in Christ:

Saturday, Jan. 12 [1723]. in the morning. I have this day solemnly renewed my baptismal covenant and self-dedication, which I renewed when I was received into the covenant of the church. I have been before God; and have given myself, and all that I am and have to God, so that I am not in any respect my own: I can challenge no right in myself, I can challenge no right in this understanding, this will, these affections that are in me; neither have I any right to this body, or any of its members: no right to this tongue, these hands, nor feet: no right to these senses, these eyes, these ears, this smell or taste. I have given myself clear away, and have not retained any thing as my own. I have been to God this morning, and told Him that I gave myself *wholly* to Him. I have given every power to Him; so that for the future I will challenge

[1] I am indebted to Daniel B. Shea for pointing out the superiority of Hopkins' text of the "Personal Narrative"; so far as we know, all modern reprints of Edwards' narrative follow an incorrect nineteenth-century version. The chief differences are discussed briefly in Mr. Shea's excellent book *Spiritual Autobiography in Early America* (Princeton, 1968).

no right in myself, in any respect. I have expressly promised him, and do now promise almighty God, that by His grace I will not. I have this morning told Him, that I did take Him for my whole portion and felicity, looking on nothing else as any part of my happiness, nor acting as if it were; and His law for the constant rule of my obedience: and would fight with all my might against the world, the flesh, and the devil, to the end of my life. And did believe in Jesus Christ, and receive Him as a Prince and a Saviour; and would adhere to the faith and obedience of the gospel, how hazardous forever the profession and practice of it may be. That I did receive the blessed Spirit as my teacher, sanctifier, and only comforter; and cherish all His motions to enlighten, purify, confirm, comfort and assist me. This I have done. And I pray God, for the sake of Christ, to look upon it as a self-dedication; and to receive me now as entirely His own, and deal with me in all respects as such; whether He afflicts me or prospers me, or whatever He pleases to do with me, who am His. Now, henceforth I am not to act in any respect as my own.—I shall act as my own, if I ever make use of any of my powers to any thing that is not to the glory of God, and don't make the glorifying Him my whole and entire business; if I murmur in the least at affliction; if I grieve at the prosperity of others; if I am any way uncharitable; if I am angry because of injuries; if I revenge: if I do any thing, purely to please myself, or if I avoid any thing for the sake of my ease: if I omit any thing because it is great self-denial: if I trust to myself: if I take any of the praise of any of the good that I do, or rather God does by me; or if I am any way proud.

The written covenant had been a customary private act among Puritans for more than a century, and Edwards' mixture here of meditation with affirmation is also perfectly conventional. What seems remarkable in this document written by a young man soon after his nineteenth birthday is the degree of explanation, the insistence on enumerating the senses given over to divine command and on defining the many tempting ways of acting "as my own." Here Edwards follows both the advice and the practice of Cotton Mather, and with an intensity equaled by few eighteenth-century diarists besides Mather himself. Like Mather, moreover (though in a different tone), Edwards expresses two strongly paradoxical qualities. He casts his resolution of self-surrender in a language that asserts not only self-control but a very strong personality. The might of the character that will fight the world, the flesh, and the devil will also lead it sometimes to be proud.

By printing this critical passage from Edwards' diary, Hopkins thus gives us one of the best views we have of the Puritan mind. Here the Puritan mind achieves discipline, declares an exalted willingness to surrender the self to God, resolves to strive for His purposes, then begs that its devotion be certified as genuine, and at last warns itself of the kinds of action that will mark its devotion as counterfeit.

In Edwards' day as in Cotton Mather's, the Puritan could never be absolutely sure of his election. When Edwards looked back on these early days more than fifteen years later, he noted that his own experience had taught him a major lesson: that the more his sense of God's excellency increased, the more sensibly convinced he was of his own wickedness. Permanent self-doubt was built into the system. Just as selfish action made one question whether one had really submitted one's will to God's service, so a convicting awareness of one's selfishness was a sign justifying hope. And although strenuous action in the Lord's cause could not give anyone perfect assurance of his own salvation, it was a better sign than the selfish acts against which Edwards warned himself, and it left little time for them. Hopkins lets his biographical narrative and the less important quotations from Edwards show how Edwards' subsequent life was ruled by the early covenant I have quoted. Some of the Resolutions that Hopkins reprints have properly been compared to similar resolutions by Benjamin Franklin and Cotton Mather, whose *Bonifacius* (or *Essays to Do Good*) was surely one of young Edwards' models. What those Resolutions demand is a life saturated with pious effort, both in public and private action: study, worship, thoughts of parents and neighbors, family government, preaching, theological and philosophical dispute, pastoral duty in Northampton, leadership of the revival, writing on the psychology of conversion and the nature of true virtue.

Hopkins helps us to see, then, that the intellectual achievement for which we honor Edwards was an expression of his piety. He also helps us to see that the tragedy of Edwards' dismissal by the Northampton congregation after twenty-five years of service issues

from the same resolve foreshadowed in the renewal of the covenant that I have quoted. Serving the Lord, Edwards encourages the
religious revival of the 1730's and 1740's even though he is
troubled by its excesses, including the suicide of his despairing
uncle. Then, as the revival subsides, Edwards stands firm in his
role as teaching elder during a controversy over "lascivious and
obscene" reading among young boys in the congregation; by his
standards compromise on such matters is unthinkable, and he
provokes the resentment of many parishioners. When he tries a
few years later to re-establish serious tests of conversion as a
prerequisite to church membership, the congregation not only
votes for his dismissal, but also refuses to let him preach a group
of sermons explaining his theological reasons for insisting on the
tests! The greatest religious thinker of his day is silenced by
people who fear he might convince them. He teaches them any-
way, if only in his farewell sermon, and he warns them there that
their conduct and his own will be considered at the Judgment.

In all this activity the hellfire preacher who terrified the Enfield
community with the sermon that became known as *Sinners in the
Hands of an Angry God* seems not to be present. I have not meant
to hide him, but it is necessary to see him, as most scholars of the
last thirty years have come to see him, in the context that Samuel
Hopkins and Perry Miller have established. This Jonathan Edwards
is the man who had resolved in his youth "to endeavor to my
utmost to act as I can think I should do, if I had already seen the
happiness of heaven, and hell torments." Hellfire is not his characteristic mode of preaching, but to bring sinners to a sense of their
true danger he is willing to preach a sermon on the text "Their foot
shall slide in due time" and to fill every auditor with a sense of
heavy weight, pressing downward toward hell. You stand on a
rotten covering over hell, you tend downward with a great weight,
heavy as lead, he tells them in 1741, and the only thing that keeps
you from dropping into hell at this very moment is the merciful
hand of an angry God, who holds you up. Edwards hopes they
will act just as he had long ago hoped that he would act "if I had
already seen the happiness of heaven, and hell torments."

The strength of Edwards' intellect, and its significance in American history, have been more effectively studied in modern scholarship than in the writings of a Hopkins. Williston Walker, a liberal church historian of the early twentieth century, tries to set Edwards' thought in the history of Congregationalism; sympathetic but prevented by his liberal Christianity from sharing Hopkins' evaluation of Edwards' piety, Walker nonetheless presents a clear, brief exposition of Edwards' critique of free will and of Edwards' definition of virtue.

Walker also reminds us briefly that we must consider the tiny scale of Edwards' Northampton, with its population of only two hundred families, but I have relied on chapters from Henry Bamford Parkes and Ola Elizabeth Winslow to supplement Hopkins' biography with more modern accounts of Edwards' early life in Connecticut and Northampton. It is the nature of Edwards' religious experience, Parkes argues, that kept him from being tempted by deism and other freethinking. Ola Elizabeth Winslow deepens our sense of that experience by providing a clear description of the Edwards family—the father, the mother, and the sisters—in the years before Jonathan's conversion.

Perry Miller, John E. Smith, and James Carse represent here the intensive study that has been accorded Edwards' philosophical and religious ideas during the last thirty years. In different ways all three of these scholars treat Edwards as a historical figure whose ideas not only foreshadow modern attitudes but also speak intelligently about modern issues. In his chapter on "The Objective Good," Miller portrays the youth whose reflections on Newton and Locke propelled him into a new atomic world. There the very definition of the atom implies a power constantly exercised rather than a substance visually apprehended. Smith's exposition of Edwards' great *Religious Affections* commends us to a mind that refuses to oversimplify its hard-won observations of psychological reality. Carse, like Miller, insists on a modern portrait, but in the chapter reprinted here he gives generous space to the most terrifying "maledictions" in Edwards' sermons. He reads these as social criticism and as tributes to the crucial importance of the human will, and he places them beside Edwards' memoir of the saintly model, David Brainerd.

Peter Gay, though admiring and sympathetic, regards Edwards as a tragic figure not because he was the first modern American but largely because he was "the last medieval American—at least among the intellectuals." Concentrating on Edwards' projected history of the work of redemption, Gay has written one of the best briefs for the dissent in the argument over Edwards' modernity. His lucid essay stands here as representative of that dissent, other spokesmen for which are cited both in the Selected Bibliography below and in Gay's notes.

Perhaps the Edwards characterized in this Profile is too sweet to serve as a just representation of the historical actuality. Although his battle with his congregation expresses the political cost of the uncompromising toughness that Miller and Smith celebrate, to finish the portrait we ought to have some glimpse of the Edwards who rode joyfully into a polemical paragraph to demolish the enemies of truth:

So that, according to their [Arminian] notion of an act, considered with regard to its consequences, these following things are all essential to it, viz., that it should be necessary, and not necessary; that it should be from a cause, and no cause; that it should be the fruit of choice and design, and not the fruit of choice and design; that it should be the beginning of motion or exertion, and yet consequent on previous exertion; that it should be before it is; that it should spring immediately out of indifference and equilibrium, and yet be the effect of preponderation; that it should be self-originated, and also have its original from something else; that it is what the mind causes itself, of its own Will, and can produce or prevent, according to its choice or pleasure, and yet what the mind has no power to prevent, it precluding all previous choice in the affair.

So that an act, according to their metaphysical notion of it, is something of which there is no idea; it is nothing but a confusion of the mind, excited by words without any distinct meaning, and is an absolute nonentity, and that in two respects: (1), there is nothing in the world that ever was, is, or can be, to answer the things which must belong to its description, according to what they suppose to be essential to it; and (2) there neither is, nor ever was, nor can be, any notion or idea to answer the word, as they use and explain it. For if we should suppose any such notion, it would many ways destroy itself. . . .

The passion that could lead this mind to open new views of God's excellency and a new definition of true virtue could also exult in deadly combat. And in the power of such paragraphs one can see perhaps the best explanation of Edwards' strength in the revival pulpit. It is the sheer force of his cumulative argument, as much as the heat from incendiary images, that communicates emotion to auditor and reader. We feel the passionate strength of a pious mind, driving the intellect forward to the Lord's work. Some sense of a modern response to that strength is expressed through many of Edwards' own words in the poems by Robert Lowell that complete the Profile.

DAVID LEVIN

Stanford, California
May 1, 1968

Jonathan Edwards, 1703–1758

Jonathan Edwards was born on October 5, 1703, in East Windsor, Connecticut, the son, grandson, and great-grandson of Protestant ministers. Educated under his father's care, he entered Yale College in his early teens and was graduated in 1720. It was during these undergraduate years that he read John Locke's *Essay concerning Human Understanding* and wrote his own "Notes on the Mind," in which he stated principles that affected the rest of his intellectual and religious life. "That which truly is the substance of all bodies," he declared, *"is the infinitely exact, and precise, and perfectly stable idea, in God's mind, together with His stable will, that the same shall gradually be communicated to us, and to other minds, according to certain fixed and exact established methods and laws."*

Edwards continued to study at Yale, spent one winter as a minister in New York, returned to Yale as a tutor, and was called in 1726 to join his grandfather, Solomon Stoddard, as pastor of the congregation at Northampton, Massachusetts. Edwards married Sarah Pierpont in 1727. For the next twenty-five years he served this congregation in "the most enthusiastical town in New England." Even before the religious revivals that made him famous, he made some stir in Boston with a lecture published under the title *God Glorified in the Work of Redemption by the Greatness of Man's Dependence upon Him in the Whole of It*

(1731). But the chief pastoral work for which he is known came in two swelling revivals, the first in 1734 and the second—part of the Great Awakening—in 1740–1742. He not only preached and counseled in these religious upheavals but also wrote major works in defense of the revival. Aware of the excesses that accompanied these remarkable works of redemption, he was nonetheless determined to find ways of distinguishing false from true conversions, and these experiences led him to write some of his most important tracts and books: *A Faithful Narrative of the Surprising Work of God* (1737), *The Distinguishing Marks of a Work of the Spirit of God* (1741), "Personal Narrative" (published only after his death), *Some Thoughts concerning the Present Revival in New England,* and *A Treatise concerning Religious Affections* (1746).

In 1744 Edwards made a number of enemies in his own congregation by refusing to compromise his belief in church discipline when a group of young people were discovered reading and exchanging "lascivious and obscene" books. The bad feelings continued to develop over more complex issues in the next few years, and in 1750 he was dismissed by the congregation because he insisted on maintaining a new set of requirements for church membership. He had become convinced that his grandfather Stoddard had erred in admitting every professing Christian whose behavior was not openly scandalous; after years of following Stoddard's practice, Edwards now contended that a new rigor had to be exercised by the elders in evaluating professed conversions. The struggle was protracted and devious, but in the end a special committee of ministers from the area ruled against Edwards, and although one of these men later published a posthumous apology to Edwards (confessing animosity as a leading motive for his negative vote), the forty-eight-year-old minister was forced to leave Northampton.

In 1751 Edwards accepted a position at Stockbridge, Massachusetts, as missionary to the Housatonic Indians and as pastor for the local congregation. This isolated assignment freed him to write several of the major works of his life: *A Careful and Strict Enquiry into the Modern Prevailing Notions of that Freedom of the Will which is supposed to be Essential to Moral Agency,*

Vertue and Vice, Reward and Punishment, Praise and Blame (1754); "The Nature of True Virtue" and "Concerning the End for Which God Created the World" (written 1755; published in 1765 as *Two Dissertations*); and *The Great Christian Doctrine of Original Sin Defended* (1758).

In 1758, Edwards reluctantly agreed to accept the presidency of the new college at Princeton, New Jersey, but soon after his arrival there he died after being inoculated for smallpox.

D.L.

JONATHAN EDWARDS

✪

The Life and Character of the Late Reverend Mr. Jonathan Edwards

THE PREFACE

President Edwards, in the esteem of all the judicious, who were well acquainted with him, either personally, or by his writings, was one of the *greatest—best—*and *most useful* of men, that have lived in this age.

He discovered himself to be one of the *greatest of divines,* by his conversation, preaching and writings: One of remarkable strength of mind, clearness of thought, and depth of penetration, who well understood, and was able, above most others, to vindicate the great doctrines of Christianity.

And no one perhaps has been in our day, more universally esteemed and acknowledged to be a *bright Christian,* an eminently *good man.* His love to God and man; his zeal for God and his cause; his uprightness, humility, self-denial, and weanedness from the world; his close walk with God; his conscientious, constant and universal obedience, in all exact and holy ways of living: In one word, the goodness, the holiness of his heart, has been as evident and conspicuous, as the uncommon greatness and strength of his understanding.

And that this distinguished light has not shone in vain, there are a cloud of witnesses. God, who gave him his great talents, led him into a way of improving them, both by preaching and writing,

---

The Life and Character of the Late Reverend Mr. Jonathan Edwards was originally published in Boston in 1765.

which has doubtless proved the means of converting many from
the error of their ways; and of greatly promoting the interest of
Christ's church, both in *America* and *Europe*. And there is reason
to hope, that though he is now dead, he will yet speak for a great
while yet to come, to the great comfort and advantage of the
church of Christ; that his publications will produce a yet greater
harvest, as an addition to his joy and crown of rejoicing in the day
of the Lord.

But the design of the following memoirs, is not merely to
publish these things, and tell the world how eminently great, wise,
holy and useful President *Edwards* was; but rather to inform in
what way, and by what means he attained to such an uncommon
stock of knowledge and holiness; and how, in the improvement of
this, he did so much good to mankind; that others may hereby be
directed and excited to go and do likewise.

The reader is therefore not to expect a mere encomium on the
dead, but a faithful and plain narration of matters of fact, together
with his own internal exercises, expressed in his own words; and is
desired not to look on the following composure so much an act of
friendship to the *dead,* as of kindness to the *living;* it being only an
attempt to render a life that has been greatly useful, yet more so.
And as this is designed for the reader's good, he is desired to
remember, that if he gets no benefit hereby; is not made wiser nor
better, gains no skill or disposition to live a holy and useful life, all
is in vain as to him.

In this world, so full of darkness and delusion, it is of great
importance that all should be able to distinguish between true
religion and that which is false. In this, perhaps none has taken
more pains, or labored more successfully, than he whose life is set
before the reader. And it is presumed that his religious resolutions,
exercises and conduct here exhibited, will serve well to exemplify
and illustrate all that he has wrote on this subject. Here pure and
undefiled religion, in distinction from all counterfeits, appears in
life and practice, exhibiting a picture which will tend to instruct,
strengthen and comfort all those, who in their religious sentiments
and exercises, are built on the foundation of the apostles and
prophets, of which Jesus Christ is the chief cornerstone; while

their hearts and practice in some measure answer to it, as in water, face answereth to face. And here, they who have hitherto unhappily been in darkness and delusion, in this infinitely important affair, may have matter of instruction and conviction.

This is a point about which, above many other, the Protestant world is in the dark, and needs instruction, as Mr. *Edwards* was more and more convinced, the longer he lived; and which he was wont frequently to observe in conversation. If therefore these his remains are adapted to answer this end, and may be considered as a word behind all to whom they shall come, "saying, THIS IS THE WAY, walk ye in it," and shall in this view, be blessed to many, it will be a relief under one of the greatest calamities that attend the Christian world, and promote that important end, so worthy the attention and pursuit of all; and in which he from whom this mantle falls, was zealously engaged, and which he pursued to the end of his life.

In this view especially, is the following life offered to the public, with an earnest desire that every reader may faithfully improve it to this purpose; while he candidly overlooks any improprieties and defects which he may observe to be chargeable on the compiler; who is he knows, in a great degree unequal to what is here attempted.

August 20, 1764

PART I *Containing the* HISTORY *of his* LIFE, *from his* BIRTH, *to his* SETTLEMENT *in the Work of the* MINISTRY

Mr. Jonathan Edwards was born October 5, 1703, at Windsor, a town in Connecticut. His father was the Reverend Mr. Timothy Edwards, minister of the gospel on the east side of Connecticut River in Windsor. He began to reside and preach at Windsor in November, 1694, but was not ordained till July, 1698. He died January 27, 1758, in the eighty-ninth year of his age, not two months before this his son. He was in the work of the ministry above fifty-nine years: and from his first beginning to reside and preach there, to his death, are above sixty-three years; and was able to attend on the work of the ministry and preach constantly till within a few years before his death. He was very universally esteemed and beloved as an upright, pious, exemplary man, and faithful minister of the gospel; and was greatly useful. He was born at Hartford in Connecticut, May 14, 1669, received the honors of the college at Cambridge in New England, by having the degrees of Bachelor and Master of Arts given him the same day, July 4, 1694, one in the forenoon, and the other in the afternoon.

On the sixth day of November, 1694, he was married to Mrs. Esther Stoddard, in the twenty-third year of her age, the daughter of the late famous Mr. Solomon Stoddard of Northampton; whose great parts and zeal for experimental religion are well known in all the churches in America; and will probably be transmitted to posterity yet unborn, by his valuable writings. They lived together in the married state above sixty-three years. Mrs. Edwards was born June 2, 1672, and is now living in her eighty-ninth year, remarkable for the little decay of her mental powers at so great an age.

They had eleven children: all which lived to adult years, viz. ten daughters, seven of whom are now living, and this their only son and fifth child.[1]

---

[1] *As the following more large and particular account, of Mr.* Edwards's *ancestors may gratify some readers, 'tis inserted here in the margin.*

Mr. Edwards's grandfather was Mr. Richard Edwards. His first wife was Mrs. Elisabeth Tuttle, daughter of Mr. William Tuttle of New Haven in Connecticut, and Mrs. Elisabeth Tuttle his wife, who came out of Northamptonshire in England. His second wife was Mrs. Talcot, sister to Governor Talcot: by his first wife he had seven children, the oldest of which was the Reverend Mr. Timothy Edwards of Windsor, his father, before mentioned. By his second wife, Mrs. Talcot, he had six children.

The father of Mr. Richard Edwards was Mr. William Edwards, who came from England young and unmarried. His wife, Mrs. Agnes Edwards, who also came out of England, had two brothers in England, one of them Mayor of Exeter, and the other of Barnstable. Mr. William Edwards's father was the Reverend Mr. Richard Edwards, minister of the gospel in London. He lived in Queen Elisabeth's day, and his wife, Mrs. Anne Edwards, assisted in making a ruff for the Queen. After the death of Mr. Edwards she married to one Mr. James Cole. She, with her second husband and her son William Edwards, came into America, and all died at Hartford in Connecticut.

Mr. Edwards's grandfather (Mr. Solomon Stoddard, and his predecessor at Northampton) married Mrs. Mather, the relict of the Reverend Mr.

Mr. Edwards entered Yale College in the year 1716, and received the degree of Bachelor of Arts in September, 1720, a little before he was seventeen years old. He had the character of a sober youth, and a good scholar while he was a member of the college. In his second year at college, and thirteenth of his age, he read Locke on the human understanding, with great delight and profit. His uncommon genius, by which he was, as it were by nature, formed for closeness of thought and deep penetration, now began to exercise and discover itself. Taking that book into his hand, upon some occasion, not long before his death, he said to some of his select friends, who were then with him, that he was beyond expression entertained and pleased with it, when he read it in his youth at college; that he was as much engaged, and had more

---

Mather his predecessor, and the first minister at Northampton. Her maiden name was Esther Warham, daughter and youngest child of the Reverend Mr. John Warham, minister at Windsor in Connecticut, who came out of England, before which he was minister in Exeter in England: he had four children, all daughters; and Mrs. Warham survived him, and had two daughters by Mr. Newbury, her second husband.

Mrs. Esther Warham had three children by Mr. Mather, viz. Eunice, Warham, and Eliakim. And she had twelve children by Mr. Stoddard, six sons and six daughters: three of the sons died in infancy. The three that lived to adult years were Anthony, John, and Israel. Israel died in prison in France. Anthony was the Reverend Mr. Anthony Stoddard, late minister of the gospel at Woodbury in Connecticut, who lived to a great age, and was in the work of the ministry sixty years: he died September 6, 1760, in the eighty-second year of his age. John was the Honorable John Stoddard, Esq. who lived at Northampton, and who often, especially in his younger years, served the town as their representative at the great and general court in Boston; and was long head of the county of Hampshire as their chief colonel, and chief judge of the court of common pleas: and he long served his Majesty, and the province of the Massachusetts Bay, as one of His Majesty's council. He was remarkable as a politician, and for his spirit of government; a wise counsellor, an upright and skillful judge, a steady and great friend to the interest of religion. He was a great friend and admirer of Mr. Edwards, and greatly strengthened his hands in the work of the ministry while he lived. A more particular account of the life and character of this truly great man may be seen in the sermon which Mr. Edwards preached and published on the occasion of his death.

Mr. Stoddard's father was Anthony Stoddard, Esq. of Boston, a zealous congregational man. He had five wives, the first of which, Mr. Stoddard's mother, was Mrs. Mary Downing, sister to Sir George Downing, whose other sister married Governor Bradstreet. Mr. Solomon Stoddard was their oldest child.

satisfaction and pleasure in studying it, than the most greedy miser in gathering up handfuls of silver and gold from some new discovered treasure.

Though he made good proficiency in all the arts and sciences, and had an uncommon taste for Natural Philosophy, which he cultivated to the end of his life, with that justness and accuracy of thought which was almost peculiar to him; yet Moral Philosophy or Divinity was his favorite study. In this he early made great progress.

He lived at college near two years after he took his first degree, designing and preparing for the work of the ministry. After which, having passed the prerequisite trials, he was licensed to preach the gospel as a candidate. And being pitched upon, and applied to by a number of ministers in New England, who were instructed to act in behalf of the English Presbyterians at New York, as a fit person to be sent to them, he complied with their request, and went to New York the beginning of August, 1722; and preached there to very good acceptance about eight months. But by reason of the smallness of that society, and some special difficulties that attended it, he did not think they were in a capacity to settle a minister, with a rational prospect of answering the good ends proposed. He therefore left them, the next spring, and retired to his father's house; where he spent the summer in close study. He was indeed earnestly solicited by the people he had been among at New York to return to them again; but for the reason just mentioned, he could not think himself in the way of his duty to gratify them.

In September, 1723, he received his degree of Master of Arts; about which time he had invitations from several congregations to come among them in order to his settlement in the work of the ministry; but being chosen tutor of Yale College the next spring, in the year 1724, being in the twenty-first year of his age, he retired to the college, and attended the business of tutor there above two years.

While he was in this place he was applied to by the people at Northampton, with an invitation to come and settle in the work of the ministry there, with his grandfather Stoddard, who, by reason of his great age, stood in need of assistance. He therefore resigned his tutorship, in September, 1726, and accepted of their invitation; and was ordained in the work of the ministry at Northampton, colleague with his grandfather Stoddard, February 15, 1727, in the twenty-fourth year of his age, where he continued in the work of the ministry till June 22, 1750, twenty-three years and four months.

Between the time of his going to New York and his settlement at Northampton, he formed a number of resolutions, and committed them to writing: the particular time, and special occasion of his making many of them, he has noted in his Diary which he then kept; as well as many other observations and rules, which related to his own exercises and conduct. And as these resolutions, together with the things noted in his Diary, may justly be considered as the foundation and plan of his whole life, it may be proper here to give the reader a taste and idea of them: which will therefore be done in the following extracts.

PART II   *Containing* EXTRACTS *from his* PRIVATE WRITINGS, *etc.*

Section I   HIS RESOLUTIONS

Being sensible that I am unable to do any thing without God's help, I do humbly intreat Him by His grace to enable me to keep these resolutions, so far as they are agreeable to His will, for Christ's sake.

Remember to read over these resolutions once
a week.

1. Resolved, That I will do whatsoever I think to be most to God's glory, and my own good, profit and pleasure, in the whole of my duration, without any consideration of the time, whether now, or never so many myriads of ages hence. Resolved to do whatever I think to be my duty, and most for the good and advantage of mankind in general. Resolved to do this, whatever difficulties I meet with, how many and how great soever.

2. Resolved, To be continually endeavoring to find out some

new invention and contrivance to promote the fore-mentioned things.

4. Resolved, Never to do any manner of thing, whether in soul or body, less or more, but what tends to the glory of God; nor be, nor suffer it, if I can avoid it.

5. Resolved, Never to lose one moment of time; but improve it the most profitable way I possibly can.

6. Resolved, To live with all my might, while I do live.

7. Resolved, Never to do any thing, which I should be afraid to do, if it were the last hour of my life.

9. Resolved, To think much on all occasions of my own dying, and of the common circumstances which attend death.

11. Resolved, When I think of any theorem in divinity to be solved, immediately to do what I can towards solving it, if circumstances do not hinder.

13. Resolved, To be endeavoring to find out fit objects of charity and liberality.

14. Resolved, Never to do any thing out of revenge.

15. Resolved, Never to suffer the least motions of anger to irrational beings.

17. Resolved, That I will live so as I shall wish I had done when I come to die.

18. Resolved, To live so at all times, as I think is best in my devout frames, and when I have clearest notions of things of the gospel, and another world.

20. Resolved, To maintain the strictest temperance in eating and drinking.

21. Resolved, Never to do any thing, which if I should see in another, I should count a just occasion to despise him for, or to think any way the more meanly of him.

24. Resolved, Whenever I do any conspicuously evil action, to trace it back, till I come to the original cause; and then both carefully endeavor to do so no more, and to fight and pray with all my might against the original of it.

28. Resolved, To study the Scriptures so steadily, constantly and frequently, as that I may find, and plainly perceive myself to grow in the knowledge of the same.

30. Resolved, To strive to my utmost every week to be brought

higher in religion, and to a higher exercise of grace, than I was the week before.

32. Resolved, To be strictly and firmly faithful to my trust, that that in Prov. xx. 6. *a faithful man who can find?* may not be partly fulfilled in me.

33. Resolved, Always to do what I can towards making, maintaining and establishing peace, when it can be without overbalancing detriment in other respects.

34. Resolved, In narrations never to speak any thing but the pure and simple verity.

36. Resolved, Never to speak evil of any, except I have some particular good call for it.

37. Resolved, To inquire every night, as I am going to bed, wherein I have been negligent, what sin I have committed, and wherein I have denied myself: also at the end of every week, month and year.

38. Resolved, Never to speak any thing that is ridiculous, or matter of laughter on the Lord's day.

39. Resolved, Never to do any thing that I so much question the lawfulness of, as that I intend, at the same time, to consider and examine afterwards, whether it be lawful or no: except I as much question the lawfulness of the omission.

41. Resolved, To ask myself at the end of every day, week, month and year, wherein I could possibly in any respect have done better.

42. Resolved, Frequently to renew the dedication of myself to God, which was made at my baptism; which I solemnly renewed, when I was received into the communion of the church; and which I have solemnly re-made this twelfth day of January, 1722–3.

43. Resolved, Never hence-forward, till I die, to act as if I were any way my own, but entirely and altogether God's, agreeable to what is to be found in Saturday, January 12.

46. Resolved, Never to allow the least measure of any fretting uneasiness at my father or mother. Resolved to suffer no effects of it, so much as in the least alteration of speech, or motion of my eye: and to be especially careful of it, with respect to any of our family.

47. Resolved, To endeavor to my utmost to deny whatever is

not most agreeable to a good, and universally sweet and benevolent, quiet, peaceable, contented, easy, compassionate, generous, humble, meek, modest, submissive, obliging, diligent and industrious, charitable, even, patient, moderate, forgiving, sincere temper; and to do at all times what such a temper would lead me to. Examine strictly every week, whether I have done so.

48. Resolved, Constantly, with the utmost niceness and diligence, and the strictest scrutiny, to be looking into the state of my soul, that I may know whether I have truly an interest in Christ or no; that when I come to die, I may not have any negligence respecting this to repent of.

50. Resolved, I will act so as I think I shall judge would have been best, and most prudent, when I come into the future world.

52. I frequently hear persons in old age say how they would live, if they were to live their lives over again: Resolved, that I will live just so as I can think I shall wish I had done, supposing I live to old age.

54. Whenever I hear anything spoken in conversation of any person, if I think it would be praise-worthy in me, Resolved to endeavor to imitate it.

55. Resolved, To endeavor to my utmost to act as I can think I should do, if I had already seen the happiness of heaven, and hell torments.

56. Resolved, Never to give over, nor in the least to slacken my fight with my corruptions, however unsuccessful I may be.

57. Resolved, When I fear misfortunes and adversities, to examine whether I have done my duty, and resolve to do it; and let it be just as Providence orders it, I will as far as I can, be concerned about nothing but my duty and my sin.

62. Resolved, Never to do any thing but duty; and then according to Eph. vi. 6, 7, 8. do it willingly and cheerfully as unto the Lord, and not to man; knowing that whatever good thing any man doth, the same shall he receive of the Lord.

65. Resolved, Very much to exercise myself in this all my life long, viz. with the greatest openness I am capable of, to declare my ways to God, and lay open my soul to him: all my sins, temptations, difficulties, sorrows, fears, hopes, desires, and every thing,

and every circumstance, according to Dr. Manton's twenty-seventh sermon on the 119th Psalm.

67. Resolved, After afflictions, to inquire, what I am the better for them, what good I have got by them, and what I might have got by them.[2]

Section II EXTRACTS FROM HIS PRIVATE DIARY

Saturday, Dec. 22, 1722. This day revived by God's Spirit. Affected with the sense of the excellency of holiness. Felt more exercise of love to Christ than usual. Have also felt sensible repentance of sin, because it was committed against so merciful and good a God. This night made the thirty-seventh Resolution.

Sabbath-Day Night, Dec. 23. Made the thirty-eighth Resolution.

Monday, Dec. 24. Higher thoughts than usual of the excellency of Jesus Christ and His kingdom.

Wednesday, Jan. 2, 1722–3. Dull. I find by experience, that let me make resolutions, and do what I will, with never so many inventions, it is all nothing, and to no purpose at all, without the motions of the Spirit of God: for if the Spirit of God should be as much withdrawn from me always, as for the week past, notwithstanding all I do, I should not grow; but should languish, and miserably fade away.—There is no dependence upon myself. It is to no purpose to resolve, except we depend on the grace of God; for if it were not for His mere grace, one might be a very good man one day, and a very wicked one the next.

Sabbath-Day, Jan. 6. at night. Much concerned about the improvement of precious time. Intend to live in continual mortification, without ceasing, as long as in this world.

Tuesday, Jan. 8. in the morning. Higher thoughts than usual, of the excellency of Christ, and felt an unusual repentance of sin therefrom.

Wednesday, Jan. 9. at night. Decayed. I am sometimes apt to

[2] The Resolutions are seventy in number. But part of them are here transcribed, as a specimen of the whole. The number here affixed to them, is that by which they are numbered in the original manuscript; and retained here for the sake of the references made to some of them in the Diary, as the reader will presently see.

think, I have a great deal more of holiness than I have. I find now and then, that abominable corruption which is directly contrary to what I read of eminent Christians.—How deceitful is my heart! I take up a strong resolution, but how soon does it weaken!

Thursday, Jan. 10. about noon. Reviving. 'Tis a great dishonor to Christ, in whom I hope I have an interest, to be uneasy at my worldly state and condition. When I see the prosperity of others, and that all things go easy with them; the world is smooth to them, and they are happy in many respects, and very prosperous, or are advanced to much honor etc. to grudge and envy them, or be the least uneasy at it; to wish or long for the same prosperity, and that it would ever be so with me. Wherefore concluded always to rejoice in every one's prosperity, and to expect for myself no happiness of that nature as long as I live; but depend upon afflictions, and betake myself entirely to another happiness.

I think I find myself much more sprightly and healthy, both in body and mind, for my self-denial in eating, drinking and sleeping.

I think it would be advantageous every morning to consider my business and temptations; and what sins I shall be exposed to that day: and to make a resolution how to improve the day, and to avoid those sins. And so at the beginning of every week, month and year.

I never knew before what was meant by not setting our hearts upon these things. 'Tis, not to care about them, to depend upon them, to afflict ourselves much with fears of losing them, nor please ourselves with expectation of obtaining them, or hope of the continuance of them. At night made the forty-first Resolution.

Saturday, Jan. 12. in the morning. I have this day solemnly renewed my baptismal covenant and self-dedication, which I renewed when I was received into the communion of the church. I have been before God; and have given myself, all that I am and have to God, so that I am not in any respect my own: I can challenge no right in myself, I can challenge no right in this understanding, this will, these affections that are in me; neither have I any right to this body, or any of its members: no right to this tongue, these hands, nor feet: no right to these senses, these eyes, these ears, this smell or taste. I have given myself clear away, and have not retained any thing as my own. I have been to God this morning, and told Him that I gave myself *wholly* to Him. I have given every power to Him; so that for the future I will challenge no right in myself, in any respect. I have expressly promised Him, and do now promise Almighty God, that by His grace I will not. I have this morning told Him, that I did take Him for my whole portion and felicity, looking on nothing else as any part of my happiness, nor acting as if it were; and His law for the constant rule of my obedience: and would fight with all my might against the world, the flesh and the devil, to the end of my life. And did believe in Jesus Christ, and receive Him as a Prince and a Saviour; and would adhere to the faith and obedience of the gospel, how hazardous and difficult soever the profession and practice of it may be. That I did receive the blessed Spirit as my teacher, sanctifier and only comforter; and cherish all his motions to enlighten, purify, confirm, comfort and assist me. This I have done. And I pray God, for the sake of Christ, to look upon it as a self-dedication; and to receive me now as entirely His own, and deal with me in all respects as such; whether He afflicts me or prospers me, or whatever He pleases to do with me, who am His. Now, henceforth I am not to act in any respect as my own.—I shall act as my own, if I ever make use of any of my powers to any thing that is not to the glory of God, and don't make the glorifying Him my whole and entire business; if I murmur in the least at afflictions; if I grieve at the prosperity of others; if I am any way uncharitable; if I am angry because of injuries; if I revenge: if I do anything, purely to please myself, or if I avoid any thing for the sake of my ease: if I omit any thing because it is great self-denial: if I trust to myself: if I take any of the praise of any good that I do, or rather God does by me; or if I am any way proud.

This day made the forty-second and forty-third Resolutions.

Monday, Jan. 14.—The dedication I made of myself to my God, on Saturday last, has been exceeding useful to me. I thought I had a more spiritual insight into the Scripture, reading the eighth chapter to the Romans, than ever in my life before.

Great instances of mortification are deep wounds given to the body of sin, hard blows that make him stagger and reel: we thereby get great ground and footing against him.—While we live without great instances of mortification and self-denial, the old man keeps whereabouts he was; for he is sturdy and obstinate, and will not stir for small blows. After the greatest mortifications, I always find the greatest comfort.

Supposing there was never but one complete Christian, in all respects of a right stamp, having Christianity shining in its true luster, at a time in the world; resolved to act just as I would do, if I strove with all my might to be that one, that should be in my time.

Tuesday, Jan. 15. It seemed yesterday, the day before and Saturday, that I should always retain the same resolutions to the same height; but alas, how soon do I decay! O, how weak, how infirm, how unable to do any thing am I! What a poor, inconsistent, what a miserable wretch, without the assistance of God's Spirit! While I stand, I am ready to think I stand in my own strength, and upon my own legs; and I am ready to triumph over my enemies, as if it were I myself that caused them to flee: when alas! I am but a poor infant, upheld by Jesus Christ; who holds me up, and gives me liberty to smile to see my enemies flee, when He drives them before me; and so I laugh, as though I myself did it, when it is only Jesus Christ leads me along, and fights Himself against my enemies. And now the Lord has a little left me, and how weak do I find myself! O, let it teach me to depend less on myself, to be more humble, and to give more of the praise of my ability to Jesus Christ. The heart of man is deceitful above all things, and desperately wicked, who can know it?

Saturday, Feb. 16. I do certainly know that I love holiness, such as the gospel requires.

At night. I have been negligent for the month past in these three things; I have not been watchful enough over my appetite in eating and drinking; in rising too late a-mornings; and in not applying myself with application enough to the duty of secret prayer.

Sabbath-Day, Feb. 17. near sun-set. Renewedly promised, that I will accept of God, for my whole portion; and that I will be contented, whatever else I am denied. I will not murmur, nor be grieved, whatever prosperity, upon any account, I see others enjoy, and I am denied.

Saturday, March 2.—O, how much pleasanter is humility than pride! O, that God would fill me with exceeding great humility, and that he would evermore keep me from all pride! The pleasures of humility are really the most refined, inward and exquisite delights in the world. How hateful is a proud man! How hateful is a worm that lifts up itself with pride! What a foolish, silly, miserable, blind, deceived, poor worm am I, when pride works!

Wednesday, March 6. near sun-set. Felt the doctrines of election, free grace, and of our not being able to do any thing without the grace of God; and that holiness is entirely, throughout, the work of God's Spirit, with more pleasure than before.

Monday Morning, April 1. I think it best not to allow myself to laugh at the faults, follies and infirmities of others.

Saturday Night, April 6.* This week I found myself so far gone, that it seemed to me, that I should never recover more. Let God of His mercy return unto me, and no more leave me thus to sink and decay! I know, O Lord, that without Thy help, I shall fall innumerable times, notwithstanding all my resolutions, how often soever repeated.

Saturday Night, April 13.† I could pray more heartily this night, for the forgiveness of my enemies, than ever before.

Wednesday, May 1. forenoon. Last night I came home, after my melancholy parting from New York.

I have always, in every different state of life, I have hitherto been in, thought the troubles and difficulties of that state, to be greater than those of any other that I proposed to be in; and when I have altered with assurance of mending myself, I have still thought the same; yea, that the difficulties of that state, are greater than those of that I left last. Lord, grant that from hence I may learn to withdraw my thoughts, affections, desires and expectations, entirely from the world, and may fix them upon the heavenly state; where there is fulness of joy; where reigns heavenly, sweet, calm and delightful love without alloy; where there are continually the dearest expressions of this love: where there is the enjoyment of the persons loved, without ever parting: where those persons, who appear so lovely in this world, will really be inexpressibly

* Edwards miscalculated these dates as April 7 and 14, respectively [ed.].
† Northampton.

more lovely, and full of love to us. How sweetly will the mutual lovers join together to sing the praises of God and the Lamb! How full will it fill us with joy to think, this enjoyment, these sweet exercises, will never cease or come to an end, but will last to all eternity.

Remember, after journeys, removes, overturnings, and alterations in the state of my life, to reflect and consider, whether therein I have managed the best way possible, respecting my soul? and before such alterations, if foreseen, to resolve how to act.

Thursday, May 2.—I think it a very good way to examine dreams every morning when I awake, what are the nature, circumstances, principles and ends of my imaginary actions and passions in them, to discern what are my chief inclinations etc.

Saturday Night, May 4. Although I have in some measure subdued a disposition to chide and fret, yet I find a certain inclination, which is not agreeable to Christian sweetness of temper and conversation: either by too much dogmaticalness, too much of the egoism; a disposition to be telling of my own dislike and scorn; and freedom from those that are innocent, yea common infirmities of men; and many other such like things. O that God would help me to discern all the flaws and defects of my temper and conversation, and help me in the difficult work of amending them: and that he would fill me so full of Christianity, that the foundation of all these disagreeable irregularities may be destroyed, and the contrary sweetnesses and beauties may of themselves naturally follow.

Sabbath-Day, May 5. in the morning. This day made the forty-seventh Resolution.

Sabbath-Day, May 12. I think I find in my heart to be glad from the hopes I have that my eternity is to be spent in spiritual and holy joys, arising from the manifestation of God's love, and the exercise of holiness and a burning love to him.

Saturday Night, May 18. I now plainly perceive what great obligations I am under to love and honor my parents. I have great reason to believe, that their counsel and education have been my making; notwithstanding, in the time of it, it seemed to do me so little good. I have good reason to hope that their prayers for me, have been in many things very powerful and prevalent; that God has in many things, taken me under his care and guidance, provision and direction, in answer to their prayers for me. I was never made so sensible of it as now.

Wednesday, May 22. in the morning. *Memorandum.* To take special care of these following things; evil speaking, fretting, eating, drinking and sleeping, speaking simple verity, joining in prayer, slightiness in secret prayer, listlessness and negligence and thoughts that cherish sin.

Saturday, May 25. in the morning. As I was this morning reading the seventeenth Resolution, it was suggested to me, that if I was now to die, I should wish that I had prayed more that God would make me know my state, whether it be good or bad; and that I had taken more pains to see and narrowly search into this matter. Wherefore, *Mem.* For the future most nicely and diligently to look into our old divines' opinions concerning conversion. Made the forty-eighth Resolution.

Friday, June 1. Afternoon. I have abundant cause, O my merciful Father, to love Thee ardently, and greatly to bless and praise Thee, that Thou hast heard me in my earnest request, and hath so answered my prayer for mercy to keep from decay and sinking. O, graciously, of Thy mere goodness, still continue to pity my misery, by reason of my sinfulness. O my dear Redeemer, I commit myself, together with my prayer and thanksgiving into Thine hand.

Monday. July 1. Again confirmed by experience of the happy effects of strict temperance, with respect both to body and mind. Resolved for the future to observe rather more of meekness, moderation and temper in disputes.

Thursday, July 18. near sun-set. Resolved to endeavor to make sure of that sign the Apostle James gives of a perfect man, Jam. iii. 2. *If any man offend not in word, the same is a perfect man, and able also to bridle the whole body.*

Monday, July 22. I see there is danger of my being drawn into transgression by the power of such temptations as a fear of seeming uncivil, and of offending friends. Watch against it.

Tuesday, July 23. When I find those groanings which cannot be uttered, the Apostle speaks of; and those soul-breakings, for the longing it hath, the Psalmist speaks of, Psal. cxix. 20. to humor and promote them to the utmost of my power, and be not weary of earnestly endeavoring to vent my desires.

To count it all joy when I have occasion of great self-denial, because then I have a glorious opportunity of giving deadly wounds to the body of sin, and greatly confirming and establishing the new nature: to seek to mortify sin, and increase in holiness: these are the best opportunities, according to *January 14*.

To improve afflictions of all kinds as blessed opportunities of forcibly bearing on in my Christian course, notwithstanding that which is so very apt to discourage me, and to damp the vigor of my mind, and to make me lifeless: also as opportunities of trusting and confiding in God, and getting a habit of that, according to the fifty-seventh Resolution. And as an opportunity of rending my heart off from the world, and setting it upon heaven alone. To improve them as opportunities to repent of, and bewail my sin, and abhor myself. And as a blessed opportunity to exercise patience; to trust in God, and divert my mind from the affliction, by fixing myself in religious exercises. Also, let me comfort myself, that it is the very nature of afflictions to make the heart better; and if I am made better by them, what need I be concerned, however grievous they seem for the present?

Friday Afternoon, July 26. To be particularly careful to keep up inviolable, a trust and reliance, ease and entire rest in God in all conditions, according to fifty-seventh Resolution; for this I have found to be wonderfully advantageous to me.

Monday, July 29. When I am concerned how I shall perform any thing to public acceptance, to be very careful that I have it very clear to me, that I do what is duty and prudence in the matter.

Wednesday, July 31.—Never in the least to seek to hear sarcastical relations of others' faults. Never to give credit to any thing said against others, except there is very plain reason for it; nor to behave in any respect the otherwise for it.

Wednesday, Aug. 7. To esteem as some advantage, that the duties of religion are difficult, and that many difficulties are sometimes to be gone through in the way of duty. Religion is the sweeter, and what is gained by labor, is abundantly more precious: as a woman loves her child the better for having brought it forth with travail. And even to Christ Jesus Himself, His mediatorial glory, His victory and triumph, His kingdom which He hath obtained; how much more glorious is it, how much more excellent and precious, for His having wrought it out by such agonies!

Friday, Aug. 9.—One thing that may be a good help towards thinking profitably in time of vacation is, when I light on a profitable thought, that I can fix my mind on, to follow it as far as possibly I can to advantage.

Sabbath-Day, after meeting, *Aug. 11.* Resolved always to do that which I shall wish I had done when I see others do it. As for instance, sometimes I argue with myself, that such an act of good nature, kindness, forbearance, or forgiveness, etc. is not my duty, because it will have such and such consequences: yet, when I see others do it, then it appears amiable to me, and I wish I had done it; and I see that none of those feared inconveniences follow.

Tuesday, Aug. 13. I find it would be very much to advantage, to be thoroughly acquainted with the Scriptures. When I am reading doctrinal books or books of controversy, I can proceed with abundantly more confidence; can see upon what footing and foundation I stand.

Thursday, Aug. 29.—The objection my corruptions make against doing whatever my hand finds to do with my might is, that it is a constant mortification. Let this objection by no means ever prevail.

Monday, Sept. 2.—There is much folly, when I am quite sure I am in the right, and others are positive in contradicting me, to enter into a vehement or long debate upon it.

Monday, Sept. 23. I observe that old men seldom have any advantage of new discoveries; because they are beside a way of thinking, they have been so long used to. Resolved, if ever I live to years, that I will be impartial to hear the reasons of all pretended discoveries, and receive them, if rational, how long soever I have been used to another way of thinking.

Thursday, Oct. 18. To follow the example of Mr. *B——* who, though he meets with great difficulties, yet undertakes them with a smiling countenance, as though he thought them but little; and speaks of them as if they were very small.

Thursday, Nov. 26. 'Tis a most evil and pernicious practice in meditations on afflictions, to sit ruminating on the aggravations of the affliction, and reckoning up the evil, dark circumstances thereof, and dwelling long on the dark side; it doubles and trebles the affliction. And so when speaking of them to others, to make them as bad as we can, and use our eloquence to set forth our own troubles, and are all the while making new trouble, and feeding and pampering the old; whereas the contrary practice would starve our afflictions. If we dwelt on the light side of things in our thoughts, and extenuated them all that possibly we could, when speaking of them, we should think little of them ourselves; and the affliction would really, in a great measure, vanish away.

Thursday Night, Dec. 12. If at any time I am forced to tell others of that wherein I think they are something to blame; for the avoiding the important evil, that would otherwise ensue, not to tell it to them, so that there shall be a probability of their taking it as the effect of little, fretting, angry emotions of mind.

Dec. 31. at night. Concluded never to suffer nor express any angry emotions of mind more or less, except the honor of God calls for it, in zeal for Him, or to preserve myself from being trampled on.

Wednesday, Jan. 1, 1723–4. Not to spend too much time in thinking even of important and necessary worldly business. To allow everything its proportion of thought, according to its urgency and importance.

Friday, Jan. 10. [After having wrote considerable in a short-hand, which he used when he would have what he wrote, effectually concealed from everybody but himself, he notes the following words in round hand], remember to act according to Prov. xii. 23, "A prudent man concealeth knowledge."

Monday, Feb. 3. Let everything have the value now, that it will have on a sick-bed: and frequently in my pursuits of whatever kind, let this come into my mind: "how much shall I value this on my death-bed?"

Wednesday, Feb. 5. Have not in time past in my prayers, enough insisted upon the glorifying God in the world, and the advancement of the kingdom of Christ, the prosperity of the church and the good of men. Determined that this objection is without weight, viz. That 'tis not likely that God will make great alterations in the whole world, and overturnings in kingdoms and nations, only for the prayers of one obscure person, seeing such things used to be done in answer to the united, earnest prayers of the whole church: and if my prayers should have some influence, it would be but imperceptible and small.

Thursday, Feb. 6. More convinced than ever of the usefulness of a free religious conversation. I find by conversing on natural philosophy, I gain knowledge abundantly faster, and see the reasons of things much clearer, than in private study. Wherefore earnestly to seek at all times for religious conversation; for those that I can with profit and delight and freedom so converse with.

Sabbath-Day, Feb. 23.—If I act according to my resolution, I shall desire riches no otherwise than as they are helpful to religion. But this I determine, as what is really evident from many parts of Scripture, that to fallen man they have a greater tendency to hurt religion.

Saturday, May 23. How it comes about I know not; but I have remarked it hitherto, that at those times when I have read the Scripture most, I have evermore been most lively, and in the best frames.

Saturday Night, June 6. This week has been a remarkable week with me with respect to despondencies, fears, perplexities, multitudes of cares and distraction of mind; being the week I came hither to New Haven, in order to entrance upon the office of Tutor of the College. I have now abundant reason to be convinced of the troublesomeness and vexation of the world, and that it never will be another kind of world.

Tuesday, July 7. When I am giving the relation of a thing, to abstain from altering either in the matter or manner of speaking, so much, as that if every one afterward should alter as much, it would at last come to be properly false.

Tuesday, Sept. 2. By a sparingness in diet, and eating, as much as may be, what is light and easy of digestion, I shall doubtless be able to think clearer, and shall gain time. 1*st.* By lengthening out my life. 2*dly.* Shall need less time for digestion after meals. 3*rdly.* Shall be able to study closer without wrong to my health. 4*thly.*

Shall need less time to sleep. *5thly.* Shall seldomer be troubled
with the headache.

Sabbath-Day, Nov. 22. Considering that by-standers always
espy some faults which we don't see ourselves, or at least are not
so fully sensible of: there are many secret workings of corruption
which escape our sight, and others only are sensible of: resolved
therefore, that I will, if I can by any convenient means, learn what
faults others find in me, or what things they see in me, that appear
any way blame-worthy, unlovely or unbecoming.

Section III   REFLECTION ON THE FOREGOING EXTRACTS

The foregoing extracts were wrote by Mr. Edwards in the
twentieth and twenty-first years of his age, as appears by the dates.
This being kept in mind, the judicious reader will make proper
allowance for some things, which may appear a little juvenile, or
like a young Christian, as to the matter, or manner of expression;
which would not have been found, had it not have been done in
early life. Which, indeed are no blemishes, the whole being taken
together: as by this, it appears more natural, and the strength of
his resolution, and fervor of mind; and his skill and discerning in
divine things, so seldom found even in old age, are the more
striking. And in this view, we shall be led to admire his conscientious strictness, his zeal and painfulness, his experience and judgment in true religion, at so early an age. For here are not only the
most convincing evidences of sincerity and thorough religion, of
his engaging in a life devoted to God in good earnest, so as to
make religion his only business; but through his great attention
to this matter, he appears to have the judgment and experience of
gray hairs.

This is the beginning of a life so eminently holy and useful as
Mr. Edwards's was. He who became one of the greatest divines in
this age; has had the applause and admiration of America, Britain,
Holland and Germany, for his piety, and great judgment and skill
in divinity; and has been honored above most others in the
Christian world, in this century; in his being made the instrument

of doing so much good: he began his life thus: he entered on a public life with such views, such exercises, such resolutions.

This may serve as a direction and excitement to those who are young, to devote themselves to God in good earnest, and enter on the business of strict and thorough religion without delay: especially those who are looking towards the work of the ministry, as they would take the most direct, the only way to answer the good ends which they profess to seek.

It is to be lamented, that there is so much reason to think, there are so few instances of such early piety in our day. If the Protestant world abounded with young persons of this stamp; with young men, who were preparing for the work of the ministry, with such a temper, such exercises, such resolutions, what a delightful prospect would this afford, of the near approach of happier days, than the church of God has ever yet seen! what pleasing hopes that the great, the merciful Head of the church, was about to send forth laborers, faithful, successful laborers into His harvest; and bless His people with "pastors which shall feed them with knowledge and understanding"!

But if our youth neglect all proper improvement of the mind; are shy of seriousness and strict piety; choose to live strangers to it, and keep at a distance from all appearance of it; are wanton, and given to carnal pleasures; what a gloomy prospect does this afford! If they who enter into the work of the ministry; from a gay, careless, and what may justly be called a vicious life, betake themselves to a little superficial study of divinity, and soon begin to preach; while all the external seriousness and zeal they put on, is only from worldly motives; they being without any inward, experimental acquaintance with spiritual, divine things, and even so much as any taste for true divinity, no wonder if the churches "suck dry breasts"; and there are many ignorant watchmen.

But, as the best comment on the foregoing Resolutions and Diary; and that the reader may have a more particular, full and instructive view of Mr. Edwards's entrance on a religious life, and progress in it, as consisting in the views and exercises of his mind; a brief account thereof is here inserted, which was found among his papers, in his own handwriting: and which, it seems, was wrote near twenty years after, for his own private advantage.

Section IV   AN ACCOUNT OF HIS CONVERSION, EXPERIENCES, AND RELIGIOUS EXERCISES, GIVEN BY HIMSELF

I had a variety of concerns and exercises about my soul from my childhood; but had two more remarkable seasons of awakening, before I met with that change, by which I was brought to those new dispositions, and that new sense of things, that I have since had. The first time was when I was a boy, some years before I went to college, at a time of remarkable awakening in my father's congregation. I was then very much affected for many months, and concerned about the things of religion, and my soul's salvation; and was abundant in duties. I used to pray five times a day in secret, and to spend much time in religious talk with other boys; and used to meet with them to pray together. I experienced I know not what kind of delight in religion. My mind was much engaged in it, and had much self-righteous pleasure; and it was my delight to abound in religious duties. I, with some of my school-mates joined together, and built a booth in a swamp, in a very secret and retired place, for a place of prayer. And besides, I had particular secret places of my own in the woods, where I used to retire by myself; and used to be from time to time much affected. My affections seemed to be lively and easily moved, and I seemed to be in my element, when engaged in religious duties. And I am ready to think, many are deceived with such affections, and such a kind of delight, as I then had in religion, and mistake it for grace.

But in process of time, my convictions and affections wore off; and I entirely lost all those affections and delights, and left off secret prayer, at least as to any constant performance of it; and returned like a dog to his vomit, and went on in ways of sin.

Indeed, I was at some times very uneasy, especially towards the latter part of the time of my being at college. 'Till it pleas'd God, in my last year at college, at a time when I was in the midst of many uneasy thoughts about the state of my soul, to seize me with a pleurisy; in which he brought me nigh to the grave, and shook me over the pit of hell.

But yet, it was not long after my recovery, before I fell again into my old ways of sin. But God would not suffer me to go on with any quietness; but I had great and violent inward struggles: 'till after many conflicts with wicked inclinations, and repeated resolutions, and bonds that I laid myself under by a kind of vows to God, I was brought wholly to break off all former wicked ways, and all ways of known outward sin; and to apply myself to seek my salvation, and practice the duties of religion: But without that kind of affection and delight, that I had formerly experienced. My concern now wrought more by inward struggles and conflicts, and self-reflections. I made seeking my salvation the main business of my life. But yet it seems to me, I sought after a miserable manner: Which has made me some times since to question, whether ever it issued in that which was saving; being ready to doubt, whether such miserable seeking was ever succeeded. But yet I was brought to seek salvation, in a manner that I never was before. I felt a spirit to part with all things in the world, for an interest in Christ. My concern continued and prevailed, with many exercising thoughts and inward struggles; but yet it never seemed to be proper to express my concern that I had, by the name of terror.

From my childhood up, my mind had been wont to be full of objections against the doctrine of God's sovereignty, in choosing whom he would to eternal life, and rejecting whom he pleased; leaving them eternally to perish, and be everlastingly tormented in hell. It used to appear like a horrible doctrine to me. But I remember the time very well, when I seemed to be convinced, and fully satisfied, as to this sovereignty of God, and his justice in thus eternally disposing of men, according to his sovereign pleasure. But never could give an account, how, or by what means, I was thus convinced; not in the least imagining, in the time of it, nor a long time after, that there was any extraordinary influence of God's spirit in it; but only that now I saw further, and my reason apprehended the justice and reasonableness of it. However, my mind rested in it; and it put an end to all those cavils and objections, that had 'till then abode with me, all the preceding part of my life. And there has been a wonderful alteration in my mind, with respect to the doctrine of God's sovereignty, from that day to this; so that I scarce ever have found so much as the rising of an objection against God's sovereignty, in the most absolute sense, in showing mercy to whom he will show mercy, and hardening and eternally damning whom he will. God's absolute sovereignty, and justice, with respect to salvation and damnation, is what my mind seems to rest assured of, as much as of any thing that I see with my eyes; at least it is so at times. But I have often times since that first conviction, had quite another kind of sense of God's sovereignty, than I had then. I have often since, not only had a conviction, but a *delightful* conviction. The doctrine of God's sovereignty has very often appeared, an exceeding pleasant, bright and sweet doctrine to me: and absolute sovereignty is what I love to ascribe to God. But my first conviction was not with this.

The first that I remember that ever I found any thing of that sort of inward, sweet delight in God and divine things, that I have lived much in since, was on reading those words, I Tim. i. 17. "Now unto the king eternal, immortal, invisible, the only wise God, be honor and glory for ever and ever, Amen." As I read the words, there came into my soul, and was as it were diffused thro' it, a sense of the glory of the Divine Being; a new sense, quite different from any thing I ever experienced before. Never any words of scripture seemed to me as these words did. I thought with myself, how excellent a being that was; and how happy I should be, if I might enjoy that God, and be wrapt up to God in Heaven, and be as it were swallowed up in Him. I kept saying, and as it were singing over these words of scripture to myself; and went to prayer, to pray to God that I might enjoy him; and prayed in a manner quite different from what I used to do; with a new sort of affection. But it never came into my thought, that there was any thing spiritual, or of a saving nature in this.

From about that time, I began to have a new kind of apprehensions and ideas of Christ, and the work of redemption, and the glorious way of salvation by Him. I had an inward, sweet sense of these things, that at times came into my heart; and my soul was led away in pleasant views and contemplations of them. And my mind was greatly engaged, to spend my time in reading and meditating on Christ; and the beauty and excellency of His person, and the lovely way of salvation, by free grace in Him. I found no books so delightful to me, as those that treated of these subjects. Those words Cant. ii. I. used to be abundantly with me: *I am the Rose of Sharon, the lily of the valleys.* The words seemed to me, sweetly to represent, the loveliness and beauty of Jesus Christ. And the whole Book of Canticles used to be pleasant to me; and I used to be much in reading it, about that time. And found, from time to time, an inward sweetness, that used, as it were, to carry me away in my contemplations; in what I know not how to express otherwise, than by a calm, sweet abstraction of soul from all the concerns of this world; and a kind of vision, or fix'd ideas and imaginations, of being alone in the mountains, or some solitary wilderness, far from all mankind, sweetly conversing with Christ, and wrapt and swallowed up in God. The sense I had of divine things, would often of a sudden as it were, kindle up a sweet burning in my heart; an ardor of my soul, that I know not how to express.

Not long after I first began to experience these things, I gave an account to my father, of some things that had pass'd in my mind. I was pretty much affected by the discourse we had together. And when the discourse was ended, I walked abroad alone, in a solitary place in my father's pasture, for contemplation. And as I was walking there, and looked up on the sky and clouds; there came into my mind, a sweet sense of the glorious majesty and grace of God, that I know not how to express. I seemed to see them both in a sweet conjunction: majesty and meekness join'd together: it was a sweet and gentle, and holy majesty; and also a majestic meekness; an awful sweetness; a high, and great, and holy gentleness.

After this my sense of divine things gradually increased, and became more and more lively, and had more of that inward sweetness. The appearance of every thing was altered: there seem'd to be, as it were, a calm, sweet cast, or appearance of divine glory, in almost every thing. God's excellency, his wisdom, his purity and love, seemed to appear in every thing; in the sun, moon and stars; in the clouds, and blue sky; in the grass, flowers, trees; in the water, and all nature; which used greatly to fix my mind. I often used to sit and view the moon, for a long time; and so in the day time, spent much time in viewing the clouds and sky, to behold the sweet glory of God in these things: in the mean time, singing forth with a low voice, my contemplations of the Creator and Redeemer. And scarce any thing, among all the works of nature, was so sweet to me as thunder and lightning. Formerly, nothing had been so terrible to me. I used to be a person uncommonly terrified with thunder: and it used to strike me with terror, when I saw a thunder-storm rising. But now, on the contrary, it rejoiced me. I felt God at the first appearance of a thunder-storm. And used to take the opportunity at such times to fix myself to view the clouds, and see the lightnings play, and hear the majestic and awful voice of God's thunder: which often times was exceeding entertaining, leading me to sweet contemplations of my great and glorious God. And while I viewed, used to spend my time, as it always seem'd natural to me, to sing or chant forth my meditations; to speak my thoughts in soliloquies, and speak with a singing voice.

I felt then a great satisfaction as to my good estate. But that did not content me. I had vehement longings of soul after God and Christ, and after more holiness; wherewith my heart seemed to be full, and ready to break: which often brought to my mind, the words of the psalmist, Psal. cxix. 28. *My soul breaketh for the longing it hath.* I often felt a mourning and lamenting in my heart, that I had not turned to God sooner, that I might have had more time to grow in grace. My mind was greatly fix'd on divine things; I was almost perpetually in the contemplation of them. Spent most of my time in thinking of divine things, year after year. And used to spend abundance of my time, in walking alone in the woods, and solitary places, for meditation, soliloquy and prayer, and converse with God. And it was always my manner, at such times, to sing forth my contemplations. And was almost constantly in ejaculatory prayer, wherever I was. Prayer seem'd to be natural to me; as the breath, by which the inward burnings of my heart had vent.

The delights which I now felt in things of religion, were of an exceeding different kind, from those forementioned, that I had when I was a boy. They were totally of another kind; and what I then had no more notion or idea of, than one born blind has of pleasant and beautiful colors. They were of a more inward, pure, soul-animating and refreshing nature. Those former delights, never reached the heart; and did not arise from any sight of the divine excellency of the things of God; or any taste of the soul-satisfying, and life-giving good, there is in them.

My sense of divine things seemed gradually to increase, 'till I went to preach at New York; which was about a year and a half after they began. While I was there, I felt them, very sensibly, in a much higher degree, than I had done before. My longings after God and holiness, were much increased. Pure and humble, holy and heavenly Christianity, appeared exceeding amiable to me. I felt in me a burning desire to be in every thing a complete Christian; and conformed to the blessed image of Christ: and that I might live in all things, according to the pure, sweet and blessed rules of the gospel. I had an eager thirsting after progress in these things. My longings after it, put me upon pursuing and pressing after them. It was my continual strife day and night, and constant inquiry, How I should be more holy, and live more holily, and more becoming a child of God, and disciple of Christ. I sought an increase of grace and holiness, and that I might live an holy life, with vastly more earnestness, than ever I sought grace, before I had it. I used to be continually examining myself, and studying and contriving for likely ways and means, how I should live holily, with far greater diligence and earnestness, than ever I pursued any thing in my life: But with too great a dependence on my own strength; which afterwards proved a great damage to me. My experience had not then taught me, as it has done since, my extreme feebleness and impotence, every manner of way; and the innumerable and bottomless depths of secret corruption and deceit, that there was in my heart. However, I went on with my eager pursuit after more holiness; and sweet conformity to Christ.

The Heaven I desired was a heaven of holiness; to be with God, and to spend my eternity in divine love, and holy communion with Christ. My mind was very much taken up with contemplations on heaven, and the enjoyments of those there; and living there in perfect holiness, humility and love. And it used at that time to appear a great part of the happiness of heaven, that there the

saints could express their love to Christ. It appear'd to me a great
clog and hindrance and burden to me, that what I felt within, I
could not express to God, and give vent to, as I desired. The
inward ardor of my soul, seem'd to be hindered and pent up, and
could not freely flame out as it would. I used often to think, how in
heaven, this sweet principle should freely and fully vent and
express itself. Heaven appeared to me exceeding delightful as a
world of love. It appeared to me, that all happiness consisted in
living in pure, humble, heavenly, divine love.

I remember the thoughts I used then to have of holiness. I
remember I then said sometimes to myself, I do certainly know
that I love holiness, such as the gospel prescribes. It appeared to
me, there was nothing in it but what was ravishingly lovely. It
appeared to me, to be the highest beauty and amiableness, above
all other beauties: that it was a *divine* beauty; far purer than any
thing here upon earth; and that every thing else, was like mire, filth
and defilement, in comparison of it.

Holiness, as I then wrote down some of my contemplations on
it, appeared to me to be of a sweet, pleasant, charming, serene,
calm nature. It seemed to me, it brought an inexpressible purity,
brightness, peacefulness and ravishment to the soul: and that it
made the soul like a field or garden of God, with all manner of
pleasant flowers; that is all pleasant, delightful and undisturbed;
enjoying a sweet calm, and the gently vivifying beams of the sun.
The soul of a true Christian, as I then wrote my meditations,
appear'd like such a little white flower, as we see in the spring of
the year; low and humble on the ground, opening its bosom, to
receive the pleasant beams of the sun's glory; rejoicing as it were,
in a calm rapture; diffusing around a sweet fragrancy; standing
peacefully and lovingly, in the midst of other flowers round about;
all in like manner opening their bosoms, to drink in the light of the
sun.

There was no part of creature-holiness, that I then, and at other
times, had so great a sense of the loveliness of, as humility,
brokenness of heart and poverty of spirit: and there was nothing
that I had such a spirit to long for. My heart as it were panted after
this, to lie low before God, and in the dust; that I might be

nothing, and that God might be all; that I might become as a little child.

While I was there at New York, I sometimes was much affected with reflections on my past life, considering how late it was, before I began to be truly religious; and how wickedly I had lived 'till then: and once so as to weep abundantly, and for a considerable time together.

On January 12, 1722–3. I made a solemn dedication of myself to God, and wrote it down; giving up myself, and all that I had to God; to be for the future in no respect my own; to act as one that had no right to himself, in any respect. And solemnly vowed to take God for my whole portion and felicity; looking on nothing else as any part of my happiness, nor acting as if it were: and his law for the constant rule of my obedience: engaging to fight with all my might, against the world, the flesh and the devil, to the end of my life. But have reason to be infinitely humbled, when I consider, how much I have fail'd of answering my obligation.

I had then abundance of sweet religious conversation in the family where I lived, with Mr. John Smith, and his pious mother. My heart was knit in affection to those, in whom were appearances of true piety; and I could bear the thoughts of no other companions, but such as were holy, and the disciples of the blessed Jesus.

I had great longings for the advancement of Christ's kingdom in the world. My secret prayer used to be in great part taken up in praying for it. If I heard the least hint of any thing that happened in any part of the world, that appear'd to me, in some respect or other, to have a favorable aspect on the interest of Christ's kingdom, my soul eagerly catch'd at it; and it would much animate and refresh me. I used to be earnest to read public news-letters, mainly for that end; to see if I could not find some news favorable to the interest of religion in the world.

I very frequently used to retire into a solitary place, on the banks of Hudson's river, at some distance from the city, for contemplation on divine things, and secret converse with God; and had many sweet hours there. Sometimes Mr. Smith and I walked there together, to converse of the things of God; and our conversation used much to turn on the advancement of Christ's kingdom in

the world, and the glorious things that God would accomplish for
his church in the latter days.

I had then, and at other times, the greatest delight in the holy
Scriptures, of any book whatsoever. Often-times in reading it,
every word seemed to touch my heart. I felt an harmony between
something in my heart, and those sweet and powerful words. I
seem'd often to see so much light, exhibited by every sentence, and
such a refreshing ravishing food communicated, that I could not
get along in reading. Used often-times to dwell long on one sentence, to see the wonders contained in it; and yet almost every
sentence seemed to be full of wonders.

I came away from New York in the month of April, 1723, and
had a most bitter parting with Madam Smith and her son. My
heart seemed to sink within me, at leaving the family and city,
where I had enjoyed so many sweet and pleasant days. I went from
New York to Weathersfield by water. As I sail'd away, I kept sight
of the city as long as I could; and when I was out of sight of it, it
would affect me much to look that way, with a kind of melancholy
mixed with sweetness. However, that night after this sorrowful
parting, I was greatly comforted in God at Westchester, where we
went ashore to lodge: and had a pleasant time of it all the voyage
to Saybrook. It was sweet to me to think of meeting dear Christians in heaven, where we should never part more. At Saybrook we
went ashore to lodge on Saturday, and there kept sabbath; where I
had a sweet and refreshing season, walking alone in the fields.

After I came home to Windsor, remained much in a like frame
of my mind, as I had been in at New York, but only sometimes felt
my heart ready to sink, with the thoughts of my friends at New
York. And my refuge and support was in contemplations on the
heavenly state; as I find in my diary of May 1, 1723. It was my
comfort to think of that state, where there is fulness of joy; where
reigns heavenly, sweet, calm and delightful love, without alloy;
where there are continually the dearest expressions of this love;
where is the enjoyment of the persons loved, without ever parting;
where these persons that appear so lovely in this world, will really
be inexpressibly more lovely, and full of love to us. And how
sweetly will the mutual lovers join together to sing the praises of

God and the Lamb! How full will it fill us with joy, to think, that this enjoyment, these sweet exercises will never cease or come to an end; but will last to all eternity!

Continued much in the same frame in the general, that I had been in at New York, till I went to New Haven, to live there as tutor of the college; having some special seasons of uncommon sweetness: particularly once at Boston, in a journey from Boston, walking out alone in the fields. After I went to New Haven, I sunk in religion; my mind being diverted from my eager and violent pursuits after holiness, by some affairs that greatly perplexed and distracted my mind.

In September, 1725, was taken ill at New Haven; and endeavoring to go home to Windsor, was so ill at the North Village, that I could go no further: where I lay sick for about a quarter of a year. And in this sickness, God was pleased to visit me again with the sweet influences of His spirit. My mind was greatly engaged there on divine, pleasant contemplations, and longings of soul. I observed that those who watched with me, would often be looking out for the morning, and seemed to wish for it. Which brought to my mind those words of the psalmist, which my soul with sweetness made its own language. *My soul waitest for the Lord, more than they that watch for the morning, I say, more than they that watch for the morning.* And when the light of the morning came, and the beams of the sun came in at the windows, it refreshed my soul from one morning to another. It seemed to me to be some image of the sweet light of God's glory.

I remember, about that time, I used greatly to long for the conversion of some that I was concerned with. It seem'd to me, I could gladly honor them, and with delight be a servant to them, and lie at their feet, if they were but truly holy.

But some time after this, I was again greatly diverted in my mind, with some temporal concerns, that exceedingly took up my thoughts, greatly to the wounding of my soul: and went on through various exercises, that it would be tedious to relate, that gave me much more experience of my own heart, than ever I had before.

Since I came to this town,* I have often had sweet complacency

* Northampton.

in God, in views of his glorious perfections, and the excellency of Jesus Christ. God has appeared to me, a glorious and lovely being, chiefly on the account of His holiness. The holiness of God has always appeared to me the most lovely of all His attributes. The doctrines of God's absolute sovereignty, and free grace, in showing mercy to whom He would show mercy; and man's absolute dependence on the operations of God's Holy Spirit, have very often appeared to me as sweet and glorious doctrines. These doctrines have been much my delight. God's sovereignty has ever appeared to me, as great part of His glory. It has often been sweet to me to go to God, and adore Him as a sovereign God, and ask sovereign mercy of Him.

I have loved the doctrines of the gospel: They have been to my soul like green pastures. The gospel has seem'd to me to be the richest treasure; the treasure that I have most desired, and longed that it might dwell richly in me. The way of salvation by Christ, has appeared in a general way, glorious and excellent, and most pleasant and beautiful. It has often seem'd to me, that it would in a great measure spoil heaven, to receive it in any other way. That Text has often been affecting and delightful to me, Isai. xxxii. 2. *A man shall be an hiding place from the wind, and a covert from the tempest etc.*

It has often appear'd sweet to me, to be united to Christ; to have Him for my head, and to be a member of His body: and also to have Christ for my teacher and prophet. I very often think with sweetness and longings and pantings of soul, of being a little child, taking hold of Christ, to be led by Him through the wilderness of this world. That text, Matth. xviii. at the beginning, has often been sweet to me, *Except ye be converted, and become as little children etc.* I love to think of coming to Christ, to receive salvation of Him, poor in spirit, and quite empty of self; humbly exalting Him alone; cut entirely off from my own root, and to grow into, and out of Christ: to have God in Christ to be all in all; and to live by faith on the Son of God, a life of humble, unfeigned confidence in Him. That Scripture has often been sweet to me, Psal. cxv. I. *Not unto us, O Lord, not unto us, but unto Thy name give glory, for Thy mercy, and for Thy truth's sake.* And those words of Christ, *Luk. x. 21. In that hour Jesus rejoiced in spirit, and said, I thank thee,*

O Father, Lord of heaven and earth, that Thou hast hid these things from the wise and prudent, and hast revealed them unto babes: Even so Father, for so it seemed good in Thy sight. That sovereignty of God that Christ rejoiced in, seemed to me to be worthy to be rejoiced in; and that rejoicing of Christ, seemed to me to show the excellency of Christ, and the spirit that He was of.

Sometimes only mentioning a single word, causes my heart to burn within me: or only seeing the Name of Christ, or the name of some attribute of God. And God has appeared glorious to me, on account of the Trinity. It has made me have exalting thoughts of God, that he subsists in three persons; Father, Son, and Holy Ghost.

The sweetest joys and delights I have experienced, have not been those that have arisen from a hope of my own good estate; but in a direct view of the glorious things of the gospel. When I enjoy this sweetness, it seems to carry me above the thoughts of my own safe estate. It seems at such times a loss that I cannot bear, to take off my eye from the glorious, pleasant object I behold without me, to turn my eye in upon myself, and my own good estate.

My heart has been much on the advancement of Christ's kingdom in the world. The histories of the past advancement of Christ's kingdom, have been sweet to me. When I have read histories of past ages, the pleasantest thing in all my reading has been, to read of the kingdom of Christ being promoted. And when I have expected in my reading, to come to any such thing, I have lotted* upon it all the way as I read. And my mind has been much entertained and delighted, with the Scripture promises and prophecies, of the future glorious advancement of Christ's kingdom on earth.

I have sometimes had a sense of the excellent fulness of Christ, and His meetness and suitableness as a Saviour; whereby He has appeared to me, far above all, the chief of ten thousands. And His blood and atonement has appeared sweet, and His righteousness sweet; which is always accompanied with an ardency of spirit, and inward strugglings and breathings and groanings, that cannot be uttered, to be emptied of myself, and swallowed up in Christ.

Once, as I rid out into the woods for my health, *Anno* 1737;

* That is, counted on it [ed.].

and having lit from my horse in a retired place, as my manner
commonly has been, to walk for divine contemplation and prayer;
I had a view, that for me was extraordinary, of the glory of the Son
of God; as mediator between God and man; and his wonderful,
great, full, pure and sweet grace and love, and meek and gentle
condescension. This grace, that appear'd to me so calm and sweet,
appear'd great above the heavens. The person of Christ appear'd
ineffably excellent, with an excellency great enough to swallow up
all thought and conception, which continued, as near as I can
judge, about an hour; which kept me, the bigger part of the time,
in a flood of tears, and weeping aloud. I felt withal, an ardency of
soul to be, what I know not otherwise how to express, than to be
emptied and annihilated; to lie in the dust, and to be full of Christ
alone; to love Him with a holy and pure love; to trust in Him; to
live upon Him; to serve and follow Him, and to be totally wrapt up
in the fullness of Christ; and to be perfectly sanctified and made
pure, with a divine and heavenly purity. I have several other times,
had views very much of the same nature, and that have had the
same effects.

I have many times had a sense of the glory of the third person in
the Trinity, in His office of sanctifier; in His holy operations
communicating divine light and life to the soul. God in the
communications of His Holy Spirit, has appear'd as an infinite
fountain of divine glory and sweetness; being full and sufficient to
fill and satisfy the soul: pouring forth itself in sweet communications, like the sun in its glory, sweetly and pleasantly diffusing light
and life.

I have sometimes had an affecting sense of the excellency of the
word of God, as a word of life; as the light of life; a sweet,
excellent, life-giving word: accompanied with a thirsting after that
word, that it might dwell richly in my heart.

I have often since I lived in this town, had very affecting views
of my own sinfulness and vileness; very frequently so as to hold
me in a kind of loud weeping, sometimes for a considerable time
together: so that I have often been forced to shut myself up. I
have had a vastly greater sense of my own wickedness, and the
badness of my heart, since my conversion, than ever I had before.

It has often appeared to me, that if God should mark iniquity against me, I should appear the very worst of all mankind; of all that have been since the beginning of the world to this time: and that I should have by far the lowest place in hell. When others that have come to talk with me about their soul concerns, have expressed the sense they have had of their own wickedness, by saying that it seem'd to them, that they were as bad as the devil himself; I thought their expressions seemed exceeding faint and feeble, to represent my wickedness. I thought I should wonder, that they should content themselves with such expressions as these, if I had any reason to imagine, that their sin bore any proportion to mine. It seemed to me, I should wonder at myself, if I should express *my* wickedness in such feeble terms as they did.

My wickedness, as I am in myself, has long appear'd to me perfectly ineffable, and infinitely swallowing up all thought and imagination; like an infinite deluge, or infinite mountains over my head. I know not how to express better, what my sins appear to me to be, than by heaping infinite upon infinite, and multiplying infinite by infinite. I go about very often, for this many years, with these expressions in my mind, and in my mouth, "Infinite upon infinite. Infinite upon infinite!" When I look into my heart, and take a view of my wickedness, it looks like an abyss infinitely deeper than hell. And it appears to me, that were it not for free grace, exalted and raised up to the infinite height of all the fulness and glory of the great Jehovah, and the arm of His power and grace stretched forth, in all the majesty of His power, and in all the glory of His sovereignty; I should appear sunk down in my sins infinitely below hell itself, far beyond sight of every thing, but the piercing eye of God's grace, that can pierce even down to such a depth, and to the bottom of such an abyss.

And yet, I ben't in the least inclined to think, that I have a greater conviction of sin than ordinary. It seems to me, my conviction of sin is exceeding small, and faint. It appears to me enough to amaze me, that I have no more sense of my sin. I know certainly, that I have very little sense of my sinfulness. That my sins appear to me so great, don't seem to me to be, because I have so much more conviction of sin than other Christians, but because I am so much worse, and have so much more wickedness to be convinced of. When I have had these turns of weeping and crying for my sins, I thought I knew in the time of it, that my repentance was nothing to my sin.

I have greatly longed of late, for a broken heart, and to lie low before God. And when I ask for humility of God, I can't bear the thoughts of being no more humble, than other Christians. It seems to me, that tho' their degrees of humility may be suitable for them; yet it would be a vile self-exaltation in me, not to be the lowest in humility of all mankind. Others speak of their longing to be humbled to the dust. Tho' that may be a proper expression for them, I always think for myself, that I ought to be humbled down below hell. 'Tis an expression that it has long been natural for me to use in prayer to God. I ought to lie infinitely low before God.

It is affecting to me to think, how ignorant I was, when I was a young Christian, of the bottomless, infinite depths of wickedness, pride, hypocrisy and deceit left in my heart.

I have vastly a greater sense, of my universal, exceeding dependence on God's grace and strength, and mere good pleasure, of late, than I used formerly to have; and have experienced more of an abhorrence of my own righteousness. The thought of any comfort or joy, arising in me, on any consideration, or reflection on my own amiableness, or any of my performances or experiences, or any goodness of heart or life, is nauseous and detestable to me. And yet I am greatly afflicted with a proud and self-righteous spirit; much more sensibly, than I used to be formerly. I see that serpent rising and putting forth it's head, continually, everywhere, all around me.

Tho' it seems to me, that in some respects I was a far better Christian, for two or three years after my first conversion, than I am now; and lived in a more constant delight and pleasure: yet of late years, I have had a more full and constant sense of the absolute sovereignty of God, and a delight in that sovereignty; and have had more of a sense of the glory of Christ, as a mediator, as revealed in the gospel. On one Saturday night in particular, had a particular discovery of the excellency of the gospel of Christ, above all other doctrines; so that I could not but say to myself;

"This is my chosen light, my chosen doctrine": and of Christ, "This is my chosen prophet." It appear'd to me to be sweet beyond all expression, to follow Christ, and to be taught and enlighten'd and instructed by Him; to learn of Him, and live to Him.

Another Saturday night, January, 1738–9, had such a sense, how sweet and blessed a thing it was, to walk in the way of duty, to do that which was right and meet to be done, and agreeable to the holy mind of God; that it caused me to break forth into a kind of a loud weeping, which held me some time; so that I was forced to shut myself up, and fasten the doors. I could not but as it were cry out, "How happy are they which do that which is right in the sight of God! They are blessed indeed, they are the happy ones!" I had at the same time, a very affecting sense, how meet and suitable it was that God should govern the world, and order all things according to his own pleasure; and I rejoiced in it, that God reigned, and that his will was done.

PART III *Containing a* HISTORY *of his* LIFE *from his Entering on the* WORK *of the* MINISTRY, *unto his* DEATH

Section I. HIS GENERAL MANNER OF LIFE

Mr. Edwards made a secret of his private devotion, and therefore it cannot be particularly known: though there is much evidence, that he was punctual, constant and frequent in secret prayer, and often kept days of fasting and prayer in secret; and set apart time for serious, devout meditations on spiritual and eternal things, as part of his religious exercise in secret. It appears by his Diary that in his youth he determined to attend secret prayer more than twice a day, when circumstances would allow. He was, so far as it can be known, much on his knees in secret, and in devout reading God's word and meditation upon it. And his constant, solemn converse with God in these exercises of secret religion made his face, as it were, to shine before others. His appearance, his countenance, words and whole demeanor (though without anything of affected grimace and sour austerity) was attended with a seriousness, gravity and solemnity, which was the natural genuine indication and expression of a deep, abiding sense of divine things on his mind, and of his living constantly in the fear of God.

Agreeable to his Resolutions, he was very careful and abstemious in eating and drinking; as doubtless it was necessary so great a student, and a person of so delicate and tender a bodily make as he was, should be, in order to be comfortable and useful. When he had, by careful observation, found what kind, and what quantity of diet, best suited his constitution, and rendered him most fit to pursue his work, he was very strict and exact in complying with it; and in this respect *lived by rule;* and herein constantly practiced great self-denial: which he also did in his constant early rising, in order to redeem time for his study. He used himself to rise by four or between four and five in the morning.

Though he was of a tender and delicate constitution, yet few students are capable of close application more hours in a day than he. He commonly spent thirteen hours every day in his study. His most usual diversion in summer was riding on horseback and walking. He would commonly, unless diverted by company, ride two or three miles after dinner to some lonely grove, where he would dismount and walk a while. At which times he generally carried his pen and ink with him, to note any thought that should be suggested, which he chose to retain and pursue, as what promised some light on any important subject. In the winter he was wont almost daily to take an axe and chop wood moderately for the space of half an hour or more.

He had an uncommon thirst for knowledge, in the pursuit of which, he spared no cost nor pains. He read all the books, especially books of divinity, that he could come at, from which he could hope to get any help in his pursuit of knowledge. And in this, he confined not himself to authors of any particular sect or denomination; yea took much pains to come at the books of the most noted writers, who advance a scheme of divinity most contrary to his own principles. But he studied the Bible more than all other books, and more than most other divines do. His uncommon acquaintance with the Bible appears in his sermons, and in most of his publications: and his great pains in studying it are manifest in his manuscript notes upon it; of which a more particular account may be given hereafter. He took his religious principles from the Bible, and not from any human system or body of divinity. Though his principles were *Calvinistic,* yet he called no man father. He thought and judged for himself, and was truly very much of an original. This is evident by what he published in his lifetime, and is yet more so by his Mss. Many volumes of which he has left; and the reader may expect a more particular account of them in the sequel. For reading was not the only method he took to improve his mind; but he did this much by writing; without which, 'tis probable no student can make improvements to the best advantage. Agreeable to Resolution 11th, he applied himself with all his might to find out the truth: he searched for understanding and knowledge, as for silver, and digged for it, as for his treasures. Every thought on any subject, which appeared to him worth pursuing and preserving, he pursued, as far as he then could, with his pen in his hand. Thus he was all his days, like the busy bee, collecting from every opening flower, and storing up a stock of knowledge, which was indeed sweet to him, as the honey and the honey-comb. And as he advanced in years and in knowledge, his pen was more and more employed, and his manuscripts grew much faster on his hands.

He was thought by some, who had but a slight acquaintance with him to be stiff and unsociable; but this was owing to want of better acquaintance. He was not a man of many words indeed, and was somewhat reserved among strangers, and those on whose candor and friendship he did not know he could rely. And this was probably owing to two things. First, the strict guard he set over his tongue from his youth, which appears by his Resolutions, taking great care never to use it in any way that might prove mischievous to any; never to *sin with his tongue;* or to improve it in idle, trivial and impertinent talk, which generally makes up a great part of the conversation of those who are full of words in all companies. He was sensible, that in the multitude of words there wanteth not sin; and therefore refrained his lips, and habituated himself to *think* before he *spoke,* and to propose some good and even in all his words; which led him to be above many others, agreeable to St. James's advice, *slow to speak.* Secondly, this was in part the effect of his bodily constitution. He possessed but a comparative small stock of animal life: his animal spirits were low, and he had not strength of lungs to spare, that would be necessary in order to make him what would be called, an affable, facetious gentleman, in all companies. They who have a great flow of animal spirits, and so can speak with more ease and less expense, may doubtless lawfully practice free conversation in all companies for a lower end (*e.g.*, to please and render themselves acceptable) than he, who has not such a stock to expend upon. It becomes *him* to reserve what he has, for higher and more important service. Besides, the want of animal spirits lays a man under a *natural* inability to that freedom of conversation, at all times, and in whatever company he is; which those of more life naturally go into; and the greatest degree of a sociable disposition, humility and benevolence, will not remove this obstacle.

He was not forward to enter into any dispute among strangers, and in companies where were persons of different sentiments; as he was sensible that such disputes are generally unprofitable, and often sinful and of bad consequence; and he thought he could dispute to the best advantage with his pen in his hand: yet he was always free to give his sentiments on any subject proposed to him; and remove any difficulties or objections offered by way of inquiry, as lying in the way of what he looked upon to be the truth. But how groundless the imputation of *stiff* and *unsociable* was, his known and tried friends best knew. They always found him easy of access, kind and condescending; and though not talkative, yet affable and free. Among such whose candor and friendship he had experienced, he threw off the reserve, and was most open and free; quite patient of contradiction, while the utmost opposition was made to his sentiments, that could be by any plausible arguments or objections. And indeed, he was on all occasions, quite sociable and free with all, who had any special business with him.

In his conduct in his family he practiced that conscientious exactness which was perspicuous in all his ways. He maintained a great esteem and regard for his amiable and excellent consort. Much of the tender and kind was expressed in his conversation with her and conduct towards her. He was wont frequently to admit her into his study, and converse freely with her on matters of religion. And he used commonly to pray with her in his study, at least once a day, unless something extraordinary prevented. The time in which this used to be commonly attended, was just before going to bed, after prayers in the family. As he rose very early himself, he was wont to have his family up in season in the morning; after which, before the family entered on the business of the day, he attended on family prayers. When a chapter in the Bible was read, commonly by candle-light in the winter; upon which he asked his children questions according to their age and capacity; and took occasion to explain some passages in it, or enforce any duty recommended etc. as he thought most proper.

He was careful and thorough in the government of his children; and, as a consequence of this, they reverenced, esteemed and loved him. He took special care to begin his government of them in season. When they first discovered any considerable degree of will and stubbornness, he would attend to them till he had thoroughly subdued them and brought them to submit. And such prudent thorough discipline, exercised with the greatest calmness, and commonly without striking a blow, being repeated once or twice, was generally sufficient for that child; and effectually established his parental authority, and produced a cheerful obedience ever after.

He kept a watchful eye over his children, that he might admonish them of the first wrong step, and direct them in the right way. He took opportunities to treat with them in his study, singly and particularly about their own soul's concerns; and to give them warning, exhortation and direction, as he saw occasion. He took much pains to instruct them in the principles of religion; in which he made use of the *Assembly's Shorter Catechism:* not merely by taking care that they learned it by heart; but by leading them into an understanding of the doctrines therein taught, by asking them questions on each answer, and explaining it to them. His usual time to attend this was on the evening before the Sabbath. And as he believed that the Sabbath or holy time began at sunset the evening before the day, he ordered his family to finish all their secular business by that time, or before; when they were all called

together, and a psalm was sung and prayer attended, as an introduction to the sanctifying the Sabbath. This care and exactness
effectually prevented that intruding on holy time, by attending on
secular business, too common in families where the evening before
the Sabbath is pretended to be observed.

He was a great enemy to young people's unseasonable company-
keeping and frolicking, as he looked upon it as a great means of
corrupting and ruining youth. And he thought the excuse many
parents make for tolerating their children in it (viz. that it is the
custom, and others' children practice it, which renders it difficult,
and even impossible to restrain theirs) was insufficient and frivolous; and manifested a great degree of stupidity, on supposition the
practice was hurtful and pernicious to their souls. And when some
of his children grew up he found no difficulty in restraining them
from this pernicious practice; but they cheerfully complied with
the will of their parents herein. He allowed not his children to be
from home after nine o'clock at night, when they went abroad to
see their friends and companions. Neither were they allowed to sit
up much after that time, in his own house, when any came to make
them a visit. If any gentleman desired acquaintance with his
daughters; after handsomely introducing himself, by properly consulting the parents, he was allowed all proper opportunity for it; a
room and fire, if needed: but must not intrude on the proper hours
of rest and sleep, or the religion and order of the family.

He had a strict and inviolable regard to justice in all his dealings
with his neighbors, and was very careful to provide for things
honest in the sight of all men; so that scarcely a man had any
dealings with him, that was not conscious of his uprightness. He
appeared to have a sacred regard to truth in his words, both in
promises and narrations, agreeable to his Resolutions. This doubtless was one reason why he was not so full of words as many are.
No man feared to rely on his veracity.

He was cautious in choosing his *intimate friends,* and therefore
had not many that might properly be called such. But to them he
showed himself friendly in a peculiar manner. He was indeed a
faithful friend, and able above most others to keep a secret. To
them he discovered himself more than to others, led them into his

views and ends in his conduct in particular instances: by which they had abundant evidence that he well understood human nature; and that his general reservedness, and many particular instances of his conduct, which a stranger might impute to ignorance of men, were really owing to his uncommon knowledge of mankind.

His conversation with his friends was always savory and profitable: in this he was remarkable, and almost singular.—He was not wont to spend his time with them, in scandal, evil-speaking and back-biting, or in foolish jesting, idle chat and telling stories; but his mouth was that of the just, which bringeth forth wisdom, and his lips dispersed knowledge. His tongue was as the pen of a ready writer, while he conversed about important, heavenly, divine things, which his heart was so full of, in such a natural and free manner, as to be most entertaining and instructive: so that none of his friends could enjoy his company without instruction and profit, unless it was by their own fault.

His great benevolence to mankind discovered itself, among other ways, by the uncommon regard he showed to liberality, and charity to the poor and distressed. He was much in recommending this, both in his public discourses and private conversation. He often declared it to be his opinion, that professed Christians, in these days are greatly deficient in this duty; and much more so, than in most other parts of external Christianity. He often observed how much this is spoken of, recommended and encouraged in the holy Scripture, especially in the New Testament. And it was his opinion, that every particular church ought by frequent and liberal contributions, to maintain a public stock, that might be ready for the poor and necessitious members of that church: and that the principal business of deacons is to take care of the poor in the faithful and judicious distribution and improvement of the church's temporals, lodged in their hands. And he did not content himself with only recommending charity to others, but practiced it much himself; though, according to his Master's advice, he took great care to conceal his deeds of charity; by which means doubtless most of his alms-deeds will be unknown till the resurrection, which if known, would prove him to be as great an instance of charity as any that can be produced in this age. This is not mere conjecture, but is evident many ways. He was forward to give on all public occasions of charity, though when it could properly be done, he always concealed the sum given. And some instances of his giving more privately have accidentally come to the knowledge of others, in which his liberality appeared in a very extraordinary degree. One of the instances was this. Upon hearing that a poor obscure man, whom he never saw, or any of his kindred, was by an extraordinary bodily disorder, brought to great straits; he unasked, gave a considerable sum to a friend to be delivered to the distressed person; having first required a promise of him, that he would let neither the person, who was the object of his charity, nor anyone else know by whom it was given. This may serve both as an instance of his extraordinary charity, and of his great care to conceal it.[3]

Mr. Edwards had the most universal character of a *good preacher* of almost any minister in this age. There were but few that heard him, who did not call him a good preacher, however they might dislike his religious principles, and be much offended at the same truths when delivered by others: and most admired him above all that ever they heard. His eminency as a preacher seems to be owing to the following things:

First, The great pains he took in composing his sermons, especially in the first part of his life. As by his early rising, and constant attention to his study, he had more time than most others; so he spent more time in making his sermons. He wrote most of his sermons all out, for near twenty years after he first began to preach; though he did not wholly confine himself to his notes in his delivering them.

Secondly, His great acquaintance with divinity, his study and knowledge of the Bible. His extensive and universal knowledge, and great clearness of thought, enabled him to handle every subject with great judgment and propriety, and to bring out of his treasury things new and old. Every subject he handled was instruc-

---

[3] As both the giver, and the object of his charity are dead, and all the ends of the proposed secrecy are answered; 'tis thought not inconsistent with the above-mentioned promise, to make known the fact, as it is here related.

tive, plain, entertaining and profitable; which was much owing to his being master of the subject, and his great skill to treat it in a most natural, easy and profitable manner. None of his composures were dry speculations, or unmeaning harangues, or words without ideas. When he dwelt on those truths which are much controverted and opposed by many, which was often the case, he would set them in such a natural and easy light, and every sentiment from step to step, would drop from his lips, attended with such clear and striking evidence, both from Scripture and reason, as even to force the assent of every attentive hearer.

Thirdly, His excellency as a preacher was very much the effect of his great acquaintance with his own heart, his inward sense and high relish of divine truths, and the high exercise of true, experimental religion. This gave him a great insight into human nature: he knew what was in man, both the saint and the sinner. This helped him to skill, to lay truth before the mind, so as not only to convince the judgment, but touch the heart and conscience, and enabled him to speak out of the abundance of his heart, what he knew, and testify what he had seen and felt. This gave him a taste and discerning, without which he could not have been able to fill his sermons, as he did, with such striking, affecting sentiments, all suited to solemnize, move and rectify the heart of the hearer. His sermons were well connected, not usually long and commonly a large part taken up in the improvement; which was closely connected with the subject, and consisted in sentiments naturally flowing from it.

But no description of his sermons will give the reader the idea of them, which they have who sat under his preaching, or have even read some of his discourses which are in print. There is a great number now in manuscript, which are probably as worthy the view of the public, and at least tend as much to instruct and quicken Christians, as most that have been published in this century.

His appearance in the desk was with a good grace, and his delivery easy, natural and very solemn. He had not a strong, loud voice; but appeared with such gravity and solemnity, and spake with such distinctness, clearness and precision; his words were so full of ideas, set in such a plain and striking light, that few speakers have been so able to demand the attention of an audience as he. His words often discovered a great degree of inward fervor, without much noise or external emotion, and fell with great weight on the minds of his hearers. He made but little motion of his head or hands in the desk, but spake so as to discover the motion of his own heart, which tended in the most natural and effectual manner to move and affect others.

As he wrote his sermons out at large for many years, and always wrote a considerable part of most of his public discourses; so he carried his notes into the desk with him, and read the most that he had wrote; yet he was not so confined to his notes, when he had wrote at large, but that, if some thoughts were suggested while he was speaking, which did not occur when writing, and appeared to him pertinent and striking, he would deliver them; and that with as great propriety and fluency, and oftener with greater pathos, and attended with a more sensible good effect on his hearers, than all he had wrote.

Though, as has been observed, he was wont to read so considerable a part of what he delivered; yet he was far from thinking this the best way of preaching in general; and looked upon his using his notes so much as he did, [as] a deficiency and infirmity. And in the latter part of his life was inclined to think it had been better, if he had never accustomed himself to use his notes at all. It appeared to him that preaching wholly without notes, agreeable to the custom in most Protestant countries, and what seems evidently to have been the manner of the apostles and primitive ministers of the gospel, was by far the most natural way; and had the greatest tendency on the whole, to answer the end of preaching: and supposed that none who had talents equal to the work of the ministry, was incapable of speaking *memoriter,* if he took suitable pains for this attainment from his youth. He would have the young preacher write all his sermons, or at least most of them, out at large; and instead of reading them to his hearers, take pains to commit them to memory. Which, though it would require a great deal of labor at first, yet would soon become easier by use, and help him to speak more correctly and freely, and be of great service to him all his days.

His prayers were indeed *extempore*. He was the farthest from any appearance of a form, as to his words and manner of expression, of almost any man. He was quite singular and inimitable in this, by any who have not a spirit of real and undissembled devotion. Yet he always expressed himself with decency and propriety. He appeared to have much of the grace and spirit of prayer; to pray with the spirit and with the understanding: and he performed this part of duty much to the acceptance and edification of those who joined with him. He was not wont, in ordinary cases to be long in his prayers: an error which he observed was often hurtful to public and social prayer, as it tends rather to damp than promote true devotion.

He kept himself quite free from worldly cares. He gave himself wholly to the work of the ministry, and entangled not himself with the affairs of this life. He left the particular oversight and direction of the temporal concerns of his family, almost entirely to Mrs. Edwards; who was better able than most of her sex to take the whole care of them on her hands. He was less acquainted with most of his temporal affairs than many of his neighbors; and seldom knew when and by whom his forage for winter was gathered in, or how many milk kine he had; whence his table was furnished, etc.

He did not make it his custom to visit his people in their own houses, unless he was sent for by the sick, or he heard that they were under some special affliction. Instead of visiting from house to house, he used to preach frequently at private meetings in particular neighborhoods; and often call the young people and children to his own house: when he used to pray with them and treat with them in a manner suited to their years and circumstances; and he catechized the children in public every Sabbath in the summer. And he used sometimes to propose questions to particular young persons in writing, for them to answer after a proper time given to them to prepare. In putting out these questions, he endeavored to suit them to the age, genius and abilities of those to whom they were given. His questions were generally such as required but a short answer; and yet could not be answered without a particular knowledge of some historical part of the

Scripture; and therefore led, and even obliged persons to study the Bible.

He did not neglect visiting his people from house to house, because he did not look upon it, in ordinary cases, to be one part of the work of the gospel-minister. But he supposed that ministers should, with respect to this, consult their own talents and circumstances, and visit more or less, according to the degree in which they could hope hereby to promote the great ends of the gospel-ministry. He observed, that some ministers had a talent at entertaining and profiting by occasional visits among their people. They have words at will, and a knack at introducing profitable, religious discourse in a free, natural and, as it were undesigned way. He supposed such had a call to spend a great deal of their time in visiting their people. But he looked on his talents to be quite otherwise. He was not able to enter into a free conversation with every person he met with, and in an easy manner turn it to what topic he pleased, without the help of others, and, as it may be, against their inclination. He therefore found that his visits of this kind must be in a great degree unprofitable. And as he was settled in a great town, it would take up a great part of his time to visit from house to house; which he thought he could spend in his study to much more valuable purposes, and so as much better to promote the great ends of his ministry. For it appeared to him, that he could do the greatest good to souls, and most promote the interest of Christ by preaching and writing, and conversing with persons under religious impressions in his study; where he encouraged all such to repair; where, they might be sure, in ordinary cases, to find him: and to be allowed easy access to him, and where they were treated with all desirable tenderness, kindness and familiarity. In times therefore of the outpouring of God's spirit, and the revival of religion among his people, his study was thronged with persons to lay open their spiritual concerns to him, and seek his advice and direction: whom he received and conversed with, with great freedom and pleasure, and had the best opportunity to deal in the most particular manner with each one.

He was a skilful guide to souls under spiritual difficulties. And was therefore sought unto not only by his own people, but by many who lived scores of miles off. He became such an able guide, partly by his own experimental acquaintance with divine things, and unwearied study of God's word; and partly by his having so much concern with souls under spiritual troubles; for he had not been settled in the work of the ministry many years before the Spirit of God was wonderfully poured out on his people, by which a great concern about their souls became almost universal; and a great number were hopefully the subjects of saving conversion. This was principally in the year 1734; a particular account of which has been wrote by him, entitled, *A Faithful Narrative of the surprising Work of God in the conversion of many Hundred Souls in Northampton.* Which has been printed in England, Germany and America; to which the reader must be referred.

And there was another remarkable time of the outpouring of God's Spirit in the year 1740, and 1741, in which Northampton partook largely; though not exclusive of most other parts of the land. Mr. Edwards in this time had to deal not only with his own people, but with multitudes of others. The hearing that the same things were at Northampton some years before, and the fame Mr. Edwards had for knowledge, piety, and a great acquaintance with experimental religion, naturally led both ministers and people, in almost all parts of New England, to look to him for direction and assistance, in this extraordinary time. Being in this time earnestly solicited by the ministers and people of many places to come and preach among them, he went to many; though he was not able to gratify all who desired him. And his preaching was attended with great success.

And as many of the ministers and people in New England had been unacquainted with such things as then appeared, they were greatly exposed to *run wild,* as it were, and actually did, by the subtle temptations of the devil, taking advantage of the ignorance and wickedness of men's hearts, go into great extremes both as opposers and friends to the work of God. Mr. Edwards was greatly helpful by his direction and assistance against the two opposite extremes, both in conversation, preaching and writing. His publications on this occasion were especially of great and extensive service. Of which it may be proper to give some account here.

The first is a sermon preached at New Haven, Sept. 10, 1741, *on the distinguishing Marks of the Spirit of God, etc.*

In the year 1742, he published a book of five parts, entitled, *Some Thoughts concerning the present Revival of Religion in New England, and the Way in which it ought to be acknowledged and promoted, etc.*

In the year 1746, he published a *Treatise on Religious Affections.* All which might be justly considered by the church of Christ as a voice behind them saying, "This is the way, walk therein." Especially the last-mentioned book, which has been esteemed by many the best that has been wrote on that subject; setting the distinction between true and false religion in the most clear and striking light.

To the same purpose, is *The Life of the Rev. Mr. David Brainerd, with Reflections and Observations thereon;* published by Mr. Edwards in the year 1749.

Mr. Edwards was what by some is called a rigid *Calvinist.* Those doctrines of Calvinism, which have been most objected against, and given the greatest offense, appeared to him as Scriptural, reasonable and important as any; and he thought that to give them up, was in effect to give up all. And therefore he looked upon those who called themselves *Calvinists,* that were for palliating the matter, by, as it were, trimming off the knots of Calvinism, that they might conform it more to the taste of those who are most disposed to object against it, were really giving up and betraying the cause they pretended to espouse; and were paving the way not only to Arminianism, but to Deism. For if these doctrines, in the whole length and breadth of them were relinquished, he did not see, where a man could set his foot down with consistency and safety, short of Deism, or even Atheism itself; or rather universal Skepticism.

He judged that nothing was wanting, but to have these doctrines properly stated and judiciously and well defended, in order to their appearing most agreeable to reason and common sense, as well as the doctrines of revelation; and that this therefore was the only effectual method to convince, or silence and shame the opposers of them. All will be able to satisfy themselves of the truth of this, by reading his Treatise *On Justification,* and his two last books on *The Freedom of the Will,* and *Original Sin.*

In this view of things, he thought it of importance that ministers should be very critical in examining candidates for the ministry, with respect to their *principles,* as well as their religious dispositions and morals. And on this account he met with considerable difficulty and opposition in some instances. His opinion was, that an erroneous or unfaithful minister was likely to do more hurt than good to the church of Christ; and therefore he could not have any hand in introducing a man into the ministry, unless he appeared *sound in the faith,* and manifested to a judgment of charity, a *disposition to be faithful.*

Section II   HIS DISMISSION FROM NORTHAMPTON, WITH THE OC-
CASION AND CIRCUMSTANCES OF IT

Mr. Edwards was very happy in the esteem and love of his people for many years, and there was the greatest prospect of his living and dying so. He was the last minister almost in New England that would have been pitched upon to be opposed and renounced by his people. But by what has come to pass with respect to this, we have an instructive lesson on the instability of all human affairs, and the unreasonableness of trusting in man.

In the year 1744, Mr. Edwards was informed that some of the young persons in town, who were members of the church, had books in keeping, which they improved to promote lascivious and obscene discourse among the young people. And upon inquiring, a number of persons were found to testify, that they had heard one and another from time to time talk obscenely; as what they were led to by reading a book or books, which they had among them. Upon which Mr. Edwards thought the brethren of the church ought to look into the matter. And in order to introduce it, he preached a sermon from Heb. xii. 15, 16. "Looking diligently, lest any man fail of the grace of God, lest any root of bitterness springing up trouble you, and thereby many be defiled: lest there be any fornicator, or profane person as Esau," etc. After sermon, he desired the brethren of the church to stay, and told them what information he had got; and proposed whether they thought proper to take any measures to examine into the matter. They with one consent, and much zeal, manifested it to be their opinion, that it ought to be inquired into. And proceeded to choose a number of men to assist their pastor in examining into the affair. Upon which Mr. Edwards appointed the time for their meeting at his house: and then read a catalogue of the names of young persons, whom he desired to come to his house at the same time. Some were the accused, and some witnesses; but it was not then declared of which number any particular person was.

When the names were published, it appeared, that there were but few of the considerable families in town, to which none of the persons named did belong, or were nearly related. Whether this was the occasion of the alteration or not, before the day appointed came, a great number of heads of families altered their minds (yea many condemned what they had done, before they got home to their own houses) and declared, they did not think proper to proceed as they had done; that their children should not be called to an account in such a way for such things, etc. etc.; and the town was suddenly all on a blaze. This strengthened the hands of the accused, and some refused to appear, and others that did appear, behaved unmannerly, and with a great degree of insolence, and contempt of the authority of the church. And little or nothing could be done further in the affair.

This was the occasion of weakening Mr. Edwards's hands in the work of the ministry, especially among the young people; with whom by this means he greatly lost his influence! This seemed in a great measure to put an end to Mr. Edwards's usefulness at North-ampton, and doubtless laid a foundation, and will help to account for the surprising events which will by and by be related. To be sure he had no great visible success after this; but the influences of God's spirit were greatly withheld, and security and carnality much increased among them. That great and singular degree of visible religion and good order which had been found among them, soon began gradually to decay: and the youth have since been more wanton and dissolute.

Mr. Stoddard, Mr. Edwards's grandfather and predecessor in

the work of the ministry, was of the opinion, that unconverted persons had a right in the sight of God, or considered as such, to the sacrament of the Lord's Supper; that therefore it was their duty to come to that ordinance, though they knew they had no true goodness, or gospel-holiness. He maintained, that visible Christianity does not consist in a profession or appearance of that wherein true holiness or real Christianity consists. That therefore the profession which persons make in order to be received as visible members of Christ's church, ought not to be such as to express or imply a real compliance with, or consent to the terms of the covenant of grace, or a hearty embracing the gospel. So that they who really reject Jesus Christ, and dislike the gospel-way of salvation in their hearts, and know that this is true of themselves, may make the profession without lying and hypocrisy. Accordingly, he endeavored to form a short profession for persons to make in order to be admitted into the church and come to the sacrament, answerable to this principle. And it took place and was practiced in Northampton; and persons were admitted into the church, and to the sacrament, not under the notion of their being true saints, or that they had any real goodness.

Mr. Stoddard's appearing to maintain this principle made a great noise in the country; and he was opposed as introducing something contrary to the principles and practice of almost all the churches in New England. And the matter was publicly controverted between him and Dr. Increase Mather of Boston. However, through Mr. Stoddard's great influence and ascendance over the people at Northampton, it was introduced there, though not without opposition. And his principles by degrees spread very much among ministers and people in that county, and in other parts of New England; though no church except Northampton publicly and professedly acted upon this principle, by altering the profession that those made, who were admitted to the sacrament, to suit it to such a notion: but required of all who joined to the church a profession of that wherein true Christianity, or real godliness consists. And of late years his opinion that persons who have no real goodness, but are in a Christless state, and know themselves to be so, may make a Christian profession and come to the sacrament, without lying and hypocrisy; and that they have a right, and 'tis their duty so to do, has greatly spread in the country.

Mr. Edwards had some hesitation about this matter when he first settled at Northampton, and afterwards; but did not receive such a degree of conviction, that the admitting persons into the church, who made no pretense to real godliness was wrong, as to prevent his practicing upon it with a good conscience, for some years. But at length his doubts about the matter greatly increased, which put him upon examining it more thoroughly than he had ever before done, by searching the Scripture, and reading and examining such books, as were written to defend the admission of persons to sacraments, without a profession of saving faith. And the result was a full conviction that it was wrong, and, that he could not practice upon it with a good conscience. He was fully convinced that to be a *visible Christian* was to put on the visibility or appearance of a real Christian; that the profession of Christianity was a profession of that, wherein real Christianity consists; was therefore a profession of true respect of Christ, and a hearty embracing the gospel, etc. That therefore no person who rejected Christ in his heart, could make such a profession consistent with truth. And therefore, as the ordinance of the Lord's Supper was instituted for none but visible professing Christians, none but those who are real Christians have a real right in the sight of God to come to that ordinance: and that none ought to be admitted thereto, who do not make a profession of real Christianity, and so cannot be received in a judgment of charity as true friends to Jesus Christ, or real saints.[4]

When Mr. Edwards's sentiments were known, in the spring of the year 1744, it gave great offense, and the town was put into a great ferment: and before he was heard in his own defense, or it was known by many what his principles were, the general cry was to have him dismissed, as what alone would satisfy them. This was

[4] They who have a desire more fully to understand this controversy, and know if it is justly represented here, may do it by reading what Mr. Edwards wrote on this occasion, in order to explain and vindicate his principles; together with the Rev. Mr. Williams's answer, and Mr. Edwards's reply to him. And if they please, they may consult what Dr. Mather, and Mr. Stoddard before wrote on this subject.

evident from the whole tenor of their conduct, as they neglected and opposed the most proper means of calmly considering, and so understanding the matter in dispute, and persisted in a refusal to attend to what Mr. Edwards had to say in defense of his principles. And from beginning to end opposed the measures which had the best tendency to compromise and heal the difficulty; and with much zeal pursued those, which were calculated to make a separation certain and speedy.

Mr. Edwards thought of preaching on the subject, that they might know what were his sentiments, and what were the grounds of them (of both which he was sensible the most of them were quite ignorant) before they took any step for a separation between him and his people. But that he might do nothing to increase the tumult, but on the contrary take all those steps, which he could with a good conscience, that tended to peace, he first proposed the thing to the church's standing committee; supposing that if he entered on the subject publicly with their consent, it would prevent the ill consequences which otherwise he feared would follow. But the most of them would by no means consent to it, but strenuously opposed it. Upon which he gave it over for the present, as what in such circumstances would rather raise a tumult, and blow the fire up to a greater height, than answer the good ends proposed.

Mr. Edwards being sensible that his principles were not understood, and much misrepresented through the country; and finding that his people were in too much of a heat calmly to attend to the matter in controversy then; and were in a disposition even to refuse to hear him preach upon it, proposed to print what he had to say on the point; as this seemed to be the only way left him to have a fair hearing. Accordingly his people consented to put off the calling a council, till what he should write was published. But they manifested great uneasiness in waiting, before it came out of the press. And when it was published, it was read but by very few of them. Mr. Edwards being sensible of this, renewed his proposal to preach upon it, and, at a meeting of the brethren of the church asked their consent in the following terms, "I desire that the brethren would manifest their consent, that I should declare the reasons of my opinion relating to full communion in the church, in

lectures appointed for that end: not as an act of authority, or as
putting the power of declaring the whole counsel of God out of my
hands; but for peace sake, and to prevent occasion of strife." But
it passed in the negative.

Mr. Edwards then proposed that it should be left to a few of the
neighboring ministers, whether it was not, all things considered,
reasonable that he should be heard in this matter from the pulpit,
before the affair should be brought to an issue. But this also passed
in the negative.

However, he having had the advice of the ministers and messengers of the neighboring churches, who met at Northampton to
advise them under their difficulties, proceeded to appoint a lecture,
in order to preach on the subject, proposing to do so weekly till he
had finished what he had to say. On Monday there was a precinct
or society meeting, in which a vote was passed to choose a
committee to go to Mr. Edwards, and desire him not to preach
lectures on the subject in controversy, according to his declaration
and appointment. And accordingly proceeded to choose a committee of three men for this purpose, who waited on him, and did their
errand. However, Mr. Edwards thought proper to proceed according to his proposal, and accordingly preached a number of sermons
till he had finished what he had to say on the subject. These
lectures were very thinly attended by his own people: but great
numbers of strangers from the neighboring towns attended them,
so many as to make above half the congregation. This was in
February and March, 1750.

The calling a decisive council to determine the matter of
difference between pastor and people, or rather to dismiss the
pastor from his church and people (for the delay of which a great
deal of impatience had been publicly manifested), was now more
particularly attended to by Mr. Edwards and the church.

Mr. Edwards had before this insisted upon it from time to time,
that they were by no means ripe for such a procedure (as they had
not yet given him a fair hearing in defense of his cause: which if
they would do, perhaps the need of such a council would be super-
seded). And besides, he thought there was abundant public evidence, that they were not yet in a temper suited to attend on, and

be active in such a transaction, as the dissolving of the relation between them and their pastor; which would, as things then stood, probably be the event. He observed, "That it was exceeding unbecoming churches of the Lamb of God to manage their religious affairs of greatest importance in a ferment and tumult, which ought to be managed with great solemnity, deep humiliation, and submission to the awful frowns of heaven, humble dependence on God, and with fervent prayer and supplication to Him. That therefore for them to go about such an affair, in such a manner as they did, would be most unbecoming the gospel, greatly to the dishonor of God and religion, and a way in which a people cannot expect a blessing. That such a great affair as this should be gone about with calm consideration; but that such a temper as the people were then in, was wholly inconsistent with this."

But having used all means which he could think of within his power to bring them to a more calm and charitable temper, and to hear and weigh what he had to say in his own defense, with attention and candor; and finding that nothing prevailed; but rather the tumult and uproar was increased; he consented that a decisive council should be called without any further delay.

But a difficulty attended the choice of a council, which was for some time insuperable. It was agreed that the council should be mutually chosen, one half by the pastor, and the other half by the church: but the people insisted upon it that he should be confined to the county in his choice. Mr. Edwards thought this an unreasonable restraint on him, as it was known that the ministers and churches in that county were almost universally against him in the controversy that divided him and his people, and made the two parties. He indeed did not suppose that the business of the proposed council would be to determine whether his opinion which was the occasion of the difficulty between him and his people, was right or not; or that what they were to judge of, depended upon this. But their business would be—to see and determine whether any possible way could be devised for an accommodation between a pastor and people, and to use their wisdom and endeavor in order to this. And if they found this impracticable, they must determine, whether things were now ripe for a separation; whether

what ought in justice to be previous to a separation had already
actually been done, so that there was nothing further in justice to
be demanded by either of the parties concerned, before a separation should take place. And if he was dismissed by them, it would
be their business to set forth to the world in what manner and for
what cause he was dismissed: how far he was innocent, and
whether he might yet be employed in the work of the ministry, etc.
All which were matters of great importance to him, and required
upright and impartial judges. And considering the great influence a
difference in religious opinions has to prejudice men one against
another; and the close connection of the point, in which most of
the ministers and churches in the county differed from him, with
the matter to be judged of, he did not think they could be reasonably looked upon so impartial judges, as that the matter ought to
be wholly left to them. Besides, he thought the case being so new
and extraordinary, required the ablest judges in the land. For
these, and some other reasons, which he offered, he insisted upon
liberty to go out of the county for those members of the proposed
council in which he was to have a choice. In this, as was just now
said, the people strenuously and obstinately opposed him. They at
length agreed to leave the matter to a council consisting of the
ministers and messengers of the five neighboring churches: who,
after they had met twice upon it, and had the case largely debated
before them, were equally divided, and therefore left the matter
undetermined.

However, they were all agreed, that Mr. Edwards ought to have
liberty to go out of the county for *some* of the council. And at the
next church meeting, which was on the 26th of March, Mr.
Edwards offered to join with them in calling a council, if they
would consent that he should choose *two* of the churches out of
the county, in case the council consisted of but *ten* churches. The
church however refused to comply with this at one meeting after
another repeatedly; and proceeded to warn a church meeting and
choose a moderator, in order to act without their pastor.

But, to pass by many particulars, at length at a meeting of the
church, warned by their pastor, May 3, they voted their consent to
his proposal of going out of the county for two of the churches,

that should be applied to. And then they proceeded to make choice of the ten ministers and churches, of which the council should consist. Accordingly, the churches were sent to, and the council convened on the 19th of June. Who, after they had made some fruitless attempts for a composition between the pastor and church, passed a resolve, by the majority of one voice[5] only, to the following purpose: "That 'tis expedient that the pastoral relation between Mr. Edwards and his church be immediately dissolved, if the people still persist in desiring it." And it being publicly put to the people, whether they still insisted on Mr. Edwards's dismission from the pastoral office over them? A great majority (above two hundred against twenty) zealously voted for his dismission. And he was accordingly dismissed June 22, 1750.

The dissenting part of the council, entered their protest against this proceeding, judging that it was too much in a hurry, as they were by no means ripe for a separation, considering the past conduct, and present temper of the people. And some of that part of the council that were active, expressed themselves surprised at the uncommon zeal and engagedness of spirit, publicly manifested by the people in their voting for a dismission; which evidenced to them, and all observing spectators, that they were far from a temper of mind becoming such a solemn and awful transaction, considered in all its circumstances.

Being thus dismissed, he preached his farewell sermon on the first of July, from 2 Cor. 1. 14. The doctrine he observed from the words was this, "Ministers and the people that have been under their care, must meet one another before Christ's tribunal, at the day of judgment." It was a remarkably solemn and affecting discourse, and was published at the desire of some of the hearers.

After Mr. Edwards was dismissed from Northampton, he preached there sometimes occasionally when they had no other preacher to supply the pulpit, till at length a great uneasiness was

[5] One of the churches which Mr. Edwards chose did not see fit to join the council. However, the minister of that church being at Northampton at the sitting of the council, was desired by Mr. Edwards and the church to sit in council and act, which he did. But there being no messenger from the church, the council was not full, and there was a disparity; by which means doubtless, there was *one* vote more for an immediate dismission, than against it.

manifested by many of the people, at his preaching there at all.
Upon which, the committee for supplying the pulpit, called the
town together, to know their minds with respect to that matter:
when they voted that it was not agreeable to their minds, that he
should preach among them. Accordingly, when Mr. Edwards was
in town, and they had no other minister to preach to them, they
carried on public worship among themselves, and without any
preaching, rather than to invite Mr. Edwards!

Every one must be sensible that this was a great trial to Mr.
Edwards. He had been near twenty-four years among that people;
and his labors had been, to all appearance, from time to time
greatly blessed among them: and a great number looked on him as
their spiritual father, who had been the happy instrument of
turning them from darkness to light, and plucking them as brands
out of the burning. And they had from time to time professed that
they looked upon it as one of their greatest privileges to have such
a minister, and manifested their great love and esteem of him, to
such a degree; that (as St. Paul says of the Galatians), if it had
been possible, they would have plucked out their own eyes, and
given them to him. And they had a great interest in *his* heart: he
had borne them on his heart and carried them in his bosom for
many years; exercising a tender concern and love for them: for
their good he was always writing, contriving, laboring; for them he
had poured out ten thousand fervent prayers; in their good he had
rejoiced as one that findeth great spoil; and they were dear to him
above any other people under heaven.

Now to have *this people* turn against him, and thrust him out
from among them, in a great tumult and heat, with haste, and a
great degree of violence; like the Jews of old stopping their ears
and running upon him with furious zeal, not allowing him to defend himself by giving him a fair hearing; and even refusing so
much as to hear him preach; many of them surmising and publicly
speaking many ill things as to his ends and designs! To have the
tables turned so suddenly and the voice so general and loud against
him. This surely must come very near to him, and try his spirit.
The words of the Psalmist seem applicable to this case, "It was not
an enemy that reproached me, then I could have borne it; neither
was it he that hated me, that did magnify himself against me, then

I would have hid myself from him. But it was thou—my guide and mine acquaintance. We took sweet counsel together, and walked unto the house of God in company."

Let us therefore now *behold the man!*

The calm and sedateness of his mind; his meekness and humility in great and violent opposition, and injurious treatment; his resolution and steady conduct through all this dark and terrible storm, were truly wonderful, and cannot be set in so beautiful and affecting a light by any description, as they appeared in to his friends, who were eye-witnesses.

Mr. Edwards had a numerous and chargeable family, and little or no income, exclusive of his salary: and considering how far he was advanced in years; the general disposition of people who want a minister, to prefer a young man who has never been settled, to one who has been dismissed from his people; and what misrepresentations were made of his principles through the country, it looked to him not at all probable that he should ever have opportunity to be settled again in the work of the ministry, if he was dismissed from Northampton: and he was not inclined or able to take any other course, or go into any other business to get a living. So that beggary as well as disgrace stared him full in the face, if he persisted in his principles. To be sure, he viewed himself as taking the most direct way to these, according to the natural course of things, by discovering and adhering to his principles, in the situation he then was. For he foresaw all this, before it came upon him; and therefore had the opportunity and the temptation to escape it, by concealing his principles. When he was fixed in his principles, and before they were publicly known, he told some of his friends, that if he discovered and persisted in them, it would most likely issue in his dismission and disgrace; and the ruin of himself and family, as to their temporal interests. He therefore first sat down and counted the cost, and deliberately took up the cross, when it was set before him in its full weight and magnitude; and in direct opposition to all worldly views and motives. And therefore his conduct in these circumstances, was a remarkable exercise and discovery of his conscientiousness; and his readiness to deny himself, and forsake all that he had, to follow Christ.

A man must have a considerable degree of the spirit of a martyr,

not to flinch in such a case as this; but go on with the steadfastness
and resolution with which he did. He, as it were, put his life in his
hand, and ventured on where truth and duty appeared to lead him,
unmoved at the threatening dangers on every side.

However, God did not forsake him. As He gave him those
inward supports by which he was able in patience to possess his
soul, and calmly and courageously row on in the storm, as it were,
in the face of boisterous winds, beating hard upon him, and in the
midst of gaping waves threatening to swallow him up: so He soon
appeared for him, in His providence, even beyond all his expectations. His correspondents and other friends in Scotland, hearing of
his dismission, and fearing it might be the means of bringing him
into worldly straits, generously contributed a handsome sum, and
sent it over to him.

And God did not leave him without tender, valuable friends at
Northampton; for a small number of his people who opposed his
dismission from the beginning, and some who acted on neither
side, who joined with him after his dismission, and adhered to him,
under the influence of their great esteem and love of Mr. Edwards,
were willing and thought themselves able to maintain him: and
insisted upon it that it was his duty to stay among them, as a
distinct and separate congregation from the body of the town, who
had rejected him.

Mr. Edwards could not see it to be his duty to stay among them,
as circumstances were; as this would probably be a means of
perpetuating an unhappy division in the town; and there was to
him no prospect of doing the good there, which would counter-
balance the evil. However, that he might do all he could to satisfy
his tender and afflicted friends; and because in the multitude of
counsellors there is safety, he consented to ask the advice of an
ecclesiastical council. Accordingly, a council was called, and convened at Northampton on the 15th of May, 1751.

The town on this occasion was put into a great tumult and fire.
They who were active in Mr. Edwards's dismission supposed,
though without any ground, and contrary to truth, that he was
contriving and attempting with his friends, again to introduce himself at Northampton. They drew up a remonstrance against their

proceedings, and laid it before the council (though they would not acknowledge them to be an ecclesiastical council), containing many heavy, though groundless insinuations and charges against Mr. Edwards, and bitter accusations of the party who had adhered to him: but refused to appear and support any of their charges, or so much as to give the gentlemen of the council any opportunity to confer with them, about the affair depending; though it was diligently fought.

The council having heard what Mr. Edwards, and they who adhered to him, and any others who desired to be heard, had to say, advised, agreeable to Mr. Edwards's judgment and expectation, that he should leave Northampton, and accept of the mission to which he was invited at Stockbridge; of which a more particular account will be given presently.

Many other facts relative to this sorrowful, strange, surprising affair (the most so doubtless of any of the kind, that ever happened in New England; and perhaps, in any part of the Christian world) might be related; but as this more general history of it, may be sufficient to answer the ends proposed, viz. to rectify some gross misrepresentations that have been made of the matter, and discover the great trial Mr. Edwards had herein, 'tis thought best to suppress other particulars. As a proper close to this melancholy story; and to confirm, and further illustrate what has been related, the following letter from Joseph Hawley, Esq. (a gentleman who was well acquainted with, and very active in the transactions of this whole affair, and very much a head and leader in it) to the Rev. Mr. Hall of Sutton, published in a weekly newspaper in Boston, May 19, 1760, is here inserted.

To the Rev. Mr. HALL *of* SUTTON

Northampton, May 9, 1760

Rev. Sir,

I have often wished that every member of the two ecclesiastical councils (that formerly sat in Northampton upon the unhappy differences between our former most worthy and Rev. pastor Mr. Jonathan Edwards and the church here) whereof you was a member; I say, Sir, I have often wished every one of them truly knew my real sense of my own conduct in the affairs that the one and the other of said council are privy to; and as I have long apprehended it to be my duty not only to humble myself before God for what was un-Christian and sinful, in my conduct before said councils, but also to confess my faults to them, and take shame to myself therefor before them. I have often studied with myself in what manner it was practicable for me to do it; and when I understood that you, Sir, and Mr. Eaton were to be at Cold Spring at the time of their late council, I resolved to improve the opportunity fully to open my mind there to you and him thereon; and thought that probably some method might be then thought of, in which my reflections on myself touching the matters above hinted at, might be communicated to most if not all the gentlemen aforesaid, who did not reside in this county: but you know, Sir, how difficult it was for us to converse together by ourselves when at Cold Spring, without giving umbrage to that people; I therefore proposed writing to you upon the matters which I had then opportunity only most summarily to suggest; which you, Sir, signified would be agreeable to you; I therefore now undertake what I then proposed, in which I humbly ask the divine aid; and that I may be made most freely willing fully to confess my sin and guilt to you and the world in those instances which I have reason to suppose fell under your notice, as they were public and notorious transactions, and on account whereof, therefore, you, Sir, and all others who had knowledge thereof, had just cause to be offended at me.

And in the first place Sir, I apprehend that with the church and people of Northampton, I sinned and erred exceedingly in consenting and laboring that there should be so early a dismission of Mr. Edwards from his pastoral relation to us, even upon the supposition that he was really in a mistake in the disputed point: not only because the dispute was upon matters so very disputable in themselves and at the greatest remove from fundamental, but because Mr. Edwards so long had approved himself a most faithful and painful pastor to said church; and also changed his sentiments in that point wholly from a tender regard to what appeared to him to be truth; and had made known his sentiments with great moderation and upon great deliberation, against all wordly motives, and from mere fidelity to his great Master, and a tender regard to the souls of his flock, as we had the highest reason to judge: which considerations now seem to me sufficient; and would (if we had been of a right spirit.) have greatly endeared him to his people, and made us to the last degree, reluctant to parting with him, and disposed us to the exercise of the greater candor, gentleness and moderation: how much of the reverse whereof appeared in us, I need not tell you Sir, who was an eye-witness of our temper and conduct.

And although it does not become me to pronounce decisively on a point so disputable as what was then in dispute; yet I beg leave to say, that I really apprehend that it is of the highest moment to the body of this church, and to me in particular, most solicitously to inquire, whether like the Pharisees and Lawyers in John Baptist's time, we did not reject the council of God against ourselves, in rejecting Mr. Edwards and his doctrine; which was the ground of his dismission. And I humbly conceive that it highly imports us all of this church, most seriously and impartially to examine what that most worthy and able divine, about that time, published in support of the same, whereby he being dead yet speaketh.

But there were three things Sir, especially in my own particular conduct before the first council, which have been justly matter of great grief and much trouble to me almost ever since, viz.

In the first place I confess Sir, that I acted very immodestly and abusively to you, as well as injuriously to the church and myself, when, with much zeal and unbecoming assurance, I moved the council that they would interpose to silence and stop you in an address you was making one morning to the people, wherein you was, if I don't misremember, briefly exhorting them to a tender remembrance of the former affection and harmony that had long subsisted between them and their Rev. Pastor, and the great comfort and profit which they had apprehended that they had received from his ministry; for which Sir, I heartily ask your forgiveness; and I think, that we ought, instead of opposing an exhortation of that nature, to have received it with all-thankfulness.

Another particular of my conduct before that council, which I now apprehend was criminal, and was owing to the want of that tender affection and reverend respect and esteem for Mr. Edwards which he had highly merited of me, was my strenuously opposing the adjournment of the matters submitted to that council, for about two months; for which I declare myself unfeignedly sorry; and I with shame remember, that I did it in a peremptory, decisive, vehement and very immodest manner.

But Sir, the most criminal part of my conduct at that time, that I am conscious of, was my exhibiting to that council a set of arguments in writing, the drift whereof was to prove the reasonableness and necessity of Mr. Edwards's dismission in case no accommodation was then effected with mutual consent; which tract by clear implication contained some severe, uncharitable, and if I don't misremember, groundless and slanderous imputations on Mr. Edwards, and expressed in bitter language; and although the original draft thereof was not done by me, yet I foolishly and sinfully consented to copy it: and, as agent for the church, to read it, and deliver it to the council, which I could never have done, if I had not had a wicked relish for perverse things: which conduct of mine, I confess was very sinful; am persuaded was highly provoking to God, and for which I am ashamed, confounded, and have nothing to answer.

As to the church's remonstrance (as it was called), which their committee preferred to the last of said councils, to all which I was consenting, and in the composing whereof I was very active, as also in bringing the church to their vote upon it: I would in the first place only observe, that I don't remember anything in that small part of it which was plainly discursive of the expediency of Mr. Edwards's resettlement here as pastor to a part of the church, which was very exceptionable; but as to all the residue, which was much the greatest part thereof (and I am not certain that any part was wholly free), it was everywhere larded with unchristian bitterness, sarcastical and unmannerly insinuations, contained divers direct, grievous and criminal charges and allegations against Mr. Edwards; which I have since good reason to suppose were all founded on jealous and uncharitable mistakes, and so were really gross slanders, also many heavy and reproachful charges upon divers of Mr. Edwards's adherents, and some severe censures of them all indiscriminately; all of which (if not wholly false and groundless) yet were altogether unnecessary, and therefore highly criminal. Indeed I am fully convinced, that the whole of that composure, excepting the small part thereof above mentioned, was totally unchristian, a scandalous, abusive, injurious libel, against Mr. Edwards and his particular friends; especially the former, and highly provoking and detestable in the sight of God; for which I am heartily sorry and ashamed; and pray I may remember it with deep abasement and penitence all my days. Nor do I now think that the church's conduct in refusing to appear and attend before that council to support the charges and allegations in said remonstrance against Mr. Edwards and said brethren, which they demanded, was ever vindicated by all the subtle answers that were given to said demand; nor do I think that our conduct in that instance was capable of a defense, for it appears to me, that by making charges of scandalous matters against them before said council, we necessarily so far gave that council jurisdiction; and I own with sorrow and regret, that I zealously endeavored, that the church should perseveringly refuse to appear before said council for the purpose above said; which I humbly pray God to forgive.

Another part of my conduct, Sir, of which I have long repented, and for which I hereby declare my hearty sorrow, was my obstinate opposition to the last council's having any conference with the church; which said council earnestly and repeatedly moved for, and which the church finally denied (as you know). I think it discovered a great deal of pride and vain sufficiency in the church, and showed them to be very opiniative, especially the chief sticklers, one of whom I own I was, and think it was running a most presumptuous risk, and acting the part of proud scorners, for us to refuse hearing and candidly and seriously considering what that council could say or propose to us; among whom there were divers justly in great reputation for grace and wisdom.

In these instances Sir, of my conduct, and others (to which you was not privy) in the course of that most melancholy contention with Mr. Edwards, wherein I now see that I was very much influenced by vast pride, self-sufficiency, ambition and vanity. I appear to myself vile, and doubtless much more so to others who are more impartial; and do in the review thereof, abhor myself, and repent sorely; and if my own heart condemns me, it behooves me solemnly to remember, that God is greater, and knoweth all things; and I hereby own, Sir, that such treatment of Mr. Edwards, as is herein before mentioned, wherein I was so deeply concerned and active, was particularly and very aggravatedly sinful and ungrateful in me, because I was not only under the common obligations of each individual of the society to him, as to a most able, diligent pastor; but I had also received many instances of his tenderness, goodness and generosity to me, as a young kinsman, whom he was disposed to treat in a most friendly manner.

Indeed, Sir, I must own, that by my conduct in consulting and acting against Mr. Edwards within the time of our most unhappy disputes with him, and especially in and about that abominable remonstrance, I have so far symbolized with Balaam, Ahitophel and Judas, that I am confounded and filled with terror oftentimes when I attend to the most painful similitude.

And I freely confess that on account of my conduct above mentioned, I have the greatest reason to tremble at those most solemn and awful words of our Saviour, Matth. xviii. 6. and those Luke x. at the 16.: and I am most sorely sensible, that nothing but that infinite grace and mercy which saved some of the betrayers and murderers of our blessed Lord, and the persecutors of his martyrs, can pardon me; in which alone I hope for pardon, for the sake of Christ, whose blood (blessed be God) cleanseth from all sin. On the whole, Sir, I am convinced, that I have the greatest reason to say as David, "Have mercy upon me, O God, according to Thy loving kindness, according to the multitude of Thy tender mercies, blot out my transgressions, wash me thoroughly from mine iniquity, and cleanse me from my sin; for I acknowledge my transgressions, and my sin is ever before me: hide Thy face from my sins, and blot out all mine iniquities: create in me a clean heart, O God, and renew a right spirit within me; cast me not away from Thy presence, and take not Thy holy Spirit from me. Restore unto me the joy of Thy salvation, and uphold me with Thy free Spirit."

And I humbly apprehend that it greatly concerns the church of Northampton most seriously to examine whether the many hard speeches, spoken by many particular members against their former pastor, some of which the church really countenanced, and especially those spoken by the church as a body, in that most vile remonstrance, are not so odious and ungodly, as to be utterly uncapable of defense; and whether said church were not guilty of great sin in being so willing and disposed for so slight a cause, to part with so faithful and godly a minister as Mr. Edwards was. And whether ever God will hold us guiltless till we cry to Him for Christ's sake to pardon and save us from that judgment which such ungodly deeds deserve, and publicly humble and take shame to ourselves therefor. And I most heartily wish and pray that the town and church of Northampton would seriously and carefully examine whether they have not abundant cause to judge that they are now lying under great guilt in the sight of God; and whether those of us who were concerned in that most awful contention with Mr. Edwards, can ever more reasonably expect God's favor and blessing, till our eyes are opened, and we become thoroughly convinced that we have greatly provoked the Most High, and been injurious to one of the best of men; and until we shall be thoroughly convinced that we have dreadfully persecuted Christ by persecuting and vexing that just man and servant of Christ; until we shall be humble as in the dust therefor, and till we openly in full terms, and without baulking the matter, confess the same before the world, and most humbly and earnestly seek forgiveness of God, and do what we can to honor the memory of Mr. Edwards, and clear it of all the aspersions which we unjustly cast upon him, since God has been pleased to put it beyond our power to ask his forgiveness. Such terms I am persuaded the great and righteous God will hold us to, and that it will be in vain for us to hope to escape with impunity in any other way. This I am convinced of with regard to myself, and this way I most solemnly propose to take myself (if God in His mercy shall give me opportunity,) that so by making free confession to God and man of my sin and guilt, and publicly taking shame to myself therefor, I may give glory to the God of Israel, and do what in me lies, to clear the memory of that venerable man from the wrongs and injuries I was so active in bringing on his reputation and character; and I thank God that He has been pleased to spare my life and opportunity therefor to this time, and am sorry that I have delayed the affair so long.

Altho' I made the substance of almost all the foregoing reflections in writing, but not exactly in the same manner to Mr. Edwards and the brethren who adhered to him, in Mr. Edwards's life, and before he removed from Stockbridge, and I have reason to believe that he, from his great candor and charity, heartily forgave me and prayed for me: yet because that was not generally known, I look on myself obliged to take further steps; for while I kept silence, my bones waxed old, etc.

For all these my great sins therefore, in the first place, I humbly and most earnestly ask forgiveness of God; nextly, of the relatives and near friends of Mr. Edwards. I also ask the forgiveness of all those who were called Mr. Edwards's adherents; and of all the members of the ecclesiastical councils above mentioned; and lastly, of all Christian people, who have had any knowledge of the matters above said, or any of them.

I have no desire, Sir, that you should make any secret of this letter; but desire, you would communicate the same to whom you shall judge proper; and I purpose (if God shall give me opportunity) to procure it to be published in some one of the public newspapers; for I can't devise any other way of making known my sentiments of the foregoing matters to all who ought to be acquainted therewith, and therefore I think I ought to do it, whatever remarks I may foresee will be made thereon.

Probably when it comes out, some of my acquaintance will pronounce me quite over-run with vapors; others will be furnished with matter for mirth and pleasantry; others will cursorily pass it over as relating to matters quite stale; but some I am persuaded will rejoice to see me brought to a sense of my sin and duty; and I myself shall be conscious that I have done something of what the nature of the case admits, towards undoing what is, and long has been, to my greatest remorse and trouble that it was ever done.

Sir, I desire that none would entertain a thought from my having spoken respectfully of Mr. Edwards, that I am disaffected to our present pastor; for the very reverse is true; and I have a reverend esteem, real value, and hearty affection for him, and bless God, that He has notwithstanding all our unworthiness, given us one to succeed Mr. Edwards, who (as I have reason to hope) is truly faithful.

I conclude this long letter, by heartily desiring your prayers, that my repentance of my sins above mentioned may be unfeigned and genuine, and such as God in infinite mercy for Christ's sake will accept; and I beg leave to subscribe myself,

Sir, your real, though very unworthy friend,
and obedient servant,
Joseph Hawley

Section III   HIS MISSION TO THE INDIANS AT STOCKBRIDGE, ETC.

The Indian mission at Stockbridge (a town in the western part of the province of the Massachusetts Bay, sixty miles from Northampton) being vacant by the death of the late Rev. Mr. Sergeant, the honored and reverend commissioners for Indian affairs, in Boston, who have the care and direction of it, applied to him, as the most suitable person they could think of to betrust with that mission. And he was at the same time invited by the inhabitants of Stockbridge; and being advised by the council, above mentioned, to accept of the invitation, he repaired to Stockbridge, and was introduced and fixed as missionary to the Indians there by an ecclesiastical council called for that purpose, August 8, 1751.

When Mr. Edwards first engaged in the mission, there was a hopeful prospect of its being extensively serviceable, under his care and influence; not only to that tribe of Indians which was settled at Stockbridge, but among the Six Nations: some of whom were coming to Stockbridge to settle, and bring their own, and as many of their neighbors' children as they could get; to be educated and instructed there. For this end, a house for a boarding-school, which was projected by Mr. Sergeant, was erected on a tract of land appropriated to that use by the Indians at Stockbridge: where the Indian children, male and female were to be educated, by being clothed and fed, and instructed by proper persons in useful learning. And the boys to be learned husbandry or mechanic trades, and the girls all sorts of women's work. For the encouragement of which, some generous subscriptions were made both in England and America. And the great and general court of the province of the Massachusetts Bay, did much to promote the affair, and provided lands for the Mohawks to settle on, who should incline to come. And the generous Mr. Hollis, to encourage the thing, ordered twenty-four Indian children to be educated on the same footing, wholly at his cost. Also the society in London, for propagating the gospel among the Indians in and about New England, directed their commissioners in Boston to do considerable towards this design.

But partly by reason of some unhappy differences that took place among those who had the chief management of this affair at Stockbridge, of which a particular account would not be proper in this place; and partly by the war's breaking out between England and France, which is generally very fatal to such affairs among Indians, this hopeful prospect came to nothing.

Mr. Edwards's labors were attended with no remarkable visible success while at Stockbridge: though he performed the business of his mission to the good acceptance of the inhabitants in general, both English and Indians, and of the commissioners, who supported him honorably, and confided very much in his judgment and wisdom in all matters relating to the mission.

Stockbridge proved to Mr. Edwards a more quiet, and, on many accounts, a much more comfortable situation than he was in before. It being so much in one corner of the country, his time was not so much taken up with company, as it was at Northampton, though many of his friends, from almost all parts of the land, often made him pleasant and profitable visits. And he had not so much concern and trouble with other churches as he was obliged to have when at Northampton, by being frequently sought to for advice, and called to assist in ecclesiastical councils. Here therefore he followed his beloved study more closely, and to better purpose than ever. In these six years he doubtless made swifter advances in knowledge than ever before, and added more to his manuscripts than in any six years of his life.

And this was probably as useful a part of his life as any. For in this time he wrote the two last books that have been published by him (of which a more particular account will be given hereafter), by which he has doubtless greatly served the church of Christ, and will be a blessing to many thousands yet unborn.

Thus, after his uprightness and faithfulness had been sufficiently tried at Northampton, his kind Master provided for him a quiet retreat, which was rendered the more sweet by the preceding storm; and where he had a better opportunity to pursue and finish the work God had for him to do.

Section IV   HIS BEING MADE PRESIDENT OF NEW JERSEY COL-
LEGE; HIS SICKNESS AND DEATH

On the 24th of Sept., 1757, the Rev. Mr. Aaron Burr, President of New Jersey College, died.—And at the next meeting of the trustees, Mr. Edwards was chosen his successor. The news of which was quite unexpected, and not a little surprising to him. He looked on himself in many respects so unqualified for that business, that he wondered that gentlemen of so good judgment, and so well acquainted with him, as he knew some of the trustees were, should think of *him* for that place. He had many objections in his own mind against undertaking the business, both from his unfitness, and his particular circumstances; yet could not certainly determine, that it was not his duty to accept. The following extract of a letter which he wrote to the trustees will give the reader a view of his sentiments and exercises on this occasion, as well as of the great designs he was deeply engaged in, and zealously prosecuting.

Stockbridge, 19th October, 1757
Reverend and Honored Gentlemen,
   I was not a little surprised, on receiving the unexpected notice of your having made choice of me to succeed the late president Burr, as the head of Nassau Hall.—I am much in doubt whether I am called to undertake the business, which you have done me the unmerited honor to choose me for—If some regard may be had to my outward comfort, I might mention the many inconveniences and great detriment, which must be sustained, by my removing with my numerous family, so far

from all the estate I have in the world (without any prospect of disposing of it, under present circumstances, without losing it, in great part) now when we have scarcely got over the trouble and damage sustained by our removal from Northampton, and have but just begun to have our affairs in a comfortable situation for a subsistence in this place; and the expense I must immediately be at to put myself into circumstance tolerably comporting with the needful support of the honor of the office I am invited to; which will not well consist with my ability.—But this is not my main objection: The chief difficulty in my mind, in the way of accepting this important and arduous office, are these two: First my own defects, unfitting me for such an undertaking, many of which are generally known; besides other, which my own heart is conscious to.—I have a constitution in many respects peculiarly unhappy, attended with flaccid solids, vapid sizzy and scarce fluids and a low tide of spirits; often occasioning a kind of childish weakness and contemptibleness of speech, presence and demeanor; with a disagreeable dulness and stiffness, much unfiting me for conversation, but more especially for the government of a College.—This poorness of constitution makes me shrink at the thoughts of taking upon me, in the decline of life, such a new and great business, attended with such a multiplicity of cares, and requiring such a degree of activity, alertness and spirit of government; especially as succeeding one, so remarkably well qualified in these respects, giving occasion to every one to remark the wide difference. I am also deficient in some parts of learning, particularly in Algebra, and the higher parts of Mathematics and in the Greek Classics; my Greek learning having been chiefly in the New Testament.—The other thing is this; that my engaging in this business, will not well consist, with those views, and that course of employ in my study, which have long engaged, and swallowed up my mind, and been the chief entertainment and delight of my life.—

And here, honored Sirs (emboldened by the testimony, I have now received of your unmerited esteem, to rely on your candor), I will with freedom open myself to you.

My method of study, from my first beginning the work of the ministry, has been very much by writing; applying myself in this way, to improve every important hint; pursuing the clue to my utmost, when anything in reading, meditation or conversation, has been suggested to my mind, that seemed to promise light, in any weighty point.—Thus penning what appeared to me my best thoughts, on innumerable subjects for my own benefit.—The longer I prosecuted my studies in this

method, the more habitual it became, and the more pleasant and profitable I found it.—The further I traveled in this way, the more and
wider the field opened, which has occasioned my laying out many
things, in my mind, to do in this manner, if God should spare my life,
which my heart hath been much upon: particularly many things against
most of the prevailing errors of the present day, which I cannot with
any patience see maintained (to the utter subverting of the gospel of
Christ) with so high a hand, and so long continued a triumph, with so
little control, when it appears so evident to me, that there is truly no
foundation for any of this glorying and insult—I have already published something on one of the main points in dispute between the
Arminians and Calvinists: and have it in view, God willing (as I have
already signified to the public) in like manner to consider all the other
controverted points, and have done much towards a preparation for it
—But besides these, I have had on my mind and heart (which I long
ago began, not with any view to publication) a great work, which I
call a *History of the Work of Redemption,* a Body of Divinity in an
entire new method, being thrown into the form of an history, considering the affair of Christian theology, as the whole of it, in each part,
stands in reference to the great work of redemption by Jesus Christ;
which I suppose is to be the grand design, of all God's designs, and the
summum and ultimum of all the divine operations and decrees; particularly considering all parts of the grand scheme in their historical
order.—The order of their existence, or their being brought forth to
view, in the course of divine dispensations, or the wonderful series of
successive acts and events; beginning from eternity and descending
from thence to the great work and successive dispensations of the infinitely wise God in time, considering the chief events coming to pass
in the church of God, and revolutions in the world of mankind, affecting the state of the church and the affair of redemption, which we have
account of in history or prophecy; 'till at last we come to the general
Resurrection, Last Judgment and consummation of all things; when it
shall be said, *It is done. I am Alpha and Omega, the Beginning and the
End.* Concluding my Work, with the consideration of that perfect state
of things, which shall be finally settled, to last for eternity.—This history will be carried on with regard to all three worlds, heaven, earth
and hell: considering the connected, successive events and alterations,
in each so far as the Scriptures give any light; introducing all parts of
divinity in that order which is most scriptural and most natural: which
is a method which appears to me the most beautiful and entertaining,

wherein every divine doctrine, will appear to greatest advantage in the brightest light, in the most striking manner, showing the admirable contexture and harmony of the whole.

I have also for my own profit and entertainment, done much towards another great work, which I call *the Harmony of the old and New Testament* in three Parts—The first considering the prophecies of the Messiah, His Redemption and Kingdom; the Evidences of their references to the Messiah etc. comparing them all one with another, demonstrating their agreement and true scope and sense; also considering all the various particulars wherein these prophecies have their exact fulfillment; showing the universal, precise, and admirable correspondence between predictions and events. The second part: Considering the types of the Old Testament, showing the evidence of their being intended as representations of the great things of the gospel of Christ: and the agreement of the type with the antitype.—The third and great part, considering the harmony of the Old and New Testament, as to doctrine and precept.—In the course of this work, I find there will be occasion for an explanation of a very great part of the holy scripture; which may, in such a view be explained in a method, which to me seems the most entertaining and profitable, best tending to lead the mind to a view of the true spirit, design, life and soul of the scriptures, as well as to their proper use and improvement.

I have also many other things in hand, in some of which I have made great progress, which I will not trouble you with an account of.—Some of these things, if divine Providence favor I should be willing to attempt a publication of—So far as I myself am able to judge of what talents I have, for benefiting my fellow creatures by word, I think I can write better than I can speak.

My heart is so much in these studies, that I cannot find it in my heart to be willing to put myself into an incapacity to pursue them any more, in the future part of my life, to such a degree as I must, if I undertake to go thro' the same course of employ, in the office of a President, that Mr. Burr, did, instructing in all the languages, and taking the whole care of the instruction of one of the classes in all parts of learning, besides his other labors.—If I should see light to determine me to accept the place offered me, I should be willing to take upon me the work of a President, so far as it consists in the general inspection of the whole society and subservient to the school, as to their order and methods of study and instruction, assisting myself in immediate instruction in the arts and sciences (as discretion should direct and occasion serve, and the state of things require) especially the senior class: and added to all, should be willing to do the whole work of a professor of divinity, in public and private lectures, proposing questions to be answered, and some to be discussed in writing and free conversation, in meetings of graduates and others, appointed in proper seasons for these ends.—It would be now out of my way, to spend time, in a constant teaching of the languages; unless it be the Hebrew tongue, which I should be willing to improve myself in, by instructing others.

On the whole, I am much at a loss, with respect to the way of my duty in this important affair: I am in doubt, whether if I should engage in it, I should not do what both you and I should be sorry for afterwards. Nevertheless, I think the greatness of the affair, and the regard due to so worthy and venerable a body, as that of the Trustees of Nassau Hall, requires my taking the matter into serious consideration: And unless you should appear to be discouraged, by the things which I have now represented, as to any further expectation from me, shall proceed to ask advice, of such as I esteem most wise, friendly and faithful; if after the mind of the Commissioners in Boston is known, it appears that they consent to leave me at liberty, with respect to the business they have employed me in here.

In this suspense he determined to ask the advice of a number of gentlemen in the ministry, on whose judgment and friendship he could rely, and to act accordingly. Who upon his, and his people's desire, met at Stockbridge, Jan. 4, 1758. And having heard Mr. Edwards's representation of the matter, and what his people had to say by way of objection against his removal, determined it was his duty to accept of the invitation to the presidency of the college.

When they published their judgment and advice to Mr. Edwards and his people, he appeared uncommonly moved and affected with it, and fell into tears on the occasion; which was very unusual for him, in the presence of others: and soon after said to the gentlemen, who had given their advice, that it was a matter of wonder to him, that they could so easily, as they appeared to do, get over the objections he had made against his removal, to be the head of a college; which appeared great and weighty to him. But as he thought it his duty to be directed by their advice, he should now endeavor cheerfully to undertake it, believing he was in the way of his duty.

Accordingly, having had, by the application of the trustees of the college, the consent of the commissioners to resign their mission; he girded up his loins, and set off from Stockbridge for Princeton in January. He left his family at Stockbridge, not to be removed till spring. He had two daughters at Princeton, Mrs. Burr, the widow of the late President Burr, and his oldest daughter that was unmarried.

His arrival at Princeton was to the great satisfaction and joy of the college. And indeed all the greatest friends to the college, and to the interest of religion, were highly satisfied and pleased with the appointment of Mr. Edwards to the presidency of that college, and had their hopes and expectations greatly raised hereby. And his correspondents and friends, and well-wishers to the college in Scotland, greatly approved of it.

The corporation met as soon as could be with conveniency, after his arrival in the college, when he was by them fixed in the president's chair.

While at Princeton, before his sickness, he preached in the college-hall from Sabbath to Sabbath, to the great acceptance of the hearers: but did nothing as president, unless it was to give out some questions in divinity to the senior class, to be answered before him; each one having opportunity to study and write what he thought proper upon them. When they came together to answer them, they found so much entertainment and profit by it, especially by the light and instruction Mr. Edwards communicated in what he said upon the questions, when they had delivered what they had to say, that they spoke of it with the greatest satisfaction and wonder.

During this time, Mr. Edwards seemed to enjoy an uncommon degree of the presence of God. He told his daughters, he had had great exercise, concern and fear, relative to his engaging in that business; but since it now appeared, so far as he could see, that he was called of God to that place and work, he did cheerfully devote himself to it, leaving himself and the event with God, to order what seemed to him good.

The smallpox had now become very common in the country, and was then at Princeton, and likely to spread. And as Mr. Edwards had never had it, and inoculation was then practiced with great success in those parts, he proposed to be inoculated, if the physicians should advise to it, and the corporation would give their consent.

Accordingly, by the advice of the physician, and consent of the corporation, he was inoculated February 13. He had it favorably, and it was thought all danger was over: but a secondary fever set in; and by reason of a number of pustules in his throat, the obstruction was such, that the medicines necessary to staunch the fever, could not be administered. It therefore raged till it put an end to his life on the 22d of March, 1758, in the fifty-fifth year of his age.

After he was sensible that he would not survive that sickness, a little before his death, he called his daughter to him, who attended him in his sickness, and addressed her in a few words, which were immediately taken down in writing, as near as could be recollected, and are as follows:

Dear Lucy,

It seems to me to be the will of God that I must shortly leave you; therefore give my kindest love to my dear wife, and tell her, that the uncommon union, which has so long subsisted between us, has been of such a nature, as I trust is spiritual, and therefore will continue forever: and I hope she shall be supported under so great a trial, and submit cheerfully to the will of God. And as to my children, you are now like to be left fatherless, which I hope will be an inducement to you all to seek a Father, who will never fail you. And as to my funeral, I would have it to be like Mr. Burr's; and any additional sum of money that might be expected to be laid out that way, I would have it disposed of to charitable uses.[6]

[6] President Burr ordered, on his death bed, that his funeral should not be attended with that pomp and cost, by procuring and giving away a great number of costly mourning-scarfs, etc. and the consumption of a great quantity of spirituous liquors; which is an extravagance that is become too customary in those parts, especially at the funerals of the great and the rich: and that nothing should be expended but what was agreeable to the dictates of Christian decency. And that the sum which must be expended at a modish funeral, over and above the necessary cost of a decent one, should be given to the poor out of his estate.

It is to be wished and hoped, that the laudable example of these two worthy presidents, in which they bear their dying testimony against a practice so unchristian, and of such bad tendency so many ways, may have some good effect.

He said but very little in his sickness; but was an admirable instance of patience and resignation to the last. Just at the close of his life, as some persons, who stood by, and expecting he would breathe his last in a few minutes, were lamenting his death not only as a great frown on the college, but as having a dark aspect on the interest of religion in general; to their surprise, not imagining that he heard, or ever would speak another word, he said, "TRUST IN GOD, AND YE NEED NOT FEAR." These were his last words. And what could have been more suitable to the occasion! And what need of more! In these is as much matter of instruction and support, as if he had wrote a volume. This is the only consolation to his bereaved friends, who are sensible of the loss they, and the church of Christ have sustained in his death; *God is all-sufficient, and still has the care of His church.*

He appeared to have the uninterrupted use of his reason to the last, and died with as much calmness and composure, to all appearance, as that with which one goes to sleep.

The physician who inoculated and constantly attended him in his sickness, has the following words in his letter to Mrs. Edwards on this occasion: "Never did any mortal man more fully and clearly evidence the sincerity of all his professions, by one continued, universal, calm, cheerful resignation and patient submission to the divine will, through every stage of his disease, than he. Not so much as one discontented expression, nor the least appearance of murmuring through the whole. And never did any person expire with more perfect freedom from pain: not so much as one distorted hair, but in the most proper sense of the words, he really fell asleep."

PART IV   *Containing an Account of his* MANUSCRIPTS, *and the* BOOKS *published by him*

Section I   HIS MANUSCRIPTS

Mr. Edwards has left a great many volumes in manuscript, which he wrote in a miscellaneous way on almost all subjects in divinity; which he did, not with any design they should ever be published in the form in which they are; but for the satisfaction and improvement of his own mind, and that he might retain the thoughts, which appeared to him worth preserving. Some idea of the progress he had made, and the materials he had collected in this way, he gives in the foregoing letter to the Trustees of Nassau-Hall; he has wrote much on the prophecies of the Messiah, Justification, the divinity of Christ and the eternity of hell torments. He wrote a great deal on the Bible, in the same way, by opening his thoughts on particular passages of it, as they occurred to him in reading or meditation; by which he has cast much light on many parts of the Bible, which has escaped other interpreters. And by which his great and painful attention to the Bible, and making it the only rule of his faith, are manifest.

If the public was willing to be at the cost, and publishing books of divinity met with as much encouragement now, as it has sometimes, there might be a number of volumes published from his manuscripts, which would afford a great deal of new light and entertainment to the church of Christ: though they would be more imperfect, than if he himself had prepared them for public view.

As the method he took to have his miscellaneous writings in such order, as to be able with ease to turn to anything he had wrote upon a particular subject, when he had occasion, is perhaps as good as any, if not the best that has been proposed to the public; some account of it will here be given, as what may be of advantage to young students, who have not yet gone into any method, and are disposed to improve their minds by writing.

He *numbered* all his miscellaneous writings. The first thing he wrote is No. 1. the second No. 2. and so on. And when he had occasion to write on any particular subject, he first set down the number, and then wrote the subject in capitals or large character, that it might not escape his eye, when he should have occasion to turn to it. As for instance, if he was going to write on the happiness of angels, and his last No. was 148, he would begin thus—149. ANGELS, their happiness.—And when he had wrote what he designed at that time on that subject, he would turn to an alphabetical table which he kept, and under the letter A, he would write, Angels, their happiness, if this was not already in his alphabet; and then set down the Number, 149, close at the right hand of it. And if he had occasion to write any new thoughts on this same subject;

if the number of his miscellanies was increased, so that his last number was 261, he would set down the number 262, and then the subject, as before. And when he had done writing for that time, he turn'd to his table, to the word angels; and at the right hand of the Number 149, set down 162. By this means he had no occasion to leave any chasms; but began his next subject where he left off his last. The number of his miscellaneous writings rang'd in this manner, amounts to above 1400. And yet by a table contained on a sheet or two of paper, any thing he wrote can be turned to, at pleasure.

Section II   HIS PUBLICATIONS

Mr. Edwards was greatly esteemed and famed as an author, both in Europe and America. His publications naturally raised in the reader of taste and judgment, an opinion of his greatness and piety. His books met with a good reception in Scotland especially, and procured him great esteem and applause there. A gentleman of note there for his superior genius and talents has the following words concerning Mr. Edwards, in a letter to one of his correspondents in America.

I looked on him as incomparably the greatest divine and philosopher in Britain or her Colonies; and rejoiced that one so eminently qualified for teaching divinity was chosen President of New Jersey College.

And in another letter the same gentleman says,

Ever since I was acquainted with Mr. Edwards's writings, I have looked upon him as the greatest divine this age has produced. And a rev. gentleman lately from Holland, says, That Mr. Edwards's writings, especially on the *Freedom of the Will,* were had in great esteem there: that the professors of the celebrated academy, presented their compliments to President Edwards. Several members of the Classis of Amsterdam gave their thanks, by him, to pious Mr. Edwards, for his just observations on Mr. Brainerd's life; which book was translated in Holland, and was highly approved of by the University of Utrecht——.

A brief Account of what he published is therefore here subjoined.

A Sermon preached at Boston, on I Cor. i. 29, 30, 31. With a Preface by one of the Ministers of Boston.

A Sermon preached at Northampton, in the year 1734, from Math. xvi. 17. entitled, A divine and supernatural Light immediately imparted to the Soul by the Spirit of God.

The narrative which has been mentioned, wrote Nov. 6, 1736. which was first printed in London, and recommended by Dr. Watts, and Dr. Guyse; and had two editions there. And then it had another Edition in Boston, in the year 1738. recommended by four of the senior ministers in Boston. To which were prefixed five Discourses on the following subjects.

I. Justification by Faith alone. II. Pressing into the Kingdom of God. III. Ruth's Resolution. IV. The Justice of God in the Damnation of Sinners. V. The Excellency of Jesus Christ.

Deliver'd at Northampton, chiefly at the time of the wonderful pouring out of the Spirit of God there.

The Discourse on Justification by Faith alone, may be recommended as one of the best things that has been wrote on that Subject; setting this truth in a most plain, Scriptural and convincing light; and as well worthy the careful perusal of all Christians; especially candidates for the ministry. The other Discourses are excellent, having much divinity in them, and tending above most that are published, to awaken the conscience of the sinner, and instruct and quicken the Christian.

A Sermon preached at Enfield, July 8, 1741. entitled, Sinners in the Hands of an angry God. Preached at a time of great awakenings there; and attended with remarkable impressions on many of the hearers.

A Sermon on the distinguishing Marks of a work of the Spirit of God, preached at New Haven, Sept. 10, 1741. from I Job. iv. I. published with great enlargements. This was re-printed in Scotland.

Some thoughts concerning the present revival of religion in New England, and the way in which it ought to be acknowledged and promoted humbly offered to the public, in a treatise on that subject, in five parts. Published in the year 1742. This had a second edition in Scotland.

A Treatise concerning religious Affections. Published in the year 1746. These three last have been mentioned before, with the particular occasion and design of their publication.

A treatise entitled, An humble attempt to promote explicit agreement, and visible union of God's people in extraordinary prayer, for the revival of religion etc. Recommended by five of the principal ministers in Boston. Published in 1747. In which he shows his great acquaintance with Scripture, and his attention to, and good understanding of the prophetic part of it.

An account of the life of the rev. Mr. David Brainerd, minister of the gospel and missionary to the Indians etc. with reflections and observations thereon. Published in the year 1749.

An enquiry into the qualifications for full communion in the visible church. Published in the year 1749. intended as an explanation and vindication of his principles in the matter, which occasioned his dismission from Northampton.

A reply to the rev. Mr. William's answer to the forementioned inquiry. Published in the year 1752.

A Sermon preached at Newark, before the Synod, Sept. 28, 1752. from Jam. ii. 19. entitled, True grace distinguished from the experience of Devils.

A careful and strict inquiry into the modern prevailing notion of that freedom of will, which is supposed to be essential to moral agency etc. Published in the year 1754.

This is justly thought by good judges to be one of the greatest efforts of the human mind, that has appeared, at least, in this century. In which the author shows that force and strength of mind, that judgment, penetration and accuracy of thought, that justly entitles him to the character of one of the greatest geniuses of this age. This treatise doubtless goes further towards settling the main points in controversy between Calvinists and Arminians, than anything that has been wrote: he having herein abundantly demonstrated the chief principles on which Arminians build their whole scheme, to be false and most absurd. Whenever therefore this book comes to be generally attended to, it will doubtless prove fatal to Arminian and Pelagian Principles. This was re-printed in London Anno 1762: and has been introduced by the Rev. T. Clap, President of Yale College, to be recited there by the Students.

The great Christian doctine of Original Sin defended; evidences of its truth produced and arguments to the contrary answered. Containing, in particular, a reply to the objections and arguings of Dr. John Taylor etc. Published in the year 1758. This was in the press when he died.

Besides these, he published, several Ordination Sermons, and some others, preached upon particular occasions.

WILLISTON WALKER

✪

Jonathan Edwards

To come to Andover with a lecture on Jonathan Edwards seems well-nigh an impertinence. Here, where his name has been honored more, if it be possible, than anywhere else in New England, where his life and works have long been familiarly and affectionately studied, where most of his unpublished manuscripts are guarded, there is nothing novel that a lecturer can offer; nor can he expect his knowledge of his theme to compare in thoroughness with that of several of his hearers. Yet the lecturer is reminded that this is a course on Congregationalism, not on unfamiliar Congregationalists; and to treat of the eighteenth century without glancing up, at least for a few moments, at the towering figure of our most original New England theologian, is like shutting out from memory the Presidential Range as one thinks of the White Mountains.

Passing along the sandy road that skirts the edge of the low bluff above the level meadowland, that borders the east bank of the Connecticut River, in the town of South Windsor, one sees by the roadside the site where stood, till the beginning of the nineteenth century, the "plain two-story house"[1] in which Jonathan Edwards was born. Though pleasant farming country, there is little in the immediate surroundings to detain the eye; but the blue

[1] See J. A. Stoughton, *Windsor Farmes* (Hartford, 1883), p. 46; H. R. Stiles, *History and Genealogies of Ancient Windsor* (Hartford, 1891), I, 556. The house stood till 1813.

From Williston Walker, *Ten New England Leaders* (New York: Silver, Burdett and Company, 1901), pp. 217–263.

hills beyond the river to the westward stretch away into the distance as attractively now as they did then when, if tradition is to be trusted, Jonathan's autocratic father, the parish minister, warned a neighbor whose refusal to remove a wide-spreading tree annoyed him, that if this disrespectful conduct was continued he would not baptize that contumacious neighbor's child. Behind the house, to the eastward a few rods, rises a low, tree-covered hill, cutting off the view in that direction, and affording a retreat to which father and son were accustomed to withdraw in pleasant weather for meditation or for prayer.[2] Here at what is now South Windsor, Timothy Edwards, Jonathan's father, exercised an able, spiritual, and conspicuously learned ministry from 1694 to his death in 1758.[3] Grandson of William Edwards, an early settler of Hartford, and son of Richard Edwards, a prominent merchant of Hartford, and of his erratic wife, Elisabeth Tuthill,[4] Timothy Edwards had graduated with distinction from Harvard College in 1691, and was always a man of marked intellectual power. The considerable list of boys fitted in his home for college[5] bears witness to his abilities as a teacher, and the judgment of his congregation that he was a more learned man and a more animated preacher than his son, Jonathan,[6] reflects the esteem in which he was held by the people of his charge. His wife, Jonathan's mother, was a daughter of Solomon Stoddard, of Northampton, the ablest minister of the Connecticut Valley when the seventeenth century passed into the eighteenth, and granddaughter of John Warham, the first pastor of Windsor.

Into this intellectual, strenuous, and yet cheerful home in this bit of rural New England Jonathan Edwards was born on October 5, 1703. Here he grew up, the fifth among eleven children and the only brother among ten tall sisters. Here he was fitted for college in his father's study, and the intellectual sympathy thus begun between father and son was to be a lifelong bond.

Youthful precocity is by no means an infallible prophecy of

[2] Stoughton, pp. 46, 47.
[3] *Ibid., passim.*
[4] See *Colonial Records of Connecticut,* IV, 59; Stoughton, pp. 39, 69.
[5] For some of these names see Stoughton, pp. 77, 78, 101–103.
[6] S. E. Dwight, *Life of Pres. Edwards* (New York, 1830), p. 17.

mature strength, but with Jonathan Edwards the mind received an early development and manifested a grasp that was little less than marvelous at an age when most schoolboys are scarcely emerging from childhood. His observations on nature, notably the well-known paper on the habits of the spider, apparently written when Edwards was about the age of twelve; and even more his notes on the mind, some at least of which seem to have been the immediate fruit of his reflections upon Locke's famous *Essay,* which he had read when fourteen, witness to his early intellectual maturity. The same precocious strength of mind is apparent in his less easily dated, but youthful, attainment of some of the positions of Berkeley or Malebranche—an attainment that seems to have been due to an independent development, rather than to acquaintance with their writings.[7]

Naturally, such a boy went early to college; and we find Edwards entering Yale in September, 1716, about a month before the close of his thirteenth year. The institution whose distinguished graduate he was to become was far enough removed from the university of the present. Founded in 1701, and therefore only two years older than Edwards himself, its precarious existence had thus far been spent at Saybrook; but the question of removal to New Haven was in heated debate just at the time that Edwards entered,[8] and a month after the beginning of his freshman year was decided by the trustees. Their decision in favor of New Haven was unpopular in the section of the colony in which Edwards' home was situated; and, before the close of 1716, a considerable portion of the students of the distracted college had gathered at Wethersfield under the instruction of two tutors, one, a recent graduate of Harvard, the other, three years an alumnus of Yale.[9] Of these

[7] *Ibid.,* pp. 22–63, 664–702; G. P. Fisher, *Discussions in History and Theology* (New York, 1880), pp. 228–232; Alexander V. G. Allen, *Jonathan Edwards* (Boston, 1889), pp. 3–31; E. C. Smyth, in *Proceedings of the American Antiquarian Society* for 1895, pp. 212–236; Fisher, *History of Christian Doctrine* (New York, 1896), pp. 396, 403. H. N. Gardiner, *Jonathan Edwards: A Retrospect* (Boston, 1901), pp. 115–160.

[8] F. B. Dexter, *Biographical Sketches of the Graduates of Yale College,* I, 159, 160.

[9] Elisha Williams, Harvard, 1711, afterward president of Yale, speaker of the Connecticut lower house, judge of the Superior Court, and colonel of the Connecticut troops; and Samuel Smith, Yale, 1713.

emigrating dissenters Edwards was one; and at Wethersfield he remained till the healing of the division in the early summer of 1719 carried him to New Haven.[10] Here he lived in the newly erected hall and dormitory, then known distinctively as Yale College, in a room rented at the moderate rate of twenty shillings a year; and here, too, he boarded in commons at a charge of five shillings—83⅓ cents—a week. These prices were in no way exceptionally moderate, nor is there any evidence of which I am aware that Edwards' student days were not as comfortable from a pecuniary standpoint as those of any of his position in the commonwealth. Here at New Haven he graduated, in September, 1720, at the head of a class of ten, after a course involving little more than an acquaintance with a few books of Virgil and orations of Cicero, the Greek Testament, the Psalms in Hebrew, the elements of logic, Ames' *Theology* and *Cases of Conscience,* and a smattering of physics, mathematics, geography, and astronomy.[11] In Edwards' case, however, this course had been greatly supplemented by the reading at Wethersfield of such books as he could borrow or purchase, and at New Haven by the use of the largest and best selected library then in Connecticut, which the diligence of Jeremiah Dummer and of other friends in England had procured for the college. It was doubtless the opportunity afforded by this library that kept Edwards at New Haven engaged in the study of theology till the summer of 1722, when, it seems probable, he was licensed to preach.[12]

Somewhere in this period of study, probably about the time of his graduation,[13] Edwards passed through the deepest experience that can come to a human soul, a conscious change in its relations to God. As John Wesley was a Christian and a minister before he was "converted," and yet was wrought upon mightily by that spiritual experience that came to him as he heard Luther's Preface to the *Commentary on Romans* read in the Moravian Chapel in

---

[10] See Edwards' letter of March 26, 1719, Dwight, pp. 29, 30.

[11] Dexter, pp. 115, 141–143, 177, 200, 203; Dwight, p. 32.

[12] Hopkins, *Life and Character of the Late Reverend Mr. Jonathan Edwards* (Boston, 1765; Northampton, 1804), p. 4; Dwight, p. 63.

[13] Dwight, p. 58. He is supposed to have joined the church of which his father was pastor soon after his graduation.

Aldersgate Street, London, at a quarter before nine on the evening of May 24, 1738, so Edwards, moved by religious convictions when a boy and again when in college, yet rebellious against the absoluteness of the divine sovereignty which his theology and his philosophy alike demanded, came in an instant to a "sense of the glory of the divine Being"[14]—to quote his own words—which thenceforth changed the entire conscious attitude of his soul toward God. And as Calvin, after the severe struggle involved in the submission of his will to that of God, made the divine sovereignty the cornerstone of his system, so Edwards now found that doctrine "exceedingly pleasant, bright, and sweet." But it was not, as with Calvin, a submission to an infinite authority that was the central thought of the experience that came to Edwards as he read the words "Now unto the King eternal, immortal, invisible, the only wise God, be honor and glory forever and ever, Amen." Rather it was the high-wrought, mystic conception of the excellence of the God to whom his heart went out in a flood of devotion that mastered him with an overwhelming sense of the divine presence and majesty. With true mystic outflowing of affection he seems to have had relatively little sense of a burden of the guilt of sin; he was above the plane which makes the question of one's own interests central. By him sin was felt chiefly in a profoundly humiliating sense of his own infinite unlikeness to God. But he longed with all the power of an ardent nature to "enjoy that God, and be rapt up to him in heaven, and be, as it were, swallowed up in him forever." And this new apprehension of "the glorious majesty and grace of God" found poetic satisfaction in enjoyment of Solomon's Song, in sympathy with external nature, the sky, clouds, "grass, flowers, trees," or the majesty of the lightning and the power of the storm.

This new sense of the divine glory, almost a pure intuition of the majesty, holiness, and power of God, satisfied the mystic and imaginative side of Edwards' nature, no less than the speculations which found in all being but the manifestation of spirit, and especially of the potent Spirit of God operating directly on the human spirit, satisfied the philosophic tendency so strangely joined with

[14] See Hopkins, pp. 24–42; Dwight, pp. 60, 61.

an almost oriental wealth of fancy in this remarkable man. And from both sides of his thinking his theology flowed: rock-ribbed in its speculative logic, in its limitation of the power of human freedom, in its recognition of the immediate agency of God in all events, in its emphasis on the absolute and arbitrary sovereignty of the Creator over his creatures; yet insistent on a "conversion" the chief resultant of which was an affectionate delight in God, and finding the highest Christian experience in a mystical and almost incomprehensible sense of the divine glory manifested to the loving human soul.

This experience, no less than Edwards' belief in the immediacy and power of the operations of the divine Spirit on the soul of man, led him to emphasize a struggling and conscious "conversion," rather than a scarce-observed process of growth, as the normal instead of the occasional method of entrance into the Kingdom of God. This is a view always widely prevalent in times of deep religious quickening. It was preached in early New England by Hooker, Cotton, Shepard, and the founders generally. Wesley and Whitefield taught it. And it was set forth with such persuasiveness by Edwards as an underlying principle of his conception of the religious life as profoundly to affect New England for a century after his death. Emphasizing as it does the great truth of the divine origin of all Christian life, its overemphasis as a necessary law tends to rob baptism of significance, to minimize the covenant relationships of Christian households, and to leave the children of the truest servants of God presumptively outside the Christian fold till consciously touched by the transforming power of the Spirit. Edwards' own son and namesake could write years later: "Though I had, during my father's life, some convictions of sin and danger, yet I have no reason to believe I had any real religion, till some years after his death."[15]

In the power of these thoughts Edwards entered on his first pastoral experience, taking charge of a small Presbyterian church in New York City from August, 1722, to April, 1723—a relation which the congregation would gladly have made permanent. This

[15] Letter of March 30, 1789, Hawksley, *Memoirs of the Rev. Jonathan Edwards* (London, 1815), p. 255.

practical experience but deepened his previous aspirations and convictions into a remarkable series of seventy resolutions. Some are the familiar maxims of earnest men, as "To live with all my might while I do live"; but more represent the peculiar coloring of Edwards' religious life, as "Never to do any manner of thing, whether in soul or body, less or more, but what tends to the glory of God, nor be, nor suffer it, if I can possibly avoid it."[16]

New York, though pleasant, did not seem to Edwards a hopeful field for his life work, and in May, 1723, he was back in his father's house in South Windsor. But other churches speedily sought his services. North Haven called him in vain in September, 1723; and, in November of that year, he accepted an invitation to the pastorate at Bolton, a little eastward of his home. Yet, for some reason now unknown he did not enter upon this ministry, and June, 1724, found him, instead, in a tutorship at Yale College.[17]

The period was one of great distraction in that much vexed institution. Without a president since the defection of Rector Cutler to Episcopacy in 1722, its government and instruction were in the hands of two young and frequently changed tutors. During Edwards' incumbency, begun when he was not yet twenty-two, the work was done with credit to himself and benefit to the college; and he might have continued in it for several years longer had not a most attractive invitation come to him from the people of Northampton to become the colleague of his grandfather, the venerable Solomon Stoddard. Induced by family ties, drawn by the prominence of the congregation, then esteemed the largest in Massachusetts outside of Boston, and by that repute for a certain aristocratic and social charm which Northampton then, as now, enjoyed, he resigned his tutorship and, on February 15, 1727, was ordained to the colleague pastorate of the Northampton church. The death of Stoddard two years later[18] left him in sole charge.

The establishment of these ties was speedily followed by the formation of others of a more personal character. On July 28,

[16] In full in Dwight, pp. 68–73.
[17] Dexter, pp. 218, 219.
[18] February 11, 1729.

1727, he married Sarah Pierpont, daughter of Rev. James Pierpont of New Haven, and great-granddaughter of Thomas Hooker, the founder of Hartford. Our New England ancestors married early— the bride and groom were seventeen and twenty-four—but Edwards had long been attracted by the character, even more than by the beauty, of the young woman who thus linked her life with his; and his description of her at the age of thirteen is one of the few striking bits of poetic prose which the rather arid literature of eighteenth-century New England produced.[19] Mrs. Edwards was well worthy of his regard. Hers was a nature not only of remarkable susceptibility to religious impression, but of executive force, cheerful courage, social grace, and sweet, womanly leadership.[20] She added cheer to his house, supplemented his shyness and want of small talk, and it was no inapt, though facetious, tribute to her general repute that affirmed "that she had learned a shorter road to heaven than her husband."[21] Devoted to that husband, whose frail health required constant care, administering a large part of the business affairs of the home with cheerful forgetfulness of her own disabilities that he might be free to spend his accustomed thirteen hours daily in his study, or to take his solitary meditative walks and rides,[22] she brought up eight daughters and three sons and bore her full share of labor in the vicissitudes of Edwards' life. Warmly attached to each other, husband and wife were but briefly separated by death, she surviving him less than seven months.[23] Every recollection of Edwards' achievements should also involve a remembrance of the devoted and solicitous care which made much of his work possible.

Edwards' ministry was marked from the first; and it was not

[19] In full in Dwight, pp. 114, 115; Allen, pp. 45, 46.
[20] Sketch by Hopkins in his *Life and Character of the Late Reverend Mr. Jonathan Edwards* (Boston, 1765); see also Dwight, pp. 113–115, 127–131, 171–190; Allen, pp. 44–49.
[21] Allen, pp. 47, 48.
[22] Hopkins, p. 43; Dwight, pp. 110–113. Professor F. B. Dexter informs me that an examination of Edwards' unpublished correspondence shows that he was more of a man of business than his older biographers believed him to be. He certainly left a larger estate than most New England ministers of his time.
[23] Died October 2, 1758.

long before the Northampton pulpit was strongly felt in Massachusetts and Connecticut in a direction largely counter to the religious tendencies of the time. Taken as a whole, no century in American religious history has been so barren as the eighteenth. The fire and enthusiasm of Puritanism had died out on both sides of the Atlantic. In this country the inevitable provincialism of the narrow colonial life, the deadening influence of its hard grapple with the rude forces of nature, and the Indian and Canadian wars rendered each generation less actively religious than its predecessor; and, while New England shone as compared with the spiritual deadness of Old England in the years preceding Wesley, the old fervor and sense of a national mission were gone, conscious conversion, once so common, was unusual, and religion was becoming more formal and external.

Then, too, it seems to be the law of the development of a declining Calvinism everywhere, whether in Switzerland, France, Holland, England, or America, that it passes through three or four stages. Beginning with an intense assertion of divine sovereignty and human inability, it ascribes all to the grace of God, a grace granting common mercies to all men, and special salvatory mercy to the elect. This special grace has its evident illustrations in struggling spiritual births, lives of high consecration, and conscious regeneration. In seasons of intense spiritual feeling, like the Reformation or the Puritan struggle in England, it is easy to ascribe all religious life to the special, selective, irresistible, tranforming power of God. But, in time, the high pressure of the spiritual life of a community or of a nation, which has passed through such a crisis-experience as had the founders of New England, abates. Men desirous of serving God do not feel so evidently the conscious workings of the divine Spirit, and they ask what they can do, not indeed to save themselves—this second stage of Calvinism with no less emphasis than the first asserts that God alone can accomplish salvation by special grace—but what they can do to put themselves in a position where God is more likely to save them. And the answer from the pulpit and in Christian thought is an increased emphasis on the habitual practice of prayer, faithful attendance at church, and the reading of God's Word, not as of themselves salvatory but as "means" by which a man can put himself in a more probable way of salvation. From this the path to the third stage is easy; to the belief that religion is a habit of careful attention to the duties of the house of God and observance of the precepts of the gospel in relation to one's neighbors—a habit possible of attainment by all men, and justifying the confidence that though men cannot render an adequate service to God, yet if each man labors sincerely to do what he can under the impulse of the grace that God sends to all men God will accept his sincere though imperfect obedience as satisfactory. This stage was known in Edwards' day on both sides of the Atlantic as "Arminianism," and it was accompanied by an unstrenuous or negative attitude toward the doctrines which the first stage of Calvinism had made chief. From this position it was an easy transition for some to the fourth stage, in which the essence of the Christian life is made to consist in the practice of morality, and the need of man is represented to be education and culture, not rescue and fundamental transformation. English Puritanism had reached the fourth stage in some of its representatives when Edwards began his ministry; New England had not gone farther than the third as yet, and was chiefly in the second; but an Arminian point of view was rapidly spreading, even among those who would warmly have resented classification as Arminians. Rev. Samuel Phillips of Andover, who was certainly thought a Calvinist, thus expressed a prevalent feeling in 1738:

> I can't suppose, that any one . . . who at all Times, faithfully improves the *common Grace* he has, *that is to say,* is diligent in attending on the appointed Means of Grace with a Desire to profit thereby; . . . and in a Word, who walks up to his Light, to the utmost of his Power, shall perish for want of *special* and saving Grace.[24]

Now it was Edwards' great work as a religious leader to be the chief human instrument in turning back the current for over a century in the larger part of New England to the theory of the method of salvation and of man's dependence on God which marked the earlier types of Calvinism. Yet it was not wholly a return. While he emphasized the arbitrary and absolute character

[24] *Orthodox Christian,* 1738, p. 75.

of the divine election as positively as the older Calvinists, and even more strenuously asserted the immediacy of the divine operations in dealing with the human soul, he tried to find place for a real and still existent, if unused and unusable, natural human power to turn to God, and hence a present, as well as an Adamic and racial, responsibility for not so doing.

Edwards' stimulating preaching soon had a marked effect on the little Northampton community of two hundred families.[25] The town was not unfamiliar with religious quickenings. At least five had occurred under the able ministry of Solomon Stoddard. But Edwards' sermons were on themes calculated to stir a community, and especially an isolated rural community. Two sudden deaths in the spring of 1734 excited the concern of the little town—a concern which was deepened by a vague alarm lest the spreading Arminianism which the Northampton pulpit denounced was a token of the withdrawal of God's redemptive mercy from sinful men. And the preacher set forth, in sermons which read with power after a lapse of more than a hundred and sixty years, the complete right of God to deal with his creatures as he saw fit, the enmity of human hearts against God, the terrors of the world to come, and the blessedness of acceptance with God. "I have found," said Edwards, "that no sermons have been more remarkably blessed, than those in which the doctrine of God's absolute sovereignty with regard to the salvation of sinners, and his just liberty with regard to answering the prayers or succeeding the pains of mere natural men, continuing such, have been insisted on." By December, 1734, a movement of spiritual power was manifest in the community which resulted in six months' time in "more than three hundred" conversions. The experience of those wrought upon, in large measure, corresponded to the type of preaching to which they had listened; and Edwards describes it as normally involving three definite stages. Of these the first was an "awful apprehension" of the condition in which men stand by nature, so overwhelming as to produce oftentimes painful physical

[25] Edwards gave a full account of these events in his *Narrative of Surprising Conversions* (1736–1737), S. Austin, ed., *Works of Jonathan Edwards* (Worcester, 1808–1809), III, 9–62, from which the statements in this paragraph are taken.

effects. Next followed, in cases which Edwards believed to be the genuine work of the Spirit of God, a conviction that they justly deserved the divine wrath, not infrequently leading to expressions of wonder that "God has not cast them into hell long ago." And from this valley of humiliation the converts emerged, often suddenly, into "a holy repose of soul in God through Christ, and a secret disposition to fear and love him, and to hope for blessings from him," and into such "a sense of the greatness of his grace" as to lead, in many instances, to laughter, tears, or even to a "sinking" of the physical frame, as if the inward vision of God's glory were too much for mortal spirits to endure.

This type of Christian experience is foreign to the altered and unemotional age in which we live, but it was not peculiar to Edwards' congregation. The Puritan founders of New England had entered the Kingdom of Heaven by the same door; and one finds in the sermons of Hooker or of Shepard the same analysis of the inmost feelings of the sinful human heart, the same sense of the exceeding difficulty and relative infrequency of salvation, and the same consciousness of desert of the divine wrath. It was to appear again not merely in the Great Awakening of 1740–1742, but in the remarkable series of revivals which, beginning in the last decade of the eighteenth century, lasted nearly to the Civil War. But in Edwards' sermons the view of conversion of which this experience is the normal accompaniment is put with a relentlessness of logic and a fertility of imagination that have never been surpassed. We trace his steps as he argues, in terms in which no parent would estimate the misdeeds of his child, that sin is infinite in its guilt because committed against an infinite object.[26] We follow his reasoning with a recoil that amounts to incredulity that such is the latent hatred of the unregenerate human mind that it would kill God if it could.[27] We revolt as we read Edwards' contention that the wicked are useful simply as objects of the destructive wrath of God;[28] as he beholds the unconverted members of the congregation before him withheld for a brief period by the restraining hand

---

[26] Sermon on Romans 4:5, *Works,* VII, 27, 28.
[27] *Ibid.,* 5:10, *Works,* VII, 168, 175.
[28] Sermon on Ezekiel 15:2–4, *Works,* VIII, 129–150.

of God from the hell into which they are to fall in their appointed time;[29] as he pictures the damned glow in endless burning agony like a spider in the flame;[30] and heightens the happiness of the redeemed by the contrast between the felicities of heaven and the eternal torments of the lost, visible forever to the saints in glory.[31] No wonder one of his congregation was led to suicide and others felt themselves grievously tempted.[32]

Repulsive as this presentation is, it is but fair to Edwards to remember that it seemed to him to be demanded no less by his philosophic principles than by his interpretation of the Bible. And it is merely justice to recall, also, that though the terrors of the law fill a large place in his pulpit utterances, no man of his age pictured more glowingly than Edwards the joys of the redeemed,[33] the blessedness of union with Christ, or the felicities of the knowledge of God. When all deductions have been made from his presentation of Christian truth—and much must be made—he remains a preacher such as few have been of the eternal verities of sin, redemption, holiness, judgment, and enjoyment of God.

It is evidence that this awakening at Northampton was not the effect of Edwards' preaching alone, that a similar stirring took place within a few months throughout that section of Massachusetts and in a number of towns of Connecticut.[34] The news of this then unusual work drew attention to the young Northampton minister, not only from all parts of New England but from across the Atlantic. His sermons and methods brought some enemies, but many friends; and, at the request of the Rev. Drs. Isaac Watts and John Guyse, the leading Congregational ministers of England, Edwards prepared, and these ministers published at London, in 1737, an extended account of the revival.[35]

---

[29] Sermon on Deuteronomy 32:35, *Works,* VII, 487, 491, 496, 502.
[30] Sermon on Ezekiel 22:14, *Works,* VII, 393.
[31] *Ibid.,* 15:2–4, *Works,* VIII, 141–143.
[32] *Narrative of Surprising Conversions, Works,* III, 77, 78.
[33] E. g., his sermon on John 14:27, *Works,* VIII, 230–247.
[34] *Narrative of Surprising Conversions, Works,* III, 77, 78.
[35] *A Faithful Narrative of the Surprising Work of God in the Conversion of Many Hundred Souls in Northampton and the Neighbouring Towns* (London, 1737). Generally known as the *Narrative of Surprising Conversions.* A briefer account by Edwards had been published at Boston late in 1736.

Known thus far and wide as one whose ministry had been
signally distinguished by dramatic manifestations of spiritual
power, it was natural that when the coming of Whitefield to the
Congregational colonies, in the autumn of 1740, gave the human
impetus to the marvelous religious overturning known as the
"Great Awakening," Edwards should be regarded as the best
American representative of the revival spirit which then had its
most extensive manifestation. The story of that momentous stirring
will be told in the next lecture more fully than our time will permit
today. To Edwards it seemed at first the very dawning of the
millennial age, and the visible manifestation of the divine glory.[36]
It appeared but the repetition, not merely in Edwards' own parish,
but on a scale coextensive with the American colonies, of the
revival of his early ministry. He welcomed the youthful Whitefield
to his pulpit; who, in turn, recorded an approval of the occupants
of the Northampton parsonage in the words: "He is a Son himself,
and hath also a Daughter of *Abraham* for his wife"; and said of
Edwards, "I think I have not seen his Fellow in all *New England.*"[37]
Edwards himself preached as an evangelist in many pulpits
besides his own. And when criticism arose and waxed to denuncia-
tion in many quarters as the more radical elements of the movement ran their violent and divisive course, he defended the revival
as a true work of the Spirit of God, which every Christian ought to
favor to the utmost of his power, while deprecating the excesses of
many of the exhorters, in his treatise of 1742, entitled *Some
Thoughts concerning the Present Revival of Religion in New England.*

But though Edwards distrusted, in this volume, the weight laid
by many of the friends of the revival on the bodily effects which so
frequently accompanied the preaching of Whitefield, Tennent,
Parsons, Bellamy, or his own, he nevertheless insisted that they
were oftentimes a real product of the Spirit of God, and he cites in
proof an experience of his wife begun probably near the close of
1738 and reaching its culmination in the revival scenes of 1742. In

[36] *Some Thoughts concerning the Present Revival of Religion in New
England* (Boston, 1742), pp. 96–103.
[37] Whitefield's *Seventh Journal,* pp. 47, 48.

so doing he gave a part of one of the most interesting chapters in mystic biography anywhere recorded[38]—the complement to it being contained in Mrs. Edwards' own account published by Dr. Dwight.[39] It is one which shows how Edwards' thought had in it the germ of a development of his theology fully reached by his disciples as to the extent to which a Christian must be cordially submissive to the divine disposal. Edwards did, indeed, deprecate the statements of converts that they were willing to be damned, if God so chose. "They had not clear and distinct ideas of damnation," he says; "nor does any word in the Bible require such self-denial as this."[40] And he also held that an impenitent man might rightfully pray for God's mercy.[41] But Edwards taught that the essence of virtue is the preference of the glory of God to any personal interests. And the burden of Mrs. Edwards' struggle was this crucial problem of submission. It is illustrative of the wifely devotion of this remarkable woman that the very crises of her trial were her willingness to endure, if necessary, the disapproval of her husband, and to see another more successful than he in his Northampton pulpit, if God so desired. After these battles had been won, it was easy to go on to a sense of readiness to "die on the rack, or at the stake," or "in horror" of soul, rising at last to a willingness to suffer the torments of hell in body and soul "if it be most for the honour of God."[42]

These experiences were accompanied not once, but repeatedly by such a sense of the divine glory that[43]

the Strength of the Body [was] taken away, so as to deprive of all Ability to stand or speak; sometimes the Hands clinch'd, and the Flesh cold, but Senses still remaining;

and the result was

[38] *Thoughts,* pp. 62–78.
[39] Dwight, pp. 171–186.
[40] *Narrative of Surprising Conversions, Works,* III, 37.
[41] Letter of 1741, Dwight, p. 150: "There are very few requests that are proper for an impenitent man, that are not also, in some sense, proper for the godly."
[42] Dwight, p. 182.
[43] *Thoughts,* pp. 63, 76.

all former Troubles and Sorrows of Life forgotten, and all Sorrow and Sighing fled away, excepting Grief for past Sins, and for remaining Corruption . . . a daily sensible doing and suffering every Thing for GOD, . . . eating for GOD, and working for GOD, and sleeping for GOD, and bearing Pain and Trouble for GOD, and doing all as the Service of Love.

What shall we say to these things? Not that they are not the real experiences of sensible men and women, in a period of high-wrought religious feeling. They are; or we must deny the Christian consciousness of Paul, of Bernhard, of Francis. But they are not the experiences of the normal religious life, and to insist on them as such is to make a great mistake.

And Edwards also came to feel that it was in some sense a mistake. When the Great Awakening was over, he published, in the light of that tremendous wave of excitement and its disappointing results, his noblest purely religious exposition, the *Treatise concerning Religious Affections,* of 1746. None but a man of remarkable poise of judgment could have written it. It betrays no reaction against the movement which had so come short of what he hoped. It sees the good and the bad in it; and, rising above the temporary occasion, seeks to answer the question, "What is the Nature of True Religion?"[44]

Edwards,[45] unlike modern psychologists, divided the soul into two "faculties," understanding and affections—the latter including, but not separating, the will and the inclinations. Each faculty is the realm of religion, but that of the affections most of all—that is to say, no religion can be genuine which remains merely a matter of intellectual knowledge of truth without prompting to acts of will and outgoings of emotion.

But to be moved by strong emotions, Edwards perceived, is not necessarily to be religious. This was the mistake that many had made in the recent revival, and it was as great an error, Edwards thought, as the denial that the affections had to do with religion, which reaction from the excesses of the revival had produced in some. That emotion is greatly stirred, or that bodily effects are

---

[44] *Religious Affections,* Preface.
[45] In this paragraph I have tried to give a brief synopsis of the book.

produced, are no signs that men are truly religious—though Edwards here sticks to his guns and declares that to affirm that bodily effects are not of themselves evidences of religion is not to affirm that true religious emotion may never have bodily effects. Nor are we to trust to a fluent tongue, a ready recollection of Scripture, an "appearance of love," a peculiar sequence of religious experiences, a sense of assurance, a zeal for attending meetings, or an ability to give a well-sounding account of an alleged work of grace, as proving a man a Christian. Rather, true Christian affections involve a "new spiritual sense," which comes not by nature, but by the indwelling power of the Holy Spirit, inducing a new attitude of the heart toward God; an unselfish love for divine things because they are holy; a spiritual enlightenment which leads to a conviction of the certainty of divine truth and a humiliating sense of unworthiness; and a change of disposition which shows itself in love, meekness, tenderness of spirit, producing symmetry of character, increasing longing for spiritual attainments, and a life of Christian conduct in our relations to our fellow-men.

The ideal that Edwards held up is of exceeding loftiness—too high to be made, as he and his followers made it, the test of all Christian discipleship. But it is a noble ideal for a Christian man, and especially for a Christian minister, to hold before himself as that toward the realization of which his Christian life is striving in feeling and animating purpose.

It is as a personal illustration of the *Religious Affections,* I think, that we should view the biographical edition of the diary of his young friend, David Brainerd, the missionary to the Indians, which Edwards published in 1749.[46] Betrothed to Edwards' daughter Jerusha, and dying at Edwards' house, in 1747, at the age of twenty-nine, Brainerd's story has the pathetic interest always attaching to frustrated promise; and his missionary zeal has made his consecration a stimulus to others. But, though one of the most popular of Edwards' books at the time of its publication, his *Life*

---

[46] "There are two Ways of representing and recommending true Religion and Virtue to the World, which GOD hath made Use of: The one is by Doctrine and Precept; the other is by Instance and Example." *An Account of the Life of the Late Reverend Mr. David Brainerd* (Boston, 1749), Preface.

of Brainerd is a distressing volume to read. The morbid, introspective self-examinations and the elevations and depressions of the poor consumptive are but a sorry illustration at best of the noble ideal of the full-rounded, healthful Christian life.

Edwards shared with Brainerd what our generation looks upon as the young sufferer's most winsome trait—his missionary sympathy; but opportunities for manifesting it in a rural New England parish in the middle of the eighteenth century were few. One such came in 1746, when a proposition reached New England from a number of Scotch ministers that Christians unite in a "concert of prayer for the coming of our Lord's kingdom" throughout the earth.[47] Edwards welcomed it eagerly, and, in 1747, published an extensive treatise in furtherance of the suggestion.[48] In the course of this essay he took occasion not only to urge the desirability of united prayer and to answer some objections to union which seem rather absurd to our age, though they were then regarded as real difficulties, but to set forth his interpretation of prophecy and his ardent hope for the speedy coming of a brighter religious day.

Edwards' own personal trials were thickening in the years following the revival at which we have just been glancing. Some of the causes of growing estrangement between him and his Northampton people are patent enough; some are obscure. Two are distinctly in evidence. The first was a case of discipline, apparently of the year 1744, wherein proceedings against a number of young people in his congregation for circulating what he deemed, doubtless truly, impure books, were so managed or mismanaged, as to alienate from him nearly all the young people of the town.[49]

The other evident cause was the controversy over the terms of church membership, which was the ostensible ground of his dismission.[50] In a former lecture some account was given of the rise of the "Halfway Covenant"—that system approved by the second

[47] *Works,* III, 370–372.

[48] *An Humble Attempt to promote Explicit Agreement and Visible Union of God's People in Extraordinary Prayer for the Revival of Religion and the Advancement of Christ's Kingdom on Earth* (Boston, 1747).

[49] Dwight, pp. 299, 300.

[50] Dwight gives a full and documentary account of this controversy, *ibid.,* pp. 300–448.

generation on New England soil, by which the children of church members, though themselves not consciously regenerate, were admitted to sufficient standing in the church to bring their children in turn to baptism, although themselves barred from the Lord's table. Hence the nickname "Halfway Covenant," indicating that those who stood in this relation were members enough to enjoy the privileges of the one sacrament for their children, but not members enough to participate in the other.

This system became general in New England by the beginning of the eighteenth century; but in some places the earlier practice was yet further modified. Some argued that if earnest-minded though unregenerate children of church members were themselves sufficiently church members, by reason of the divine promise, "to be a God unto thee, and to thy seed after thee,"[51] to bring their children in turn to baptism, they were sufficiently members to come to the Lord's Supper. Indeed, it was their duty to come thither, if sincerely desirous of leading a Christian life, for they would find the communion, like prayer and public worship, a means tending to conversion. This view was made popular in the upper Connecticut Valley by the great influence of Edwards' grandfather and predecessor, Solomon Stoddard. Held by him as early as 1679, he did not introduce the practice into the Northampton church till after 1700; but it soon after became the custom in that church and in most of its immediate neighbors.[52] Edwards was settled under it and practiced it for nearly twenty years.

Edwards' own lofty conceptions of the Christian life and his emphasis on conversion as its beginning led him gradually, however, to the conclusion that no church privileges should be given to those not conscious, in some degree, of a work of the Spirit of God in their own souls. He intimated this change of view in his *Religious Affections* of 1746;[53] but it illustrates the spiritual torpor that followed the fever of the Great Awakening, and possibly the alienation between Edwards and his young people, that he waited

[51] Genesis 17:7.
[52] Some account may be found in Walker's *Creeds and Platforms*, pp. 279–282.
[53] Edwards' own statement, in Dwight, p. 314.

from 1744 to December, 1748, for a single candidate for church membership to come forward even under the easy terms of the Northampton church. When an applicant at last appeared he made known his change of opinion, and intended change of practice, temperately and moderately. There was, indeed, a good deal to be said against such a modification as the pastor proposed. His honored grandfather had introduced the existing system; he had been settled, well knowing what it was; he had practiced it. It might be urged that it was a breach of contract for him to abandon it. But, even granting this, one hardly understands the virulence of the opposition which Edwards encountered from those who must almost all have been his spiritual children. One hardly sees sufficient ground for the hostility that led to charges that Edwards planned a Separatist congregation; that refused to hear his arguments; that sought to induce prominent ministers to answer the admirable book which he published in 1749 in defense of his position;[54] that appears in the long wrangle over the composition of the council which should consider his further relations to the Northampton congregation; or in the bitter enmity of some of his kinsfolk in and out of the ministry of the county. Edwards himself once declared that he had little skill in conversation; "he was thought by some . . . to be stiff and unsociable"; he held himself aloof from pastoral calling save in cases of real need;[55] and one can but suspect that he lacked the art of leading men. Honest and conscientious to the core—in this change of practice, as in the case of discipline, he seems to have taken none of the preparatory measures which often make all the difference between success and failure in swaying a democratic body. Stoddard had certainly held his peculiar views for nearly thirty years before they became the practice of his congregation, but such careful nurturing of a desired measure was apparently foreign to Edwards' nature. That the matter was intellectually clear to him was sufficient; it ought to be so to others.

But, however explainable, the fact remains that in this crisis

[54] *An Humble Inquiry into the Rules of the Word of God, concerning the Qualifications Requisite to a compleat Standing and full Communion in the Visible Christian Church* (Boston, 1749).
[55] Hopkins, pp. 44–46, 54.

Edwards had the support of no considerable portion of his congregation, nor did the strong sense of professional unity characteristic of the clergy of the eighteenth century prevent a majority of his neighboring ministers from opposing him. A council of nine churches met on June 19, 1750.[56] That advisory body having decided that Edwards' dismission was necessary if his people still desired it, the Northampton church voted by more than two hundred to twenty-three to dismiss its pastor. That action the council approved by a majority of one on June 22. And the town added what was an insult to the burdens of the deposed pastor by voting, probably in November, 1750, that Edwards should not preach in the community. It is interesting to note that one, at least, of those of Edwards' congregation prominent in procuring his removal, and esteemed by the Northampton pastor his most energetic opponent, Joseph Hawley, Edwards' cousin, and a leading lawyer and politician, afterward not only privately but publicly avowed his regret and repentance for what had been done.[57] And Edwards' contention in the principal subject of this controversy was not without abundant ultimate fruitage. His friends, notably his pupil, Rev. Dr. Joseph Bellamy, carried forward his attack on Stoddardeanism and the Halfway Covenant, with the result that, by the first decade of the nineteenth century, when Edwards had been fifty years in his grave, the system had been generally set aside by the Congregational churches.

Turned out from his pastorate thus, at the age of forty-seven with a family of ten living children,[58] he had to look about for a new charge. His friend, Rev. Dr. John Erskine, suggested a settlement in Scotland, where Erskine was a leader in the church;[59] the people of Canaan, Connecticut, heard him with approval;[60] but

[56] Dwight gives the documents, pp. 398–403; Edwards wrote a most interesting account in letters of July 5, 1750, to Erskine, and of July 1, 1751, to Gillespie, *ibid.,* pp. 405–413, 462–468.

[57] Letter of May 9, 1760, *ibid.,* pp. 421–427. See Edwards' characterization of him, *ibid.,* pp. 410, 411.

[58] Two daughters, however, were married in the year of Edwards' dismission.

[59] Edwards' letter of July 5, 1750, Dwight, p. 412.

[60] Dexter, *Biographical Sketches of the Graduates of Yale College,* I, 219, 220.

the place of his next seven-years sojourn was determined by a two-fold call that came to him through the efforts of his friend and pupil, Samuel Hopkins, in December, 1750, from the church in the little frontier village of Stockbridge to become its minister, and from the English "Society for the Propagation of the Gospel in New England," which had grown out of Eliot's labors a century before, to become its missionary to the Housatonic Indians at the same place.[61] Thither he and his household removed in the summer of 1751. But Stockbridge was not without its serious controversies between the new pastor and missionary and those who were exploiting the Indians for pecuniary advantage; and the chief of his new foes was a relative of some of his leading opponents in the Northampton separation. These disputes distressed the first years of his new settlement, but Edwards' position was so manifestly just that, with the support of the commissioners whose missionary agent he was, victory and peace came to him.[62]

Edwards doubtless conscientiously fulfilled his stipulated duty of preaching to the Indians once a week through an interpreter,[63] besides ministering to the English-speaking Stockbridge congregation, but he was too settled in scholastic ways to make a successful missionary. His own judgment of himself he expressed when he wrote to Erskine, in 1750, that he was "fitted for no other business but study."[64] And at Stockbridge opportunity came to him, even amid the distractions of the great military struggle between France and England in which little Stockbridge was at times a turmoiled frontier outpost,[65] for studies which produced the four treatises by which he is best known—his *Careful and Strict Enquiry into the Modern Prevailing Notions of Freedom of Will*,[66] his "Concern-

---

[61] Dwight, p. 449; see also Hopkins' statement, West, *Sketches of the Life of the Late Rev. Samuel Hopkins* (Hartford, 1805), pp. 53–57.

[62] For some aspects of this controversy, see Dwight, pp. 450–541.

[63] There is an outline of one of these sermons in Grosart, *Selections from the Unpublished Writings of Jonathan Edwards* (Edinburgh: Privately printed, 1865), pp. 191–196.

[64] Dwight, p. 412.

[65] Compare Edwards' letter of April 10, 1756, to McCulloch, Dwight, p. 555.

[66] First edition, Boston, 1754.

ing the End for which God Created the World," his "Nature of True Virtue,"[67] and his *Great Christian Doctrine of Original Sin Defended.*[68]

This is not the time and place, even if the lecturer possessed the ability, to enter on any thorough criticism, or even on any elaborate exposition, of these works. Viewed simply as feats of intellectual achievement they present the highest reach of the New England mind and have given their author a permanent place among the philosophers of the eighteenth century. Were Edwards' writings subtracted from the literature of colonial New England the residue would embrace little more than the discussions of a narrow and provincial society, aside from the course of the world's affairs. It was Edwards who gave to the thought of eighteenth-century New England about whatever interest and lasting repute it bears in other lands. Edwards' treatises involved no changes in his theology. Rather they were the logical formulation of what he had long taught.

Edwards' volume on the *Will*, usually esteemed his crowning work, was long planned,[69] but was not written till 1753. It was his supreme effort against the Arminianism which had been the horror of his early ministry. Calvinism, in this feature of its strenuous creed, had fallen low. Its contemporary defenders in England, like Watts and Doddridge, had been compelled, as Edwards' son Jonathan phrased it, to "bow in the house of Rimmon, and admit the *Self-Determining Power*" of the will.[70] In the *Discourse* published by Daniel Whitby, rector at the English Salisbury, in 1710, predestination in the Calvinistic sense was widely believed to have received its deathblow; and we may imagine that the arguments therein advanced had often been pressed upon Edwards' attention by his keen-minded kinsman and opponent in Northampton, Joseph Hawley, when the latter was a student in his household.[71] But whatever of local and personal interest there may have been for Edwards in the theme, the general defense of what he deemed the

---

[67] These two treatises were first published at Boston in 1765.
[68] First edition, Boston, 1758.
[69] Dwight, p. 507.
[70] "Improvements in Theology," *ibid.*, p. 614.
[71] *Ibid.*, pp. 410, 411.

truth against widely prevalent error was motive enough to rouse a
man of his temperament to utmost endeavor.

To Edwards' thinking,[72] human freedom signifies no more than
a natural power to act in accordance with the choice of the mind.
With the origin of that choice the will has nothing to do. Man is
free to do as he chooses, but not free to determine in what direction his choice shall lie. His will always moves, and moves freely,
in the line of his strongest inclination, but what that inclination
will be depends on what man deems his highest good. While man
has full natural power to serve God—that is, could freely follow a
choice to serve God if he had such an inclination—he will not
serve God till God reveals himself to man as his highest good and
thus renders obedience to God man's strongest motive. Moral
responsibility lies in his choice, not in the cause of the choice; and
hence a man of evil inclination deserves condemnation, since each
choice is his own act, even though the direction in which the
choices are exercised is not in his control. Man cannot choose
between various choices, nor can his choice originate without some
impelling cause external to the will; but his will acts in the direction in which he desires to move, and is free in the sense that it is
not forced to act counter to its inclination.

In this treatise Edwards took up conceptions essentially re-
sembling those advanced by Hobbes, Locke, and Collins, with
whose religious speculations he had no sympathy; but his use of
these ideas was profoundly original. He appears to have been
acquainted with the writings of Locke only, and his grasp of the
points involved is far surer than that of the English philosopher.
The volume was, till comparatively recent times, in extensive use,
being esteemed by Calvinists generally an unanswerable critique of
the Arminian position. It has met, however, with growing dissent,
and though not often directly opposed of late years, is largely felt
to lie outside the conceptions of modern religious thought; but it
has acceptance still, especially with those who hold a necessitarian
view of the universe, and may be said never to have had a positive

[72] In describing Edwards' books I have borrowed some sentences from
my *History of the Congregational Churches in the United States* (New York,
1894), pp. 283–286.

and complete refutation, though suffering a constantly increasing neglect.

The preparation of this treatise on the *Will* was followed by the composition of two smaller essays, probably in 1755[73]—that "Concerning the End for which God Created the World," and that on the "Nature of True Virtue." Of the former investigation into a profound and mysterious theme it may be sufficient to say that Edwards' immediate interpreters, notably his son Jonathan, regarded it as uniting the two heretofore supposedly mutually exclusive explanations of the universe as created either for the happiness of finite beings or as a manifestation of the glory of the Creator. This union Edwards would effect by showing that both results "were the ultimate end of the creation," and that, far from being incompatible, "they are really one and the same thing." The universe in its highest possible state of happiness is the ultimate exhibition of the divine glory.[74]

The second of these treatises—that on the "Nature of True Virtue"—though incomplete, expresses in metaphysical form the feature of the teaching of Edwards that has probably most affected New England thought. He asserted that the elemental principle in virtue is benevolence, or love to intelligent being in proportion to the amount of being which each personality possesses.[75] Other things being equal, the worth of each personality is measured by the amount of being which it has. To use Edwards' illustration, "an *Archangel* must be supposed to have more existence, and to be every way further removed from *nonentity,* than a *worm.*"[76] And the benevolence which constitutes virtue must go out to all in proportion to their value thus measured in the scale of being. Closely connected with this benevolence toward being in general is a feeling of love and attraction toward other beings who are actuated by a similar spirit of benevolence. But any love for being less wide than this, or springing from any motive narrower than general benevolence cannot be true virtue.

[73] Dwight, p. 542.
[74] "Improvements in Theology," Dwight, pp. 613, 614.
[75] "The Nature of True Virtue," *Works,* II, 394–401.
[76] *Ibid.,* p. 401.

This theory profoundly influenced New England theology. Reduced to popular thought, it taught that selfishness is sin, and that disinterested love to God and to one's fellow-men is righteousness. It seemed to furnish a self-evident demonstration of the necessity of a divinely wrought change of heart. It gave a ground also for holding that virtue is identical in its nature in God and man by showing that benevolence toward intelligent personalities in proportion to the amount of being that each possesses leads God, as the Infinite Being in comparison with whom the rest of the universe is infinitesimal, to seek first his own glory, while man, if actuated by the same motive of general benevolence, seeks first the glory of God. Nor was this doctrine less effective in giving a basis for philanthropy. It was no accident that classed Samuel Hopkins, sternest of the pupils of Edwards, or Jonathan Edwards the younger, clearest-minded expounder of the Edwardean system, among the earliest New England opponents of Negro slavery, or drew the earliest missionaries of the American Board from Edwardean ranks. Like the *Treatise concerning Religious Affections,* this essay holds love to be the basal element in piety; but in its banishment of self-interest it left room for the assertion by some of Edwards' successors that no true benevolence could be present till the soul was ready to submit willingly to any disposition of itself which God saw was for the best good of the universe, even if that disposition was the soul's damnation. We have already noted that though Edwards never asserted this necessity, Mrs. Edwards reached this degree of self-renunciation in the revival of 1742.

The fourth important fruit of Edwards' studies was a volume that was passing through the press at the time of his death—that on *Original Sin.* Of all his works none is more ingenious or intellectually acute, but none has met so little acceptance. The subject of original sin, like that of the powers of the will, was one on which the eighteenth-century opponents of the historic Augustinian view were widely supposed to have got much the better of its defenders. Chief among these opponents in popular regard was John Taylor, a Presbyterian Arian minister at Norwich, England, whose *Scripture Doctrine of Original Sin,* of 1738, argued that sorrow, labor, and physical death are consequences to us of

Adam's transgression, but we are in no sense guilty of Adam's sin, our rational powers are in no way disabled, nor are we on account of that sin in any state of natural corruption so as to be now without capacity fully to serve God.

These opinions were reflected in eastern Massachusetts; and, in 1757 and 1758, a lively exchange of pamphlets took place in which Rev. Samuel Webster of Salisbury and Rev. Charles Chauncy of Boston attacked the doctrine of original sin, while Edwards' friend, Rev. Peter Clark of Danvers, and his pupil, Rev. Joseph Bellamy, defended it. Edwards had probably written most of his volume when this American discussion opened; but though he had Taylor primarily in mind, it was doubtless hastened through the press in view of the debate on this side of the Atlantic.[77]

In his volume on original sin Edwards argued, with great wealth of illustration, the innate corruption of mankind at whatever stage of their existence from earliest infancy to old age, with proofs drawn from Scripture and experience. This corruption amounts in all, of whatever age, to utter ruin. It has its root in Adam's sin, and that sin is ours, but not by any Augustinian presence of humanity in Adam.[78] On the contrary, Edwards explained our guilt of that far-off transgression by a curious theory of the preservation of personal or racial continuity—a theory drawn in part from Locke's speculations on Identity and Diversity.[79] That which makes you and me today the same beings that thought or walked or studied yesterday is the constant creative activity of God. God, by a "constitution," or appointment of things, that is "arbitrary" in the sense that it depends on his will alone, sees fit to appoint that the acts and thoughts of the present moment shall be consciously continuous of those of the past; and it is this ever-renewed creation that gives all personal identity to the individual.[80] What is true of each man is also true of the race. God has constituted all men one

[77] Some account of this controversy may be found in my *History of the Congregational Churches*, pp. 273–276.
[78] Here again I borrow from the volume above cited.
[79] Compare Fisher, *History of Christian Doctrine*, p. 403.
[80] See *Original Sin* (1758), pp. 338–346.

with Adam, so that his primal sin is really theirs, and they are viewed as *"Sinners,* truly guilty, and *Children of Wrath* on that *Account."*[81]

Mr. Lecky has characterized this volume as "one of the most revolting books that have ever proceeded from the pen of man."[82] Without at all sharing the severity of his criticism, it may fairly be said to be a work that renders more difficult, if anything, one of the most mysterious problems of religion—the origin and universal pervasiveness of evil.

Our glance at Edwards' principal writings has necessarily been fleeting; but it has sufficed to show that he impressed several principles on the minds of his contemporaries and successors. Teaching that the sinner possesses the natural power, but not the inclination, to do the will of God, he held that a change of disposition, wrought by a conversion through the transforming work of the Spirit of God, was not merely the primary, but the only important, thing in beginning a Christian life. He taught, also, that the essential characteristic of that life was love to God and to his creatures rather than to self, and that there could be no true religious life which did not have its seat in the emotions and will even more than in the intellect. Edwards did not live long enough to work out a full-rounded system. But besides the evident features of his teachings at which we have glanced, he dropped many hints and half-elaborated suggestions which made his work not merely the beginning of a development carried much farther by his followers, but have led to the claim that he was the father of most various tendencies in later New England thought.

Edwards' pastorate at Stockbridge was the harvest-time of his intellectual activity; but it was followed by a brief episode that had the promise of usefulness for him as a former of character and a leader of young men. The death of Rev. Aaron Burr, the husband of Edwards' third daughter, Esther, in September, 1757, left vacant the presidency of Princeton College, which Burr had occupied since 1748. The "College of New Jersey" had been founded,

[81] *Ibid.,* p. 355.
[82] *History of the Rise and Influence of the Spirit of Rationalism in Europe* (New York, 1866), I, p. 368; see also Allen, *Jonathan Edwards,* p. 312.

in 1746, as an institution in more hearty sympathy with the revival movement to which Edwards was attached than were Harvard or Yale. Nine of its trustees were graduates of Yale.[83] The college had recently been permitted (1753) by the Connecticut legislature to raise funds in Edwards' native colony by means of a lottery, "for the encouragement of religion and learning," as the act read.[84] It appealed to New England as much as to the Middle States, and represented what was then freshest and most spiritually warmhearted in New England thought. Naturally the trustees looked to Edwards; and, two days after Burr's death, elected him to the vacant presidency.[85]

Edwards hesitated. He wished to complete his *History of the Work of Redemption,* which should set forth his conceptions of theology as a whole.[86] Yet the call was one he felt to be pressing, and with the supporting advice of an ecclesiastical council which met at Stockbridge early in January, 1758, he accepted the appointment. But he was destined to assume the work of the proffered office only to lay it down. Inoculated with smallpox as a protective measure, on February 13, 1758, the disease, usually mild under such circumstances, took an unfavorable turn, and he died at Princeton, March 22, in his fifty-fifth year, leaving his work, from a human point of view, incomplete.

Jonathan Edwards the controversialist, the revival preacher, and the metaphysician is the figure oftenest in our thought. It is necessary that it should be so, for in all these respects he was a leader of men. But as we think of him in these attributes he seems remote. His controversies are over questions in which our age takes languid interest, his denunciatory sermons we read with reluctance, his explanations of the will, of the constitution of the human race, or of the end for which God created the world we admire as feats of intellectual strength; but they do not move our hearts or altogether command the assent of our understandings. The thought I wish to leave with you is rather of the man who walked with God.

[83] Dexter, *Biographical Sketches,* I, 220.
[84] *Colonial Records,* X, 217, 218.
[85] Dwight, p. 565.
[86] Letter to the Trustees of the College of New Jersey, *ibid.,* p. 569.

No stain marred his personal character, no consideration of personal disadvantage swayed him from what he deemed his duty to the truth in the controversy at Northampton which led to his dismission. He was the type of a fearless, patient, loyal scholar. But this steadfast-mindedness was based on more than personal uprightness. To him God was the nearest and truest of friends, as well as the strongest of sovereigns. In his narrative of his religious experience he noted the delight and the strength that he found in the saying of the old Hebrew prophet regarding the Saviour: "A man shall be as an hiding place from the wind, and a covert from the tempest; as rivers of water in a dry place, as the shadow of a great rock in a weary land."[87] Above all his other gifts and acquisitions he had, and he made men feel that he had, a vision of the glory of God that transfigured his life with a beauty of spirit that makes his memory reverenced even more than his endowments of mind are respected.

[87] Isaiah 32:2; see Hopkins, p. 36; Dwight, p. 132.

✪

The Young Philosopher

It would not have been surprising if a boy educated under such conditions had learned nothing at all; but Edwards seems to have profited from the very freedom which he enjoyed.

Probably the Wethersfield curriculum was similar to that which Rector Pierson had instituted at Saybrook; but it was not quite so medieval in spirit. Elisha Williams, like Samuel Johnson, realized that the philosophers of Europe had not been inactive in the ninety years since the fathers of New England had taken their degrees at Cambridge; and the political pamphlet which he wrote eighteen years later shows a profound admiration for the philosophy of John Locke. Presumably it was he that introduced Locke to his pupil; for in his second year at Wethersfield Edwards read the *Essay concerning Human Understanding,* and derived from it, as he related many years afterwards, a greater pleasure "than the most greedy miser finds, when gathering up handfuls of silver and gold, from some newly discovered treasure."

Stimulated by his reading of Locke, the fourteen-year-old schoolboy began on his own account a series of notes on philosophical problems. The first was a definition of "excellency," so long and elaborate that we may suppose it to have been a frequent subject of meditation. He could not have started more appropriately.

He began by defining material beauty; and with the aid of

Reprinted by permission of the author from Henry Bamford Parkes, *Jonathan Edwards: The Fiery Puritan* (New York: Minton, Balch & Company, 1930), pp. 52–65.

several geometrical designs, he satisfied himself that it was all a matter of symmetry; beauty was a harmony in which the details were balanced against each other. "The beautiful shape of flowers, the beauty of the body of man, and of the bodies of other animals"; the pleasures of music, and colors, and sweet tastes and smells: all were derived from harmony. His explanations were inadequate enough; but what interested him was to pass on to spiritual beauty. That too was based on harmony: the harmony of the separate souls with each other and with God, which is called love.

To the young dreamer, walking alone in the fields at Wethersfield, the whole universe was a single harmony, the whole universe was beautiful; and if any of the details seemed ugly, that was because the universe, like a complicated melody, required "a vastly larger view" to comprehend it. For the universe was God's artistic creation; it was God expressing Himself, for His own aesthetic delight. And the beauty of each soul was to participate in the melody of the universe, by loving the universe and God. "A lower kind of love," he said, a love for a woman or a possession, "may be odious, because it hinders, or is contrary to, a higher and a more general. Even as a lower proportion is often a deformity, because it is contrary to a more general proportion."

The boy passed on still further. Why was harmony beautiful? What was the highest good? What was the ultimate reality? To Edwards, exulting in the powers of his mind and in aesthetic delights, it was life itself; life was the highest good; harmony was good because it promoted life, disharmony was ugly because it contradicted life. God was life in excelsis; and the human being was most beautiful and most alive when it loved God, most ugly and nearest to nothingness when it hated Him.

These ideas were new; no other New Englander had ever approached them; the boy Edwards worked them out by himself; and forty years later he was still elaborating them; for after he was converted, his God-intoxication united with the traditional theology of Calvinism to form a new compound.

There were seventy-two notes in all. The schoolboy meditated upon a great variety of philosophical topics. Incidentally—for the fact is not important—he worked out an idealism similar to that of

Berkeley in England; he also anticipated some of the most important suggestions of Hume and Kant; and played with ideas of the relativity of motion and the finiteness of the universe in words which might have been written yesterday. But his central theme was the glory of God, the God whom he had found in sweet sensations and natural beauties, a God who loved Himself and all things living, not the Calvinist God who punished men in hell. There is all the charm of innocence and novelty, and sometimes also an unearthly mystic beauty, about these early notes, which disappeared from the treatises of the theologian.

He took all knowledge as his field; and after reading Newton and Rector Pierson, began a second series of notes on natural science. He was not a scientist: his purpose was to prove the existence of God, not to discover truth. Upon a suggestion or an observation, wholly unproved, he would build the most magnificent fancies. He was a poet, playing with possibilities; he took an exuberant delight in striking out hypotheses, in exercising his mind with logical speculations. Of the scientific skepticism, the need to experiment, the search for proof, he had not a trace. The most memorable passages in these notes are poetic: as when he describes "nothing" as "the same that the sleeping rocks do dream of." Typical of them are memoranda like: "To find out a thousand things by due observation of the Spheroid of the Universe"; and, after discussing the refraction of light rays, "To seek out other strange phenomena, and compare them together, and see what qualities can be made out of them: And if we can discover them, it is probable we may be let into a New World of Philosophy." The sense of wonder is magnificent, worthy of a Leonardo; but it is not science.

He used the Newtonian theory to prove that if the smallest atom were misplaced, the whole universe would, in the course of infinite time, be thrown into confusion; hence it must have had an all-wise designer. This was the core of his speculations.

In the eighteenth century it did not occur to people that the universe might have evolved by accident, or that it was already in confusion.

The scope of his observations was prodigious: the human anatomy, the saltness of the sea, the structure of light waves, the nature of stars and atoms, the cause of lightning, the erosion of valleys, the growth of trees, the content of fogs, the color of the sun's rays when they passed through the leaves of a tree on to the pages of a book—he had new theories to propound about them all.

He proved thus that water could be compressed. The solid earth, according to the second of the ten commandments, rested upon water; obviously that water was compressed. But nobody had actually been able to compress water; that however was merely for lack of power.

He had some remarkable suggestions to offer about planetary influence on human history. The heavenly bodies, he suggested, discharged streams of particles which hit the earth, and caused direct alterations in terrestrial affairs; such alterations must have been stronger before the flood, when the atmosphere of the earth was less disturbed; and the antediluvian patriarchs, being long-lived, had enjoyed special opportunities for observing them scientifically; thus a tradition, handed down by Noah, had probably caused the general opinion that the moon and the planets affected the movement of events.

As the notes increased, and with them his pride in his own intellectual capacity, he began to dream of glory; he would publish a great philosophical treatise, and become famous in Europe. He drew up a scheme for it: it was to have two parts, the first on the mind, the second on the external world. For the treatise on the mind he enumerated fifty-six subjects, covering every branch of psychology. For the treatise on the external world he wrote an introduction, and some preliminary propositions, and notes on "being" and "atoms," and a series of eighty-eight topics to be "written fully about."

On the inside page of the cover of his notebook he wrote down a number of rules to guide him in writing this work. Those in long-hand were naïve but harmless. "Let much modesty be seen in the style," he reminded himself. And "let there be much compliance with the reader's weakness, and according to the rules in the Ladies' Library, Vol. 1, p. 340." He resolved "to be very moderate in the use of terms of art. Let it not look as if I was much read, or was conversant with books, or with the learned world." And he decided that the preface should form part of the body of the work; "then I shall be sure to have it read by every one."

But several of the notes were written in shorthand, in order that they might be illegible to his classmates. Two of these were: "Before I venture to publish in London, to make some experiment in my own country, to play at small games first. That I may gain some experience in writing, first to write letters to some in England and to try my hand in lesser matters before I venture in great." And, "The World will expect more modesty because of my circumstances, in America, young, etc. Let there therefore be a superabundance of modesty and, though perhaps 'twill otherwise be needless, it will wonderfully make way for its reception in the world. Mankind are by nature proud and exceeding envious and evermore jealous of such upstarts, and it exceedingly irritates and affronts them to see them appear in print."

Such self-confidence, from a youth of seventeen in a backward province on the edge of the civilized world, is amazing; almost as amazing as the speculative genius which prompted it.

Meanwhile his attitude to religion was ambiguous. He accepted Christianity; he even began a series of notes on the Bible, and another on theology; but he had not been converted; he had no appreciation of the depravity of man, and the imminence of hellfire; he was, in fact, like most other New Englanders of his day, a nominal believer.

His conversion occurred when he was seventeen years old, in the first of his two years as a graduate student. This event has had such an enormous influence on the future of America that it is necessary to study it carefully; unfortunately the evidence is scanty, and any account of why it happened must be based partly on guesswork.

The dogma of original sin, upon which Christianity is built, is a mythological explanation of the feeling that something is wrong with life in this world. It has reference both to the inner life of the soul and to the external world. Calvinist theology declared that the inner life was corrupted first, by deliberate choice in Adam but by an inevitable inheritance in his descendants, and that God's anger then blasted the external world.

To young Edwards, in the woods of the Connecticut Valley, the world was beautiful. In his last year at college he learned that it was also ugly.

He realized that some day he must die; perhaps he would die quite soon, before he had finished his speculations, before he had published his treatise and earned applause in London. He fell ill with pleurisy, and for a time his life was in danger. He had a delicate constitution and there was no knowing what might happen to him. Sudden death was the commonest of occurrences in New England; strong men went to bed in health, awoke in the night with violent pains, and died in a few hours; doctors were worse than useless; food might easily cause horrible diseases, and worms many feet long were sometimes found inside men's bodies. A myriad accidents might await a young philosopher: Red Indians and Frenchmen descending from the Berkshire Hills, a rattlesnake in the grass or a mettlesome horse, a sudden storm at sea.

Children often died before they were properly alive. This was a very puzzling phenomenon; and Edwards watched their death-pangs with a kind of fascination. The "throat-distemper," apparently what we call diphtheria, descended upon the New England towns, one after another, in the twenties and thirties, and slew the children by scores; entire families were wiped out. The accepted remedy was to beat together mustard, pepper, and the rind of elder bark, and apply it to the nape of the neck; this was supposed to "draw away the malignity." Why, asked Edwards, should innocent creatures endure these dreadful pains? The young man saw their feverish brows, their anguished cries, their tortured expressions, as they passed out of a life which they had scarcely entered. It seemed to him that the children offered up to Moloch in the fire or roasted inside the brazen bull could scarcely have suffered such torments. How could this be reconciled with a God of beauty and all-embracing love?

The theology of his forefathers gave him an explanation: God had given man a law; man had disobeyed God and broken the law; God was therefore angry with man and with the world.

In his own soul there were phenomena equally puzzling. His ambition was to live passionately the life of a philosopher; he wanted to live intensely with his whole being every hour of the day. But his body was weak; he was attacked by headaches; he became tired and dull; he was easily upset by eating wrong foods. His consciousness was beset by alien impulses; desires, not included in the system which he had imposed upon himself, sprang up from his subconsciousness and distracted him; sensuality, which he had banned from the circle of life, became the enemy of life; to Edwards it was not an aid to passionate living, but an encumbrance; he used arithmetic as an anaphrodisiac, but he knew now that there was a devil.

Once more the theology of his forefathers gave him an explanation: the first man had sinned; and hence all his descendants, born in sin, were unable to be perfect and heirs of corruption.

Intellectually convinced, he turned to religion; he abandoned all habits which were considered sinful, and practiced many religious duties. But he took no delight in behaving piously; and he still rebelled against hellfire and predestination.

One day he was reading, from the Book of Timothy, "Now unto the King eternal, immortal, invisible, the only wise God, be honour and glory for ever and ever, Amen." The rhythm of the words, with their slow repetitiveness, like the music of a Catholic mass, threw a spell upon him, and he fell into a trance. There was a God, eternal, immortal, invisible; there was a God, who knew all things, who could do all things; there was a God, beautiful, mighty, majestic; there was a God, matchless in all perfections; there was a God, who was life in excelsis, who was passionate yet immovable. "Oh, if only I might enjoy that God! If only I might be rapt up to Him in heaven, and swallowed up in Him for ever!" he cried. He began chanting to himself, again and again, "Now unto the King eternal, immortal, invisible, the only wise God, be honour and glory." For God was all that he could never be; He was that beauty which filled his dreams; He was that power for which he pined. He had forgotten himself; he thought only of the glory of God.

"It never came into my thought," said Edwards, "that there was any thing spiritual, or of a saving nature in this." Several years afterwards he came to regard it as his conversion. But it violated all the regulations which the theologians had laid down, because it was not caused by fear of hell; so for a long time Edwards was not sure whether he had really been saved.

According to the theologians a necessary preliminary to conversion was to become very heartily terrified of hellfire. The unconverted man was completely depraved; he was not merely sinful; everybody was sinful; the unconverted man was incapable of a single deed or word or thought which was not wicked. For everything not done for the glory of God was wicked; and unconverted men were men who acted to please themselves or to please other people or to benefit the world, and not for God's glory. Consequently it was useless to tell the unconverted man how good God was or how beautiful virtue was; he was unable in his wickedness to appreciate anything good; he must be thoroughly terrified by telling him about the pains of hell; this first stage in the conversion of a sinner was called "legal repentance." When the sinner was thus prepared, God, if He so willed it, gave him His grace; He poured into the sinner's soul the knowledge of Himself and His own perfection; henceforth the sinner, having something good inside him, endeavored to obey God's law, and to act only for the glory of God; he was now capable of "evangelical repentance."

Edwards, however, had scarcely been terrified of hell at all; he had never had any strong sense of sin; he had never felt that he was disobedient to God; he had been dissatisfied with the world, and had had a mystic experience. This difference between what he had actually experienced and what, according to the theologians, he ought to have experienced, caused him much perplexity; even four years later he was still worried about it.

If he had thought about it more deeply, he might have become the greatest figure in the history of American thought; he might have altered the whole of the future history of America.

But, when one considers his environment and the possible alternatives, his acceptance of the Calvinist system is easy to understand: it explained the beauty of the natural world; it explained why men and innocent children lived such miserable lives and were tormented by such horrible diseases; it explained Edwards' dissatisfaction with his own personality. Most other kinds of Christianity would have explained these problems equally well. But for Edwards, in New England, in 1721, the only alternatives were deism and the Anglicanism of the eighteenth century. The deists offered no explanation at all for what puzzled Edwards. They went about saying that God was benevolent; God benevolent, when infant children were allowed to die in torment! The Anglicans—those at least whom Edwards knew—were hardly an improvement. They affirmed that God punished men for their good; but how were infant children benefited by being slain with the throat distemper? It was like justifying a parent who broke the bones of his children, not because they had sinned, but for fear they might sin. They believed in free will, and denied the necessity of conversion; but Edwards had himself experienced conversion, and he knew that it was not his own willing that had caused it, but the grace of God showered upon him from above. Moreover, to be an Anglican meant to deny the wisdom of the founders of New England, to belong to the same confession as royal governors in Boston and persecuting bishops in Great Britain, to increase the subserviency of the New World to the Old; Edwards was becoming patriotic.

So from the spring of 1721 he adopted the Calvinist creed and the Calvinist moral code, and set himself to school his nature to it and to convert other people.

In the course of years he accepted predestination and hellfire, as he accepted the belief in the imminence of the millennium, because they formed part of the theology which corresponded in other ways to his experience. He found for the mystery of hell a new and strange solution, growing out of his old conviction of the beauty of the universe. He explained it by the necessity of contrast. Goodness was impossible without wickedness, beauty without ugliness, and happiness without misery; a universe which contained a maximum of goodness must contain also a maximum of evil; a universe all white would be a universe of gray, and therefore there must also be black. For this reason God, when He made the world, had withdrawn His light from a part of it, in order that He might shine more brightly on the remainder. The world was a drama, a picture, a melody, the most beautiful which God could have made;

and men were puppets whom God elected, as He thought best, for goodness or wickedness. Those elected for goodness, having fought in this world against evil, would in the next be lifted up to an infinite happiness; and looking down out of heaven, they would realize their own ecstasy by contrasting it with the infinite misery of the sinners in the flames of hell. Thus the beauty of the Calvinist universe satisfied the laws worked out by the pantheist schoolboy; it was a harmony in which the details—heaven and hell—were balanced against each other.

✪

The Life of a New England Minister

The last years of the 1730's are uneventful. There is time to pause, and describe the daily life of the minister of Northampton. His main occupation is study. At four in the morning he leaves his bed, and lights his single candle; thirteen hours a day he spends poring over the tiny lettering of his volumes of theology, until his eyes, like those of almost all his colleagues, grow astigmatic; he reads always with a pen in his hand, and writes illegible notes which accumulate year by year. His studies, however, are not wholly theological; he devours every book on which he can lay his hands; most of the classics of English literature appear in his reading lists, and a few French books in English translations; he subscribes to an English monthly magazine; and, soon after publication, reads the novels of Fielding and Richardson. His opinion of Fielding is not recorded; but Richardson, whose *Pamela* is advertised, to suit the taste of New England, as likely to "cultivate the Principles of Virtue and Religion in the Minds of the Youth of Both Sexes," and is read all over the country by colonels' daughters and ministers' daughters, wins his strong commendation; Sir Charles Grandison is, in his opinion, "wholly favorable to good morals and purity of character"; when he reads it, he regrets his own inattention to the graces of good writing.

Reprinted by permission of the author from Henry Bamford Parkes, *Jonathan Edwards: The Fiery Puritan* (New York: Minton, Balch & Company, 1930), pp. 124–137.

After dinner, every midday, he rides out for three miles to a lonely grove, where he dismounts and meditates; or in winter he sometimes chops wood for half an hour. In the evening he enjoys an hour's relaxation, when he and his wife smoke their long clay pipes by the fireside and talk with their children. Only by the strictest regularity of life and the most careful attention to diet is the minister, with his sickly constitution, able to spend such long hours in study.

The details of household business he leaves to his wife. Their closest friend describes her as "a most judicious and faithful mistress of a family, habitually industrious, a sound economist, managing her household affairs with diligence and discretion. She is conscientiously careful, that nothing should be wasted or lost; and often, when she herself takes care to save any thing of trifling value, or directs her children or others to do so, or when she sees them waste anything, she repeats the words of our Saviour—'That nothing be lost.' " The minister must sometimes attend to the business of the farm; he writes letters to a friend, arranging for the purchase of sheep, in order that his family may have wool. But his salary is the largest in New England, outside Boston, and is paid with quite unusual regularity; so in general he can leave his farm to the care of his wife and their hired man; and in course of time he becomes more and more aloof and absent-minded.

Nevertheless it is necessary always to exercise the strictest economy. Owing to the depreciation of the currency all New England is in distress; the law courts are crowded with debtors; and the ministers, with their fixed salaries which, even when paid, are usually quite inadequate, are everywhere complaining of their poverty to God, to their parishes, and to the General Assembly. They eat meat once a day; their breakfast and supper consist solely of bread and milk; their only wine is what is left over from communion services; and coffee, chocolate, rum, tobacco, and books are considered as luxuries.

Children come to the minister and his wife with Puritan regularity, one every two years; there are eleven in all; no less than six are born on the Sabbath, thus disproving the old superstition that children born on the Sabbath were conceived on the Sabbath, and, being the fruit of wickedness, should be denied baptism. Mrs. Edwards has the chief care of them: and her dreadful responsibility in bringing into the world yet another sinner worthy of damnation causes her to pray vehemently to God for the conversion of the future babe as soon as she is pregnant. She never speaks angrily to them, and never uses heavy blows; very rarely does she punish them at all. An eyewitness reports that they never quarrel with each other; and that "when their parents come into the room, they all rise instinctively from their seats, and never resume them until their parents are seated; and when either parent is speaking, no matter with whom they have been conversing, they are all immediately silent and attentive."

Mr. Edwards is bowed down by the fear that even one of them may go to hell, and cares infinitely more about their spiritual welfare than about the health of their bodies. Unconverted children, he believes, go to hell like unconverted adults; and it would be a terrible breach of duty not to describe to them the terrors of eternal punishment; how many souls, dying in childhood, he asks, must curse their parents for such false kindness? "As innocent as children seem to be to us," he declares, "yet, if they are out of Christ, they are not so in God's sight, but are young vipers and are infinitely more hateful than vipers; . . . they are naturally very senseless and stupid, being born as the wild ass's colt, and need much to awaken them. Why should we conceal the truth from them?" When his daughters are away from home, he writes them curious solemn letters. To Sarah he says: "You have very weak and infirm health, and I am afraid are always like to have; and it may be, are not to be long-lived; and while you do live, are not like to enjoy so much of the comforts of this life, as others do, by reason of your want of health; and therefore, if you have no better portion, will be miserable indeed." And to Mary, who is visiting friends in Portsmouth: "If you should be taken with any dangerous sickness, that should issue in death, you might probably be in your grave, before we could hear of your danger. But yet, my great concern is not for your health, or temporal welfare, but for the good of your soul." When young Timothy at New York is in danger of smallpox, he tells him: "If I hear that you have escaped—either that you have not been sick, or are restored—though I shall rejoice, and have great cause of thankfulness, yet I shall be concerned for you. If your escape should be followed with carelessness and security, and forgetting the remarkable warning you have had, and God's great mercy in your deliverance, it would in some respects be more awful than sore sickness." Jonathan, at the age of nine, he sends to live among the Indians, in order that he may learn their language, and be able to preach the gospel to them when he is a man.

Nevertheless his family are not miserable. A happy home is the truest proof of Christianity; and Mrs. Edwards and her children all adore him passionately; she can scarcely endure a reprimand from him; and except Pierpont, who is less than eight years old when Mr. Edwards dies, they are all devout Edwardeans, and continue so through life. For he can be indulgent to them; one day he spends four and sixpence on a child's plaything; and Mrs. Edwards buys, for her adornment, a gold locket and chain which costs eleven pounds. When their daughters grow to be sixteen and eighteen, and ministers and Northampton gentlemen come to court them, they are allowed every freedom to become well acquainted.

To his parishioners he is not so human; they love him less and fear him more; he is so absorbed in his studies that, except at times of awakening, they see too little of him. He preaches twice on the Sabbath and once during the week; he also preaches often at private meetings in particular neighborhoods; and he calls the children to his home and prays with them, and also catechizes them every Sabbath. But he is too shy and aloof, and too absorbed in the things of eternity, to indulge with freedom in worldly conversation; he does not mix well; and any attempt to exchange gossip with his neighbors about the crops or the Indians, and twist it round to religion, results only in a lowering of his dignity. "I have a constitution, in many respects peculiarly unhappy," he says, "attended with flaccid solids, vapid, sizzy, and scarce fluids, and a low tide of spirits; often occasioning a kind of childish weakness and contemptibleness of speech, presence, and demeanor, with a disagreeable dullness and stiffness, much unfitting me for conversation." So he never visits his people unless they send for him. They know him as a solitary horseman, riding out every afternoon for communion with God among the trees; and only Colonel Stoddard, perhaps, is intimate with him.

Some of the neighboring ministers, however, know him more closely, and consider him the greatest genius of the age; for he is a faithful and stimulating friend, with a talent for making disciples. A burly loud-voiced aggressive divinity student, named Bellamy, comes in 1738 to study in his house; he remains for eighteen months before being ordained, and is utterly dominated by the more gentle personality of his teacher; they become most intimate friends, and meet often to discuss the problems of theology; Bellamy is so saturated with the ideas of Edwards that his writings would be indistinguishable from his master's but for his more prosaic style. Three years later a young man from Yale, named Hopkins, having heard Edwards preach, rides to Northampton and presents himself at the house, though he is an utter stranger; Edwards is away, but Mrs. Edwards makes him welcome and invites him to stay the winter. He is gloomy and dejected, and spends most of the time alone in his bedchamber. Mrs. Edwards after some days comes to his room and asks if she can help him. The young man replies that he fears he is damned. Mrs. Edwards replies that she has been praying for him, and promises him speedy comfort. He stays in the family until the following autumn, when he becomes a minister. Bellamy and Hopkins are united in their passionate devotion to Edwards and his theology; they are united too in their admiration for the beauty and charm of Mrs. Edwards; her tactful hospitality makes them immediately feel at home, whenever they visit her husband.

For twenty-three years this is the life of the minister of Northampton. For twenty-three years he sits in his study, elucidating the high problems of divinity. The sun rises over the barren table-land of central Massachusetts, and sets beyond the ranges of the Berkshires; the maples put out their leaves in April, and become yellow and scarlet in October; the thunderstorms break over Mount Holyoke, and the moonlight is reflected in the waters of the stately river Connecticut. The pile of notes grows higher, and the outlines of a complete theological system steadily take form and shape.

Behind him is always the framework of the seasons. In the

spring there is sowing of corn and wheat, and the calves and lambs
are born; in the summer there is hay-making, and the barns are
repaired for harvest; in the autumn the crops are gathered in, the
apples are garnered, and the beer and cider are brewed; then the
sheep and oxen are slaughtered, and the river freezes over, and
the snow prevents all but the most necessary communication with
the world outside; and always there are horses to be fed, and cows
to be milked, and butter and cheese to be made. Northampton is
dominated by the slow rhythms of nature, and any caprice of the
powers that govern it may result in famine.

Life, however, is not one round of duty in a single spot.
Through New England there is much coming and going of ministers, who ride along the dirt tracks from town to town. They ride
to visit each other or to preach in each other's pulpits. They ride to
association meetings, where they discuss obstinate heretics and the
smallness of their salaries. Sometimes they ride to a council, where
ministers and delegates from half a dozen churches meet to
arbitrate a quarrel between another minister and his church; they
hear how the minister has admitted members and appointed
officers without securing the consent of his people, how it is
shrewdly suspected that he drinks too much and is overfond of his
maid-servant; the minister replies that his efforts to discipline
sinners have been ignored, that his people no longer come to
meeting, that his salary has not been paid for several years. The
council sits all day and through the night, and, if God favors them,
have agreed before sunrise on a "result," which may, with God's
help, reconcile the parties.

From Northampton Edwards rides almost every year down the
valley to New Haven for Yale commencement, or across the hills
to the ministers' convention at Boston. Boston is the longer distance and he spends two nights on the journey at the houses of
fellow-ministers. As he rides he meditates systematically upon
some theological problem; and amid the hum of the grasshoppers
and the rustle of apple orchards, he formulates a theory about the
happiness of the angels, or the relationship of God the Father to
the Holy Ghost; when he has finished, he fastens a piece of paper
to some part of his clothing, to remind himself to write down his

conclusion when he comes home. On the morning of the third day he is soon clattering over the cobblestones of Boston, on his way to the house of Benjamin Colman or of Thomas Prince, his two chief friends among the clergy of the town.

Boston is a very gay town. If Edwards were more observant and less absorbed in divinity, he would see young ladies in scarlet hoods and great hooped petticoats tripping along the streets to dances and singing lessons; if he were not so obviously a minister somebody might put into his hands an advertisement for a dancing assembly. He passes a pillory, where a cheater is being pelted by the onlookers; or his way is blocked by a funeral procession of many carriages, all loaded with mourners, winding its way up to Cop's Hill burial ground. Sometimes there is a wild animal on show, a catamount or a leopard, a "tyger-lyon" or a two-headed foal; or the streets are filled with servants gaping at a distinguished visitor—Shick Sidi, the Syrian, for example, who has a swarthy complexion and wears the Turkish costume, and is said not to like Boston very well. On the Sabbath as he walks down with Dr. Prince to the Old South Meeting House, he may find the streets all lined with noisy crowds; they are waiting to see a murderer, under sentence of death, brought from the prison to the church. And when he comments on how the Bostonians pollute the Sabbath, Dr. Prince may reply that the crowd is nothing compared with that which awaited the pirates in 1726, when a group of men captured on the high seas by the vigilance of a private citizen were all condemned to die; when they were brought through the streets to hear Dr. Benjamin Colman preach their last sermon, says Dr. Prince, some of them were penitent, but one hardened rascal wore a nosegay and gallantly ogled the ladies who craned their necks to see him. If Edwards is in Boston on Guy Fawkes day he sees troops of children marching round the town, demanding money from householders, and breaking the windows of those who refuse. Whenever there is a birthday or a marriage in the British royal family, there is a festival: all the church bells ring out peal after peal; the militia parades and is inspected by the Governor; and in the evening there is a banquet and a ball. Every day of the week but two there is a newspaper, relating the latest news from Europe,

mixed with a tale of a Negro slave who has hanged himself, or of
two Connecticut farmers who have got drunk, fallen through the
ice, and been drowned, and followed by an advertisement of a wet
nurse or a parcel of slaves to be sold.

But Boston is not congenial to ministers from the Connecticut
Valley. Boston is halfway to London, and London, to judge from
family traditions, from its heretical books, and from the tales of
wicked noblemen and ladies of easy virtue which the Boston newspapers reprint with such willingness, is obviously a very wicked
place. So Edwards cares only for talking with the ministers, and
turning over the latest importations in the bookshops on Cornhill;
and even the ministers' conventions are marred for him by the
liberalism of so many of the Harvard graduates who attend them.
He accepts these facts, as he accepts everything, as ordained in
God's inscrutable providence. But he thanks God that Northampton is less obviously predestined for hell than Boston.

To Boston, on the other hand, with its dignified merchants, its
smart shopkeepers and lawyers, he is a provincial, though less
round-eyed and easily impressed than most. They despise the
westerners; they are people without refinement, who scarcely know
how to use forks and knives, who are startled and horrified by the
organs in the Episcopalian churches. They have read in the
Courant about the practice of bundling, which appeals to them as
especially crude and ridiculous; modesty out west, they tell each
other with decorous sniggers, is measured by bastards. In Boston,
of course, there is a double standard of morals, and the favors of
lower-class women are not gratuitous.

The few who can appreciate Edwards become his friends. He
makes acquaintances among some high political officers, and
corresponds regularly with some of the clergy. His first publication
is a sermon preached at the public lecture in Boston in 1731. Dr.
Colman and his colleague write a preface, in which they explain
that "it was with no small difficulty that the author's youth and
modesty were prevailed on, to let him appear a preacher in our
public lecture, and afterwards to give us a copy of his discourse."
And they "heartily rejoice in the special favor of Providence, in
bestowing such a rich gift on the happy church of Northampton."

His wife and children, also, visit his Boston friends; and Miss Esther Edwards becomes the close friend of Miss Sally Prince. But probably Edwards is glad when he turns his horse westward, and on the morning of the third day sees the ridge of Holyoke once more loom up to the left and the spire of his own meeting house visible among the trees in front of him.

While the years slip by, his devotion to his religion only grows more ardent. As he contemplates the infinite beauty of God and appreciates it more vividly, he becomes more conscious of his own feeble and fallible humanity. "Often since I lived in this town," he relates, "I have had very affecting views of my sinfulness and vileness; very frequently to such a degree as to hold me in a kind of loud weeping, sometimes for a considerable time together; so that I have often been forced to shut myself up. . . . It has often appeared to me, that if God should mark iniquity against me I should appear the very worst of all mankind; of all that have been since the beginning of the world to this time; and that I should have by far the lowest place in hell. . . . My wickedness, as I am in myself, has long appeared to me perfectly ineffable, and swallowing up all thought and imagination; like an infinite deluge, or mountains over my head. I know not how to express better what my sins appear to me to be, than by heaping infinite upon infinite, and multiplying infinite by infinite. . . . And it appears to me, that were it not for free grace . . . I should appear sunk down in my sins below hell itself. . . . And yet it seems to me that my conviction of sin is exceedingly small and faint."

With a curious reversed pride, not uncommon in the annals of Christianity, he adds that "when I ask for humility I cannot bear the thought of being no more humble than other Christians. It seems to me, that though their degrees of humility may be suitable for them, yet it would be a vile self-exaltation in me, not to be the lowest in humility of all mankind."

He has times of especial fervor. Once, when walking among the trees, he has "a view that for me was extraordinary, of the glory of the Son of God, as Mediator between God and man"; for an hour he is in a flood of tears, weeping aloud, because he longs to be "emptied and annihilated; to lie in the dust, and to be full of Christ alone." And on one Saturday night he "had such a sense, how sweet and blessed a thing it was to walk in the way of duty; to do that which was right and meet to be done, and agreeable to the holy mind of God; that it caused me to break forth into a kind of loud weeping, which held me some time, so that I was forced to shut myself up, and fasten the doors."

But, in spite of his own wickedness and the wickedness of his parish, he still finds in the natural world beyond his doorstep a shadow of God's excellency. In gentle breezes and singing birds, in the lily and the fragrant rose, in the murmur of rivers and in the golden edges of an evening cloud, "in comets, in thunder, in the hovering thunderclouds, in rugged rocks and the brows of mountains," "in that beauteous light with which the world is filled on a clear day," and in the beauty of the human body, he sees emanations of Christ's glory and goodness.

✪

A Frontier Childhood

Jonathan Edwards was born in the East Windsor parsonage on October 5, 1703. This was precisely nine years after Timothy Edwards had come with his bride, Esther Stoddard, to the newly gathered congregation across the river. He was now thirty-four years old and his wife was thirty-one. Four daughters had already been born into their home and six more were to follow. Jonathan was their first and only son. Was he named Jonathan for what the name means, "Gift of Jehovah," for some English ancestor now lost to view, or for the Welsh theologian and controversialist, Jonathan Edwards of Jesus College, Oxford, whose *Preservative Against Socinianism* had been completed and published earlier in the year 1703? Any one of these reasons might have seemed the best reason to Timothy Edwards.

One cannot but remember that three months earlier, in a Lincolnshire parsonage on the Isle of Axholme, another son had been born to another minister and his godly, strong-minded wife. The two great religionists were never to meet, or even to know why such a meeting would have seemed significant to historians of another century. On two continents John Wesley and Jonathan Edwards were to go their separate and quite different ways, changing the meaning of religion for many thousands, and with it also the cultural pattern of their generation.

In 1703 the East Windsor parish was still a young enterprise, full of promise. During the nine years he had been among them as their pastor, Timothy Edwards had definitely succeeded. The bitter controversy incident to the separation of his small flock from the parent congregation across the river had gradually slipped into the background and, in spite of occasional reminders that the new parish was made up of both factions in the dispute, withdrawal had abundantly justified itself in the growth and contentment of the new congregation. To go safely to meeting on their own side after years of perilous canoe crossings in all weathers was blessing untold. Month by month new families had come to reside on their fertile holdings across the river and the six-year-old meetinghouse was already too small. The new parish was now a separate township with full power to order its own affairs. This too was a great blessing. For the most part the pews liked the minister, and though no revival had yet come to bless his labors among them they believed God was merely testing their faith; and they waited confidently.

By 1703 life in this far-flung settlement had taken on a fairly settled character and was growing steadily safer year by year in spite of periodic alarms and very real dangers. When Jonathan Edwards was four months old the ever present Indian peril came close to the parsonage in the murder at Deerfield, Massachusetts, of Eunice Williams, half-sister of Esther Edwards. Two of Mrs. Williams' children were also killed, her husband and four more children carried into captivity. The news brought deep personal grief; it was also a grim reminder of the time when churchgoing Windsor had been fined for not carrying muskets to meeting, according to order. Indians were not very numerous in Connecticut by this time, and they were for the most part friendly; but there was still cause for fear. Not for another generation could a child grow up without the memory of a thousand cautions as to what was by no means a phantom danger. From all perils within and perils without, the village must be sufficient unto itself, for this part of the "Lord's Waste" was still a remote frontier. Except for Timothy Edwards and a few other great ones of the village, who occasionally took horse and rode away to Boston, the town limits were the very boundaries of life. One was born, had children, and died without ever going so far as Hartford—two centuries later, only twenty minutes away. As for the vast worries of the land of their grandfathers—Whigs and Tories battling over the nature of the monarchy at home, the War of the Spanish Succession raging abroad, and a stupid queen on the throne—these things were no longer the realities of life. Connecticut colony, East Windsor in particular, was all the world.

Agricultural pursuits made up the background of village life and, as in all country parishes of the day, the minister was perforce a farmer among farmers. He divided his time between his study and his acreage, directing the spring plowing or taking a hand at skinning a cow quite as naturally as he expounded the Scriptures or conducted a funeral. The isolation of East Windsor made the separation between parsonage and parish, sacred and secular, even less sharp than would have been true of Hartford or Northampton. In consequence, Timothy Edwards, for all his austere dignity, was not a man apart from his people. They cut and carted his wood as part of his "rate," made his children's shoes, brought him sugar and mutton and spice as they happened to have abundance, and advised him when to cut the hay. He gave them credit in his *Rate Books* for their services and donations, and in his turn taught their children for pay, bought their cider, distilled it into brandy and sold it back to them again, and engaged in many other sorts of barter convenient to both parties. He was their pastor whom they respected, to a degree feared, and sometimes opposed bitterly; but he was also their neighbor whom they knew in his second-best clothes. On Sundays and Thursdays he preached and assumed the full dignity of his priestly office; on other days he was one of themselves, taking part with them in the exchange of commodities and services by which this isolated little community maintained its independent life.

According to family tradition he was irked by these weekday details and inclined to delegate responsibility for them to his capable wife. Possibly, for he had been town-bred and as a boarding pupil in Mr. Glover's home had escaped chores at an early age; but as an East Windsor husbandman he could not have claimed immunity from farm tasks. The Edwards acres were fairly extensive: there were fields to be fertilized, crops to be harvested, woods to be cut down and put under cultivation, stock to be cared for, hides to be tanned, extra acres to be rented for pasture, and numerous routine chores to be performed daily. Some supervision of all these multiple concerns fell to him as head of the house, no matter how distasteful it may have been. Besides, there is plenty of evidence that he knew the details first-hand and had some share in the actual labors which came with the seasons.

By his son in his own country parish days, these tasks would be assumed far more naturally. Born part villager, part farmer, he would be able throughout life to accept the routine of field and barnyard as a necessary, normal part of life, to be performed without protest or apology. The difference between father and son in this as in so many other directions was a difference of emphasis. Jonathan Edwards hewed his life to the line of his main interest, consciously subordinating those things which he considered lesser; Timothy Edwards often became confused under tasks hostile to his main interest, scattered his energies in a fretful and futile busyness, and was at times defeated by the very details he hated. Both men handled minutiae with a conscience; only the son chose to split hairs in an argument, not to measure corn to the half pint.

Jonathan Edwards grew up in the house built as the gift of Richard Edwards of Hartford at the time of Timothy's settlement in East Windsor. It stood on the east side of the present highway, about a quarter of a mile from the old burying ground. As described by Sereno E. Dwight, who saw it in 1803, and by John Stoughton, who added memories of the oldest settlers in the mid-century, the house conformed to the general plan of substantial middle-class dwellings of the 1690's. It was a severely plain, two-story structure of moderate size, built low to the ground and with the second story projecting slightly beyond the first. A single chimney separated the two first-floor rooms, one of which was the kitchen-living-room—possibly also a bedroom as the family increased—the other, called by Timothy Edwards the "parlor," was really the schoolroom. In this room, which was equipped on three sides with benches fastened to the wall, Jonathan Edwards and his ten sisters, together with the village boys who aspired to college and some who did not, received their elementary education. Like other Connecticut houses of the period the parsonage grew with the family, various lean-tos being added, and also an eight- or nine-foot projection at the middle front, spoken of as the "porch" but really a vestibule.

Tradition has built this house of somewhat better materials, more ample proportions, and more expensive appointments than the other houses in East Windsor. Possibly, although its alleged "elegant ornaments" would hardly seem consistent with the character of the donor, Richard Edwards. More probably like the Grant Mansion built in the same decade, it merely introduced architectural improvements hitherto unknown along the "Street." Any house built in the 1690's would naturally have been superior to the log houses of the first residents. Extant expense accounts show the parsonage to have been built of hewn lumber, probably brought by sledge from the nearest mill at Scantic, and of bricks carted from Podunk. The labor of building was the donation of the parishioners, who put a year of their spare time into the task. How well they did their work became a village legend to be repeated confidently generations afterward when the house was being torn down. During all its one hundred and eighteen years, said the great-grandchildren of the pioneer builders, this house had but one covering of shingles—those originally nailed in place by the brethren. Such statements are best left unchallenged, if only to perpetuate the picture of deacons in their old clothes, armed with hammer and saw to a godly end.

In this frontier parish and in this house, its recognized center, Jonathan Edwards lived for the first thirteen years of his life. In many ways he was fortunate, not only for what he missed but for what he gained by such isolation. No wonder the beauty and majesty of nature stamped themselves unforgettably on his early thought. In such a setting nature would have been the most important daily fact to a sensitive child. With a horizon in all four directions he could hardly have escaped impressions of a spacious world: a world of meadows, unending forests, the river; a world of ever changing beauty, not a world of man's making. Even today,

standing on the slight eminence which marks the site of the
Edwards parsonage, the virgin forests gone and the meadows
turned into tobacco fields, one still has a sense of spaciousness and
isolation amounting almost to loneliness. Before 1716 isolation
meant also helplessness, for danger lurked beyond the dark line of
the forest, and miles beyond there were still no habitations.

From the "Street" running in front of the house he could see to
the west, beyond the meadows and beyond the river, the turret of
the Windsor meetinghouse—larger than his father's—and the
more numerous dwellings of the parent settlement. Trips to Windsor in the homemade canoes, so much feared by the older folk,
would have been events in his boyhood. In the foreground, a little
to the right of the parsonage and just across the ravine from his
father's meetinghouse, stood the small fort or Palisado built a
generation earlier as a place of rendezvous in time of Indian
attacks, but in his boyhood used for more peaceful purposes. Even
so, to every boy in the village, acquainted with the tales of earlier
raids, a blast on the infrequent Palisado trumpet would have
sounded a hope of high adventure for his generation also.

Scattered along the "Street" beyond the meetinghouse and
beyond his own home were the houses of the other families of the
parish, fewer than one hundred in all. They stood scarcely closer
together than the farmhouses along the present highway, on which
life now goes so rapidly by; for East Windsor was not a huddled
village. Each house was built on its own acres; and the tracts,
small for farms, were large for town plots. The house nearest the
Edwards home was that of Captain Thomas Stoughton who, in the
year the parsonage was built, married Abigail, sister of Timothy
Edwards. In the Stoughton home there were also eleven children,
with ages corresponding almost exactly to those of the Edwards
eleven. Seven of these were boys—three older, three younger, and
one almost the exact age of Jonathan Edwards—so that the
companionship with boys which he missed in his own home he had
with his seven boy cousins next door. The assumption that, as the
only son in his father's house, he had to endure being petted by his
ten sisters and made to share their girl games is absurd. In addition
to the Stoughtons similar hosts could have been mustered from

almost every one of the hundred houses in the village, for in spite of the "throat distemper," upsetting canoes, and home remedies East Windsor, as well as the rest of colonial New England, was full of children.

At the rear of the house, toward the east, there was scarcely a suggestion of man and his concerns. The land slopes gently down to a brook on the Edwards side, then up a hill—at that time densely wooded. Somewhere along this brook Jonathan Edwards built the booth in which he and his boy companions used to meditate and pray. These were the fields in which "multitudes of times" he had "beheld with wonderment and pleasure" the spiders marching in the air from one tree to another, "their little shining webbs and Glistening Strings of a Great Length and at such a height as that one would think they were tack'd to the Sky by one end were it not that they were moving and floating." One may be sure he had also watched other living and growing things with the same philosophic eye. He may even have committed his observations to paper frequently, for the spider essay, so often cause for the marvel of posterity, can hardly have been his only excursion into a realm so minutely known and so confidently possessed. When he wrote of spiders, he wrote not of something which transiently caught his eye but of a world which belonged to him by right of long and deep intimacy.

Inevitably in his speculations about the universe he shared the belief of his contemporaries that the processes of nature went on by personal manipulation of the Almighty and therefore had a logical relation to the shortcomings of man; but having accepted this major tenet his mind went freely on to other queries. Although when he wrote of the rainbow he was probably still young enough to believe that the ends of it stood in basins of gold, his orthodoxy had been corrupted by no such pleasant fables. But to believe instead that it was the symbol of God's covenant with Noah did not paralyze his boyish inventiveness when it came to making a little rainbow of his own. There were several ways. He could take water in his mouth, stand between the sun and "something that looks a little Darkish," spurt the water into the air, and make a rainbow as complete and perfect as any ever seen in the heavens.

He could get the same result by dashing up drops of water from a puddle with a stick. Unfortunately (and unforgivably) he had been deprived of a visit to the sawmill at Scantic; but he had heard his "Countrymen that are Used to sawmills" say that rainbows could be seen in the violent concussion of the mill waters. It is pleasant to imagine the picture of this serious-faced and persistent small boy catechizing his sawmill countrymen for purposes of his own philosophic speculation. In the spider essay he accepted the current notion that spiders are the most despicable of the insect kind. They are the "corrupting nauseousness of the air," and yet this assumption, borrowed from his elders, did not vitiate his own clear-sighted observation as to the spider's ballooning habits, or his inspired guess (for a twelve-year-old) as to the liquid character of the unspun web.

In an eager desire to discover the child as father of the man, this unit of boyish composition, possibly written even earlier than his twelfth year, has been dignified more than once into a truly remarkable piece of scientific observation for its day and assumed to contain proofs that Jonathan Edwards had potentialities for a career in science as great as, if not greater than, in theology. Such enthusiasm is pardonable, and the conjecture is perhaps warranted. Argument spends itself vainly on such matters. The fact is that Jonathan Edwards' observation of flying spiders is accurate so far as it goes, even when tested by the findings of mature observers in a later day. As the findings of a boy who had no training in scientific observation, no microscope, no body of specialized knowledge by which to test his own observations or his conclusions from them, this juvenile effort is indeed arresting. It might do credit, in the observation alone, to an amateur twice his age.

The deductions leading from his observations are even more arresting: the basis for classification, the theory of equilibrium by which he explains the spider's navigation of the air, the character of the web, even his naïve justification of nature in providing creatures with just such equipment. That he took great pains with the essay is apparent, especially in the extant manuscript which was probably a first draft. The erasures and substitutions suggest that he had set himself to deserve a hearing from his learned correspondent, not realizing that the boyish letter accompanying his effort would easily have gained the hospitality of one not interested in spiders.

Forgive me, sir, [he wrote] that I Do not Conceal my name, and Communicate this to you by a mediator. If you think the Observations Childish, and besides the Rules of Decorum,—with Greatness and Goodness overlook it in a Child & Conceal Sir, Although these things appear very Certain to me, yet Sir, I submit it all to your better Judgment & Deeper insight. . . . Pardon if I thought it might at Least Give you Occasion to make better observations, on these wondrous animals, that should [be] worthy of Communicating to the Learned world, respecting these wondrous animals, from whose Glistening Webs so much of the wisdom of the Creatour shines. Pardon Sir

> your most Obedient humble servant,
> JONATHAN EDWARDS

As to spiders, how many kinds were there? Why did they always fly in a southeasterly direction? How was it possible for them to navigate the air? Determined to satisfy his curiosity as to the "manner of their Doing of it," he became, as he said, "very conversant with Spiders," spending in their interest days in the woods—exploring rotten logs, tracking them down, classifying them, and trying to understand how they stretched their webs from tree to tree. Like any other wide-awake boy he was sufficiently inventive to devise ways and means of finding out what he wanted to know; but unlike most boys his age he was unable to rest until he had finished what he had begun. After he had evolved a satisfactory technique of observation, he "Repeated the triall Over and Over again till I was fully satisfied of his way of working." When presently he saw the second string issuing from the tail of the spider he held on his stick, he concluded that he had "found out the Whole mystery." Stick in hand, he gave demonstrations to his companions of the spider's habit of "mounting into the air," discussed his theory with others and no doubt set his sisters and the Stoughton cousins to watching spiders and reporting their observations. One hopes also that he hoarded a collection of specimens on the parsonage windowsill.

Years later when he preached on the spider as one of the four things on earth which are exceeding small and yet exceeding wise, how did he remember this boyish attempt to solve the spider's mystery for itself, not as the prop to doctrine? Perhaps he did not remember it at all, for long before that time the door to this early world was shut, and he had lost the key.

Whatever its precise date, this precocious essay, as perhaps the earliest of his voluminous writings, is of unquestioned biographical importance. More than precocity is involved. The quality of mind revealed in these boyish observations and deductions would be equally significant whether he was eleven or thirteen when he wrote them down. The essay is a chapter in his mental development, a glimpse into the world he lived in, a world of speculative thought reached through objective fact. It is illuminating also as a personal document out of his East Windsor boyhood, testifying to long afternoons in the meadow when as a little boy he lay on his back, apparently idle, but his mind and eye intent on the life of the fields. There was no reason two and a half centuries ago for any East Windsor neighbor to set down a description of Jonathan Edwards as a child; but if his portrait were to be imagined in characteristic pose, the open fields should be the background, the figure that of a healthy boy dressed in sturdy homespun, sitting alone, doing nothing with his hands, but mentally as active as though bent over his books. Aged eleven or twelve he was no daydreamer, or even Boy of Winander, taking sensitive pleasure in bird calls and cloud movements or in listening to the rhythms of nature, heard and unheard; he was already a thinker, pushing his natural boy's curiosity about the universe as far as infinity. On such days his East Windsor boyhood was indeed "fair seed-time" for the soul of a philosopher.

In the light of his mature development one need scarcely wonder why he did not continue to devote his great powers of mind to scientific thought. The answer is that science would not have satisfied him. The physical universe was to him only the skeleton of reality, and scientific investigation was the means of stripping off only the outer layers of the mystery. From the utmost bounds of material science other speculative minds likewise have been teased along until they have leaped from the known and measurable to the intangible and infinite. To such minds only the ultimate questions as to the whence and whither of being seem worth the asking. Even as a boy, Jonathan Edwards was one of this company. Why a world at all? he was saying. "What need was there that any thing should be?" To Pascal, Newton, Swedenborg, and other giants in scientific reasoning his intellectual history would be an open book. These men also turned from physical science to religion; but they turned late in life after they had made contributions which changed the direction of scientific thought in their day. Jonathan Edwards turned away before he had made more than a bare beginning, but he obeyed the same impulse.

Had he been the son of Josiah Franklin he might have carried his boyish observations further; but as the son of Timothy Edwards he was not allowed to grow up in the meadow watching spiders, unsupervised. Like Aunt Mary Emerson's famous nephew he was "born to be educated," and indications are that the process began as early as speech. The setting was favorable. Whether Timothy Edwards had begun to prepare boys for Harvard College as early as Jonathan's infancy is not clear, but there were already four other Edwardses needing his services, and the "parlor" was in daily use. Under a discipline more rigorous than obtained in any "dame school" of the period, Jonathan Edwards laid substantial foundations for his ministerial career from the time he could first read. He began with the "Tongues."

Some few hints of the pedagogical process survive in several letters written by Timothy Edwards to his wife, when she was obliged during his absence on military duty in the fall of 1711 to take over his schoolroom duties. He admonished her not to let Jonathan, aged seven, lose the Latin he had already learned by heart, suggesting that she have him "say pretty often" to the girls from the Latin *Accidence* and both sides of "propria Quae moribus," and also that he help his younger sisters to read as far as he had learned. More than economy of effort for the teacher was back of this law of the Edwards schoolroom, by which the older child taught the younger. Timothy Edwards knew that, by the time the young Latinist had said "pretty often" to one group and heard "pretty often" the "sayings" of another group, he would have the Latin *Accidence* and both sides of "propria Quae moribus" for life; and to learn them less permanently was not to learn them at all.

His parent-teacher could hardly have been one whose teaching brought joy of the vision or made discipline seem more than an end in itself; but by his tireless persistence, which brooked no indolence and no half-knowledge, Timothy Edwards fortified his son for life against textual errors, major and minor, and made thoroughness one of the ten commandments. Unlike the tutor of Cotton Mather he did not encourage his pupils to compose poems of devotion in the tongues they were set to master. He preferred that they be letter-perfect in their verbs. Jonathan Edwards accepted his father's standard when he was too young to question it, and several years later, when the unlucky "Stiles" who was also a "parlor" product could not tell the "Preteritum of Requiesco" in a Yale examination, Jonathan shared his father's humiliation. The fact that Stiles committed no error in Tully's Orations, which "he had never Construed before he came to Newhaven, nor in any other Book, whether Latin, Greek or Hebrew," would seem to a modern college board examiner something of an extenuating circumstance, if indeed he could believe the sight of his eyes; but not to Timothy Edwards. No wonder Harvard and Yale were glad to accept his pupils. The lesson of strict accuracy was perhaps the most valuable lesson which Jonathan Edwards learned in the East Windsor schoolroom, along with his own unforgettable preterits.

Parental discipline was not limited to schoolroom exercises. The other minutiae of daily life were likewise under a supervision all but omniscient though never harsh, and filial obedience was the first law of the household. Timothy Edwards' elaborate catalogues of instruction, written on march and sent back to his partner in authority, re-create more fully than it has been elsewhere preserved the panorama of parsonage life as it was lived under the watchful eyes of the heads of the house. These letters are therefore an important part of Jonathan Edwards' childhood story. Written in homesick mood, they constitute a kind of last will and testament of affection to those Timothy Edwards had left behind and might not see again. In the light of his phrase "If I Live to come home," his exaggerated worries become understandable. As he called up the familiar round, his homesickness took the form of imagined disaster for each child of the flock. In his absence something might go wrong. Hence the pyramid of hypothetical woes and multiple cautions which, taken out of their emotional context, appear almost ludicrous.

The letter of August 7 is the richest in household detail. It is also a strange medley and a revealing glimpse into a man's mind.

Tuesday
Newhaven Aug/ 7th/ 1711

My Dear

This comes to express my Dearest Love to thee, and to Informe Thee y^t I am (Through the goodness of God) yet in Good health, & do expect to Go towards Albany in a few days; ye Govn:^{or} Intends ye part at Least of ye Regiments Shall March to morrow, & talks of Going himself on Friday next at furthest.

I desire thee to take care y^t Jonathan don't Loose w^t he hath Learned but y^t as he hath got ye accidence, & above two sides of *propria Quae moribus* by heart so y^t he keep what he hath got, I would therefore have him Say pretty often to ye Girls; I would also have ye Girls keep what they have Learnt of ye Grammar, & Get by heart as far as Jonathan hath Learnt: he can help them to Read as far as he hath Learnt: and would have both him and them keep their writing, and therefore write much oftener than they Did when I was at home. I have left Paper enough for them which they may use to ye End, only I would have you reserve enough for your own use in writing Letters &c.

I hope thou wilt take Special care of Jonathan y^t he dont Learn to be rude & naught &c. of wch thee and I have Lately Discoursed. I wouldnt have thee venture him to ride out into ye woods with Tim.

I hope God will help thee to be very carefull y^t no harm happen to ye little Children by Scalding wort, whey, water, or by Standing too nigh to Tim when he is cutting wood: and prithee take what care thou canst about Mary's neck, which was too much neglected when I was at home, & Let her also sometimes read over what She hath Learnt in the Grammar y^t she Maynt Loose it: and Let a new rope be speedily put upon ye well pole, if it be not done already: And Let Esther & Betty Take their powders as Soon as the Dog Days are Over, & if they dont help Esther, talk further with ye Doct^r: about her for I wouldnt have her be neglected: Something also Should be done for Anne who as thou knowest is weakly: & Take Care of thy Self, and Dont Suckle little Jerusha too Long.

My horse Got a bad wound her in Broth^r: Mathers Pasture, I would have due Care taken y^t he May be well lookt to, and thoroughly cured, If he Should be Neglected, or Ridden much before he be pretty well, It may be of very Ill consequence.

I herewith Sent you a Bill of 40^{sh}, because I would not have thee want mony in My Absence; this & ye other I Left with thee thou knowest are Loose papers, & if they be not carefully Laid up they may Soon be Lost. ye Lord Jesus Christ be with thy Spirit my Dear, & Incourage thee to hope and trust in him, & discover his Love to thy Soul to whom I commit thee & all thine and mine, to whom Remember my Love, & also to Mercy Brooks & Tim: Demming & tell him y^t I shall much Rejoice If I Live to come home to know y^t he hath been a Good Boy, & tell my Children y^t I would have Them to pray dayly for their Father, and for their own Souls, and above all things to Remember their Creator and Seek after ye Lord Jesus Christ now in ye Days of their youth. God be with & bless you all.

> I am my Dear, ever Thine in y^e
> Dearest Love and affection
>
> Tim^o: Edwards

If any of ye children should at any time Go over ye River to meeting I would have them be exceeding carefull, how y^y Sit or Stand in ye boat Least they should fall into ye River.[1]

I like thy Letter so well my dear both as to ye hand, and ye framing of it, y^t I Desire more of y^m one at Albany would be exceeding well-come to me towards which I am going tomorrow.

Let care be taken y^t ye cattle dont get into ye orchard & wrong ye trees.

& y^t ye barn ben't left open to ye Cattle, thy^r Dung be carried out & Laid in ye orchard where there is most need before winter, & y^t ye flax be not spoiled.

The fleet sailed Last Monday was Sev'n night (consisting of 100 Sail of all Sorts, & as is computed here of about 20 men of war. this I had from ye post Last Friday evry Sev'n night: Col. Whiting also sent it to ye Govn:^{r} in a Letter, as I have been told.

Let Mary write pretty often as well as the Rest of ye Girls &c.

[1] These last instructions are written in the margins.

If the legend of Esther Edwards' strong-mindedness be true, these marginal additions must have somewhat mitigated her joy in the pleasure her letter had given. For one of her instincts and her breeding to be reminded of what she could not possibly forget— her children's safety, and, on one later occasion, her manners— would seem to have been a severe strain on her Christian forbearance.

In these multiple admonitions Timothy Edwards sat for his own mental portrait. Like his son he had the kind of mind which visualizes its concepts, an excellent kind of mind to possess if one would be a preacher of the Last Judgment, but requiring sterner terrors than scalding whey, flying chips, and neglected medicine to summon its powers appropriately. The son's resources of imagination were, by contrast, reserved for the agonized suspense of the final day and the subsequent tortures of the damned, not unleashed to conjure up minor injuries to the children around the kitchen stove. As he lays bare his characteristic ways of thought in these intimate letters Timothy Edwards shows himself to be a man careful and troubled about many things, one who forgot nothing and yet assumed that everyone else forgot everything continually, one who busied himself unnecessarily with the obligations of others and half enjoyed the self-imposed burden of details innumerable. In all these counsels, which by long habit he usually delivered in the negative, there is not the slightest hint of a peevish or unpleasant spirit. He merely could not help thinking for everyone else and compiling ubiquitous lists of tasks to be done, with all conceivable hazards present to his mind at every turn.

Instead of quieting childish fears he raised them, as though parental guidance consisted in advance notice of potential disaster. A letter written to his daughter Mary when she was attending school in Hatfield, begins with cautions against wet feet and going "too thin to meeting," proceeds through warnings against losing her good name (especially since she is a woman), and ends with an injunction to remember she has an immortal soul lodged in a frail mortal body. This letter might well stand as a father's legacy to his daughter in the days when one was permitted to live in order to get ready to die.

Such counsels were by no means unique. Children of Jonathan Edwards' generation, who were not sons and daughters of ministers, were made to live in the ever present consciousness of death. Every Sunday might be the last. Every parting was for eternity. Newspaper accounts of accident were invariably framed to suggest that no one dare boast himself of tomorrow. It was as though life were indeed lived in the formula of the Middle Ages: "What is this our life but a march toward death?" Children might as well learn it early as late. The chance legend

REMEMBER YOU WAS BORN TO DIE

surviving as a child's copy on the flyleaf of an old almanac, and painstakingly scrawled nine times down the page, was no morbid reflection. It was merely the inevitable truth brought home afresh with each new onslaught of pestilence or other disaster, born of isolation and man's impotence.

Jonathan Edwards like other children of his day grew up with this as a settled conviction, although his own childhood was singularly protected from loss of those near him. Almost phenomenally the Edwards family circle remained unbroken for thirty-five years, and when Sister Jerusha died in 1729, aged twenty, Jonathan Edwards was a man grown and had been away from East Windsor for thirteen years. This unusual record, be it said in all fairness, may have owed something to Timothy Edwards' tiresome vigilance, and that vigilance in turn may have owed something to the supposed mythology of his own boyhood, reputed to have been a succession of remarkable deliverances from drownings, freezings, scaldings, killing of playmates, and swallowing of peach stones. If these tales be not the sheerest invention memory doubtless aided imagination whenever he saw his own children set foot in a rocking boat or ride away on horseback.

The potential naughtiness of Jonathan, mentioned in the Albany letter, may have been only another parental chimera, although allusion to the late conference on the subject suggests that, thanks to Tim the chore boy, Jonathan, aged seven, may have manifested symptoms of taint. One hopes so, since his story includes all too few hints of a childlike childhood. East Windsor would have had its corrupting influences of course, like all towns small and large; but by comparison with less remote communities these would certainly have been less numerous. Samuel Hopkins, born in 1721, made the astonishing statement that up to his fifteenth year he had never heard a profane word from any of the children with whom he grew up in Waterbury, Connecticut. The answer is of course that he had not been listening for profanity. His ears were stopped against all sinful matter because his head was full of something else. Jonathan Edwards at no time in his life was given to such impressive personal statements, but he too had been protected in childhood by the strength of his impulses in the opposite direction. From his birth he had lived in an atmosphere of respect for all things holy and had deep concern for the exercises of piety after the earlier American pattern. Until he rationalized and justified these attitudes by his own thought he accepted them as unquestioningly as he accepted the sunrise and the seasons.

It is in the light of such boyhood training that his later guidance of the Northampton boys and girls must be judged. Playing leap-frog in the parsonage yard while they waited their turn to be reproved by the minister was a gigantic impropriety in comparison with his own boyhood standard. Had he or any one of the Stoughton boys felt inclinations toward such blasphemous behavior they would not have dared indulge them in the very shadow of the meetinghouse turret. Satan would have been too much pleased.

Of Jonathan Edwards' earliest religious experiences there is no contemporary record; only his own later allusion to his first "awakening" which, as he wrote, took place "some years before I went to college," and the well-known detail of the booth in the swamp, belonging to the same period. This may have been at any time from his eighth to his tenth year, for Timothy Edwards was having annual revivals during that period. Looked back upon, this first awakening did not seem to him a profound experience. It was rather a greatly quickened delight in the outward duties of religion which he had been performing all his life, but in which he now took intense new pleasure. The building of the booth in the swamp was a group response to the same quickening of religious interest and is not so strange as it has sometimes seemed to later generations. In part a boy enterprise, interesting in the doing, and in part imitation of adult action during a revival season, it probably surprised none of the parents whose sons were associated in the scheme. In a sense the boys who went to the booth to pray and to talk about their own salvation were playing at religion, as children of a later generation played at vast Tory and Continental hatreds, and re-enacted the drama of adult action. The significant detail in this episode for the understanding of Jonathan Edwards is that praying with his companions did not satisfy him. Even as a child he felt religion as too personal an experience to be shared so intimately; hence, unknown to his companions, he had his own place of secret prayer deeper in the woods. This was years before his mind acknowledged that religion must be an individual experience, else it was nothing; but even as a child he felt it so, and in this solitary quest was responding to the deepest instinct of his nature. Going back and forth to the meetinghouse, keeping the Sabbath as the son of Timothy Edwards was expected to keep it—these things were not enough. Religion was more than the mere observances of it. What it was, he could not have said, except that his mind was "deeply engaged in it" and no other delights were comparable.

There is not the slightest suggestion that either at this time or at any time later in his life he courted austerity for its own sake, or that in his solitary devotions he sought deliberately to mortify the flesh in order to develop the spirit. Always his mind was on the end, not the means, and the discipline itself was of so little importance that he was usually oblivious of it. Moreover, at this time, going to the woods to pray was something of a practical necessity in a household so numerous that privacy was all but impossible at any hour in the twenty-four. In addition to the Edwards flock guests were frequent, sometimes staying for weeks and paying board as was the custom. Some of Timothy Edwards' pupils from other towns also lived at the parsonage. One wonders how or where. Certainly there must have been times when, between parental supervision, sisterly criticism, and the presence of perhaps twenty persons under one sloping roof, those "little nervous strings" which, according to Jonathan Edwards' boyhood reasoning, proceed from the "soul in the brain" must at least have been "jarred" by these external things. For one to whom solitude was an unquestioned necessity, to be obliged—not only in his boyhood but throughout his life—to live in houses which were more like hostelries than private dwellings seems unkindness indeed.

Particularly in connection with these earliest religious experiences one would like to know more than the records tell of his relation to his mother Esther Edwards. No letters to her or from her are extant for any time in his life. She takes on individuality only in his father's numerous epistles filled with everyday details testifying to her resourcefulness in the minor crises of frontier life, and to her unsparing vigilance as she nursed one after another of them through serious illnesses. "We find your absence, (especially So Long) makes a great empty place in the house," he wrote on one occasion. One might think it would. She was the shadow of a great rock to them all. Did she, in addition to her practical gifts, her intellectual vigor and zeal in good works, have also an understanding of her son's deeply spiritual nature, his sensitive approach to religious experience? There is no recorded answer to these questions. An unauthenticated tradition that during one of her husband's revivals she made public profession of conversion would certainly suggest, if true, that she had not only the courage of her convictions in a difficult test but also a capacity for religious emotion which might have given her a sympathetic understanding of his young ecstasies; but, if so, the evidence does not appear. He spoke freely of his experiences to his father, but there is no record that he confided them also to his mother. She lives only in the filial idiom "Remember my Duty to my honored Mother" unfailingly included in his letters to his father.

The fact that Sister Jerusha, six years younger than Jonathan, was also given to solitary walks and prolonged devotions, with corresponding abhorrence of "froth and levity in conversation" and delight in weighty discourses, particularly books of divinity, may mean that she was consciously or unconsciously imitating him, or more probably that something in their joint heritage prompted these similar yearnings and in a sense unfitted them both to live in the world as they found it. In Jerusha there is no hint of mystical raptures. She was merely engaging in devotions, with more than a hint of childish asceticism in the manner of them. It was her custom on Saturday nights to stay up later than the rest of the family, in preparation for the Sabbath, and in the morning to walk alone to the house of God in solemn meditation. When she returned from the afternoon service, if the weather were not too severely cold, she diligently improved the remainder of the holy day in an unheated upper room, as the saying was, "filling in all the chinks of the Lord's day with useful thoughts." When she attended any merry meeting of young people she took no part in the merriment, but instead sat on "one side of ye Company with some person who would entertain her upon some sollid and profitable subject." Not that she was an "enemy to something of innocent Jesting," her sisters protested; she merely chose to use her wit as sauce, thinking it "very improper food, for ye soul."

Even after allowance is made for sisterly overstatement, this picture of Jerusha Edwards with her beautiful countenance, her blameless life, and "Quiet Virtue" has its ludicrous side, even for a minister's daughter in a godly age. Her extravagant pieties, however modestly she attempted to hide them, must have made her something of a village oddity and none too welcome at the merry meetings she rebuked by her soberness. She judged by a standard too high for weekday living, yet thought it her duty, for the good of others, to speak her criticism frankly. When on one occasion she so far overshot the mark as to attempt to improve the virtue of her sweetheart and "preserve him against ye infection of vice" by telling him what was wrong with his behavior, the sally cost her a budding romance. But she had done her duty as she saw it and in the sequel bore herself like a true Edwards, her calm unruffled by the ferment of gossip which ensued. So great was her personal triumph (so said her sisters) that she took no pains to contradict the story that he had jilted her but went serenely to meeting, all eyes upon her. Such was the Edwards code.

With all his flat-footed good sense Timothy Edwards applauded these unyouthful rigidities. He was, in fact, responsible for most of them. Jerusha was the eloquent embodiment of the Christian virtues he preached; only, being her father's child, she had taken them somewhat too literally. Had she lived, her wit might have helped her to attain a better balance, but she was denied the chance. Even before her death she seems to have been all but canonized in the Edwards household where she lived with her sisters "in love, not unlike to y^t which is in ye heavenly regions."

Had Jerusha been nearer to him in age Jonathan Edwards might have found much in common with her; but when he left home for college she was a child of six, whom he was to know later only in brief vacations. It was to his practical sister Mary, two years older than himself, that he turned for companionship through all his young life. When she went away to school in Hatfield he sent her the family news; and when later he went away to Yale College she did the same for him. These letters tell a story of affectionate comradeship and mutual dependence pleasant to read. It was to Mary that his first extant letter, written when he was twelve years old, was sent. In the news of the revival with which he begins, he talks more like a deacon than a twelve-year-old boy; but with his own awakening behind him he was already on the side of the pulpit and yearning toward the unconverted. By his twelfth year, also, he had learned the formalities of polite correspondence, and out of respect for a missive which must be carried by hand (sometimes by several hands) he did not fill his pages with light matter but appropriately subordinated the trivialities of chickenpox and toothache to lists of the newly converted and the newly dead. He wrote in a neat hand and made the customary epistolary flourishes. The letter reveals much as to his childhood background of thought and his standards of value.

Windsor May 10 1716

Dear Sister

Through the Wonderful Mercy and Good[ne]ss of God there hath in this Place Been a verry Remarkable stirring and pouring out of the Spirrit of God, And Likewise now is But I think i have Reason to think it is in Some Mesure Diminished but I hope not much. About thirteen Have been joyned to the Church in an estate of full Comunion These are those which by Enquiry I Find you have not heard of that

have joyn'd to the Church, viz; John Huntington, Sarah Loomas the
Daughter of Thomas Loomas, and Esther Elsworth. And their are five
that are Propounded which Are not added to the Church, namely, John
Loomas, John Rockwell's wife, Serg.ᵗ Thomas Elsworth's wife, Isaac
Bissels wife, and Mary Osband I think there Comes Commonly a
Momdays above thirty Persons to Speak with Father about the
Condition of their Souls.

It is a time of Generall Health here in this Place. There Has five
Persons Died in this Place Since you have been gone, viz. Old Good-
wife Rockwell, Old Goodwife Grant, and Benjamin Bancroft who was
Drowned in a Boat many Rods from Shore wherein were four young
women and many others of the other Sex, which were verry Remarkably
Saved, and the two others which Died I suppose you have heard of,
Margaret peck of the New Town who was once margaret Stiles hath
Lost a Sucking Babe who died very Suddenly and was buried in this
Place.

Abigail Hannah and Lucy have had the Chicken Pox and are recovered but jerusha has it now but is almost well I myself Sometimes
am much Troubled with the tooth ack but these two or three Last
Days I have not Been troubled with it but verry little so far as i know
the whole famaly is well except Jerusha.

Sister i am glad to hear of your welfare So often as i do I should be
glad to hear from you by a Letter and therein how it is with you as to
your Crookedness.

                              Your Loving Brother Jonathan E.
Father and Mother Remember their Love
unto you. Likewise do all my Sisters and Mercy and tim

It is plain to see that already the meetinghouse had first place in
all his boyhood plan of life. It was his one extramural interest, his
larger world. He saw the whole drama of village life from the angle
of the parsonage and the pulpit. East Windsor was a parish, a little
corner of the Lord's vineyard, not a center of secular interests.
What he knew of the world outside the town limits came chiefly
from visiting clergymen who brought news of the Lord's work in
other corners of the same vineyard. The ministerial language of the
hour was as natural an idiom to him as the language he spoke in
the schoolroom. Likewise the pulpit controversies of the hour: the
Halfway Covenant and Grandfather Stoddard's bitterly opposed

amendment thereto, the old and the new way of singing in the churches—all this was familiar territory in his thought.

When East Windsor had its own village quarrel over where to set the new meetinghouse, it is safe to imagine that he listened to the long and bitter arguments detailed in nightly sessions at the parsonage, had his own opinion on the subject, discussed it with his father and was respectfully heard, and that when the church finally voted to rebuild on the old site (the usual decision after the peace of a village had been sadly frayed) he was one of those present at the demolition of the old structure and thereafter watched week by week the new meetinghouse take shape under parish labor. It would have been an absorbing drama more intensely personal to him than to the other village boys, a major event from which to date his own smaller concerns. Before the still greater village excitement of "dignifying the seats" came to pass he was a student at Wethersfield and for the first time in his life met with new scenes, new thoughts, and new ways of thinking them.

Childhood ended for Jonathan Edwards just before his thirteenth birthday. He had recited his last lesson in the "parlor" and was now ready for college. These first thirteen years had determined many things: his sober view of life, his reflective bent, his refinement of self-discipline, his pursuit of religion as the unquestioned goal of life. To some extent his mind was already his servant; he could think for himself. He had learned the benediction of solitude amid the quiet beauty of woods and fields. His calling was a straight path before him. The foundations of a deep understanding sympathy had been laid with the man who was to mean more to him throughout his life than any other human being he was ever to know—Timothy Edwards, his own father. Poles apart in temperament, in natural endowment, and in ways of thought, father and son were to enjoy for life a rare fellowship.

Outwardly, there would not be much change in the look of life. College would mean no quadrangles, no spires and deep-toned bells. Matriculation day to Jonathan Edwards meant merely exchanging a schoolroom in one Connecticut farmhouse for a similar room in another, slightly more pretentious. He was not even to be taught by strangers. His own cousin Elisha Williams, nine years his senior, was to be his tutor. In such terms the distance between life as it had been and life as it was to be does not seem very great; but to Jonathan Edwards, as to any child standing on the threshold of independence, it was a chasm. In the fall of 1716, just before his thirteenth birthday, he took horse and rode away to Yale College, leaving his childhood behind him.

The Objective Good

In vulgar modern terms Newton was profoundly neurotic of a not unfamiliar type, but—I should say from the records—a most extreme example. His deepest instincts were occult, esoteric, semantic—with profound shrinking from the world, a paralyzing fear of exposing his thoughts, his beliefs, his discoveries in all nakedness to the inspection and criticism of the world. . . . His peculiar gift was the power of holding continuously in his mind a purely mental problem until he had seen straight through it. . . . Anyone who has ever attempted pure scientific or philosophical thought knows how one can hold a problem momentarily in one's mind and apply all one's powers of concentration to piercing through it, and how it will dissolve and escape and you find that what you are surveying is a blank. I believe Newton could hold a problem in his mind for hours and days and weeks until it surrendered to him its secret. . . . He looked on the whole universe and all that is in it as a riddle, as a secret which could be read by applying pure thought to certain evidence, certain mystic clues which God had laid about the world to allow a sort of philosopher's treasure hunt to the esoteric brotherhood. He believed that these clues were to be found partly in the evidence of the heavens and in the constitution of elements (and that is what gives the false

---

From Perry Miller, *Jonathan Edwards* (New York: William Sloan Associates, 1949), pp. 71–99. Reprinted by permission of William Morrow and Company, Inc. Copyright © 1949 by William Sloan Associates, Inc.

*suggestion of his being an experimental natural philosopher), but
also partly in certain papers and traditions handed down by the
brethren in an unbroken chain back to the original cryptic revelation in Babylonia. He regarded the universe as a cryptogram set by
the Almighty—just as he himself wrapt the discovery of the
calculus in a cryptogram when he communicated with Leibnitz. By
pure thought, by concentration of mind, the riddle, he believed,
would be revealed to the initiate.*

                                             —JOHN MAYNARD KEYNES

A stray copy of Locke might have found its way to Wethersfield in
1717, but that Williams' little band owned a copy of *Principia* is
unlikely. Many entries in the "Notes" probably attained their
present form only after Edwards had moved back to New Haven
in 1719, and some passages may date from his tutorship in
1724–26. After the College forcibly reclaimed the Dummer collection from Saybrook, Edwards could hold in his hands the actual
Principia and *Opticks* Newton himself took down from his shelves
and gave to Dummer for a gift to the new college in the wilderness.
(In 1723 Harvard owned the *Opticks* but no *Principia*.) We know
that Samuel Johnson read this *Principia* and vainly tried to teach
himself enough mathematics to understand it. Edwards never
understood fluxions or other higher mathematics, but to the extent
that a man can read Newton without such proficiency, he read
him, and though like most admirers he accepted the "sublime
geometry" on Newton's say-so, he appreciated the more literary
"Scholia" with a profundity not to be rivaled in America until the
great John Winthrop took over the Hollis professorship as successor to Greenwood in 1738, or until a printer in Philadelphia
succeeded in keeping his shop until it kept him in sufficient leisure
to allow time for reading. Consequently, when we go behind
Edwards' early publications to find the hidden meanings, we discover in the "Notes" not one key but two, a dual series of reflections, often intermingled but not yet synthesized. The one proceeds
out of Locke and becomes what posterity has called his "idealism"; the other begins with Newton and becomes what has been
less widely appreciated, his naturalism. In his mind there was an

equilibrium, more or less stable, of the two, which is the background of his cabalistic dichotomy, set up in the Boston lecture as though it were too apparent to need explaining; if his proposition about the "inherent good" requires for full comprehension a knowledge of Locke, his assertion of the "objective good" demands an equally rigorous study of Newton.

Edwards would not compartmentalize his thinking. He is the last great American, perhaps the last European, for whom there could be no warfare between religion and science, or between ethics and nature. He was incapable of accepting Christianity and physics on separate premises. His mind was so constituted—call it courage or call it naïveté—that he went directly to the issues of his age, defined them, and asserted the historic Protestant doctrine in full cognizance of the latest disclosures in both psychology and natural science. That the psychology he accepted was an oversimplified sensationalism, and that his science was unaware of evolution and relativity, should not obscure the fact that in both quarters he dealt with the primary intellectual achievements of modernism, with the assumptions upon which our psychology and physics still prosper: that man is conditioned and that the universe is uniform law. The importance of Edwards—I cannot insist too strongly—lies not in his answers, which often are pathetic testimonies to his lack of sophistication or to the meagerness of his resources, but in his inspired definitions. Locke is, after all, the father of modern psychology, and Newton is the fountainhead of our physics; their American student, aided by remoteness, by technological innocence, and undoubtedly by his arrogance, asked in all cogency why, if the human organism is a protoplasm molded by environment, and if its environment is a system of unalterable operations, need mankind any longer agonize, as they had for seventeen hundred years, over the burden of sin? By defining the meaning of terms derived from Locke and Newton in the light of this question, Edwards established certain readings so profound that only from the perspective of today can they be fully appreciated.

"The whole burden of philosophy," said Newton, "seems to consist in this—from the phenomena of motions to investigate the forces of nature, and then from these forces to demonstrate the other phenomena." Conceiving the universe as motion—which, unlike the concepts hitherto taught in New England, such as substance, form, and accident, could be expressed in mathematical formulae—Newton arrived at such an earth-shaking discovery as this: "If you press a stone with your finger, the finger is also pressed by the stone." Of course, no farmer in Connecticut needed to be told, "If a horse draws a stone tied to a rope, the horse (if I may say so) will be equally drawn back towards the stone." But every farmer was told, and professed to believe, what Luther had put succinctly over a century before the *Principia:* "For though you were nothing but good works from the sole of your foot to the crown of your head, yet you would not be righteous, nor worship God, nor fulfill the First Commandment, since God cannot be worshipped unless you ascribe to Him the glory of truthfulness and of all goodness, which is due Him." By the logic of that other science, called divinity or theology, upon which New England was founded, the best of deeds were "insensate things," which in themselves reflect no slightest glory upon the Creator. "Faith alone is the righteousness of a Christian man." If a man has faith, according to Luther—and after him Calvin and the Puritans—he "is free from all things and over all things."

For a century Yankees had believed this, but they had not been free from and over such things as the stones in their pastures, which broke both their own and their horses' backs. In the old-fashioned physics a stone was a concatenation of form and substance, with a final cause, and so its weight could be "improved" in theology as a trial laid upon man in punishment of his sin; but if now the obstinacy of the resisting body was an inherent mathematical product of its density and its bulk, if it lawfully possessed an inertia of its own which man must comprehend by the analogy of muscular effort, how could a man struggling with a rock in his field become persuaded that by faith he might be "free" of it? A more logical conclusion was that since weight is a natural force, the profitable method of freeing himself from it was by the law of levers, by a better breed of horses, but not by moralizing that the presumption of good works means the instant loss of faith and its benefits. There was—as Edwards perceived the situation—an organic connection between Newton's laws of motion and that law of salvation by faith which Calvin had made, once and for all, "the principal hinge by which religion is supported."

Luther, Calvin, and the founders of New England frequently utilized the physics of their day, which was still scholastic, for illustration or confirmation of their doctrines, but they never dreamed of resting the case for Protestantism upon the laws of nature. Edwards saw in a glance that no theology would any longer survive unless it could be integrated with the *Principia*. Newton claimed that in so far as we can learn the first cause from natural philosophy, "so far our Duty towards Him, as well as towards one another, will appear to us by the Light of Nature." This was not a boast, it was a threat. The *Principia* meant that henceforth there was to be no intelligible order apart from the actual. Although Newton discreetly left unanswered certain basic queries, he did show beyond question that the method of inquiry, in theology no less than in science, must be conformed to physical reality: "For Nature is pleased with simplicity, and affects not the pomp of superfluous causes."

In 1734 Edwards preached a series of sermons on justification by faith, the "principal hinge" of Protestantism; he reworked them into a sustained tract which he published in 1738. It was the most elaborate intellectual production he had yet attempted, and it figures in his development—or rather in the public exhibition of the development he had already undergone—as the first effort in American history to coordinate with the doctrine of Puritan revelation the new concept of science, in which such a superfluity of causes as had been the stock-in-trade of Edwards' predecessors became an affectation of pomp. He was resolved to prove that justification must in all simplicity be merged with the order of causality, and that if salvation was to be called an effect, of which faith was in some sense the cause, then the sequence must be formulated anew in language compatible with Newton's.

The still regnant doctrine, which no respectable Puritan had openly questioned, went back to Calvin himself, who as usual reduced Lutheran eloquence to legalism. Justification by faith, he said, is entirely a "forensic" transaction: a sovereign God is pleased, for no other reason than that He is pleased, to accept the righteousness of Christ in place of the obedience which no man can achieve, and He "imputes" Christ's perfections to a chosen few who in fact fall far short of perfection. These are saved "as if" they were Christ Himself: "He is justified who is considered not as a sinner, but as a righteous person, and on that account stands in safety before the tribunal of God, where all sinners are confounded and ruined." In the realm of objective fact, salvation was conceived by the Puritans as the transfer of a balance on the divine ledger, wherein God arbitrarily accepted another's payment for the debt which all men owed Him by the sin of Adam, and condemned those for whom the debt was not paid, though in life there might be little to distinguish one from another. In its published form, Edwards' treatise on justification reaffirmed the stereotyped doctrine: "A person is said to be justified, when he is approved of God as free from the guilt of sin and its deserved punishment; and as having that righteousness belonging to him that entitles to the reward of life." Had he been concerned, like Prince and Sewall, with no more than restating old doctrines, his tract would have said only this, as indeed no other American publication of the 1730's did.

The necessity of saying something more was, to Edwards' sense of the times, thrust upon him. For over a century Puritans in both Englands had drifted into the habit of calling faith the "condition" of justification. They started speaking in this fashion because they adhered to the "Federal Theology." At first it was merely a manner of speaking. They meant simply that if you believe you may be saved. Their rhetoric, in its early stages, was a natural result of Calvin's version of the whole procedure as a forensic transaction in which the recipient got credit for deeds he had not done. But the legalistic bent of primitive Calvinism, once carried to England, was there accelerated by the alliance of the English Puritans with the Parliamentary lawyers. Concepts taken from the common law pervaded theology, and even before the founding of New England the Puritans had theorized Calvinism anew into an idiom of what the lawyers called a contract or a covenant. Every New Englander before Edwards was a "Federalist," and because he put aside all this sort of thinking, he became a new point of departure in the history of the American mind. All his predecessors would have denied that Federalism was anything different from Calvinism—or Protestantism. They believed that it was simply a more precise way of phrasing the doctrine, on the premise that an absolute God, like an absolute monarch, could be held to nothing but what He had covenanted. Federal theologians, of whom Stoddard was a great example, liked to say that Jehovah, out of sheer indulgence, signed a set of contracts with both Christ and Abraham, in which He covenanted to accept the performance of Christ as though it had been rendered by individuals among the seed of Abraham, on the "condition" that they believe in Christ. As long as the theorists also pointed out that belief was an act of God, and that no man could muster it by himself, they were technically good Calvinists; they merely obtained in the language of the contract a greater precision, or at least a more precise metaphor, with which to argue that God does all, while man is impotent, but that nevertheless there exists a recorded transaction in which the recipient of grace can be accorded, and is assured, the bounty.

Actually, with a century of repetition, and after the political triumphs of 1649 and 1689, the Covenant of Grace came to mean in Puritan circles, in both the Englands, not what God was pleased to grant, but what He was obliged to concede. Faith gradually became so identified, at least in general parlance, with the condition of the covenant that it ceased to mean a decree enacted outside and above the human sphere. It became, bit by bit, something which a man might obtain, and which, once he had it, gave him a claim that God was bound to honor. Even in a theology of predestination, it was declared that a man could do his part and then relax, waiting upon God to do His. The theory of faith as a condition, said Edwards in 1734, is "ambiguous, both in common use, and also as used in divinity." New England had so perverted the language of the founders—the language lent itself rather too easily to perversion—that faith had come to mean "any thing that may have the place of a condition in a conditional proposition, and as such as is truly connected with the consequent."

In these sentences Edwards spoke with restraint, but he was

none the less declaring a break with the New England past, a break which his Boston sermon only subtly insinuated. He was putting his finger upon the point at which, as he saw it, the real declension of New England had set in. He maneuvered a revolt by substituting for seventeenth-century legalisms the brute language of eighteenth-century physics. He cast off habits of mind formed in feudalism, and entered abruptly into modernity, where facts rather than prescriptive rights and charters were henceforth to be the arbiters of human affairs. If the experience of regeneration is real, then "what is real in the union between Christ and his people, is the foundation of what is legal." The language of revolution in this undramatic sentence is difficult to catch across the centuries, but taken in the context of the 1730's it is as decisive, and as fundamental, as that of the more historic declarations. In 1734 Edwards was applying to theology a critique which assumed that theology should derive from experience and not from logic or from convention. His society, having slipped into a way of calling faith the condition of a covenant, had made the gratuitous assumption that faith was therefore the actual producer of the effect. It was heedlessly supposing that faith is the cause of salvation, and had insensibly come to assume that a man's belief worked his spiritual character exactly as by his physical exertion he shoved a stone out of a meadow. The people had succumbed to a metaphor, and had taken a shallow analogy for a scientific fact. Hence religion, which can thrive only upon realities, was fallen into decay.

Thus without openly proclaiming a revolution, Edwards effectively staged one. The object of his attack was what his society had hitherto assumed to be the relation of cause to effect, on which assumption it was constructed. If a ball that strikes another is called the cause of motion in the other, it then works the effect and determines the consequences; if, however, the first can be said only to transmit force to the second, it is but the first in a series of events determined by a law higher than itself. Puritanism all unwittingly had made the fatal mistake—it has proved equally disastrous for other cultures—of supposing that an event in one realm can cause effects in a totally other realm, that a man's act of belief can oblige the will of God. It had tried to make the tran-

scendent conform to the finite, and pretended that it had succeeded. Edwards drew upon his study of Newton for a contra-
dictory conception: "There is a difference between being justified
by a thing, and that thing universally, and necessarily, and inseparably attending or going with justification." He went to physics for
a cause that does not bind the effect by producing it; he found in
the new science (few besides Newton himself understood that this
was the hidden meaning of the *Principia*) the concept of an
antecedent to a subsequent, in which the subsequent, when it does
come to pass, proves to be whatever it is by itself and in itself,
without determination by the precedent.

He never bewildered his auditors by expounding scientific anal-
ogies beyond their grasp, but he quietly took into the realm of
theology the principles he had learned—or believed were obvious
—in his inspired reading of Newton. Obviously his imagination
had taken fire from such remarks of Newton's as, "It is not to be
conceived that mere mechanical causes could give birth to so many
regular motions." Thousands of Newtonians in the eighteenth and
nineteenth centuries took this to mean only that "God" created the
universe; Edwards took it to mean that cause in the realm of
mechanics is merely a sequence of phenomena, with the inner
connection of cause and effect still mysterious and terrifying. He
interpreted the sequence of belief and regeneration by the same
insight. His people, of course, were still ignorant of the "Notes on
the Mind." Had they been permitted to take them from his desk,
they might have comprehended how, in his view, the old Aristote-
lian array of causes—final, formal, and material—had been dissolved before the triumph of the now solitary efficient cause.
Hence they might have understood that for him the secret of
nature was no longer that an efficient cause of itself works such
and such an effect, but is to be defined as "that after or upon the
existence of which, or the existence of it after such a manner, the
existence of another thing follows." All effects must therefore have
their causes, but no effect is a "result" of what has gone before it.

The metaphysics of this idea were profound, but Edwards'
statement is so enigmatic that we may rightly doubt whether many
good burghers in Northampton had any notion what he was talking

about. Still, the import was clear: a once harsh doctrine, which for over a century had been progressively rendered harmless and comfortable, was once more harsh. It was imperiously brought back to life. And there were many among the river gods, and in the counting houses of Boston, who were eager to let sleeping dogmas lie. What right had this grandson of Stoddard—whom the town had employed to carry on his grandfather's ecclesiastical organization—to raise again, and in so disturbing a form, theological issues which New England had settled long since? The society had learned how to live with Calvinism; why make it something with which men could no longer live, or at least could not live on the basis of a profit and loss economy? Edwards began quickly to make converts, but almost as rapidly he made enemies, and most promptly among his cousins.

In five or six compact pages of the sermons that later made up the discourse *Justification by Faith Alone,* pages marked by no rhetorical flourishes, uttered in the calm, impersonal manner that never stooped to the capacities of his audience but bore them down with imperturbable assertion, Edwards pointed out that if the loveliness of a person is what wins faith, if the human achievement is at all a "reward"—which to speculation divorced from the heart might seem, as we have heard, no more than reasonable—then faith is a cause that may or may not be put into action. Indeed, considering the general unloveliness of human beings, it is apt never to get started at all. Furthermore, if faith is an effect of merit, then it too becomes an event which in turn is the cause of still another event, and so on, *ad infinitum.* Every man can be a fresh cause every day of his life, as though he had never lived yesterday, and the universe will be the sum total of today's contingencies, which tomorrow will become still more contingent. Edwards might have called this heresy solely on the strength of the traditional creed or of the Bible, but he took a startling line: "Because the nature of things will not admit of it." By appealing to nature Edwards set up his thesis:

The wisdom of God in his constitutions doubtless appears much in the fitness and beauty of them, so that those things are established to

be done that are fit to be done, and that those things are connected in
his constitution that are agreeable one to another. . . . This is something different from faith's being the condition of justification, only so
as to be inseparably connected with justification: . . . yet nothing
in us but faith renders it meet that we should have justification assigned
to us.

By this conception any act, either faith or lust, is not an instrument
which works an effect, but is part of a sequence within a system of
coherence. God is "a wise being, and delights in order and not in
confusion, and that things should be together or asunder according
to their nature." The connection between a subjective state and an
objective fact is not the subject's conviction that his loveliness
ought to be rewarded, but is "a natural suitableness," which means
that the qualification and the circumstance go together. The difference is fundamental: in the theory of faith as an instrument—as in
all "instrumentalism"—the world is supposedly so constituted that
it regards the beauty or utility of acts committed by some Ebenezer
or Jonathan; in the scientific conception, the ecstasy resides not in
a "hypothetical proposition" but in the fact itself, in "the entire,
active uniting of the soul." In the first scheme, God waits upon
man, and if man elects to be worthy, a grateful cosmos yields to
his virtues, or at least to his industry. In the order of the objective
good, "Goodness or loveliness of the person in the acceptance of
God, in any degree, is not to be considered prior but posterior in
the order and method of God's proceeding in this affair." To the
bewilderment of an energetic America, intent upon commerce and
real estate, where an ounce of effort meant a pound of sterling,
Edwards declared that "the nature of things will not admit of a
man's having an interest given him in the merits or benefits of a
Saviour, on the account of any thing as a righteousness, or virtue,
or excellency in him."

If so, the nature of things must in fact be opposed to the
appearances of American society. There had always been in
Calvinism a vague feeling that Protestant doctrine had a connection with the structure of the physical universe; Calvin himself,
searching for metaphors, compared the light of grace to the rising
sun that blots out the stars, or the persuasion of our own right-

eousness to a foolish eye that prides itself on its perspicacity in viewing adjacent objects and then is dazzled when it looks directly upon the sun. But Edwards, with Newton behind him, saw in the phenomena of nature, as employed in Christ's own discourse, not metaphors to adorn a discourse, but factual embodiments of eternal law. "These things," he confided to his notebooks, "are not merely mentioned as illustrations of his meaning, but as illustrations and evidences of the truth of what he says."

In Newton, Edwards found, as illustrations not of meaning but of the truth of what he would say, two primary conceptions: atoms and gravity. If there was a lion's mouth to be met with, Edwards would put his head in it. In ancient Greece, Democritus had laughed at the superstition of the senses that takes for reality the sweet or the bitter, the hot, the cold, or the purple, when "in truth there are atoms and a void." It is a startling fact about the rise of experimental science that, by the middle of the seventeenth century, scientists took the material universe to be made up of millions of particles which they had never seen, measured, or subjected to experiment, and in which they believed out of sheer faith. Thanks to Gassendi, Galileo, Boyle, and other physicists, this staggering assumption was one of the major premises of Newton:

It seems probable to me, that God in the Beginning form'd Matter in solid, massy, hard, impenetrable, moveable Particles, of such Sizes and Figures, and with such other Properties, and in such Proportion to Space, as most conduced to the End for which he form'd them; and that these primitive Particles being Solids, are incomparably harder than any porous Bodies compounded of them; even so very hard, as never to wear or break in pieces; no ordinary Power being able to divide what God himself made one in the first Creation.

Newton knew that this doctrine raised the specter of Lucretius and of "materialism"; a major reason for the distrust of the new science which Johnson found active at Yale in 1714 was a fear of its atheistical atomism. But in 1721 Cotton Mather's *Christian Philosopher* laid New England's fears to rest by advertising that the Newtonian world, far from denying, actually proved the existence of God and of design in the cosmos; he invited New England "to avoid philosophical romances" by getting an insight "into the principles of our perpetual dictator, Sir Isaac Newton." Cotton Mather made out of Newton those generalities of law, order, and symmetry that were becoming the commonplaces of eighteenth-century optimism. His "insight" did not go deep, but Edwards' did, and it went to the crucial point: if atoms are so hard that they never break, how small is the smallest atom? And then, if they are massy, hard, and impenetrable, what holds them together?

These were annoying problems for Newton also, and he who boasted of making no hypotheses never gave an answer. Lucretian naturalism had supposed that the atoms were "hooked" and so got fastened together; Newton rejected this fantasy, but he did allow his mind to play with the possibility that some medium might pervade the interstices of bodies and act as a sort of glue to hold atoms together; yet all this, he agreed, was speculation, and the most he could say factually was, "I had rather infer from their Cohesion, that their Particles attract one another by some Force, which in immediate Contact is exceeding strong." When we get behind the brilliant façade of Newtonianism, the apparently rational system of which poets sang and which Cotton Mather embraced, we are brought more terribly face to face with the dark forces of nature than any Puritan had been while staring into the dazzling glare of predestination. That element in the early Newton which Lord Keynes calls necromancy, which was deliberately masked in his last years and was ignored in his panegyrics, was an intuition of pure magic.

> Matters that vexed the minds of ancient seers,
> And for our learned doctors often led
> To loud and vain contention, now are seen
> In reason's light, the clouds of ignorance
> Dispelled at last by science.

Behind the mathematical analysis which by its perfection of form inspired such hymns as this, concealed so carefully that only the most astute might catch a glimpse of it, moved a power that could not be seen by reason's light or dispelled by science, that hid itself in matter to hold the atoms in cohesion, and betrayed its existence by resisting the pressure of a finger. It was to Newton the necromancer that Edwards, who was of the same brotherhood, responded. This Newton, turning from his imaginings of a subtle medium that might give a rational explanation for the solidity of bodies, let slip the intelligence that just how primitive particles, which obviously touch each other only at a few points, "can stick together, and that so firmly as they do, without the assistance of something which causes them to be attracted or press'd towards one another, is very difficult to conceive." The best of Newton's popularizers, Colin Maclaurin, whose *Account* of 1748 was known to Edwards, admitted that while Newton had not quite explained everything, he "left valuable hints and intimations of what yet lies involved in obscurity." The best hint he could leave on this obscure but basic problem was that there must be some agents in nature able to make atoms hang together in bodies, "And it is the Business of experimental Philosophy to find them out." Edwards had the temerity, although he had no laboratory, to take him at his word.

The difficulty was that this problem was in reality a double problem, each aspect of which elusively played into the other: to think how atoms cohered soon became to wonder how large or how small the atom was. Imagine it to be as small as possible, it still occupies space: why cannot it be divided as a stone is split by a wedge? For a century Cartesians had challenged atomists, asserting that unless matter were conceived as completely indivisible, atheism would follow. Newton and his followers were devout men, but they hated Cartesians and believed passionately in atoms and the void. With dogged persistence Newton asserted again and again that the extension, hardness, impenetrability of all objects are founded upon the same qualities in each of the atoms, "and this is the foundation of all philosophy." If so, the Age of Enlightenment was founded on a mystery, but was incapable, except in a few Blakes or Edwardses, of recognizing it. Newton did not want to say that the atom could never be split, and he foresaw that if it could be, we should have to conclude that divided particles may be subdivided to infinity; but for the moment he called a halt before the irreducible minimum, the atom that cannot be shattered and is the stuff of bodies. "We have ground to believe," said his grateful followers, "that these subdivisions of matter have a termination." He warned them not to indulge in fancies nor "to recede from the analogy of Nature, which is wont to be simple, and always consonant to itself." On this basis we may occupy ourselves with formulae of velocity and prediction of comets, concealing even from ourselves that we do not know the size of the atom or how one atom hangs on to another, and above all keep well hidden from view that we suspect but dare not identify too closely some agent, some active "vis," who hides in the stone and makes for its resistance.

By the analogy of nature, this dark power might, of course, be the same that operates in gravity, but Newton would never say so. When he let his mind range over the possibilities of the subtle medium or ether, he saw that in addition to gluing atoms together it might exert pressure from the edges of the solar system and so impress centripetal force upon bodies within the gravitational field. In that case we should have a wholly mechanical explanation. The eighteenth century often had occasion to lament that Newton lent himself to such vagaries; in 1756 Edmund Burke was to deplore that this great man, "if in so great a man it be not impious to discover anything like a blemish," stooped from his mathematical eminence to such trivialities as "a subtle elastic ether," a subject which, Burke added, "leaves us with as many difficulties as it found us," But on the whole, Newton was faithful to Burke's notion of sublimity; he could not, or he would not, give a cause for gravity. He left his greatest discovery so wrapped in mystery that the only permissible conclusion was his "Scholium" to Book III: the one cause which can penetrate to the centers of the sun and planets, that can operate not according to the quantities of the surfaces of the particles (as do "mechanical" causes), but according to the quantity of the solid matter, must be God. Only He can be omnipresent both virtually and substantially, as the ultimate cause must be present for a world to exist at all; only He can suffer nothing from the motion of bodies and only in Him can bodies find no resistance. Since His inward substance is as inaccessible to us as the inward substance of stones, which speak to our senses only from outer surfaces, so "We know him only by his most wise and excellent contrivances of things, and final causes; we admire him for his perfections; but we reverence and adore him on account of his dominion." Newton's champions could present the Newtonian system as a method of approaching God, offering proof of His existence out of natural powers and laws "from the difficulty we find to account for them mechanically"—which was to say, out of the deficiencies of physics.

Thus Newton tried strenuously to say that it was enough, whatever the cause, that "gravity does really exist, and act according to the laws which we have explained, and abundantly serves to account for all the motions of the celestial bodies, and of our sea." But it is clear that this was actually not enough for Newton, and it certainly was not enough for Edwards. It was not enough because there were two problems, the cause of gravity and the cohesion of atoms, left unsolved, both of which threatened to yield up answers that Newton dreaded: he preferred leaving them as riddles to coming out with solutions that might prove the world Godless and mechanical. There could be no question that gravity was universal, but it simply could not be allowed to operate at a distance across the void, with no material intermediary. If there is no ether through which the force can be transmitted, then we had better leave unanswered the question of how the various solar systems are so wonderfully synchronized. All matter is subject to gravity, and every particle gravitates to every other, but under no circumstances could we allow ourselves to speak as though gravity were essential and inherent to matter: "Pray do not ascribe that notion to me." The way his popularizers elide the difficulty is a sign of their underlying anxiety: "From so many indications," wrote Maclaurin, "we may at length conclude, that all bodies in the solar system gravitate toward each other; and tho' we cannot consider gravity as essential to matter, we must allow that we have as much evidence, from the phenomena, for its universality, as for that of any other affection of bodies whatsoever."

The real motive for these maneuvers among the Newtonians is not far to seek, although recent studies have for the first time made clear its strength: Newton was a religious man first, and a scientist secondarily. What Newton wanted above all else was to give such an account of the cosmos as would make evident that God rules the world, in the words of Maclaurin, "not as its Soul but as its Lord, exercising an absolute sovereignty over the universe, not as over his own body but as over his work; and acting it according to his pleasure, without suffering any thing from it." Newton suffered an obscure nervous collapse in 1692–1693, after which he abandoned natural philosophy and devoted himself to theology and prophecies. Perhaps he believed that the clues he was following would lead him through nature to God, but at the point where the certainty of approaching divinity grew shaky, he stopped. The Newtonian mechanics came to Edwards apparently a complete system of the world, but committed to two dogmatic presuppositions: that gravity at a distance is absurd, and that gravity is not synonymous with solidity. Gravity, said the Newtonians, is "an original and general Law of all Matter impressed upon it by God, and maintained in it by some efficient power, which penetrates the solid Substance of it." This result was all that Cotton Mather or most eighteenth-century theologues desired, and they betrayed little or no awareness that it was founded upon unprovable surmises and upon dogmatic evasions of mysteries. Edwards was the one man (or rather boy) in New England who refused to pretend that the questions of the cohesion of atoms and of the universality of gravity either were solved or were unimportant. He was prepared to venture in thought where Newton would not tread, into the hiding places of nature, to run down the force that was both the cohesion of atoms and the power of gravity, and to risk the possibility that could he find it or name it, the force might turn out to be simply monstrous.

Edwards was the forthright boy who knew no better than to use his eyes and cry that the emperor had no clothes. He asked what, after all, is an atom? Gassendi, Boyle, Newton had never held one in their hands nor even seen one in a microscope. Yet fervent apostles of experiment believed in this untested thing, and men who scorned hypotheses universally embraced this supposition. Of course, as a workable theory, atomism justified itself in Boyle's chemistry and Newton's physics; but it worked, Edwards made out, because it did not have to be proved: it was a way of thinking, not a thing. The scientists, talking exclusively in what Edwards called the "old way," did not listen to themselves long enough to catch on that their real difficulty was not in fixing the position of atoms in space or in measuring them, but in the confusions of their speech. If atomism was, as Newton declared, the foundation of philosophy, it was time that philosophy was taken in hand by a clear-headed theologian.

In all scientific discourse about the atom, the real point was its single oneness. So Edwards offered a succinct definition (he underscored it), *"a body which cannot be made less."* Therefore a body, no matter what its size, that cannot be lessened is all that scientists mean by an atom: "an Atom may be as big as the Universe; because any body, of whatsoever bigness, were an atom, if it were a perfect solid." This did not mean that Edwards took reality into the mind and treated matter as a dream; he was as thoroughgoing an atomist as any in the age, and commenced his thinking with Newton's definitions:

God, in the beginning, created such a certain number of Atoms, of such a determinate bulk and figure, which they yet maintain and always will, and gave them such a motion, of such a direction, and of such a degree of velocity; from whence arise all the Natural changes in the Universe, forever, in a continued series.

What has been miscalled his idealism never meant to him that the world resides inside a man's head. Things are where they are, and Edwards had no intention of flouting "the science of the Causes or Reasons of corporeal changes." He was simply applying to the problem the method that was Newton's own, for Newton had once explained that he was not a genius except in so far as "when an idea first came to him, he pondered over it incessantly until its final results became apparent." Convinced that the "proportion of God's acting" would be the same, whether we suppose the world material or mental, Edwards set himself to ponder the nature of atoms and of gravity, an occupation which absorbed him for the rest of his life.

The first result was a group of the "Notes" to which he gave a title, "Of Atoms and of Perfectly Solid Bodies," which his editors believe to be among the earliest of his cogitations; the manuscript journals devote literally hundreds of pages to the same theme, and though many of these are possibly of greater literary interest, all confirm the first insight. Proposing that we cease to fool ourselves by taking an atom to be some small segment of space, as though we were speaking of a chair or a table, he said that all we mean by it is indivisibility. Therefore to talk of it as broken is to annihilate it. Hence it is evident that we really mean a point to which we can apply Newton's third law of motion: we are saying that an atom *resists*. Newton's stone, the farmer's stone, resists the pull of the horse, and by resistance stones have achieved the identity they so jealously guard. It would be easy to say, along with those who openly broached "schemes of a pernicious and fatal tendency," that God works from the outside and so compresses atoms together to form a stone. The danger of that position, as Newton had intimated, is that a more exact mathematical analysis of the inner structure of the nucleus may achieve a logic so sufficient unto itself that God will be relieved of the only work left for Him. It would also be easy to go to the other extreme of outright materialism, or at least of mechanism. When Newton toyed with the notion of a fluid that acts as glue among the atoms, he was trying to avoid the first extreme by veering in the direction of the second. Edwards instinctively rejected the subtle fluid, along with hooked atoms. The danger of the mechanistic extreme was not its atheism but its unscientific method: based on the fiction of the atom, it took the myth for a fact. Until it could isolate and draw a diagram of the atom, it was just as "speculative" as the rationalized theism of the optimists.

Both schemes were pernicious because both insisted upon treating atoms as pieces, as "particles," of existing substance. For Edwards, as for us, the whole question was altered as soon as he realized that the atom is a concept. It was useful in physics, not because it had spatial dimensions, but because it played only the one role, though an essential one, of providing a point on which resistance could be concentrated. It was, as Maclaurin put it, "a termination." It was what a more highly developed mathematics would call a "limit." And what resists is, by the act of resistance (not necessarily by substance), solid, because what else does solid mean? To speak of two atoms as *perfectly* joined is nonsense because the two, if absolutely united, must be "one and the same atom or perfect solid." Obviously no imaginable physical power can break up solidity; to split a stone into a thousand pieces, and each piece into another thousand, is not approaching termination.

It must needs be an Infinite power, which keeps the parts of atoms together; or, which with us is the same, which keeps two bodies touching by surfaces in being; for it must be infinite power, or bigger than any finite, which resists all finite power, how big soever, as we have proved these bodies to be.

Of the two dangers, optimistic theism or deterministic materialism, Edwards feared the second less than the first. Materialism, aside from its initial fallacy about the atom, gave a more truthful description of reality than was offered by "those modern divines." Edwards was mainly concerned to prove that the statement, "the constant exercise of the Infinite power of God is necessary, to preserve bodies in being," did not mean that God acts *ab externo* to press a million pieces of stone into the form of a rock. But it did mean that the principle of coherence is in the stone, because that principle is the being of the stone. Individuality is not merely the "hardness": it is "the immediate exercise of God's power." The substance of an object—a stone, a horse, a man—is a single event, "nothing but the Deity, acting in that particular manner, in those parts of space where he thinks fit." The grand, but to Calvinists the hitherto dangerous, conclusion was "that, speaking most strictly, there is no proper substance but God himself."

Edwards was apprehensive lest he sound like a Thomas Hobbes holding that God is matter, whereas what he intended was "that no matter is, in the most proper sense, matter." One may say that Edwards was making a distinction without a difference, that the world is one whether we call it all matter or all mind, and so he was actually a materialist. The charge has, I believe, more pertinence than the customary label of "idealist," but both labels are beside the point. He was trying to say something simpler than either, which modern students may find more intelligible than could his contemporaries or, for that matter, most readers in the last century—namely, that the corporeal universe results from concentrations of resistance at various centers in space, which have a power of communicating, through gravity and through collision, from one point to another, according to stated conditions which infinite wisdom perpetually observes. In such a cosmos there is no such thing as mechanism "if that word is intended to denote that, whereby bodies act, each upon the other, purely and properly by themselves," but there is a perpetual determination of sequences of events. The cohesion of thought makes possible both the idea of the atom and of bodies made of atoms joined together: "that Ideas shall be united forever, just so, and in such a manner, as is agreeable to such a series." If we hold the world to be composed of a number of atoms, ten millionths of an inch in diameter, and then try to deal with it as an assemblage of atoms, we can never be vigilant enough to keep every one under control; a few will slip loose and run wild through the system. But any experience with stones in a Connecticut field is enough to show that there are no wandering atoms. "The existence and motion of every Atom, has influence, more or less, on the motion of all other bodies in the Universe." No motion, either of the proud or of the contrite heart, is lost. Not that thinking makes the atoms law-abiding, for in that case thought might be only a kind of private vice, but that thinking, originating in the senses, is a true representation of what prevails. "The secret," cried the boy, trying at last to put it all into one searing paragraph, is that the true substance of all bodies "is the infinitely exact, and precise, and perfectly stable Idea, in God's mind, together with his stable Will, that the same shall gradually be communicated to us, and to other minds, according to certain fixed and exact established Methods and Laws."

A fixed and exact method was, according to Newton, a characterization of gravity. Therefore Edwards, having so read the riddle of the atom as to discover that every object is a continuing event, and God is within it and not outside it, plunged head-first into the thought which Newton most feared and avoided: gravity is a function of solidity and so inherent in matter. Edwards' religion differed fundamentally from Newton's in that he did not need to reserve to God the honor (he more than divined that it could easily become an empty title) of being the "immaterial" cause of gravity. He was never more clairvoyant than when he warned that gravity ought not any more "be attributed to the immediate operation of God, than everything else which indeed arises from it." To suppose God the creator of the world, and then over and above that the stage manager of gravity, was a way of dispensing with God entirely. But by seeing the universe as a system of stable ideas, Edwards could see exactly why gravity should have the same proportions across the immensities of space without any material medium. This was why Newton's speculations on the ether seemed to him as frivolous as they did to Burke, "the folly," he called it, "of seeking for a mechanical cause of Gravity."

Nothing in Edwards' mind is more original or more exciting than this insight, but we need not wonder why, having reached it, he became cautious. Had he baldly proclaimed it, he would have been denounced in every corner of the land as a traitor to New England's Calvinism, by none more loudly than by those who long since had lost any real sympathy or understanding for the creed. They would have pounced upon him for identifying the laws of nature, not with the decrees of a transcendent sovereign situated somewhere above and outside the world, but with "a principle by which Matter acts on Matter"; by calling him the materialist and the Lucretian, they would have diverted attention from their own worldliness. I suspect Edwards would feel that most of the comment written about him since his time has been so motivated! But in the secrecy of the "Notes," Edwards could say what Newton dared not: "Solidity is gravity, so that, in some sense, the Essence of bodies is Gravity." Discretion was clearly advisable when speaking in public, but a thinker really should not handle the law of gravity quite so gingerly as did Sir Isaac; if body is a specification in one place rather than in another of a focus of resistance, then coordination among the several centers is to be expected. It is, in fact, the presupposition of there being any world at all, and the danger of atheism is infinitely greater if we pretend that it is not than if we frankly recognize it. To Edwards' clear eyes, Newton's fear, and still more the fear of his followers, that if gravity became a function of mass, science would become Godless, was what Bunyan called Little-faith; it was a failure to see what was written before their eyes.

Therefore, we may infallibly conclude, that the very being, and the manner of being, and the whole, of bodies depends immediately on the Divine Being. To show how that, if Gravity should be withdrawn, the whole Universe would in a moment vanish into nothing; so that not only the well-being of the world depends on it, but the very being.

The failure of Newton, and of the age, was a failure of intelligence. They were ready to call mobility a quality of matter without supposing themselves in danger of becoming atheists; but gravity, more than mobility, is essential in order for existence to exist, though for many reasons "the mind does not so intuitively see how." But actually, once Newton's laws are grasped, it seemed to Edwards logical, inescapable, that gravity does operate at a distance, for what is distance but, like time, a principle of stability for organizing a sequence of ideas?

Edwards could not know that a philosopher of the twentieth century, profoundly versed in a still more subtle and powerful physics, would deduce that cognition, having a unity of its own as an event, "knows the world as a system of mutual relevance, and thus sees itself as mirrored in other things." He would, I am sure, agree that Whitehead put thus simply the heart of his meaning, and he would agree further with Whitehead that men of thought, by virtue of this perception, are ultimately rulers of the world, but he knew more than Whitehead ever did of what is actually required for ruling a New England town. Though he was born to the purple, and though the society still bowed or curtseyed to the pulpit upon entering the meetinghouse, a ruler could not tell them all his thought. Hence, could the good people (or those not so good) of Northampton be expected to comprehend that the young pastor they had chosen to be, like his grandfather, the administrator of their ecclesiastical foundation was inwardly and incessantly concerned with testing whether an assertion of *how* the universe acts can be made identical with the *why?* Could they comprehend that he had a new vision of the cosmos as a system of causes, atoms, and gravity, and that for the mind to achieve regeneration, it would need to strip itself of all verbal substitutes for physical reality, of all metaphor and similitude, and look squarely upon the purely factual? Could they understand that in this scientific version of grace, the perception of beauty is that which determines both value and reality, that only in such a perception can the natural world and the world of religious experience become one? Could they even begin to grasp that for him the sheer naked reality was enough?

We should claim too much did we call Edwards' metaphysical intuitions about gravity anticipations of Planck and Einstein. He was not, let me repeat, an experimental scientist, nor was he a trained mathematician, and he could never even have approximated the conception that laws may be formulated without reference to any particular space-time manifold. He was a man of his century, though his thought was in the forefront of it; he was a docile Newtonian, who believed in absolute and objective space, and he assumed absolute time; he accepted this very same space which we see and this daily time which we experience. Still, it is not extravagant to point out that, by his argument that an atom is not a thing but a way of speaking about a locus of attraction and repulsion, Edwards was divining the great line of the future. That he was predisposed to some such divination by his theology, and that he meant no more than would confirm his doctrines, cannot be doubted, but at least it is clear that he saw through the genial and obtuse rationalism which most of his contemporaries thought was the import of Newton.

In his sermons on justification, in 1734, he needed to draw upon the "Notes" for only one statement: the relation of event to event in a causal sequence, whether of atoms, planets, or of grace, flows "only from the natural concord or agreeableness there is between such qualifications and such circumstances." If atomic entities are really entities in enduring conception (and otherwise men can never know what they are), and are related one to another because

God delights in order and not in confusion, then a cause is not one occurrence which is instrumental in producing the other, but properly speaking is "that, after or upon the existence of which, or the existence of it after such a manner, the existence of another thing follows." In this sense faith may be called a "cause" of justification, but not in the pernicious sense of that which brings it to pass. If the nature of things is a system of stable ideas which does not depend on the capricious goings or comings of atoms, why should the grace of God wait upon an uncaused achievement of virtue by this or that individual? Salvation, along with the atom and the law of gravity, can be only a manifestation of God's regard, not to the pretensions of individuals, but to "the beauty of that order that there is in uniting those things that have a natural agreement, and congruity, and unition the one with the other." For humanity this must mean, instead of a justification built upon the merit of our finite virtues, that "the acceptableness, and so the rewardableness of our virtue, is not antecedent to justification, but follows it, and is built entirely upon it." In the order of causation, a man is not a saint because he is good, but if he is a saint he is caused to be good. In more conventional language, he is elected.

Had Newton, or such of his disciples as Clark or Maclaurin, read Edwards' "Notes," they would not have been impressed as are we today. The scientists waged a hard fight to get their experimental, empirical method not only understood but even tolerated; they found that their chief enemies were those who "hastily," as they put it, resolve material motions "into immediate volitions of the supreme cause, without admitting any intermediate instruments," who thus "put an end to our enquiries at once." The physicists felt it essential for good science, and therefore they claimed for sound theology, that God be severely limited to governing the world not as His own body but as His work; in that sense alone, they would agree that God is "omnipotent." Persons who confounded God's lordship with His substance—the scientists said this in a hundred ways—"hurt those very interests which they would promote." Consequently, the majority of Newtonians, scientific and theological, would have called Edwards a brash boy who was perverting the incomparable Newton back to the obscurantism of immediate volitions of the supreme cause. They would not have appreciated that in fact Edwards gave over the material world to a chain of "intermediate" terms even more consistently than did the pious Newtonians.

Furthermore, they would not have understood that the sensitive Edwards was looking ahead to what they could only vaguely foresee; Maclaurin found himself stating, though with reluctance, a new problem which, in the very wake of Newton's success, appeared to be distracting the European mind. The intellectual world, he lamented, is becoming divided into two camps (where he thought they ought to be all one): those who from their fondness for explaining things by mechanism "have been led to exclude every thing but matter and motion out of the universe," and those with a contrary disposition, who will "admit nothing but perceptions, and things which they perceive," some of whom have gone to such extremes that "they have admitted nothing but their own perceptions." The majority of Newtonian rationalists were unable to figure out why these strange divisions had come about when it seemed that Newton had settled all such foolish arguments.

In the Boston lecture, Edwards exhibited the two orders, the objective and the inherent. The one, we find, forced us back to Newton and natural law, the other to Locke and perception. We cannot be certain how much was fully explicit in Edwards' mind, but considering how caution and reticence were thrust upon him, it appears that Edwards saw exactly where the modern problem is centered, upon this incompatibility of Newton and Locke, of the objective and the subjective, of the mechanical and the conscious. The effort of his life was to unite the two. The line of his speculation might well seem to less subtle Newtonians a slighting of "subordinate instruments and agents," but if so, they would again betray, as many in New England were soon to do, the shallow dogmatism which prevented them from comprehending what the age had really to grapple with, as it was to prevent Chauncy and his circle from ever seeing what Edwards was driving at.

His problem, then, was to get the two orders together—or else to confess that the modern world is incoherent. A stone transmits force to another by collision, and so is a "cause" of motion; in perception, there is a "fitness" of the antecedent sensation to the subsequent act. Is perception, then, just another form of collision, in which an object transmits motion through the senses? A moved stone receives what it must receive, no more, no less; but is man merely another kind of stone? Human perceptions notoriously vary in depth and width; is causality the same in either realm? In perception, may there not be a fitness between response and object that is still freedom of action? When the stone resists, is not the farmer at liberty either to curse or to pray? Does the tavern irresistibly attract the toper, does the woman inescapably arouse the lust of the adulterer? Are the principles of nature, the implacable sequences of things, applicable without change to human nature and society? If the inherent good is excellency and pleasure, while the objective good is the possession and enjoyment of that object which is good for the organism, is there not an incurable conflict between the two? Perception, either as pleasure or as beauty, is value, but if it is illusion, then reality is only the dance of atoms. The civilization of more than New England was at stake if the life of the spirit was henceforth to be a civil war between atoms and perceptions. Unless Edwards could merge, or at least reconcile, his objective good and his inherent, neither he nor, as he saw the predicament, anyone else would be able to locate the good where it might be of help to mankind.

JOHN E. SMITH

✪

Edwards' *Religious Affections*

THE ARGUMENT: THE "TWELVE SIGNS OF GRACIOUS AFFECTIONS"

The *Affections* is a masterful treatment of a basic theological problem; it is also a work of remarkable literary power. We are grasped by the earnestness of the author, by his concern that we understand him aright, and by the pains he has taken to capture our imagination. In directing attention to his style, we cannot overlook the fact that many readers have found the *Affections* difficult going, nor should we ignore what is implied in the activity of the many editors who thought it necessary to rewrite the text. It is admittedly an exacting work; it calls forth a reader's best effort. But there are rewards if we are willing to raise ourselves to the level of Edwards' austere standards; nothing is to be gained by bringing him down to a more facile plane in order to make him say what we would like to hear.

Edwards was in tight control of his ideas; he knew exactly what he wanted to say and he said it in an uncompromising way. The result is a meticulous form of expression, a precision in language and an intricacy which reveals a deep and subtle mind. He would not let a subject drop until he had exposed it from every side, nor would he move on to another theme until he had expressed the

Reprinted with permission from Jonathan Edwards, *Religious Affections,* ed. John E. Smith (New Haven: Yale University Press, 1959), pp. 8–24, 40–52. Copyright © 1959 by Yale University Press.

results of his analysis incisively and arrestingly. A careful reader will be delighted by Edwards' ability to guide him through a long line of argument and he will come to exercise his own ingenuity in anticipating some of the surprising turns in the road.

The most striking features of the *Affections,* then, are the exactitude and vividness of the language. Edwards always sought the right word, the one which exactly expressed his intended meaning. When, for example, he wished to emphasize the need for the heart in genuine religious conviction, he found expressions like "assent" or "allow" too pale and lifeless. A man may "allow," he says, that something is so and he may give assent to it in a merely notional way, but unless he is willing to "profess" that conviction, his heart is not in it. Professing is an affectionate believing and stems from the whole man. If we forget that Edwards chose his language with care and are led to suppose that some other form of expression would have done as well, we shall misunderstand him and lose the fruit of his efforts to make difficult things clear.

The vividness and imaginative power of his style are intimately connected with the fundamental theme of the work; doctrine and style flow together. Edwards was convinced that if religion consists in holy affections, the proclamation of that doctrine must be made in an affecting way. In one of his earlier writings we find him criticizing a minister he had heard for his failure to adapt the form of his expression to the content of his message. Edwards saw incongruity and even contradiction in the attempt to communicate the truth about life in a lifeless way. When we must convey a *sense* of what we say, just because what we say is of no account unless it grasps the sense of the hearer, an affecting style is needed. Edwards never lost sight of this principle in the *Affections.*

Consider, for example, the magnificent comparison between the true saints and those merely puffed up by the experience of vigorous but fleeting emotions. Hypocrites are likened to meteors which flare up suddenly in a blaze of light trailing showers of many sparks but soon falling back to earth, their light dissipated; all is over in a twinkling. The true saints are like the fixed stars; they shine by a light which is steady and sure, a light which continues to show itself over time and through the infinite spaces. Thus is

expressed the central doctrine that the true saints have the sense of
the heart, a steady and abiding principle in their own natures;
something not to be confused with the spectacular emotions and
commotions of revivalism.

The affecting style compels the reader to understand by vicari-
ous participation in what is being described. And the remarkable
thing is that the result is achieved at the same time that an intricate
analysis is taking place. Like Henri Bergson, Edwards had the gift
of analyzing an experience in great detail before our eyes at the
same time that his language leads us to participate in the experience itself. This gift represents the fusion of the descriptive and
evocative functions of language; we are made to see the anatomy
of experience at the same time that the language in which the
analysis is couched lays hold upon us, making us participate in
that experience with all its directness and warmth.

The continuing power of the *Affections* is to be found in the
success with which Edwards brought together the essential ingredients of a theological work. It must express a synthesis of clear
argument and the quickening spirit of direct experience. If a
formula is needed, it must combine information and inspiration. In
contrast to devotional writing, a theological work must contain
analysis and argument; it must exercise and enlighten the mind.
But the nature of its subject requires that it touch the heart and
engage the inner man; it cannot be a compendium of doctrine
alone. The *Affections* furnishes both; as one follows the line of
argument defining the nature of genuine piety, one is led to understand and to feel its power at the same time. Analysis and experience converge.

There has been a tendency among interpreters to view the
Affections not as a sustained analysis in its own right but as an
historian's document pointing beyond itself to the past or to events
in Edwards' life that were yet to come. Thus the work has been
viewed simply as commentary upon the Great Awakening, or as an
indication of the position Edwards was to take in the communion
controversy which came to a head in 1750. In both cases the
Affections is made to appear as an interlude between historical
events. Important as the historical setting may have been, the fact

remains that Edwards' real story is to be found in the life of the mind. His works must therefore be treated as attempts to answer basic and perennial theological problems. Moreover, the *Affections* has been praised in vague descriptions; it must now be read and analyzed in a way consistent with a work of its stature. The highest praise of a book should proceed not from uncritical acceptance but from a willingness to treat it as important enough to be argued about.

Edwards poses his central problem in the Preface: "What are the distinguishing qualifications of those that are in favor with God, and entitled to his eternal rewards?" In expanding upon his theme he is led to identify this question with a second, "What is the nature of true religion?" Even if he had not told us that this problem had been at the center of his mind "ever since I first entered on the study of divinity," we could still trace it from his earliest writings and sermons to the publication of the *Affections* in 1746. What continued to puzzle and vex him was the mixture of evil with good in the revival and among the saints, and consequently the problem of finding a way to distinguish the one from the other so that the evil might be exposed and rejected and the good retained. He was not blind to the presence of tares among the wheat, nor did he overlook, as Wesley accused him of doing, the mixture of purity and corruption in those genuinely favored of God. Indeed, it was his acknowledgment of counterfeit piety that forced him to find criteria for distinguishing false from true religion.

The *Affections* is especially distinguished by the intensity of its concern with the religious life of the individual; all but essentials are stripped away and a frontal assault is made upon the underlying problem. Edwards had previously described religion as it could be found in the depths of the individual soul, but these discussions had been more concerned with the fates and fortunes of the revival at large than with the gracious operation of the Spirit. He recognized this fact himself; in the *Affections* he was anxious to center attention on the gracious activity of the Spirit in the *individual* soul. This work was, so to speak, a final try at answering the crucial question, and in order to present his position in the clearest

light, he concentrated upon the activity of the Spirit in its purity
and upon the positive description of the genuine religious life.

Thus far much has been said about affections, but little attention
has been paid to exactly what they are. Here, as in all his writings,
Edwards was most circumspect; he begins with an account of the
nature of affections and a defense of the thesis that they are the
substance of true religion. Our first task, therefore, is to understand exactly what he meant by affections, how they arise, what
relation they bear to the divine Spirit, and how they stand connected with the understanding and the will. Having answered these
questions, we may consider the meaning of signs or criteria for
judging the affections. The twelve signs of gracious affections are
these criteria. Not only do they serve as tests or standards of
genuine piety, but they are themselves the very substance of the
religious life.

The first point to be stressed is that Edwards, for all his ability
to draw clear distinctions, nevertheless struggled to preserve the
unity and integrity of the self and to avoid compartmentalizing the
human functions and powers. This means that despite his rather
sharp distinction between understanding, affections, and will, we
must not overlook the extent to which these initial distinctions are
overridden in the course of the argument. The entire discussion
shows a moving back and forth between analysis and synthesis;
clarity demands distinctions within the self and between its
powers, but the integrity of the self requires that its faculties or
capacities be related to each other so as to preserve unity.

The starting point of the *Affections* is subtle; Edwards required
a biblical picture of true religion as a model, and he found it in a
word addressed to the early church during a time of persecution.
He assumed that in a time of pressure, when faith is tried in the
fire of persecution and disbelief, religion will appear in its true
form. Consequently, he chose his text for the opening section (the
part of the *Affections* most clearly in sermonic form) from I Peter
1:8: "Whom having not seen, ye love: in whom, though now ye
see him not, yet believing, ye rejoice with joy unspeakable, and full
of glory." From this text together with the historical context, he
derives his conception of true religion as consisting in the affec-

tions of love and joy in Christ; the former rests upon a spiritual sight, since the object of love is unseen with ordinary eyes, and the latter is the fruit of faith. The nature of such joy is to be "full of glory" and to Edwards this meant a filling of the mind and the whole being of the believer with a sight, a sense, and a power from beyond nature. He further derives or, as the expression ran, "raises" from the text this doctrine: "True religion, in great part, consists in holy affections"; the development of this thesis involves, first, an account of the nature of affections, and secondly, the adducing of those considerations which show "that a great part of true religion lies in the affections."

Edwards' response to his own question about the nature of affections is that they form a class of "vigorous" and "sensible" exercises of will or inclination. The special kind of such exercises entitled to the name "affections" are those that are vigorous enough to carry the self well beyond indifference, to the point where "the motion of the blood and animal spirits begins to be sensibly altered" and some change shows in the "heart." Whether or not we take the physiological trappings seriously, it is clear that Edwards wants to root affections in the inclination or central orientation of the self; affections are signposts indicating the *direction* of the soul, whether it is toward God in love or away from God and toward the world. This becomes clearer when we pay attention to his distinction between the understanding and the inclination or will. He refers initially to "two faculties" in man; one "capable of perception and speculation," which is called understanding, and the other, left for the moment without a name, which is said to be the means whereby "the soul does not merely perceive and view things, but is someway inclined with respect to the things it views or considers." On the one hand the soul may be inclined toward something and approve it, or it may be displeased and thus reject it. The judgment or inclination of the self involved in such reactions of attraction or aversion is intimately related to what Edwards meant by the "heart." This fact has been obscured in the past because of a misapprehension according to which the heart is vaguely described as "emotional" and set over against the "head," which is a symbol for reason and knowledge. *Edwards' analysis gives no warrant either for the identification or the opposition.*

The only contrast Edwards sets up is between the understanding as a grasp of meaning unaccompanied by any "inclination" or judgment of approval or disapproval, and the will or inclination as comprising such a reaction. In other words, a line is drawn between understanding and will, where the distinction means the difference between the "neutral observer" and one who "takes sides"; but there is no clear warrant for making this into an opposition between the two terms (and, *a fortiori,* it gives us no reason for opposing understanding and affections). The point almost invariably missed is that in Edwards' view the *inclination* (the faculty initially distinguished from the understanding) involves *both* the will and the mind. When inclination receives overt expression in action it is most commonly called "will," and when inclination is expressed through the mind alone it is called "heart." The latter relationship is central to the *Affections.* Those "more vigorous and sensible exercises"[1] of inclination, i.e. of being inclined and not in a state of indifference, are what Edwards calls "affections." They are thus the expressions of inclination *through the mind.* They stand in a necessary relation to the ideas of the understanding and are also the springs of actions commonly ascribed to the will. Inclination is not a blind affair, since it is based on an apprehension of the idea, the doctrine or the object which the self is attempting to judge. Nor are the affections merely mental in the sense that they have to do with the depths of the soul alone, for the sign to which Edwards attached the greatest importance, the sign of consistent practice, shows that in order to be genuine, affections must manifest themselves in an outward and visible way.[2]

---

[1] "But yet, it is not the body but the mind only, that is the proper seat of the affections."

[2] Try as we may, it is difficult to avoid confusion over the difference between will and affections and their mutual connections. JE is not clear himself, although it is obvious that the problem stems from his attempt to preserve the integrity of the self against the tendency to break it up into "faculties." We are told that "the affections are not essentially distinct from the will," and this point is repeatedly emphasized. On the other hand, will

The essential point is that the affections manifest the center and unity of the self; they express the whole man and give insight into the basic orientation of his life. Edwards was aware that the term "affections" does not ordinarily mean all of our "actings" and that it may not even be understood to involve action at all. To understand what he means we must take such phrases as "exercise of the will" and "actings of the inclination and will" to mean choice or judgment in the first instance[3] and overt action secondarily. The crucial point is that in every choice the soul likes or dislikes, and when these "inclinations" are "vigorous" and "lively" the liking or disliking coincides with love and hatred. Affections, then, are *lively* inclinations and choices which show that man is a being with a heart.

There is a further preliminary distinction; and although it occupies but a paragraph, it is of pivotal importance. "The *affections* and *passions*," he says, "are frequently spoken of as the same," but there are grounds for distinguishing them. Passions he describes as those inclinations whose "effects on the animal spirits are more violent" and in them the mind is overpowered and "less in its own command." The self becomes literally a "patient," seized by the object of a passion. With the affections, however, the situation stands quite otherwise. These require instead a clear understanding and sufficient control of the self to make choice possible. This distinction enabled him to criticize and reject a great many revival phenomena, especially those of a pathological sort, and to dissociate the heart religion he advocated from hysteria, the excesses of bodily effects and enthusiasm. His contemporaries paid

---

is said to denote *inclination expressed in action* as distinct from the "heart," which points to *inclination expressed in the mind.* Since, however, affections are most often identified with the "heart," it may appear that further identification of will and affections will need some qualification. Perhaps the attempt to be too meticulous here will only lead to confusion. If we stick to the idea that an affection is a "warm" and "fervid" inclination involving judgment, we shall not go wrong.

[3] See the introductory discussion of the nature of will in JE's *Freedom of the Will,* ed. Paul Ramsey (New Haven: Yale University Press, 1957), pp. 137–140; cf. pp. 16 ff. The analysis there definitely stresses the element of choice or judgment over that of exertion, and shows JE's insistence upon identifying "volition" and "preference."

insufficient attention to his distinctions. They thought he was defending revivalism in the sense of religious passions at the expense of intellect, whereas he was developing a conception of affections accompanied by understanding.

With this conceptual framework, with the affections separated into two principal kinds—those seeking to possess their object and those seeking to reject their object—Edwards returns to the Bible to establish more securely the thesis that genuine religion "in great part, consists in holy affections."[4] The piety which God requires, the only one he will accept, is one which engages the heart and inclines the self as a whole toward the divine glory in a love which is unmixed. Of all the aspects of human life and experience, religion is the one in which it is least possible to be "lukewarm"; piety which does not include a fixed and fervent inclination touching the heart is no genuine piety. Hearing the Word, as the Bible repeatedly emphasizes, is not enough, nor is it sufficient merely to "allow" that the doctrine may be true. What is needed is that the soul be "moved" and filled with the love of God which ultimately shows itself through right conduct in the world. Neither is possible in Edwards' view unless the soul is "affected" and the will inclined. In this sense affections are motive forces or springs, and the particular change called conversion becomes possible only if the self is affected at the heart. "I am bold to assert," he says, "that there never was any considerable change wrought in the mind or conversation of any one person, by anything of a religious nature, that ever he read, heard or saw, that had not his affections moved."[5]

We must not overlook the duality in Edwards' theory of affections rooted in the fact that love is both one of the particular

---

[4] It is important to notice that JE does not want to swallow religion in affections; they constitute the most important part of genuine piety and the testing of their character provides a test of piety, but he is most careful to qualify his position by such phrases as "in great part." His full formula is that affections are *necessary for* religion and *constitute a large part* of its nature.

[5] Here, as in the case throughout the early part of the *Affections*, the connection between affections and will is uppermost; later on, JE stresses much more the place of understanding and the divine light.

affections and the fountain of all affections. His contention is that the basis of true religion is found in that chief affection which is love to God unmixed; this defines the original relation of the soul to God. Religion, however, includes along with the basic relation to God, life in the world and in the glory to come. This means that as a life and not merely a doctrine it has further content; Edwards' view is that this content itself consists largely in affectionate life. Hope, joy, fear, zeal, compassion and others are frequently referred to in the New Testament as the substance of religion; Edwards describes them as affections and goes on to argue that they make up the religious life. To avoid confusion we must understand that he is defining the basic religious relationship as essentially the affection of love. This is what he means when he says "the essence of all true religion lies in holy love," but at the same time he maintains that the fruits of love are also affections— joy, zeal, peace—which have their proper place in the whole of religion. "For love," he says, "is not only one of the affections, but it is the first and chief of the affections, and the fountain of all the affections." There is thus a basic affection, holy love, which relates the self to God in a decisive way and it has to do with the "first fruit" of the Spirit or "sealing of the Spirit," in biblical phrasing. There are also fruits or further gifts of the Spirit which represent the substance of the religious life in the world. The dual meaning of love running throughout Edwards' analysis need not confuse us if we understand the comprehensiveness with which he uses the term.[6] Love taken as the fountain of affections is the more important sense of the term because it refers not only to the relationship between man and God at the root of all religion but also to the activity of the Holy Spirit in the individual soul. Moreover, when holy love is said to be the essence of genuine religion, it is

---

[6] The duality involved is reflected in the ordinary use of the term "affection." In the eighteenth century the term meant the whole class of attitudes and dispositions to which JE refers: love, hope, fear, etc. Because of the centrality of love, the class term "affections" came to be identified with it alone, although it is but one of the affections. The phenomenon is familiar to students of language; a class term has often become identified with one of its members when that member has come to be regarded as more basic than others.

then possible to explain sin by contrast as that equally basic and ultimate *rejection* of God, symbolized in the Bible as "hardness of heart."[7] Edwards was most acute in finding biblical support for his position; assuming such hardness and rejection of God to be the very opposite of genuine piety, he sought, among the biblical illustrations of the hard-hearted, evidence to show that what they chiefly lacked was the affection of love. And he argued in the reverse direction, declaring that if the antithesis of genuine piety is to be without holy love, there is further reason for believing that love is a mark of true religion. Those who have such religion overflow with that divine love which Pharaoh, for example, did not have.

The intention of the *Affections* is to test these fruits of the Spirit, not to praise them. Edwards never lost sight of the twofold task that followed: on the one hand, to defend the central importance of the affections against those who would eliminate them from religion; and on the other, to provide criteria for testing them lest religion degenerate into emotional fanaticism and false enthusiasm. Moreover, testing the spirits was no academic exercise; Edwards wanted to give to the individual some basis for judging the state of his own soul. It is essential here that we attend to his subtlety and depth. Simple oppositions and alternatives will not do. They allow for too much or too little. We need an approach more sophisticated than is implied in asking whether Edwards was "for" or "against" affections. Many of his contemporaries approached him in that light; they were bound to be disappointed, simply because no answer of a strict either/or type can be given. The point is that he was "for" the affections, but not in any sense you please; moreover, he was not *uncritically* for them, which is why he was at such pains to explain what they are, how you might know when you had them, and which ones marked the genuine

---

[7] It is interesting that instead of describing sin and hardness of heart as "affection" in the direction of hatred, aversion, and rejection, JE refers instead to the hard heart as an "unaffected heart," i.e., as a heart not affected by "virtuous affections." This is a minor inconsistency only, but it is apt to cause confusion. The point is simply that since JE was interested in the genuine religious affections, he identified "affection" with those which are directed toward God, and described the hard heart as devoid of affection.

presence of the divine Spirit. His book, consequently, brings together two lines of thought: it identifies the activity of the Holy Spirit with the affections in the soul and at the same time shows how these same affections when properly tested enable us to discriminate genuine from false piety. It is not difficult to understand what a precarious line Edwards marked out for himself. To those who rejected heart religion his analysis of genuine piety in terms of affections was anathema, but he was equally set upon by those who wanted their affections neat, so to speak, and had no time for bothersome inquiries into their grounds and authenticity.

In concluding the opening section of the *Affections,* Edwards proceeds to draw some concrete conclusions from his previous doctrine. He criticizes those who reject all affections because of the excesses of some and the vain zeal of others. He attacks the oscillation from one extreme to the other and he is as outspoken against those who accept all affections uncritically as against those who want to be done with them completely. He did not miss the opportunity to put a vivid biblical construction upon the New England revival experience while also preparing the ground for his own theory of signs and tests. He tells the congregation that he sees the hand of Satan both in the Revival and in those who fight against it. Satan, seeing that people were unlearned in heart religion, sowed tares in the form of false affections and thus misled and confounded many with the belief that they belonged to the Lord's elect. On the other hand, after seeing the reaction that took place after the high tide of affectionate religion, Satan set to work in another direction to establish the belief that affection itself is an evil. In both cases genuine religion is made to suffer. Against this background Edwards' position stands out most clearly: affections are essential, but since there are false as well as true affections, critical tests are required. The main concern of his book is to establish the only valid criteria for making such tests. Testing the spirits is of the essence of "experimental religion."

Edwards devotes his short second section to what were formerly called "negative signs." Here he makes his position more explicit by describing these signs as insufficient to enable us to conclude whether affections are gracious or not. The critical force of negative signs lies in the fact that their insufficiency refutes anyone who rejects all affections, by showing that an excess or exaggeration cannot be taken as conclusive. The argument attempts to demonstrate, both by biblical example and appeal to general experience, that the presence of a given characteristic does not mean either the presence or absence of the divine Spirit in its saving operations. In every case the accidental character of these signs is said to reside in the fact that they can be present without the Spirit's presence. The full extent of their insufficiency becomes apparent only after the positive signs are set forth, but taken by themselves Edwards argues that they are to be found where there is no genuine piety and that they may be absent where genuine piety exists. They cannot, therefore, be taken as necessary conditions.

There is no need to follow Edwards in detail through his discussion of all the negative signs. His analysis is clear enough and is even repetitive of much he had expressed before. There are, however, two points of special importance: the first has to do with the idea that the Spirit is bound to a definite *order* of operation and the second concerns whether it is possible to infer anything about affections from the fact that they come to be accepted by *other people* as signs of saintliness.

As regards the first point, Edwards' thesis is as follows: "Nothing can certainly be determined concerning the nature of affections by this, that comforts and joys seem to follow awakenings and convictions of conscience, in a *certain order*." Before proceeding to his final conclusion, Edwards first calls attention to the fact that God deals with human beings in a way that has a discernible pattern in it. That is to say, there are abundant evidences in the Scripture of God's having first convicted, wounded, distressed, and terrified man by the contrast between his sin and the divine majesty, and then comforted him with glad tidings. "It seems to be," says Edwards, "the natural import of the word 'gospel,' glad tidings, that it is news of deliverance and salvation, after great fear and distress." He concludes that nothing can be said against the authenticity of comforts and joys because they come after terrors and convictions of conscience, for the prevalence of this order of events in so many biblical experiences nullifies any such claim. On the other hand, he is concerned to maintain that comforts and joys cannot be accepted as genuine merely because they succeed great terrors and fears of hell; being afraid of hell is not the same as having genuine convictions of conscience. His argument at this point is apt to be confusing because he speaks of both the *nature* of the states in the soul and their *order*. The argument begins by emphasizing the order of events in the soul, but we soon discover that their nature is involved as well. The fact is, one aspect cannot be separated from the other. The problem of order is made central at this point.

As regards the nature of the states, Edwards wants to say that terror or fear is not necessarily the same as conviction of conscience; even granting that terrors and convictions have actually been produced by the Spirit in the soul, this fact by itself does not prove that true comfort *must* follow. The principal reason is revealing; the "unmortified corruption of the heart may quench the Spirit of God," he says, and this can mean only that if grace is not irresistible, the "preparation" or common influences of the Spirit are capable of being resisted or stifled by pride and the claim of a false hope. Satan, moreover is able to counterfeit the operations of the Spirit, but there is an important qualification about his power to do so: Satan can *exactly imitate the order* of affections, but not their nature. "The nature of divine things," says Edwards, "is harder for the devil to imitate, than their order," and from this fact follows the chief problem. It also explains why Edwards fastened upon the concept of order. If Satan can imitate the order exactly, then the order of operation followed by the Spirit *cannot* be a certain and decisive sign; the truly dependable signs are, as we shall see, those which Satan cannot perform. "Therefore," Edwards concludes, "no order or method of operations and experiences, is any certain sign of their divinity."

This point has several far-reaching repercussions. First, Edwards is denying the validity of many Puritan descriptions of salvation as involving a sequential process. There is thus in his thought room for a certain "variety" in religious experience and no conversion by "rule." Secondly, and even more basic, if we confine our attention to the order alone there is no necessary transition from nature to grace. The sharp separation between "common" and "saving" operations comes to the fore; we have no insight into any necessary connection between an order of events in nature and their issuance in grace. The Scripture, Edwards asserts, is silent on this point, and there is no alternative to denying the validity of order as a sign of genuine piety. He is willing to admit only that some awareness or conviction of sin on the part of the believer is necessary, but this necessary condition is not itself a sufficient ground from which to infer the presence of the Spirit. The ultimate basis for Edwards' view is not only the Bible but an appeal to experience. No better example of Edwards "the experimental divine" can be found than his appeal to the observations he made in the midst of the Revival to refute the thesis that the Spirit is bound to a single method or order in laying hold of the soul. As a final and telling word he says, "we are often in Scripture expressly directed to try ourselves by the *nature* of the fruits of the Spirit; but nowhere by the Spirit's *method* of producing them."

The second noteworthy point in Part II concerns the attempt to use the "approval of the godly" as a criterion for judging affections. Edwards' contention is of the utmost importance for his entire theory; it means that external judgment, the judgment of one man upon another, is not only unreliable but ultimately impossible. The saints, though they know "experimentally" what true religion is in their own selves, have no power of discerning the *heart* of another. Edwards liked to cite I Sam. 16:7 as an authority: "The Lord seeth not as man seeth; for man looketh on the outward appearance, but the Lord looketh on the heart." There are at least two consequences of the position taken which need to be underlined in any study of Puritan piety. First, the testing of the spirits can ultimately be done only by the self for itself; the external situation may lead a man to seek the counsel and judgment of others but no man can pronounce any final judgment concerning the status of another before God. "It is against the doctrines of Scripture," says Edwards, "which do plainly teach us that the state of others' souls toward God, cannot be known by us." Secondly, there is the consequence that the "public charity" forming the basis of acceptance between the visible saints in the visible church must not imply any *final* judgment by any man about the religious status of his neighbor. This is a touchy point. Edwards in several places argued against making a distinction *within* the visible church between the sheep and the goats. It has sometimes been objected by critics that his refusal to allow this distinction was incompatible with the position he later took in demanding conversion experiences and confession of Christ as conditions for being received into full communion. His position can be made consistent with the principle laid down in the *Affections*. When the congregation accepts a confession based upon conversion experiences, it must not suppose that this acceptance is the same as certain knowledge of the confessor's state. This is a subtle line of thought but it is consistent; some credentials are demanded of the believer who presents himself, but their acceptance by others does not mean or imply certain knowledge on their part of the status of another person. The heart of the other is known but to God; the acceptance or approval of others is no certain sign for judging religious affections.

The third and largest part of the *Affections* contains the heart of Edwards' position: the exhaustive account of the twelve signs of gracious affections. This analysis must, of course, stand or fall on its own merits. The reader will be aided greatly in approaching the text, however, if he has clearly in mind several leading ideas. He must understand what Edwards meant by a sign, what basic principle is behind each sign, and the way in which the individual is supposed to use the sign as a test of his own heart.

Since this part of the book contains the bulk of the material quoted by Edwards in defense and illustration of his position, the reader will do well to bear in mind what is said later about his relation to other writers. It would be an error to suppose that Edwards was directly dependent for his own doctrine upon the works cited; his own thought was remarkably self-contained and, furthermore, he firmly believed that his entire theory of affections was rooted in the biblical picture of the true religious life. Consequently, the works of others appear more as illustrations and confirmations of his position than as "influences" from which it might be derived. This remains true even of his use of Stoddard and Shepard, upon whom he relied most.

The positive signs are meant to delineate those affections that are "gracious" or "saving." The entire theory presupposes a distinction in kind (more obvious in the treatment of some signs than others) between "common" and "saving" operations of the Spirit. As Edwards had occasion to point out, the *Affections* is directly concerned only with those operations which are saving, as compared with the *Distinguishing Marks,* which paid more attention to the common workings of God. The whole discussion of the positive signs is prefaced by a re-emphasis upon the closing note of Part II: the signs of gracious affections are not for enabling us to distinguish true from false affections in others. Edwards repeats what he had claimed many times before: "it was never God's design to give us any rules, by which we may know, who of our fellow-professors are his, and to make a full and clear separation between sheep and goats." Edwards goes even further and allows for uncertainty in the knowledge with which the saints are supposed to know themselves. The signs are neither doubtful nor unavailable, but there are weaknesses in the person (the clouding of the eye of judgment) and seeds of corruption (the cold or carnal "frame"). These work together to make the process of discerning both difficult and uncertain when applied to the experience of a particular individual. The qualification is important; for while Edwards' theory of signs or criteria went considerably beyond what some of his contemporaries believed possible in the discerning of spirits, he claimed no infallibility for their application in a given case. The rules themselves have their own certainty, but the applications always fall short; no biblical principle is on the same level with its application.

Turning to the meaning of sign in the positive sense, we must understand a sign to be a mark through which the presence of the divine Spirit can be known. Edwards does not say that we *infer* the presence of God's grace using the signs as a basis; he does, in fact, leave that relationship vague. It is best to suppose that the sign "points to" the activity of the Spirit, especially when we consider the matter from the side of our human process of knowing. Taken apart from its evidential force, however, a sign must be understood as the very presence of the Spirit, since it is the working of divine grace in the heart of the believer. Not all signs make this point equally evident. As we attempt to discern and judge our state, the signs are viewed by us as pointing to or announcing the presence of the Spirit; considered in themselves, the signs *are* that presence. While all signs perform a common service in critical judgment, they differ on their material side. Thus a sign may be a cause or ground in one case, a quality of life or a relation in another, and even a series of deeds stretching over an extended time. Whatever its particular nature, however, a sign is of no value or interest save as it enables us to assess the nature of piety. Positive signs are the marks of the Spirit.

Since Edwards' main aim is to test affections, every sign refers to them in some specific way. Not every sign, however, fastens upon their inner nature. Some clearly do so, as in the tenth sign which singles out symmetry and proportion. Other signs point instead to the ground or stimulus of affections such as the evangelical humiliation at the heart of the sixth sign. Confusion can be avoided if we bear in mind that some signs point to affections themselves, others to their ground, and still others to what issues from them or to their consequences. Whatever aspect is made central, it is affections that are the object of the test; to test affections is to test religion.

It is a curious fact that Edwards nowhere considers the relations between the signs, whether they imply each other, whether some are more basic than others and similar questions. The signs have, to be sure, a natural affinity as belonging to the one integral religious life, but Edwards has not yet told us whether genuine piety must exhibit *all* the signs or whether perhaps one or more might be taken as a sufficient basis for judgment. The one clue we have for answering these questions is given in a principle which is common to every sign. The Spirit in its saving or gracious operation dwells in the believer in its proper form, or, in classical philosophical expression, according to its own kind. Edwards placed great emphasis upon the distinction between the Spirit as *operating on* the self and thus as still externally related to it, and as *dwelling in* the self in its own proper nature.[8] Only the latter form is the presence of the Spirit as *grace;* the former represents the "common work" of the Spirit. All signs as positive indications of gracious affections point back to the saving operation; if this indwelling fails to take place, no genuine signs can appear at all. It so happens that while the indwelling Spirit forms a common background of all signs, the fact is more explicitly stated in some (e.g., the first, fourth, and seventh signs), and we are perhaps justified in taking these as more basic than others.

● ● ● ● ●

The Twelfth Sign

Edwards devoted more space to this sign than to any other; we cannot but conclude that it loomed largest in his mind. Moreover, he makes two claims which at once set it apart from the others. First, "it is," says Edwards, "the chief of all the signs of grace"; and secondly, the public character of practice makes it a sign whereby others are granted some insight into the sincerity of the believer. Edwards is most careful not to say that other men should use the sign and judge their neighbors; he confines himself instead to saying that practice is the best evidence of a man's godliness in the eyes of others. While it is true that the state of the believer is known but to God and the individual is subject to the divine judgment alone, the daily conduct of a man is not beyond the scrutiny and provisional judgment of his neighbors. Indeed if the established practice of accepting members into the church on the basis of a "public charity" was to have any meaning at all, it is difficult to see how judgment by others could have been avoided. The heart may have its hidden side, but since practice furnishes a genuine clue to its nature, it cannot remain entirely secret.

The principle behind this sign is that holy affections must exert their influence in Christian practice; the deed is the most important "outward and visible sign of an inward and spiritual grace." Practice is a sure evidence of sincerity or, as Edwards says, "men's deeds are better and more faithful interpreters of their minds than their words." But if practice is taken as a paramount sign, it

[8] Below [in Yale edition], pp. 232 ff., where this communication of nature is said to be the "true" witness of the Spirit.

becomes necessary to see that it is not also taken as a ground of grace. Practice is a reliable sign of holy affections but it points beyond to the center of the self from which it issues and to the Spirit which makes it possible. The conduct of Christians in the world is to be guided by three demands. First, behavior must be in conformity with Christian rules; secondly, the "practice of religion" must be the chief occupation of life; and thirdly, one must persist in this practice till the end of his earthly days. As a principal means of establishing these demands, Edwards makes exhaustive use of biblical material. From all parts of both Testaments he culls illustrations supporting his thesis that true affections issue in universal obedience as the chief and enduring concern of life.

Critics of Edwards' interpretation of the revival have sometimes claimed that his view was inconsistent on the grounds that it is impossible to reconcile having a new nature with backsliding or the failure of Christian practice. If Edwards' doctrine of affections is correct, the argument runs, the true saints cannot fail in their Christian duty. In meeting this objection he claimed that "true saints may be guilty of some kinds and degrees of backsliding," but that they cannot fall away from that earnestness toward God which stems from having the new sense of the heart. If a man's behavior shows that he no longer persists in making the love of God the chief business of his life, then we have a clear sign that he was never converted and his experiences are to no avail. On the other hand, since genuine piety consists in the new heart and the change in nature, true believers may fail in their moral duty and be convicted of sin through the law without falling away from God entirely.

We have before us a distinction between the heart or essential nature of a man and the fact of his day-to-day performance in the world. Genuine piety concerns the heart and not bare conformity to the law; practice, nevertheless, is supposed to provide some clue to the heart. The question is, how can practice be used as a test? The most obvious answer is that there are certain deeds to be done and others to be avoided, and that those who do not deviate from this standard are the true saints. Such an answer Edwards could not give. True religion consists not merely in conformity to rules but in the new heart; the use of practice as a sign, however, bids us try to understand how it can be a clue to the inner nature of the self from which it comes. This is the crux of the matter; taking conduct as a sign as a matter not merely of discovering whether it conforms to rules but of learning how and in what way it reveals the heart. Practice, then, cannot be viewed merely as a doing or abstaining, for we must discover in a man's conduct the true affections of his heart. Accordingly, Edwards looked to the attitude behind practice, to the love and gratitude displayed, and to the persistence of the believer in seeking to obey the commands of religion over a course of time. It was his belief that if a change of heart is genuine, its permanent character will continue to show itself through the whole of life.

Viewed in this light, the backsliding of the saints ceases to be the insuperable problem it first appeared to be. If genuine piety has to do not with a perfect conformity to the law but with the new heart at the basis of life, there will be no inconsistency in supposing that this new heart can exist side by side with moral failure and shortcomings.

The place of practice in the Christian life may be viewed from another perspective. The Spirit is said to dwell in the believer as a living power; the body, says Edwards, is a temple of life and not a tomb. As a principle of life, the Spirit shows itself in the true believer as a vital power; the form most appropriate to its nature is that of holy practice. What this means is that a man's conduct is something more than the moral consequence of the religious relationship; it means that practice takes on a religious dimension. It may take its place as the chief among the signs of gracious affections because it is the Holy Spirit revealing itself as life in the world.

The prominence given by Edwards to practice as a test of affections is of great moment not only for his own thought but for the driving force of American Protestantism as well. In setting up practice as a cardinal test, Edwards was no mere follower of tradition. Classical Protestantism had placed considerable emphasis upon the inner workings of the Spirit and upon the primacy of faith. Puritanism went even further in the direction of making religion into an affair of the interior life. While Edwards' doctrine of affections carried this trend forward, it also took a large step in the direction of making action a center of attention. American Protestantism has never been far from believing that the most reliable test of religious sincerity is the deed; seeing what a man will do is the best test of his heart.

In Edwards' time this was a bolder step than might be imagined. He was subordinating the traditional "immanent grace" to the power of the Spirit as expressed in overt behavior, and he did so without becoming involved in a doctrine of works. There is, he says, no justification in works: "I proceed to show that Christian practice . . . is . . . much to be preferred to the method of the first convictions, enlightenings and comforts in conversion, or any immanent discoveries or exercises of grace whatsoever, that begin and end in contemplation." We need not follow Edwards through his tedious arguments in defense of the position; the conclusion to which they point is vastly more important. He was taking a long look at Protestantism's sacred domain—the inner life—and demanding that it be subjected to a public test. The ground of action, the new nature, is not displaced; in the order of essential things the sense of the heart is always prior. But from the standpoint of human knowing and testing the proof of the heart is to be found in the fruit it can produce in the world. The Holy Spirit not only dwells in the depths of the soul but is manifest in that power through which the face of nature is transformed.

The bearing of this doctrine on the relation between religion and technology in American life has still not been fully realized. American Protestantism has had no place for quietism; its robust sense of activity in the world can be traced to the strain of Puritan piety and not least to the interpretation of that piety by Jonathan Edwards. It is no small irony that a skillful and vigorous defense of the primacy of practice in religion should have found expression in a treatise on religious *affections.*

RELIGION, REVIVALISM, AND RELIGIOUS AFFECTIONS

The details of Edwards' argument in the *Affections,* while important for revealing the subtlety of his mind, may prove more distracting than enlightening unless we can come to an understanding of the central contributions made by the work. We are bound, moreover, to ask for its relevance to our present situation. A work which attacks fundamental questions has perennial importance; it is the task of each age in confronting such a work to discover where that importance lies.

All about us at present are signs of renewed interest in the things of religion, and the past decade* has witnessed not only a vigorous revival in theology but an even more vigorous upsurge of revivalism at the level of personal religion. But there are dissenting voices as well, those who view an increased emphasis upon religion with alarm, those who are convinced that morality is enough and that the idea of salvation is outmoded, those who believe that natural science alone gives reliable knowledge while all else is emotion and sentimental bias. Against such voices that of the revivalist in religion is raised even louder; the situation is urgent, secular society is godless, conversion is the answer to our ills, it is too late for discussion, the only course is to decide and have faith. We cannot, as we confront such a situation, avoid asking what light is shed upon our predicament by the thought of Jonathan Edwards. It would be strange indeed if one who labored so conscientiously in the revivalist vineyard and who thought so acutely about its problems should have nothing pertinent to say to us in the present hour.

What, then, can we find in Edwards' interpretation of heart religion that will provide us with a vantage point from which to understand and evaluate the current scene? There are three basic contributions made by the *Affections,* and each has a direct application to present religious thought and practice. Edwards recovered, through his doctrine of the new sense and the new nature, the distinctively religious dimension of life; he pointed the way to a form of understanding broad enough to retain its relation to the direct experience of the individual; he showed how piety, though ultimately rooted in the individual's relation to God, could be subject to rational scrutiny in the form of tests aimed at revealing its genuine or spurious character.

The first shows us the way to prevent the reduction of religion to

* That is, the 1950's [ed.].

something other than itself; the second makes it clear that understanding can be preserved within religion if it is not taken as a purely theoretical power which ignores the experience of the unique individual; the third gives us a basis for interpreting and evaluating the present concern over revivalistic religion. And in seeking to trace out the further implications of each of these points we do well to remember that if Edwards can aid us, our present religious situation enables us to understand him as perhaps never before. For we are falling or have fallen into some of the very pitfalls he sought to avoid; we are in a better position than any age since Edwards to understand the profundity of his contribution to theological thinking.

The properly religious aspect of man's life is always in danger of being obscured because of our tendency to identify it with something other than itself. Western society since the time of the Enlightenment has consistently manifested this misunderstanding. Religion has been taken as morality with emotional overtones or, even worse, has been made one with social and political idealisms, and thought of merely as an instrument of social change. Whatever form the corruption has assumed, loss of genuine religion has been the result. American Christianity has been especially vulnerable; the practical or pragmatic bent of much American life has led time and again to the reduction of religion to morality. The sincerity of the heart has been subordinated to action and, in its lowest terms, to appearing proper in the eyes of the world.

Edwards made no such mistake, and he can aid us in our attempts to overcome it. One of the clear declarations of the *Affections* is that religion has to do with the inner nature of a man, with the treasure on which his heart is set and with the love which supplies his life with purpose. There can be no identifying religion with morality or anything else; it is the deepest and most fundamental level of life and it goes to the *heart* of the matter. Religion, to be sure, issues in deeds, but it is not the same as right conduct. As Whitehead has pointed out in his arresting comparison between religion and arithmetic, "You use arithmetic, but you *are* religious." Edwards would have agreed. He was reviving the time-honored tradition of Augustine in finding religion in the whole man, in the fundamental inclination of his heart and in his love of the divine *gloria*. In recovering the religious dimension of life and in expressing it through the vivid idea of affections, Edwards is a guide. He has given us a means of exposing the pseudo religions of moralism, sentimentality, and social conformity. For if religion concerns the essential nature of a man and the bent of his will, it cannot be made to coincide with moral rules, with fine sentiment, or with social respectability.

If our age has been plagued by its failure to comprehend what religion means, it has suffered no less from the acceptance of a false conception of the nature of human understanding. The dazzling successes of science, and their interpretation along wholly technological lines by pragmatically minded philosophers, have led to the conception of human understanding as a purely impersonal instrument aimed at finding objective and universal truths. We have acquiesced in that view of reason which sees in it only the abstractive intelligence fitted for expressing what is so true in general that it can have no bearing upon the life of the unique individual in particular. The rational self consequently has come to be understood as a spectator or as one who must put out the light of his own personal experience in order to gain that objective knowledge which alone is deemed worthy of concern. For religion the reduction of reason to science has meant that rationality is denied to religious truth and there is left to it nothing but the domain of emotion and caprice. Few have seen that this consequence is due to our view of what human understanding is and means; as understanding became narrower in scope it inevitably lost its capacity for dealing with dimensions other than science. Exclusive emphasis, moreover, upon understanding as dealing with the universal features of things has led to the disregard of individual experience; what can only be understood by personal experience has been subordinated to the knowledge that is gained by forgetting about yourself and attending to the universal law. What escapes the scientific net, we are told, is just on that account not a fish and need be considered no further as a possible object of rational understanding.

It is no secret that the philosophy known as existentialism in our time is dedicated to challenging the sufficiency of this scientific outlook for the whole of life. The attempt is being made, often in bizarre and unconventional ways, to bring the individual back to a sense of his own individuality and to the need for a broader conception of human understanding, one that does not eliminate everything but science from its concern.

With the *Affections* before us we are now in a position to see that Edwards, though by no stretch of imagination an existentialist, was wrestling with the same problem. He saw that an understanding which excludes first-person experience is doomed to be lost in abstraction and to forfeit its relevance for religion. To deal with the problem he reinterpreted human understanding so as to include a sensible element within it. He grasped the truth that sensible experience is always first-person experience; when we think in general concepts we pass beyond our own senses to a meaning common to many selves. But in using our own senses we are aware of grasping something that each individual must grasp for himself. If a man has never tasted honey, he cannot possibly know what is meant by calling it sweet and, similarly with Edwards' new sense, if a man has not actually tasted of the divine love no combination of general concepts will be adequate for conveying to him what it means.

Following the lead of the classical British experience-philosophy, Edwards placed primary emphasis upon first-person experience; in religion it took the form of the new sense or taste without which faith remains at the merely notional level. A spiritual understanding is not confined to the apprehension of universal concepts but includes within itself a sense which a man must experience directly. If such experience is lacking, there is no way in which he can be made to understand the things of religion through general concepts alone. If, as Hegel said, the great principle of empiricism is that a man must see for himself and be in the presence of the thing he knows, the great principle of Edwards' spiritual understanding in religion is that a man must sense or taste for himself the divine love in order to understand what it means.

In the doctrine of the spiritual understanding Edwards was carrying on the tradition of Augustine and the Puritans, the tradition of the "light" in which, and through which, the things of God are to be grasped. But he qualified the purely rationalistic description of this light by bringing in the "sensible" factor. He had help in framing this conception not only from the English philosopher John Locke but from the English Puritans and the Cambridge Platonist John Smith. The latter was dissatisfied with the tendency of English Puritanism to overemphasize the purely intelligible aspect of the understanding; to correct the disbalance he developed the notion of a "spiritual sensation" or grasp of religious truth which is understanding and at the same time engagement of the individual heart. Edwards' "new sense" points in the same direction. It is the taste of the divine excellence which marks the difference between genuine piety and the merely conceptual grasp of religious doctrines that may lead a man to accept them as general truths without seeing and feeling their special bearing upon his own individual life and situation.

The doctrine of spiritual understanding shows a way in which both rationality and direct experience can be preserved within religion. It shows that understanding need not be a dry light which excludes individual experience. If, moreover, we follow Edwards in his view that understanding is a power of the whole man, we shall see that the heart and the will—the *inclination* of the self— are necessarily involved. A conception of understanding as a purely theoretical or observing power permits only what Edwards called a "speculative" approach: a man considers the problem abstractly but is not engaged. The theoretical attitude is inappropriate in religion because it leaves out the one thing which counts: the individual man and his destiny.

The contemporary relevance of these ideas is clear. If reason and understanding extend no further than the highly abstract knowledge to be found in the natural sciences, it becomes difficult to see how they can possibly have a legitimate function in religion. The original protest made by Kierkegaard against rationalism was directed against a reason which sets the individual self at a theoretical distance from everything it seeks to understand. The essence of the theoretical attitude is to ignore the peculiar bearing of what is known or contemplated upon the life and destiny of the one who knows.

Jonathan Edwards was dealing in his own way with the same problem. A merely notional understanding of Christianity is theoretical; it is inadequate because it leaves the individual soul outside as a spectator looking on at the feast. What is needed instead is engagement of the self and the inclination of the heart and will. But if we are to have such engagement and preserve understanding in religion at the same time, we shall need a conception of that power which neither shrinks it to the proportions of science nor identifies it with the theoretical grasp of general concepts. Understanding will have to be seen, as indeed Edwards viewed it, as a power of the integral self, a power related to the will and the heart. His skillful linking of the understanding to these other aspects of the self through the idea of the new sense opens up novel possibilities for attaining that broader doctrine of understanding so necessary at present.

Edwards' third contribution to the resolution of our modern predicament centers in his contention that affections can and must be subject to critical judgment. While he would not allow that there can be genuine piety which does not express itself in affections, he was equally insistent that they be put to the test. Affections do not test themselves and there can be, so to speak, no affectionate testing of affections. Critical examination calls for signs or marks that enable us to tell the true from the false. These criteria are provided by the New Testament picture of the Christian life as interpreted in a rational way.

A position seeking to recover immediate experience in religion and subject it at the same time to clearly announced tests is exactly what our present circumstance requires. It is a subtle position, one likely to be misunderstood, because it aims to combine what a one-sided way of thinking always sunders. But we must not be misled by the confusions of our forbears. Edwards' contemporaries failed to grasp the underlying consistency of the *Affections*. Some were confused by his double-barreled approach, while others were driven by frustration to anger. Edwards has declared himself for heart religion and against a narrow rationalism; to many this meant full support for revivalism even if it reached the bounds of enthusiasm and immediate revelation. But Edwards rejected enthusiasm and branded as false much of the popular piety resulting from the high tide of revivalist preaching. The heart, he contended, must be affected, for genuine religion is power and more than the verbal acceptance of doctrines. But the change of heart is not in the convulsion or the shout, the flowing tears or the inner voices. These external signs, the sensational marks of revivalism in every age, are no guarantee of genuine faith; there are other tests to be met.

The double-edged character of Edwards' doctrine gives it a peculiar relevance for the current situation because it holds out the possibility of bringing together in a fruitful way what many are concerned to separate. The present renewal of interest in religion often takes on a revivalistic form and thus stands in striking contrast to the underlying assumptions and conventions of our highly rationalistic, secular society. The opposition further widens the gap between faith and the rational disciplines. Rationalists, in order to eliminate, or at least minimize, the threat of revivalistic religion, tend to overestimate the power of reason and science while at the same time exaggerating the irrationality of all religion. On the other side many proponents of the religious revival preach the irrelevance of knowledge and the cultural disciplines, contrasting the critical attitude with the urgency of commitment and the theoretical approach with the immediate experience of the individual. The power of Edwards' doctrine of affections resides in its uncompromising demand that both sides be preserved and related in a fruitful way. The heart and the individual's direct perception are essential to genuine religion, but without critical and rational tests of the heart we cannot know when religion is genuine.

The motivation behind the revivalist in every period is a vivid sense of the personal character of religious faith. He sees that conventionalism is the death of religion and that each individual must confront the issues and make the decision for himself; there is no faith by proxy. He further sees that this truth itself may fall to the level of a general pronouncement and thus may fail to have the very impact it is meant to have in each individual case. His chief strategy for meeting the situation is to dramatize its urgency and seriousness. There is, he believes, no time to stand off and survey the situation, no room for discussion and criticism. The object of faith stands before a man as a brute fact; if its importance is impressed upon him in a vivid and moving way, he will accept. For the majority of revivalists religion is as simple as that.

Edwards saw the element of truth in this position but he was too acute to fall prey to the errors that go with it. He saw well enough that where the individual is not touched at the heart there is no genuine religion. He would have joined hands with William James in believing that there can be no religion at second hand. Edwards' sense of the heart, his defense of the necessity of affections, and his doctrine of spiritual understanding underline the fact. But despite this avowal of heart religion he failed to fall in with revivalism at two crucial points; he denied that the urgency of believing provides any criterion for the truth of religion or the sincerity of the believer, and he was unwilling to follow the pattern of most revivalists and set the religious spirit over against learning and intellect. For Edwards the Word must come in truth as well as in power.

He was second to none in his sense of the seriousness and urgency with which the individual confronts the religious issues. He had repeatedly drummed the ears and laid it upon the consciences of his hearers that each man is judged according as he makes the "business of religion" central or peripheral to his life. But he did not suppose that the urgency by itself tells us what is to be believed, whether it is true, and to what extent the believer is sincere in his profession. Insight into these problems requires more than vivid preaching; the individual must have discipline, he must understand as well as hear, and behind it all must be the sense or "taste" of the beauty of holiness. No one of these essentials is furnished by the revivalist preacher armed with nothing more than the sense of urgency.

Edwards never tired of repeating the thesis that genuine affections are not heat without light. As even Chauncy acknowledged in Edwards' own time, this meant a refusal to accept the primitivism that has often attached itself to revivalist religion. He never was willing to represent himself as a simple soul able to understand the things of the spirit just because of a lack of "book learning." The great temptation of the revivalist is to come forward in this guise, to identify innocence with ignorance and to claim that only the

soul uncorrupted by the studies and doctrines of the theologians is
in a position to receive the gifts of the spirit. Edwards, on the
contrary, was a scholar of the first rank, and he repeatedly criti-
cized those who had neither the time nor the interest to give to the
task of understanding their faith intelligently. He constantly urged
his parishioners to study to the limit of their capacity, to avoid
those who despised intellect in the belief that it is a power hostile
to religion. The Bible is still the medium through which the ancient
faith is preserved, and its treasures cannot be unlocked if learning
is given up and interpretation becomes a matter of personal whim
and individual vision. The recurrent error of the naïve revivalist is
to overlook the labor and the pains of learning; his conviction of
the truth of his own immediate insight leads him to present the
Bible as a book so clear in its import that he who runs may not
only read but understand. Edwards never wavered in his repudia-
tion of these ideas.

If, from the vantage point of the *Affections,* we view recent
attempts to harvest souls in revivalist fashion, we shall lay hold of
the enduring contribution of that treatise. In seeking for the signs
that distinguish gracious affections from fleeting emotion and from
the effects wrought by the rhetoric of an hour, Edwards was trying
to penetrate beneath the surface of things. A genuine change must
take place in the heart, and that change must show itself over a
lifetime of work and worship in the world. As we contemplate the
renewal of interest in religion, we must not fail to apply these
criteria. What permanent change is taking place in the depths of
the self and with what consistency will it show itself in practice?
More likely than not the vast majority of cases will be unable to
pass the test. And one of the principal reasons for the failure is to
be found in our by now well-established tendency to view everything as a technique used by the human will to conquer nature and
master history. Edwards had seen this source of corruptions, and
he had attacked it through the doctrine of divine love as disinterested. Religion is genuine and has power only when rooted in a
love which does not contemplate its own advantage. Religion becomes false at just the point when we attempt to make it into a
device for solving problems. Faith does indeed move mountains,

but only when it is informed by a love pure and unmixed, such as Edwards described in his fourth sign. Love of this kind overcomes the evil desires of the heart and proves itself in the Christian life, but if it is held forth as a panacea for all ills or as something to be *used* by an individual or a society to achieve benefits, its divine character is lost.

Edwards' calm word in the midst of "much noise about religion" is that religion must not be lifeless and it must be something more than doctrine or good conduct. True piety shows itself in the affections and in the fruits of the Spirit, but these must be put to the test so that we may know the gold coin from the counterfeit. To the revivalist in our time Edwards has a sobering word, one that is best expressed by biblical paraphrase: "Test the affections and see if they are of God, for many false affections have gone out into the earth."

An Urgent *Now!* for the Languid Will

The alert reader will have become increasingly aware that the course of the portraiture to this point has made at least one rather obvious circumvention. Perhaps there is the suspicion that something is being intentionally omitted, and like the official portraits of Lenin after the revolution the "message" has overwhelmed and obscured the "facts" of the original event. What every living man could have remembered about Lenin and the revolution was that it was a season of uncommon anguish in which the innocent perished in number as generous as the confusion of the age was great. Where does that appear on the epic canvas? Or like the artist whose executed work is designed merely to flatter its subject, we might be accused of having left out the withered leg. Not just once, but with surprising frequency, Jonathan Edwards delivered the most searing maledictions in the memory of the American church.

What must be said at once is that there is no way of avoiding this fact. We cannot say, for example, that Edwards was momentarily taken up into the reckless spirit of the Awakening, or that he did not "really believe" what he was saying. The eternal torment of the damned was a subject to which he repeatedly and tirelessly turned in his preaching, and even in his miscellaneous notes. There is no item in this vivid explosion of metaphoric carnage on which his imagination could not feed at length. Indeed, we might well argue that his creative powers are nowhere more in evidence than in these astonishing pages. Our task in interpreting this material is the same as it has been elsewhere: we must not merely record our reactions to it, but attempt to understand what it *meant* for Edwards to believe that there was a hell and that its purpose was to punish sinners.

In agreement with virtually every other major thinker in the Western world before him, Edwards uncritically accepted the theory of immortality. Without argument or defense he could plainly say that "intelligent beings of the world are everlasting & will remain after the world comes to an end."[1] But what gives specific shape to his thinking about the after-world comes from another more or less implicit theme, also widely shared, that the inner logic of the ethical life could be comprehended in the term "desert." A man gets what he deserves. The patient seeker after truth, the doer of righteousness, the faithful servant, each shall be rewarded for his uprightness and earnestness. But, since the world in which we live is a world largely without Edwards' "beauty" and "excellency" no such perfect recompense in the mortal life can be expected. For in this life the innocent will suffer and the wicked prosper. Therefore, final rewards and debts will be paid and collected in the world to come. Immanuel Kant was so persuaded of the idea of just deserts that he thought the ethical life made belief in immortality necessary.[2]

Consistent with these two themes there is an over-all design to the imprecatory sermons that the casual reader, interested more in amusement than in understanding, will easily overlook. First, we should observe the way in which the torments of hell have been described. With what must have been great effectiveness Edwards reaches into the common experience of his listeners to convey their imagination by means of vivid sense impression into the eternal anguish. Appealing to the universal dread of being locked into a closed place without any hope of escape, for instance, he says that hell "is a strong prison: it is beyond any finite power, or the united

---

[1] *Miscellanies,* Yale Mss., No. 547.
[2] Cf. *Critique of Pure Reason,* trans. Lewis White Beck (Indianapolis, 1956), pp. 126 ff.

strength of all wicked men and devils to unlock, or break open the door of that prison. Christ hath the key of hell; 'he shuts and no man opens.' " [3] There were few experiences in the frontier town that were more terrifying than housefires: "Some of you have seen buildings on fire; imagine therefore with yourselves, what a poor hand you would make at fighting with the flames, if you were in the midst of so great and fierce a fire."[4] In the same sermon he introduces the famous image of the spider in the flames, combining it with the common miniature drama of the moth or mayfly led by its own fascination into the candle flame.

You have often seen a spider, or some other noisome insect, when thrown into the midst of a fierce fire, and have observed how immediately it yields to the force of the flames. There is no long struggle, no fighting against the fire, no strength exerted to oppose the heat, or to fly from it; but it immediately stretches forth itself and yields; and the fire takes possession of it, and at once it becomes full of fire, and is burned into a bright coal.[5]

Once he has the wicked in the midst of the fierce heat, defenseless against it, he will not let them find any place of refuge, "any secret corner, which will be cooler than the rest, where they may have a little respite, a small abatement of the extremity of their torment. They never will be able to find any cooling stream or fountain, in any part of that world of torment; no nor so much as a drop of water to cool their tongues." Edwards wants his auditors to see that once the wrath of God has been unleashed on a sinner, he can avoid it no more easily than a worm can lift the heavy rock thrown down upon it.[6]

In perhaps the most severe of all his sermons Edwards reaches much closer to the heart. He concludes from his studies of Scripture that when the last judgment has been made and when the whole of mankind has been divided into the saved and the

---

[3] "The Future Punishment of the Wicked Unavoidable and Intolerable," *The Works of President Edwards,* a reprint of the Worcester edition, 4 vols. (New York: Jonathan Leavitt and John F. Trow, 1843), IV, 259.

[4] *Ibid.,* IV, 263 f.

[5] *Ibid.,* IV, 264.

[6] *Ibid.,* IV, 259.

damned, "the two worlds of happiness and misery will be in view of each other." "The saints in glory will see how the damned are tormented: they will see God's threatenings fulfilled, and his wrath executed upon them."[7] This gives him the chance to say that since this division will be by God's justice, and since every saint loves God's justice, there "will be none to pity you."

Look which way you will, before or behind, on the right hand or left, look up to heaven, or look about you in hell, and you will see none to condole your case, or to exercise any pity towards you, in your dreadful condition. You must bear these flames, you must bear that torment and amazement, day and night, forever, and never have the comfort of considering, that there is so much as one that pities your case; there never will one tear be dropped for you.[8]

The emotional climax of this sermon is a passage that bids fair to be cited as the moment of greatest power—or perhaps savagery—in the entire genre. He asks the unregenerate within his hearing to think of their friends, and especially their parents, when the final judgment is uttered.

How will you bear to see your parents, who in this life had so dear an affection for you, now without any love to you, approving the sentence of condemnation, when Christ shall with indignation bid you depart, wretched, cursed creatures, into eternal burnings? How will you bear to see and hear them praising the Judge, for his justice exercised in pronouncing this sentence, and hearing it with holy joy in their countenances, and shouting forth the praises and hallelujahs of God and Christ on that account? When they shall see what manifestations of amazement there will be in you, at the hearing of this dreadful sentence, and that every syllable of it pierces you like a thunderbolt, and sinks you into the lowest depths of horror and despair; when they shall behold you with a frightened, amazed countenance, trembling and astonished, and shall hear you groan and gnash your teeth; these things will not move them at all to pity you, but you will see them with a holy joyfulness in their countenances, and with songs in their mouths. When they shall see you turned away and beginning to enter into the great furnace, and shall see how you shrink at it, and hear you

[7] "The End of the Wicked Contemplated by the Righteous: or the Torments of the Wicked in Hell, No Occasion of Grief to the Saints in Heaven," *Ibid.,* IV, 289.

[8] *Ibid.,* IV, 294 f.

shriek and cry out; yet they will not be at all grieved for you, but at the same time you will hear from them renewed praises and hallelujahs for the true and righteous judgments of God, in so dealing with you.[9]

If these are the words of man become captive to an extreme religious position, they are also the words of an artist, for Edwards, with a skill as sure as that of any story teller, has collapsed the distance between his subject matter and his listeners by describing a strange and terrifying world in terms of a present and familiar world. But there is a decisive difference between what Edwards is doing here and what a teller of stories seeks to accomplish. A story is designed to arrest the fancy, freeing it from the immediate world, in order that momentarily the listener will be suspended from the presentness of his experience. Edwards' appeal is not to the fancy, but to the will. He is not giving us a world that will exist if only we can take our attention from the immediately given; he is giving us a world in which we will exist if we fail to heed the true nature of the immediately given. Edwards is giving us a world which our present wills surely will create if they persist in the spiritual languor. Look where you are now, he is saying. Not then, but NOW!

If any of the saints will need assistance in determining how their will is faring, Mr. Edwards can provide that, too, in these sermons. "Look over your past life," he calls out to them, "inquire at the mouth of conscience, and hear what that has to testify concerning it."[10] Then like a surgeon in search of the body's disease, he pokes into the private reflections of his listeners, attempting to startle them into an awareness of their peccability.

How many sorts of wickedness have you been guilty of!

How manifold have been the abominations of your life! What profaneness and contempt of God has been exercised by you!

And how have you behaved yourself in the time of family prayer! What wicked carriage have some of you been guilty of toward your parents! How far have you been from paying that honor to them that God has required!

[9] *Ibid.,* IV, 296.
[10] "The Justice of God in the Damnation of Sinners," *Ibid.,* IV, 232.

How have some of you vaunted yourselves in your apparel! Others in their riches! Others in their knowledge and abilities! How has it galled you to see others above you!

And what abominable lasciviousness have some of you been guilty of! How have you indulged yourself from day to day, and from night to night, in all manner of unclean imaginations! Has not your soul been filled with them, till it has become a hold of foul spirits, and a cage of every unclean and hateful bird?[11]

After this catalogue of personal failings comes the concluding, summarizing question: "Now, can you think when you have thus behaved yourself, that God is obliged to show you mercy? Are you not, after all this, ashamed to talk of its being hard with God to cast you off?"[12]

The most famous of all Edwards' sermons, "Sinners in the Hands of an Angry God," is not properly a description of hell as such. It is concerned rather with the fact that the time between the present and one's death is a totally unknown quantity. Death comes suddenly and unannounced.

The unseen, unthought of ways and means of persons' going suddenly out of the world are innumerable and inconceivable. Unconverted men walk over the pit of hell on a rotten covering, and there are innumerable places in this covering so weak that they will not bear their weight, and these places are not seen. The arrows of death fly unseen at noonday; the sharpest sight cannot discern them.[13]

The imagery of the sermon is designed to communicate the sense of a disaster close at hand.

There are the black clouds of God's wrath now hanging directly over your heads, full of the dreadful storm, and big with thunder; and were it not for the restraining hand of God, it would immediately burst forth upon you. The sovereign pleasure of God, for the present, stays his rough wind: otherwise it would come with fury, and your destruction would come like a whirlwind, and you would be like the chaff of the summer threshing floor.[14]

[11] *Ibid.,* IV, 233 f.
[12] *Ibid.,* IV, 235.
[13] *Ibid.,* IV, 315.
[14] *Ibid.,* IV, 317.

In the conclusion to the sermon the imagery falls away and the minister confronts his congregation with direct prose plainly describing their situation.

There is reason to think that there are many in this congregation now hearing this discourse, that will actually be the subjects of this very misery to all eternity. We know not who they are, or in what seats they sit, or what thoughts they now have. It may be they are now at ease, and hear all these things without much disturbance, and are now flattering themselves that they are not the persons; promising themselves that they shall escape. . . . But alas! . . . how many is it likely will remember this discourse in hell! And it would be a wonder, if some that are now present would not be in hell in a very short time, before this year is out. And it would be no wonder if some persons, that now sit here in some seats of this meeting-house in health, and quiet and secure, should be there before to-morrow morning.[15]

The purpose of such preaching is certainly clear enough. It can be summarized in one straightforward sentence of Edwards': "The only opportunity of escaping is in this world; this is the only state of trial wherein we have any offers of mercy, or there is any place for repentance."[16] To draw a heavy line of emphasis under this fact, he wants to make it understood by all that with death each person has lost the last chance to change the final balance of his life. After death there are no more chances, there is no hope whatsoever, for the torments of hell are eternal.

How dismal will it be, when you are under these racking torments, to know assuredly that you never, never shall be delivered from them; to have no hope: when you shall wish that you might but be turned into nothing, but shall have no hope of it; when you shall wish that you might be turned into a toad or a serpent, but shall have no hope of it; when you would rejoice, if you might but have any relief, after you shall have endured these torments millions of ages, but shall have no hope of it; when after you shall have worn out the age of the sun, moon, and stars, in your dolorous groans and lamentations, without any rest day or night, or one minute's ease, yet you shall have no hope of ever being delivered.[17]

[15] *Ibid.,* IV, 321.
[16] "The Eternity of Hell Torments," *Ibid.,* IV, 275 f.
[17] *Ibid.,* IV, 278.

The undeniable contempt the preacher is pouring out in these words serves easily to obscure another rather remarkable feature of Edwards' imprecatory sermons. While he is convinced of man's mountainous sinfulness, he is also saying that a man's entire life, both past and future, lies under the power of his present will. All of a man's debts for things past, and all of a man's responsibilities for things to come, are fully within the power of his present will to discharge. What lies behind these sermons, therefore, is Edwards' profound respect for both the importance and power of the human will. This point is made all the clearer when we see how he deals with the opposite side of this same subject matter; that is, when he addresses himself to the consequences that attend the life of a man who had seized on Christ as his most apparent good. Such a man, in Edwards' judgment, was David Brainerd.

In 1747 young Brainerd, missionary to the Indians and fiancé of Edwards' daughter, Jerusha, died of tuberculosis in the Edwards home. A few months later Jerusha, carrying Brainerd's love and his disease, followed him to the grave. Brainerd had asked Edwards on his deathbed to edit his private journals. *The Life and Diary of David Brainerd* fell into the long tradition of Puritan pieces in which the diarist painfully examines himself against standards for his performance that could not possibly be met. It reads therefore like a mournful self-condemnation, but in the idiom of the time it could be seen as the modestly composed chronicle of a spiritual hero willing to undergo any danger and hardship in the service of his Lord. Brainerd's funeral sermon was preached by Edwards, and is memorable if only because the preacher converts his transparent grief into a long discourse on the experience of the saints after death. Like the damned in hell, the saints' blessedness in heaven is eternal. And as the damned are thrown into the keeping of Satan, the saints are led into the presence of Christ.

The most intimate intercourse becomes that relation that the saints stand in to Jesus Christ; and especially becomes that most perfect and glorious union they shall be brought into with him in heaven. They are not merely Christ's servants, but his friends.[18]

[18] "Saints When Absent From the Body," *Ibid.*, III, 629.

The experience of the saint in life is, as we have seen, one of great affection. When Christ becomes one's most apparent good, he responds with love for all things. In heaven the appearance of Christ will be more direct, and the response to it all the more vivid, for there the elect

see every thing in Christ that tends to kindle and inflame love, and every thing that tends to gratify love, and every thing that tends to satisfy them: and that in the most clear and glorious manner, without any darkness or delusion, without any impediment or interruption.[19]

Edwards described the life of the saint on earth as one of vital union with Christ. After death this union becomes much more complete. The saints not only live by his life, but they also share in his power and glory; they are

exalted to reign with him. They are through him made kings and priests, and reign with him, and in him, over the same kingdom. As the Father hath appointed unto him a kingdom, so he has appointed the Son to reign over his kingdom, and the Son appoints his saints to reign in his.[20]

Here again we can focus on the mythic absurdity of these thoughts, or we can attempt to get behind them and to understand why Edwards should have voiced them in this way and on this occasion. If it is the case that the sermons on hell are designed to awaken the people into a recognition of the power of the will, then so is this sermon and the others like it. If they can choose hell, they can also choose heaven. The vast differences between heaven and hell point to the vast differences between the kinds of lives people currently are living. The one is dark and self-enclosed, turned in upon itself, feeding on its own emotions and organizing all values around its own needs and tastes. The other is brilliantly life-affirming, it is open and free, seeing in the darkness not the estuary of its self-destruction but the possibility of new and surprising kinds of caring for the world. Jonathan Edwards thought that Brainerd had lived the latter kind of life, and this sermon is a way of saying it. "Saints When Absent From the Body" is not a

[19] *Ibid.,* III, 627 f.
[20] *Ibid.,* III, 631.

disembodied, ill-informed series of speculations about some other world; it is a profound HURRAH! for the life of David Brainerd.

Therefore, I shall make no attempt here to omit from this portrait what many have regarded as the least creditable part of Jonathan Edwards' intellectual production. On the contrary, the portrait would lose much of its power and meaning if the blacker machinations of this American intelligence were left out of it. For in these sermons are combined what Americans elsewhere are wont to celebrate in the worldliness of their civilization: a hard-minded appraisal of the nature of things as they are, and a sturdy confidence that by an act of the will all things are alterable.

Edwards looked out upon his world and what he saw there was not beautiful. We are momentarily deceived by the fact that what he thought was ugliness is for us a series of petty moral failings, because the ugliness of our own age stands in such contrast to his. He was worried about children being distracted from family prayer; but we have seen the family structure itself fall into decay. He was alarmed by those who vaunted themselves in their apparel and in their riches; but we live in an age when a man's wealth brings upon him an astonishing blindness to the poverty of his fellow Americans, and even supplies him with reasons for strengthening the bonds by which others are excluded from even the merest comforts of human existence. Edwards was concerned with the unclean imaginations of his people, but we are living in a time when the imaginations of national glory fill the world with devastation. If there was any need for the languid will to exercise itself in the direction of beauty in the century of Jonathan Edwards, that need is enormously magnified in the century of the atomic bomb and the urban slum.

Edwards was an artist for his people, he was the reporter and the critic who caused them to focus on the larger world. His sermons were designed to terrify. They were for his time what Picasso's "Guernica" is for ours. They are Eisenstein's films of war and revolution, they are the photographs of police dogs and sheriff's deputies in Alabama, or the television report of American soldiers setting fire to the straw huts of Asian peasants. The earth over which we walk is no less rotten than it was for those who

were in the hearing of Jonathan Edwards that unforgettable day in
Enfield, Connecticut. "The arrows of death," he reminded them in
July of 1741, "fly unseen at noonday. The sharpest sight cannot
discern them." What man among us, 222 years later, on that unforgettable day in the November of 1963, could have thought
otherwise?

In these sermons Edwards was not wandering off the edge of a
realistic mentality into a foolish other-worldliness: rather, he was
bringing his hearers out of their irrelevant and fruitless Sunday
musings, and showing on the seachart of their lives as a people
precisely where they were and precisely whither they were bound.
What Jonathan Edwards preached and wrote in all of his sermons
was a radical this-worldliness. It is for this reason that the failure
of Jonathan Edwards is a fact of no small significance in the
American civilization. After Edwards every great American
prophet would fail in the same way. The American journey is over.
Let the dream of the ultimate society be spoken in public cere-
monies, but never dispatch the will and the intelligence in the
active attempt to achieve it. The ship is at anchor, the sails down.
There will be many men who will with great usefulness labor at
tightening her rigging, cleaning her decks, and keeping the logs of
her once great adventures. But there is no captain at the wheel,
and too few crewmen athirst for the open sea.

PETER GAY

✪

Jonathan Edwards

An American Tragedy

I

In 1739, Jonathan Edwards delivered a series of sermons on the work of redemption, a breathtaking survey of the "grand design of God" in the "form of a history."[1] It was an audacious undertaking, unprecedented in the rich theological literature produced by the Puritans in America. Beset on one side by the enthusiasm of the Great Awakening and on the other by the threat of formal religiosity and frigid rationalism, Edwards rose to an Olympian view of man's religious destiny, and spoke to his flock at Northampton about things of the last importance: Christ's activity in behalf of man from the invention of time to its abolition. He was invading treacherous territory, last traversed half a century before by the great Bossuet.[2]

[1] Jonathan Edwards to the Trustees of the College of New Jersey, October 19, 1757, *The Works of President Edwards,* ed. S. Austin, 4 vols. (New York, 1847 and several times thereafter), I, 48.

[2] Thomas Prince, it is true, published his *Chronological History of New England, In the Form of Annals,* in 1736, and it begins with Adam, "year one, first month, sixth day." But he ends with 1630, and eschatological speculation is wholly absent from it.

Reprinted by permission of author and publisher from Peter Gay, *A Loss of Mastery: Puritan Historians in Colonial America* (Berkeley and Los Angeles: University of California Press, 1966), pp. 88–117.

Edwards, like Bossuet, was a professional theologian and only an amateur historian. But, like Bossuet, Edwards saw no reason to apologize for his excursion; he was only doing his duty. After all, "The work of REDEMPTION is a work that GOD carries on from the fall of man to the end of the world";[3] it was work God performed in, and through history, and what was more urgent for man than to trace evidences of that divine work in time? Besides, and from this motive, devout historical study had long been one of Edwards' favorite pursuits. "My heart has been much on the advancement of Christ's kingdom in the world," he observed in his spiritual autobiography. "When I have read histories of past ages, the pleasantest thing in all my reading has been, to read of the kingdom of Christ being promoted." The very anticipation of coming upon such a passage was a source of rejoicing. "My mind," he said, "has been much entertained and delighted with the Scripture promises and prophecies, which relate to the future glorious advancement of Christ's kingdom upon earth."[4]

This pious, purposeful pleasure in history never left him. He importuned his European correspondents to send him the latest books on history and theology, and he continued to brood on his sermons on redemption: as late as October, 1757, eighteen years after these sermons, he told the trustees of New Jersey College that he was not sure he wanted to be president of their institution, partly because his health was uncertain, partly because his learning was sadly incomplete, but largely because he was thinking of writing a *History of the Work of Redemption*. This history had been on his "mind and heart" for many years; he had begun it "long ago, not with any view to publication." It was to be a "great work," designed on "an entire new method"—towering claims for a man who, though he knew his powers, was a modest man—a work that would consider "the affair of Christian Theology, as the whole of it, in each part, stands in reference to the great work of redemption by Jesus Christ." Since the work of redemption,

---

[3] *A History of the Work of Redemption* (first published in 1774), *Works,* I, 298.

[4] *Personal Narrative* (probably written in 1740, a year after the sermons on the work of redemption), *Works,* I, 21.

Edwards wrote, was the *"summum* and *ultimum* of all the divine operations and decrees; particularly considering all parts of the grand scheme, in their historical order," his book on redemption must be on a grand scale: it must look at "all three worlds, heaven, earth, and hell," and introduce "all parts of divinity in that order which is most scriptural and most natural."[5]

This program delighted Edwards: he was never afraid of grand architectonic designs. His plan appeared to him "the most beautiful and entertaining, wherein every divine doctrine will appear to the greatest advantage, in the brightest light, in the most striking manner, shewing the admirable contexture and harmony of the whole."[6] In the enforced solitude of his later years, Edwards wrote some ambitious books and spun out some ambitious plans, but among all his works, realized or contemplated, his history of the work of redemption was the most ambitious. He did not live to write it; in March, 1758, he died, shortly after receiving inoculation for smallpox, a victim of modern science.

We can only speculate how Edwards would have transformed his sermons on redemption into a book of history. This much is certain: he would not have discarded, or modified, their classical Puritan theology. The books, the journals, and letters of his late years, like those of his early years, betray no skepticism of miracles, no doubt of Scripture, no rebellion against God's sovereignty, no deviation from the Augustinian vision of history. In the midst of the greatest revolution in the European mind since Christianity had overwhelmed paganism, Edwards serenely reaffirmed the faith of his fathers.

He had some notion that such a revolution was going on: he even read David Hume and professed himself "glad of an opportunity to read such corrupt books, especially when written by men of considerable genius"; it gave him, he said, "an idea of the notions that prevail in our nation."[7] But he had no idea how

---

[5] Edwards to the Trustees of the College of New Jersey, *Works,* I, 48–49.
[6] *Ibid.,* I, 49.
[7] See Thomas H. Johnson, "Jonathan Edwards' Background of Reading," *Publications of the Colonial Society of Massachusetts,* XXVIII (1931), 210–211.

extensive that revolution was, and how far his own historical thinking deviated from the historical thinking about to seize control of
educated opinion in Europe. In fact, the nineteen years between
Edwards' sermons and Edwards' death were decisive years in the
rebellion of the Enlightenment against Christianity. Hume published the first two books of his *Treatise of Human Nature* in
1739; Condillac his *Essai sur l'origine des connaissances humaines*
in 1746; Montesquieu his *Esprit des lois* in 1748, and with these
books the foundations for the Enlightenment's epistemology, psychology, and sociology were firmly laid down. They were all attempts (in David Hume's words) "to introduce the experimental
Method of Reasoning into Moral Subjects";[8] attempts to found
the science of man on the ideas of Locke and the method of
Newton. They were scientific rather than metaphysical, critical
rather than credulous, naturalistic in temper, and wholly incompatible with revealed religion of any kind.

History, ready as always to follow the new currents, was bene-
ficiary, and part, of the offensive of the secular against the Christian mind. In the late 1730's, while Edwards was displaying to his
congregation the activity of Christ in history, Voltaire was at work
on his *Siècle de Louis XIV,* a book which, with its anticlericalism,
its worldliness, and its aggressive modernity, became the mani-
festo, and the model, of the new history. A few years later,
Voltaire began his vast *Essai sur les mœurs,* the Enlightenment's
answer to Bossuet. Both of these books were published in Edwards' lifetime: the first in 1751, the second in 1756. Hume
turned to historical subjects in the late 1740's; he started work on
his *History of England* in 1752, and four years later published its
first installment, covering the Stuart dynasty from the accession of
James I to the expulsion of James II. William Robertson, the great
Scottish historian whose reputation then was higher than it is now,
began the first of his masterpieces, the *History of Scotland,* in
1753. Edward Gibbon, who combined the secular mentality of the
philosophes with the technical competence of the *érudits,* was still
a young man in those years, but he had already found his vocation,
perfected his classical learning, and discovered his religious posi-

[8] Subtitle of Hume's *Treatise of Human Nature* (1739–1740).

tion; all he needed was a subject commensurate with his talents, and he found that, with the lucid finality of a religious conversion, in 1764, only five years after Edwards' death.

To turn from these books to Edwards' *History of the Work of Redemption* is to leave the familiar terrain of the modern world with its recognizable features and legible signposts for a fantastic landscape, alive with mysterious echoes from a distant past, and intelligible only—if it can be made intelligible at all—with the aid of outmoded, almost primitive maps. The philosophes' histories made secular propaganda by providing information about a real past; Edwards' history made religious propaganda by arousing memories of a religious myth. To grasp the temper of Voltaire's or Hume's histories, one must read the new philosophy and collections of state papers; to grasp the temper of Edwards' history, one must read the Church Fathers and the Scriptures. However magnificent in conception, however bold in execution, Edwards' *History of the Work of Redemption* is a thoroughly traditional book, and the tradition is the tradition of Augustine.

The very plan of the book places it in this tradition. Edwards periodizes world history by relying wholly on sacred numbers and sacred events. The first great period stretches from the Fall of Man to the Incarnation of Christ; the second, from His Incarnation to His Resurrection; the third, from His Resurrection to the end of the world. The first of these great periods, in turn, is subdivided into six "lesser periods": from the Fall to the Flood, the Flood to the calling of Abraham, Abraham to Moses, Moses to David, David to the Babylonian Captivity, and the Captivity to the Incarnation.[9] The second period, Christ's short sojourn on this earth, need not be subdivided: it is an intense, luminous, concentrated moment in the career of God's world: "Though it was but between thirty and forty years, yet more was done in it than had been done from the beginning of the world to that time."[10] The third and last period, finally, matches the first in perfect symmetry; it is marked by six steps in "Christ's coming in his kingdom":

[9] *History of the Work of Redemption, Works,* I, 306.
[10] *Ibid.,* I, 395. Edwards does subdivide this period, but only for purposes of analysis.

from the Resurrection to the destruction of Jerusalem; the destruction of Jerusalem to the advent of the Christian Emperor Constantine; Constantine to the reign of Roman Catholicism; the reign of Antichrist to the Reformation; the Reformation to the present; the present to the final overthrow of Antichrist.[11]

This periodic scheme is the appropriate, indeed the only possible scheme for Edwards: it mirrors, and perfectly expresses, his theory of historical causation and historical purpose, and his prediction of the end of time. Edwards insists that the course of events follows a predetermined plan laid down by God before the Fall, indeed before Creation. God settled everything at the beginning: man's nature, man's sin, Satan's interference, Christ's intercession; and God settled it for the sole purpose of glorifying himself. In good Calvinist fashion, Edwards despised the doctrine of foreknowledge as the refuge of timid Christians: of course, God had perfect foreknowledge of man's future conduct, but if he had dictated the course of history merely because he knew what was going to happen, he could not be said to have dictated it, but merely to have conformed his decree to necessity. This was a limitation on the divine omnipotence to which Jonathan Edwards could never assent: no theme is more consistent in his writings than the lovely and unlimited glory of God, which looks to the perfection of the creature for the sake of the perfection of the Creator: because God "infinitely values his own glory, consisting in the knowledge of himself, love to himself, and complacence and joy in himself; he therefore valued the image, communication or participation of these, in the creature. And it is because he values himself, that he delights in the knowledge, and love, and joy of the creature; as being himself the object of this knowledge, love and complacence."[12]

The historical drama, therefore, was divine in all its aspects; "this lower world," in which human history took place, "was

[11] This periodization of the third period is less obvious than the first; it is, however, implicit. See C. C. Goen, "Jonathan Edwards: A New Departure in Eschatology," *Church History*, XXVIII (1959), 26.

[12] "Concerning the End for Which God Created the World," *Works*, II, 256.

doubtless created to be a stage."[13] God was author of the drama, its director, chief actor, and, just to make sure, authoritative critic. Everything had happened precisely as Scripture described it, everything would happen precisely as Scripture prophesied it: the past fulfillment of prophecies was guarantee, if guarantees were needed, of future fulfillment of prophecies not yet realized. The course of history did more than merely offer evidence in support of the divine origins of the Bible: the Bible was incomparably the most accurate and most sublime—in fact the only accurate and sublime—history ever written.

For Edwards, secular history was on the whole insignificant, or significant only as it illustrated, illuminated, impinged upon sacred history: kings appear only as they establish, or obstruct, the true church, wars are mentioned only as they serve to spread, or to constrict, the true faith. All of parts one and two, and much of part three, of the *History of the Work of Redemption* consists of a free retelling of Scripture, with each miraculous event reported as a historical event. For Edwards, the authority of the Bible is absolute. "There were many great changes and revolutions in the world, and they were all only the turning of the wheels of Providence in order to this, to make way for the coming of Christ, and what he was to do in the world. They all pointed hither, and all issued here."[14] Characters in the Old Testament acted in behalf of purposes greater than themselves, and prefigured great events of which they knew nothing, but they were real people, real historical subjects. There was an Adam and an Eve, and they sinned and awoke to their sense of guilt; there was a Cain and an Abel, a Noah and a Moses, and while they were symbols and types, they were symbols and types in the way all creaturely beings represent both themselves and God's intentions. In the modern sense, in the sense of Voltaire and Hume, almost none of Edwards' history is history—it is Calvinist doctrine exemplified in a distinct succession of transcendent moments.

Yet history intrudes. In the time span between the establishment of the primitive church and the apocalyptic future, the Bible

---

[13] *History of the Work of Redemption, Works,* I, 300.
[14] *Ibid.,* I, 305.

provides no guidance; Edwards thus had to find other guides for the period between the first and the eighteenth centuries, and he found them in expected places. The style is the style of Jonathan Edwards, the story is the story told by Cotton Mather, by William Bradford, by John Foxe: in its first three centuries on earth, the true church was pure but suffered under persecution; then came years of prosperity and peace, as Constantine delivered the church from its travail—Satan, "the prince of darkness, that king and god of the Heathen world," was driven out.[15] But this time of rest did not last long: "Presently after, the church again suffered persecution from the Arians; and after that, Antichrist rose, and the church was driven away into the wilderness, and was kept down in obscurity, and contempt, and suffering for a long time."[16] While the true church was kept down, Satan's counterfeit church ruled the world: "The Pope and his clergy robbed the people of their ecclesiastical and civil liberties and privileges," and, just as Scripture had foretold, "robbed them of their estates, and drained all Christendom of their money, and engrossed the most of their riches into their own coffers, by their vast revenues, besides pay for pardons and indulgences, baptisms, and extreme unctions, deliverance out of purgatory, and a hundred other things." This renewed reign of Satan made "superstition and ignorance" prevail more than ever, for the Pope and his minions "industriously promoted ignorance"; in a line that David Hume might have written—and in fact did write, almost word for word—Edwards reminded his congregation that it was "a received maxim" among the Papists that "ignorance is the mother of devotion: and so great was the darkness of those times, that learning was almost extinct in the world."[17] Finally, after many centuries, Satan was driven away once again, by the "reformation of Luther and others."[18] Here was a splendid moment in the history of God's own church:

---

[15] *Ibid.*, I, 450.
[16] *Ibid.*, I, 438.
[17] *Ibid.*, I, 458. Hume quotes the maxim, *"Ignorance is the mother of Devotion"* in his *The Natural History of Religion, Philosophical Works*, 4 vols., ed. T. H. Green and T. H. Grose (1882), IV, 363.
[18] *History of the Work of Redemption, Works,* I, 438.

"God began gloriously to revive his church again, and advance the kingdom of his Son, after such a dismal night of darkness as had been before." There had been many endeavors by the witnesses to the truth, "for a reformation before," but it was only now, "when God's appointed time was come"—for in God's drama, all actors spoke their lines only on cue—that God's "work was begun, and went on with a swift and wonderful progress."[19]

Still, Edwards warned his flock, deliverance was not yet, and complacency was misplaced. The spirit of a true Christian remained what it had always been, a "spirit of suffering."[20] Satan, though wounded, was far from dead. He had risen higher and higher, and now felt himself falling once again, halfway to ruin, and with his last strength did his all to obstruct the great work of reformation. He strengthened the Papists through a great council, he fostered plots and conspiracies, he oppressed helpless minorities of true believers, he warred upon God's children. "The Heathen persecution had been very dreadful; but now persecution by the church of Rome was improved and studied, and cultivated as an art or science."[21] There was a time—a time that very old members of Edwards' congregation would remember—when Rome seemed near a decisive triumph: the king of England and "Lewis XIV. of France," both of them fanatical Papists, mounted a great conspiracy to extirpate what they called "the Northern heresy." But then, "just as their matters seemed to be come to a head, and their enterprise ripe for execution, God, in his providence, suddenly dashed all their schemes in pieces by the Revolution, at the coming in of King William and Queen Mary; by which all their designs were at an end; and the Protestant interest was more strongly established, by the crown of England's being established in the Protestant house of Hanover, and a Papist being, by the constitution of the nation, forever rendered incapable of wearing the crown of England. Thus they groped in darkness at noon-day as in the night, and their hands could not perform their enterprise, and their kingdom was full of darkness, and they gnawed their

---

[19] *Ibid.,* I, 462.
[20] *Ibid.,* I, 479.
[21] *Ibid.,* I, 465.

tongues in pain."[22] Like Cotton Mather before him, Jonathan Edwards distrusted the Anglican church, but he accepted as divinely ordained the aid of an Anglican state against the Papists.

Such victories, though impressive, were not final. A candid survey of the modern world showed Satan at work in many places. Protestants had been expelled from Bohemia and from France not long before; "Ireland has been as it were overwhelmed with Protestant blood," and there had been cruel persecutions elsewhere.[23] "Thus did the devil and his great minister Antichrist, rage with such violence and cruelty against the church of Christ! And thus did the whore of Babylon make herself drunk with the blood of the saints and martyrs of Jesus!"[24] But Satan was serpent as well as Moloch, a subtle deceiver as well as a ravening monster, and the progress of the true church had been much impeded by the spreading of corrupt opinions: Arminianism has "greatly prevailed" in the Church of England and among dissenters, and "spread greatly in New England, as well as Old."[25] Deism, which denied revelation altogether, had "very much overrun" the English nation on both sides of the Atlantic—"our nation."[26] Perhaps worst of all, indifference to religion was spreading. "The glorious outpouring of the Spirit of God that accompanied the first Reformation" had greatly diminished, and "vital piety" was now despised as *"enthusiasm, whimsy, and fanaticism."* Those who are truly religious, "are commonly looked upon to be crack-brained, and beside their right mind; and vice and profaneness dreadfully prevail, like a flood which threatens to bear down all before it."[27]

But, as Edwards knew, it was not written that the threat should become reality. The future, being the future, was hard to fathom, the history of the future hard to write. But Edwards ventured to undertake it; armed with the book of Revelation and with his interpretation of some events in his own day, he projected his history forward to give hope to the saints in his audience, and to

22 *Ibid.,* I, 464.
23 *Ibid.,* I, 466.
24 *Loc. cit.*
25 *Ibid.,* I, 467.
26 *Loc. cit.*
27 *Ibid.,* I, 471.

inspire the sinners with despair. There will be a time of darkness, then the millennium will come, than a final paroxysm of Satanic fury, and then the Judgment, the end of time, the end of history. "These sayings are faithful and true," Edwards said in conclusion, appropriately ending his cycle of sermons by paraphrasing the last chapter of Revelation, "and blessed is he that keepeth these sayings. Behold, Christ cometh quickly, and his reward is with him, to render to every man according as his work shall be. And he that is unjust, shall be unjust still; and he that is filthy, shall be filthy still; and he that is holy, shall be holy still. Blessed are they that do his commandments, that they may have right to the tree of life, and may enter in through the gates into the city: for without, are dogs, and sorcerers, and whoremongers, and murderers, and idolaters, and whatsoever loveth and maketh a lie. He that testifieth these things, saith, Surely I come quickly. Amen; even so come, Lord Jesus."[28]

Yes, Jesus would surely come. But when? Here, Edwards could remind his congregation of what they knew: there was an expectancy in the air, a self-satisfied prosperity among men of learning puffed with pride and self-sufficiency, an atmosphere reminiscent of the time around the first coming of Christ, when the pride of scholars was humbled by the divine foolishness. Besides, persecutions had lately much diminished, the wings of the Pope had been clipped, in Germany the blessed work of *"August Herman Frank"* testified that true piety was still alive. And then there was America, that vast continent so long wholly delivered over to the devil, yet recently gloriously receptive to the word of Christ: "Something remarkable has appeared of late here, and in other parts of America, among many Indians, of an inclination to be instructed in the Christian religion." Even Northampton could testify to the progress of Christ in this day: "Another thing, which it would be ungrateful in us not to take notice of, is that remarkable pouring out of the Spirit of God which has been of late in this part of New England, of which we, in this town, have had such a share." This was not egotism, not parochialism, not patriotism: Edwards only meant to suggest that small events were microcosms

[28] *Ibid.,* I, 516.

of great events, that an insignificant town might become the scene for a decisive transformation, that an obscure pastor might be the spokesman for a historic turning point. *The History of the Work of Redemption* makes no special claims for New England, for Northampton, or for Edwards; it claims only for all of these their rightful share in the divine drama.[29]

If Edwards had been an ordinary Congregationalist pastor, his history would be remarkable only for its range and its style: its underlying philosophy offers no surprises. But Edwards was a brilliant scholar, a gifted student of science, a deft dialectician; he read as widely as Cotton Mather and to greater profit; he was open to the most abstruse and most advanced works of philosophy; he was among the first in the New England colonies to study Locke and appreciate Newton. His mind was the opposite of reactionary or fundamentalist. Yet his history was both. Such apparent contradictions are a sign of something extraordinary; with Jonathan Edwards, they are the mark of tragedy.

II

When we speak of Jonathan Edwards, we are bound to speak of tragedy—perhaps all too easily. Certainly his philosophy was not tragic: it was Calvinist. Edwards was aware of man's limits and limitations, of man's futile striving, his anguish and his defeats, and these are prominent themes in authentic tragedy. But they are not of its essence. The tragic situation arises when a man of stature produces, through his actions, great conflict and great suffering. The conflict may be between the imperious urge of passion and the lucid restraint of reason, between two high but irreconcilable duties, between a corrupt society and an honorable innocent individual. However flawed he may be, the tragic hero must be neither villainous nor mediocre, and if he fails, as he is likely to, he must fail nobly, affirming the essential dignity, the essential auton-

---

[29] See *ibid.*, I, 468–470. This (as one of my listeners correctly pointed out) does not mean that Edwards was wholly immune to local pride—he was not. But his conviction that he, and New England, had a special place in the providential scheme was at best—or at worst—expressed only on rare occasions.

omy, of his human estate. Even if God, or a god, enters the tragic action, the human hero remains the hero. But Edwards set man's historical situation into a supernatural frame: man is helpless in the hands of God, incapable of resisting the influx of grace or the decree of condemnation. The Calvinist drama—it is worth saying once again—is wholly predestined: its resolution—eternal salvation or eternal damnation—is unaffected by the actions of men, and takes place not in this world but in the next. That is why Calvinism, like other Christian philosophies, but far more than they, is alien to tragedy.

But while Calvinism is not a tragic system, Calvinists may become tragic heroes, and Jonathan Edwards was the greatest tragic hero—I suspect, the only tragic hero—that American Calvinism produced. Edwards' stature was commanding, his fate inevitable; his failure evokes both pity and admiration. His heritage and his spiritual travail had nothing unusual about them: other sons of Congregationalist pastors followed their fathers into the ministry, other Congregationalist pastors endured an invincible sense of their vileness interspersed with moments of euphoric participation in Christ. But with Jonathan Edwards, such commonplace experiences rose to a high pitch of intensity: he was more intelligent—much more intelligent—than the others, suffered more poignantly—or at least more articulately—than they, probed the meaning of Puritanism more persistently than anyone. As a young man, he put down a series of resolutions, and one of them read, *"Resolved,* To live with all my might, while I do live."[30] His whole life was a commentary on this trite, laconic, fervent, totally honest declaration.

What made Edwards a tragic hero was this ruthlessly intelligent search for the meaning of Puritanism, pursued without regard to the cost. That terrible time in 1750, when his congregation dismissed him, was prefigured in all Edwards had thought and written since he entered Yale in 1716, a precocious young man of thirteen. From the beginning, he had loved God, and taken God's sovereignty seriously. He studied Newton and Locke, with hungry appetite, as he studied theology and apologetics, for the sake of

[30] *Resolutions, Works,* I, 4.

God: "More convinced than ever of the usefulness of free, religious conversation," he wrote into his diary in 1724, deliberately
merging an inferior with a superior sphere of inquiry. "I find by
conversing on Natural Philosophy, that I gain knowledge abundantly faster, and see the reasons of things much more clearly than
in private study: wherefore, earnestly to seek, at all times, for
religious conversation."[31] He was never the self-sufficient philosopher, always the strenuous servant of a higher power; he was
aware, he wrote, that he was "unable to do anything without
God." And, aware of that, he resolved with characteristic energy,
"To endeavour to obtain for myself as much happiness, in the
other world, as I possibly can, with all the power, might, vigour,
and vehemence, yea violence, I am capable of, or can bring myself
to exert, in any way that can be thought of."[32] This devout
violence marks all his work, even the most scholarly, and it led
inescapably to that day, July 1, 1750, when Edwards preached
his farewell sermon to a congregation that had voted to do without
him—without *him,* Jonathan Edwards, the grandson and successor
of Solomon Stoddard, who had for many years ruled western
Massachusetts, they said, like a Protestant Pope.

It was an inescapable day because Jonathan Edwards insisted
on rescuing the essence of the Puritan faith, on clarifying it,
defending it, and preaching it to an age that did not wish to listen.
Apologists for Edwards have made light of his most notorious
performance, the Enfield sermon of 1741; at Enfield, Edwards had
sent his hearers into fits of moaning, weeping, and lamentations by
portraying man, with horrible specificity, as a sinner in the hands
of an angry God, held over the flaming pit of hell by a thin thread,
like a spider or other loathsome insect. It is true that this was not
all of Edwards. He was as much the scholar and the polemicist as
he was the fisher of souls. And often, he preached not hellfire for
the damned but, with lyrical conviction, blissful peace for the
saved. His doctrine of God satisfied his need to humble himself, to

---

[31] *Diary,* February 6, 1724, *Works,* I, 12.
[32] *Resolution* No. 22, not in *Works;* printed in Clarence H. Faust and
Thomas H. Johnson, eds., *Jonathan Edwards, Representative Selections*
(New York, 1935), p. 39.

feel himself a vile worm before pure and ineffable Power, but it also satisfied his vigorous aesthetic appetite: his conviction of God's sovereignty, he said, was a "delightful conviction" which appeared to him "very often" as "exceeding pleasant, bright, and sweet."[33] That, after all, we know, was a central theme in his projected history of redemption: it would display God's design as "most beautiful and entertaining," musical in its "admirable contexture and harmony."[34] All this is true. But to minimize the importance, and explain away the doctrine, of the Enfield sermon is to do Edwards a dubious favor; it is to make him inoffensive by emasculating him. Edwards did not want to be inoffensive. God was omnipotent, God was angry, man was wholly lost without God: these were the pillars sustaining the structure of Edwards' theology. To dissolve them into metaphors or disguise them with quibbles and qualifications would be to play Satan's game.

The central importance of these teachings to Edwards is plain: he reiterated them often enough. He reminded himself of them over and over again in his resolutions and his private notebooks. He expounded them in Boston, in 1731, in a sermon reminding his hearers that God should be glorified in his work of redemption, and that man greatly depended on the Lord; the sermon was, significantly, Edwards' first public success.[35] He insisted upon them in his major writings, his psychological, apologetic, and metaphysical treatises: appropriately, his last book, *The Great Christian Doctrine of Original Sin Defended,* which was in the press when he died, was a refusal to make theology palatable or pretty. And he drew the last consequences of his teachings, bluntly and fatally, for his own congregation: for years, Edwards had followed his grandfather's practice of admitting to communion all who made their profession of faith, and who deserved admission by a sober walk of life. But then, in the 1740's, after the fervor of the Great Awakening, which seemed to promise an enlargement of

---

[33] *Personal Narrative, Works,* I, 15.

[34] See above, p. 233.

[35] The importance of this sermon has often been singled out, notably by Herbert W. Schneider, *The Puritan Mind* (New York, 1930), pp. 103–104, and Perry Miller, *Jonathan Edwards* (New York, 1949), pp. 3–40.

the churches with pure, converted new members, Edwards changed his mind; gradually, first obliquely and privately, then openly, he sought to restore the primitive Puritan practice of admitting only visible saints, to revive the religious aristocracy of the heroic age of Bradford and Winthrop. Reluctantly but, once certain, without hesitation, Edwards contradicted Solomon Stoddard, and reversed his own practice. It was folly, and Edwards, knowing it was folly, preached it, convinced that he must testify to the truth as he had come to see it. He was asking his Puritan congregation to accept the burden of its Puritan past, and it wrecked his career.

III

Edwards' tragedy was personal, but it was not wholly private. It participated in, and, with its poignant protagonist, illuminates a larger tragedy: the failure of the Puritan errand in America. From the days of Bradford and Winthrop down to Edwards' day, and with ever increasing acuteness, the American Puritans faced a dilemma from which there was no escape, the dilemma that besets all Utopians unfortunate enough to secure power. While the welcome confusions and complexities of their life often saved them from the agony of making clear-cut and irrevocable decisions, the American Puritans had at bottom two choices, and both threatened them with disastrous consequences. They could continue to idealize, and seek to perpetuate, the temper of the Founding Fathers; or they could try to adapt themselves to drastic changes in political, economic, and intellectual conditions. Rigid, they would turn themselves into anachronisms; flexible, they would betray their Puritanism.

This dilemma arose only because the Puritans made such high demands on themselves. Puritan theology was crisis theology, but no civilization—especially no prosperous civilization—can long sustain the tension of continuous crisis. As the founders died, as the threats of starvation and disease, treacherous Indians and persecuting Anglicans receded, the routine of living and of doing business invaded the noble dream of a religious refuge set apart from the world as a hiding place and a model. The world, this

world, loomed larger than it should for a pilgrim, whose true home
is heaven. The great crusade collapsed while, and largely because,
New England flourished.

It was a cruel and ironic fate. The American Puritans had
suffered the trauma of separation from a cherished landscape; the
first generation above all suffered in addition from the guilt of their
disobedience: no amount of political sophistry or theological
dialectic could wholly numb their awareness that they had defied,
and were continuing to defy, established authorities in church and
state. That is why the early American Puritans were even more
rigid, even more conservative, than other Puritans in easier circumstances; that is why they clung to a few certainties that time
could not touch, above all to their ideal of a religious community
that was nothing more than a large family. The social thought of
the early Puritans in America was essentially the Puritan family
ideal—hierarchical, disciplinarian, homogeneous, soberly affectionate and earnestly dedicated to a religious purpose—projected
upon society as a whole. But later generations discovered that the
sheer passage of time, and new circumstances, made this social
ideal unenforceable, reactionary, irrelevant. Thus the American
Puritans lost mastery over their society as they lost control over
their families.

This loss was troublesome enough, but the Puritan dilemma lay
deeper still, concealed in the very nature of Puritan piety. Like
other Christian churches, Puritans had many grounds for their
belief, offered many reasons for its validity. They cared nothing for
the sanctity of tradition, the authority of priesthood, or the miraculous efficacy of ritual—these superstitious innovations they left to
the Papists. Instead, they appealed to the authority of a sacred
book, the ineffable power of the divine person, the mystical certainty induced by private experience. As dialecticians and lovers of
learning, they also appealed to the rational persuasions of logic,
and to the scientific and aesthetic coherence of the natural order,
but these were inferior, if important and satisfying arguments.
They recognized man as a rational creature, and admired him as
made in God's image, but they emphasized his sin, his estrangement from his divine father, and the dimming of his reason after

the Fall. In consequence, they could be deft logicians, cultivated theologians, and competent scientists: the glacial age of American Puritanism was not an age of obscurantism, Philistinism, or superstition. But their emphasis on the divine sovereignty and on human depravity led them to confine the new philosophy—the physics of Newton and the epistemology of Locke—to a clearly marked and distinctly subordinate sphere. The Arminians, for their part, with their optimistic view of human nature, their prideful account of the capacity of human reason to penetrate the meaning of the universe, could adopt the new philosophy with little loss of theological rigor. A good Arminian could be a good Newtonian with no inner stress. But the Puritans could not permit the scientific world view to penetrate their style of thinking, although they could utilize the practical results of science to heal the sick, satisfy natural curiosity, or confirm God's glorious skill. Increasingly as time went on, there were modern Christians among the New England Congregationalists—Jonathan Edwards deplored their influence in his sermons on the Work of Redemption—but these preachers, men like Charles Chauncy or Jonathan Mayhew, paid a price for their modernity: they surrendered the citadel of their Puritan faith.

The burden of Edwards' work was a protest against this surrender. He was anything but an obscurantist, and, in his feverish intellectual excitement over the ideas of Newton and Locke, he sought to express the old religion in new ways. But the results were, as they had to be, pathetic: Jonathan Edwards philosophized in a cage that his fathers had built and that he unwittingly reinforced. The religious implications of Locke's sensationalist philosophy were inescapable, and they were drawn with surprising unanimity by Locke himself, by Locke's many followers, and by his detractors: revelation, to be true revelation, can be nothing more than an extension of reason; nearly all religious doctrine is either redundant or superstitious. For Locke, the only dogma a Christian need believe—the only dogma he can believe—is that Christ is the Messiah. But Edwards went right on accepting the testimony of Scriptures as literally true, accepting the predictions of the Apocalypse as authoritative history. He read Locke in careful isolation: Locke's psychology gave him useful material for understanding the quality of religious emotion, but little else.

Edwards' reading of Newton was equally parochial. It led him into some ingenious speculations about the nature of the physical universe and the future of mankind. Newton himself, it is true, was not a Newtonian all the time; unlike Locke, he left it to others to explicate, and to complete, his system; unlike Locke, he found pleasure in delving into biblical chronology and chiliastic prophecies. But, whatever Newton's private religious explorations—and they remain a matter of heated controversy—the ultimate religious direction of Newton's system was away from fundamentalism, away from chiliasm—away, in a word, from Puritanism—toward rationalism, Unitarianism, simple Theism. The physical universe of Edwards was not the physical universe of Newton: it was a universe created in six days, filled with angels and devils, with a heaven and a hell, a universe in the hands, and at the mercy, of an angry God. Edwards did not become a Puritan, or remain a Puritan, as a result of his philosophical and scientific inquiries; he exploited modern ideas and modern rhetoric to confirm religious convictions he had held all his life, and accepted on other grounds.

The complete incompatibility of Edwards' system of ideas with the new world of enlightened philosophy has been obscured by Edwards' vocabulary. It is not that he adopted modish words for modish purposes; but he delighted in intellectual investigation, his ear was sensitive, and his curiosity acute. Hence he felt the power of the new imagery and the new language, and freely used them in his writings. He appealed to "history, observation, and experience," and claimed, as a good empiricist, to bow to fact. But the history he cited was the infallible Scriptures; the observations he noted are the observations of biblical characters or contemporary Christians in a state of religious trance; the experience he valued was the revelation that gives man knowledge of God. Edwards' facts are of the same order.[36] The *Essay concerning Human Understanding* and the *Principia Mathematica* may have been important to him, the Pentateuch and the book of Revelation were indispensable. "A great Divine," Ezra Stiles justly called Edwards, "a good linguist" and "a good Scholar," thoroughly versed in "the

[36] I owe this illustration to Vincent Tomas' critique of Perry Miller's *Jonathan Edwards;* see "The Modernity of Jonathan Edwards," *New England Quarterly,* XXV (1952), 60–84, esp. 75–82.

Logic of Ramus and Burgersdisius, & the philosophy of Wende-
line," but not in "the Mathematics & the Ratiocina of the Newtonian Philosophy."[37]
Edwards' spiritual isolation was exacerbated by his physical
isolation.[38] In Europe, the ideas of Newton and Locke called
forth vigorous debate; they were tested and extended. The followers of Newton and Locke, goaded by their critics, gradually
constructed an enlightened intellectual system of great power and
lasting influence. Edwards had no such advantages; when he
corresponded with Europeans, it was mainly with like-minded
clerics; when he read—and he read deeply and voraciously—he
read mainly books that would feed his Puritan convictions, or
books that he thought he needed to refute. The outside world
existed mainly to supply him with echoes. Far from being the first
modern American, therefore, he was the last medieval American—
at least among the intellectuals.

IV

Every tragedy has its irony, and the tragedy of Jonathan Edwards
is no exception. The world, Edwards wrote in his sermons on the
redemption, would soon come to an end; the time of the millennium and the apocalypse was not far away. But the world, it
seemed, went on, more worldly than ever before. Americans, to be
sure, continued to worship the old God, and even advanced
clergymen welcomed the evangelical invasion of Whitefield—at
least for a while. But the old God wore new, almost unrecogniz-
able guises; his yoke was easy, and his burden light. And Americans turned to new guides in the writing of history, discarding
Providence, and seeking the causes of events within the natural

[37] Diary entry, May 24, 1779; "Presidents of Colleges with whom I have
been personally acquainted." Quoted in Ola Elizabeth Winslow, *Jonathan
Edwards, 1703–1758: A Biography* (1940; reprinted 1961), p. 337.

[38] See Edwards' letter to Edward Wigglesworth, the liberal professor of
divinity at Harvard, written in 1757: "I can't assign any particular acquaintance as my warrant for troubling you with these lines; not being one of
them that have been favored with opportunities for such an advantage."
Quoted in Johnson, "Edwards' Background of Reading," p. 196.

realm. The best history the Puritans could write was written by Thomas Prince, a diligent compiler, a discriminating book collector, a patient chronicler, but little more. It was to be other historians, rationalists like Governor Thomas Hutchinson, who were to rejoin the main stream of the European intellect. When Edwards' *History of the Work of Redemption* was finally published in 1774, the *Monthly Review* spoke for prevailing opinion, both in Old England and New, in a contemptuous notice. Far from being new, the reviewer noted, the book was "a long, laboured, dull, confused rhapsody," the revival of a medieval method that should have been buried long since: "It is merely an attempt to revive the old mystical divinity that distracted the last age with pious conundrums: and which, having, long ago, emigrated to America, we have no reason to wish should ever be imported back again." The book is visionary, presumptuous, reactionary, extravagant, a species of "pious nonsense" spouted by a "poor departed enthusiast."[39] There could be no question: the world went on. Yet, in an ironic sense, Edwards' chiliastic prediction was fulfilled, and in his lifetime. Only it was Jonathan Edwards' world, and with it the world of Puritanism, that came to an end.

[39] *The Monthly Review; or, Literary Journal,* LII (January to June, 1775), 117–120.

✪

After the Surprising Conversions

September twenty-second, Sir: today
I answer. In the latter part of May,
Hard on our Lord's Ascension, it began
To be more sensible. A gentleman
Of more than common understanding, strict
In morals, pious in behavior, kicked
Against our goad. A man of some renown,
An useful, honored person in the town,
He came of melancholy parents; prone
To secret spells, for years they kept alone—
His uncle, I believe, was killed of it:
Good people, but of too much or little wit.
I preached one Sabbath on a text from Kings;
He showed concernment for his soul. Some things
In his experience were hopeful. He
Would sit and watch the wind knocking a tree
And praise this countryside our Lord has made.
Once when a poor man's heifer died, he laid
A shilling on the doorsill; though a thirst
For loving shook him like a snake, he durst
Not entertain much hope of his estate
In heaven. Once we saw him sitting late
Behind his attic window by a light

That guttered on his Bible; through that night
He meditated terror, and he seemed
Beyond advice or reason, for he dreamed
That he was called to trumpet Judgment Day
To Concord. In the latter part of May
He cut his throat. And though the coroner
Judged him delirious, soon a noisome stir
Palsied our village. At Jehovah's nod
Satan seemed more let loose amongst us: God
Abandoned us to Satan, and he pressed
Us hard, until we thought we could not rest
Till we had done with life. Content was gone.
All the good work was quashed. We were undone.
The breath of God had carried out a planned
And sensible withdrawal from this land;
The multitude, once unconcerned with doubt,
Once neither callous, curious nor devout,
Jumped at broad noon, as though some peddler groaned
At it in its familiar twang: "My friend,
Cut your own throat. Cut your own throat. Now! Now!"
September twenty-second, Sir, the bough
Cracks with the unpicked apples, and at dawn
The small-mouth bass breaks water, gorged with spawn.

Jonathan Edwards in
Western Massachusetts

Edwards' great millstone and rock
of hope has crumbled, but the square
white houses of his flock
stand in the open air,

out in the cold,
like sheep outside the fold.
Hope lives in doubt.
Faith is trying to do without

faith. In western Massachusetts,
I could almost feel the frontier
crack and disappear.
Edwards thought the world would end there.

We know how the world will end,
but where is paradise, each day farther
from the Pilgrim's blues for England
and the Promised Land.

Was it some country house
that seemed as if it were
Whitehall, if the Lord were there?
so nobly did he live.

Gardens designed
that the breath of flowers in the wind,
or crushed underfoot,
came and went like warbling music?

Bacon's great oak grove
he refused to sell,
when he fell,
saying, "Why should I sell my feathers?"

Ah paradise! Edwards,
I would be afraid
to meet you there as a shade.
We move in different circles.

As a boy, you built a booth
in a swamp for prayer;
lying on your back,
you saw the spiders fly,

basking at their ease,
swimming from tree to tree—

so high, they seemed tacked to the sky.
You knew they would die.

Poor country Berkeley at Yale,
you saw the world was soul,
the soul of God! The soul
of Sarah Pierrepont!

So filled with delight in the Great Being,
she hardly cared for anything—
walking the fields, sweetly singing,
conversing with some one invisible.

Then God's love shone in sun, moon and stars,
on earth, in the waters,
in the air, in the loose winds,
which used to greatly fix your mind.

Often she saw you come home from a ride
or a walk, your coat dotted with thoughts
you had pinned there
on slips of paper.

You gave
her Pompey, a Negro slave,
and eleven children.
Yet people were spiders

in your moment of glory,
at the Great Awakening—"Alas, how many
in this very meeting house are more than likely
to remember my discourse in hell!"

The meeting house remembered!
You stood on stilts in the air,
but you fell from your parish.
"All rising is by a winding stair."

On my pilgrimage to Northampton,
I found no relic,
except the round slice of an oak
you are said to have planted.

It was flesh-colored, new,
and a common piece of kindling,
only fit for burning.
You too must have been green once.

White wig and black coat,
all cut from one cloth,
and designed
like your mind!

I love you faded,
old, exiled and afraid
to leave your last flock, a dozen
Houssatonic Indian children;

afraid to leave
all your writing, writing, writing,
denying the Freedom of the Will.
You were afraid to be president

of Princeton, and wrote:
"My deffects are well known;
I have a constitution
peculiarly unhappy:

flaccid solids,
vapid, sizzy, scarse fluids,
causing a childish weakness,
a low tide of spirits.

I am contemptible,
stiff and dull.

Why should I leave behind
my delight and entertainment,
those studies
that have swallowed up my mind?"

Selected Bibliography

WORKS BY JONATHAN EDWARDS:

The best edition of Edwards' complete works (begun under the general editorship of Perry Miller) is now in progress at the Yale University Press. At this writing, the following have been published: Edwards' *Strict Enquiry into . . . Freedom of the Will*, edited by Paul Ramsey; *Treatise concerning Religious Affections*, edited by John E. Smith; and *Images or Shadows of Divine Things*, edited by Perry Miller. The best edition (reprinted above) of Edwards' "Personal Narrative" is in Samuel Hopkins, *The Life and Character of the Late Reverend Mr. Jonathan Edwards* (Boston, 1765). Pending the Yale edition, the best edition of Edwards' "Notes on the Mind" is that of Leon Howard, in *"The Mind" of Jonathan Edwards: A Reconstructed Text* (Berkeley, 1963). In all these editions the editorial commentary is also extremely valuable. Although textually less reliable, the volume edited by Clarence Faust and Thomas H. Johnson, *Jonathan Edwards: Representative Selections* (New York, 1935; reissued, 1962) is the most convenient anthology of Edwards' writings.

The most important individual works of Edwards are the following (in chronological order): "Of Insects," "Of Being," "Notes on the Mind," *God Glorified in the Work of Redemption by the Greatness of Man's Dependence upon Him in the Whole of It* (1731); *A Divine and Supernatural Light, Immediately Imparted to the Soul by the Spirit of God, Shown to be both a Scriptural, and a Rational Doctrine* (1734); *A Faithful Narrative of the Surprising Work of God in the Conversion of Many Hundred Souls in Northampton, and the*

Neighboring Towns and Villages (1737); *Personal Narrative* (written 1739?); *The Distinguishing Marks of a Work of the Spirit of God* (1741); *Sinners in the Hands of an Angry God* (1741); *Some Thoughts concerning the Present Revival of Religion in New England* (1742); *A Treatise concerning Religious Affections* (1746); *An Account of the Life of the Late Reverend Mr. David Brainerd* (1749); *A Careful and Strict Enquiry into the Modern Prevailing Notions of that Freedom of Will which is supposed to be Essential to Moral Agency, Vertue and Vice, Reward and Punishment, Praise and Blame* (1754); *The Great Christian Doctrine of Original Sin Defended* (1758); "The Nature of True Virtue" and "Concerning the End for Which God Created the World" (written 1755; published in 1765 as *Two Dissertations*).

BIOGRAPHY AND CRITICISM:

The best biographies are those by Samuel Hopkins (Boston, 1765; reprinted above), Henry Bamford Parkes (New York, 1930), and Ola E. Winslow (New York, 1940). The best intellectual biography, and perhaps the most important single book on Edwards, is Perry Miller, *Jonathan Edwards* (New York, 1949); a brief, less difficult explication is Edward H. Davidson, *Jonathan Edwards: The Narrative of a Puritan Mind* (Cambridge, Mass., 1966). For the background on church membership in Congregationalism, the most useful book is Edmund S. Morgan, *Visible Saints: the History of a Puritan Idea* (New York, 1963). On Edwards' influence in American thought, three major statements deserve especial notice here: Joseph Haroutunian, *Piety versus Moralism: The Passing of the New England Theology* (New York, 1932); Perry Miller, "Edwards to Emerson," in *Errand into the Wilderness* (New York, 1956); and Alan Heimert, *Religion and the American Mind: From the Great Awakening to the Revolution* (Cambridge, Mass., 1966), which lays especial stress on the political differences between Calvinists and religious liberals. For a general study of the revival, see Edwin Gaustad, *The Great Awakening in New England* (Chicago, 1957). Among numerous literary studies one of the most valuable is the essay on Edwards' "Personal Narrative" in Daniel B. Shea, *Spiritual Autobiography in Early America* (Princeton, 1968). A good recent analysis of Edwards' theology is Douglas Elwood, *The Philosophical Theology of Jonathan Edwards* (New York, 1960), and another, emphasizing faith as the central concept in Edwards' theology is Conrad Cherry, *The Theology of Jonathan Edwards: A Reappraisal* (Garden City, N.Y., 1966).

This Profile has emphasized admiring and sympathetic studies of Edwards. Interesting arguments in support of Peter Gay's skeptical conclusions may be found in Vernon Louis Parrington, *The Colonial Mind* (1926); Vincent Tomas, "The Modernity of Jonathan Edwards," *New England Quarterly,* XXV (1952), 60–84—more critical of Perry Miller's method than of Edwards himself—and Alfred O. Aldridge, *Jonathan Edwards* (New York, 1964). Richard L. Bushman has published two excellent psychoanalytic studies of Edwards: "Jonathan Edwards and Puritan Consciousness," *Journal for the Scientific Study of Religion,* V (Fall 1966), 383–396; and "Jonathan Edwards as a Great Man," *Soundings, An Interdisciplinary Journal,* LII (Spring 1969), 15–46.

Contributors

JAMES CARSE teaches at New York University's Department of the History and Literature of Religion. He is the author of *Jonathan Edwards & the Visibility of God* and the forthcoming book *The Fourth Believer*.

PETER GAY is Professor of Comparative European Intellectual History at Yale. He has written with great distinction about European intellectual history—especially the eighteenth century—and won the National Book Award with *The Enlightenment*. His most recent book is *Weimar Culture: The Outsider as Insider*.

SAMUEL HOPKINS (1721–1803) was a student, and then a friend, of Jonathan Edwards, and he knew Edwards especially well during the first fifteen years of his pastorate at Housatonick (now Great Barrington), Massachusetts. Besides the life of Edwards, Hopkins wrote a number of influential theological works which gave him a prominent place in post-Edwardsean controversies among Calvinists and between Calvinists and their opponents. Just five years after publishing his life of Edwards, he was dismissed from his church in a theological disagreement, and he moved to Newport, Rhode Island.

ROBERT LOWELL, who now serves as Ralph Waldo Emerson Lecturer on English Literature at Harvard, has won numerous prizes (American Academy of Arts and Letters, Pulitzer, National Book Award, Bollingen) with his volumes of poetry. Much of his best work has studied and celebrated, even as it strengthened, the New England tradition.

PERRY MILLER (1905–1963) began at the University of Chicago the work that eventually distinguished him as the leading literary and intellectual historian of New England. His most important books, besides the volume on Edwards, are *Orthodoxy in Massachusetts, The New England Mind: The Seventeenth Century, The New England Mind: From Colony to Province,* and *Errand into the Wilderness.* He spent his entire teaching career at Harvard University, where he was Cabot Professor of American Literature. He was also a member of the Institute for Advanced Study at Princeton (1953–1954).

HENRY BAMFORD PARKES has served on the faculty of New York University since 1930, the year after he received a Ph.D. from the University of Michigan. Educated before then in his native England, he has specialized in American intellectual history. Besides his book on Edwards, his most important works include *The American Experience* and *Gods and Men.*

JOHN E. SMITH, Professor of Philosophy at Yale, has been chairman of the Philosophy Department there and has served as Dudleian lecturer at Harvard (1960). Trained both in philosophy (Ph.D., Columbia) and theology (B.D., Union Theological Seminary), he has written *Reason and God* and *The Spirit of American Philosophy.*

WILLISTON WALKER (1860–1922) was a prominent church historian who made a specialty of New England Congregationalism. He taught church history and American history at Bryn Mawr, Hartford Theological Seminary (where he had been a student), and Yale (where he was Titus Street Professor of Ecclesiastical History from 1901 to 1922). Besides *Ten New England Leaders,*

For
Mayor Sheila,
Happy Birthday
Happy Eatings
Happy Always
with much love,
Charlotte
February 1993

Shepherd's Garden Publishing
Felton, California

RECIPES FROM A KITCHEN GARDEN

VOLUME ONE

By Renee Shepherd

Library of Congress catalog card number: 87-090646
ISBN number: 0-9618856-0-2

Published by:
Shepherd's Garden Publishing
7389 West Zayante Road
Felton, CA 95018
(408) 335-5400

Illustrations by Mimi Osborne
Book design by Linda Lane
Typeset in Bembo by Rock & Jones, Oakland, Calif.

First edition 1987
Second edition 1990
Third edition 1991

Printed in the United States of America

To My Mother

With love and gratitude
for her support, good humor
and good cooking.

Acknowledgments

Heartfelt thanks to my longtime friend and manuscript typist, Dottie Hollinger, who has cheerfully translated my handwritten scrawl through the years of my Ph.D. thesis, six seasons of catalog copy and now this cookbook. Dottie's kindness and calm efficiency have enabled me to pull projects together against improbable deadlines.

Mimi Osborne's superb illustrations have become part and parcel of whatever muses I follow in writing. Her talents and extensive knowledge of culinary and gardening subjects make our relationship pure pleasure.

Linda Lane's sensitive approach to design provides the critical underpinnings to all our joint projects and her patience and humor have been central in seeing them to completion.

As always, I have relied heavily upon my wonderful sister, Sue Shecket, for creative ideas, encouragement, good cheer and her expert editing and proofing skills.

Jesse Cool, skilled chef/owner of the Menlo Park, California, restaurants Late for the Train and Flea St. Cafe, is the source of our best baby vegetable recipes for the catalog and I am glad to share them here with my sincere appreciation for her generosity.

Many thanks to my husband Michael for his patience and understanding on the many evenings and weekends we didn't spend together while this book was finished. He and Al Raboff were also cheerful guinea pigs at our many recipe-tasting sessions.

Accomplished author and friend Ros Creasy gave me much needed advice and support and Jennifer Runo kept the office fires burning bright. Finally, thank you to the many wonderful customers of Shepherd's Garden Seeds whose enthusiasm inspires this cookbook.

Contents

DEAR FRIENDS

My kitchen garden is a classic example of the chicken-and-egg dilemma. I really can't say if I began gardening to have the freshest, best-tasting vegetables for cooking, or if I became more interested in cooking once we had a garden of beautiful and abundant produce. Probably both are true because growing fresh vegetables and herbs finds its natural completion in preparing them well.

Over the last few years here in California, there has been a new emphasis on the pleasures of dishes that feature fresh, local vegetables and herbs. Many fine restaurants have produce grown for them by small market gardeners. But it is really the home gardener whose garden can consistently provide the full-flavored fresh ingredients necessary for this healthy and appetizing style of cooking and eating. Put in another way, in an age of supermarkets and square tomatoes, we must become our own greengrocers!

FROM GARDEN TO KITCHEN

Our catalog seed company features vegetable, herb and edible-flower seeds selected and bred for tenderness and flavor, especially fine European varieties of familiar garden favorites as well as the best domestic seeds. To help our customers enjoy what they grow, the catalog also includes as many good recipes as we can fit in. I have also found that while it is one thing to prepare a store-bought vegetable three or four times a month, it is quite another challenge finding interesting ways to use steady daily harvests of green beans or squash or tomatoes. While having an abundance of fresh basil is a luxury, after weeks of pesto sauce every basil lover appreciates new suggestions for ways to enjoy it throughout the season and beyond. This book is a collection of our recipes, designed to give both the cooking gardener and the gardening cook an array of satisfying ways of using fresh-picked, first-rate vegetables and herbs to produce good food.

These recipes can be made in a reasonable amount of time by busy cooks. We have ruled out exotic or hard-to-find ingredients beyond the kitchen garden's bounty. Our recipes are not novel or extreme, but rely on a simplicity of style that includes elegance, flavor and presentation.

HOW OUR GARDEN GROWS

Our kitchen garden is a large French Intensive organic garden. We currently have 24 raised beds, each about 20–25 feet long and 3 feet wide (so we can easily reach to the middle of any bed to tend the plants). We also garden

in fifteen large 20-inch patio pots so we can understand the needs and desires of urban patio gardeners. Our garden serves two purposes. It is a demonstration garden for visitors who come to look at and sample the varieties currently offered in our seed catalog. It also serves as one of our trial gardens for a small portion of our two-year evaluations of new varieties.

One section of the demonstration garden is always devoted to our specialty basils since everyone who comes by looks forward to seeing and tasting and smelling them. I love the colors, textures and flavors of a wide variety of salad plants, so there are usually nine or ten small plantings of different lettuces and other salads in spring and fall and five or six heat-tolerant varieties in summer. In the trial garden, we always have a section dedicated to our search for new, flavorful and early-bearing tomatoes; this season the tomato beds are filled with plants whose seeds came with high promise from Italy, England, France and Japan, as well as several American heirloom favorites to taste and compare. An assortment of pretty edible flowers rounds out the corners of the beds.

COOKING PARTNERS

The result of all this abundance is a constant supply of vegetables and herbs coming to the kitchen, perfectly ripe and ready to use. Each spring and summer as the harvests peak, we test and refine new recipes to share in our catalog and in the specialty recipe brochures we offer with our seeds. This book represents our favorite recipes, developed in large part with the collaborative skills of the two talented cooks I work with each season and would like to introduce here.

Frances Raboff is an artist who combines her considerable talents for painting and sculpture with a lively interest in cooking. While living in Los Angeles she co-authored several cookbooks and now she regularly teaches a wide variety of cooking classes at our local community college. Fran and I regularly prepare dishes in her wonderful kitchen, a light, airy and perfectly set up test kitchen located at her hillside home. Fran's fine library of cookbooks and reference materials, her encyclopedic knowledge of classic technique and inventive skill in combining flavors and textures have been invaluable. In our cooking sessions we usually make seven to ten dishes and invite our husbands and friends to try them with us. Recipes with initial approval are tested and redefined again for publication. Fran has been particularly instrumental in helping develop the edible flower recipes, an area with few traditional recipe resources.

Our other source of cooking expertise comes from Bobbie Greenlaw. Bobbie grows a huge and very successful kitchen garden that supplies her family's handsome and capacious kitchen. Besides cooking, Bobbie is an avid

bike tourer and she travels widely. An alumna of La Varenne Cooking School, Bobbie taught cooking classes in her own school for years and now does food consulting and design for magazines in the San Francisco Bay area. I met her first as a seed customer and we have become fast friends. Her years of experience have made her a confident and expert cook with a well–developed taste memory. Often I simply ask her for a good recipe for a specific vegetable or herb and she always suggests three or four excellent choices developed over the course of her career in the professional food world.

FINALLY ...

Serendipity has also presented itself with wonderful frequency in the shape of the fine recipes we receive from the many accomplished cooks who are our customers and from chefs whose restaurant gardens use our seeds. We invite readers to continue to share their favorite recipes with us.

I have served all the dishes on these pages to my family and friends frequently and with satisfaction, and hope you will enjoy them as much as we have. I began writing my catalog as a way to share my own enthusiasm for the outer and inner joys of growing and cooking from the garden and I am delighted to share these recipes as a happy extension of these passions.

With warmest regards,

Renee Shepherd

VEGETABLES

BEANS

JANICE'S PICKLED BASIL BEANS

These crispy basil-scented beans are a fine appetizer, pleasing appetites without spoiling them. They make a satisfying between-meal nibble and are one of our favorite ways to utilize a bean harvest.

> **3 to 4 pounds fresh-picked green snap beans, rinsed**
> **5 cups mild white vinegar**
> **5 cups water (not softened water)**
> **1 tablespoon sugar**
> **¼ cup pickling salt**

> **FOR EACH JAR:**
> **4 peppercorns**
> **2 garlic cloves, peeled**
> **4 to 6 large fresh basil leaves**

Wash 8 pint or 4 quart canning jars with hot soapy water and rinse, or run them through the dishwasher.

Trim the ends of the beans. Bring to a boil the vinegar, water, sugar and salt.

In the bottom of each jar, put the peppercorns, garlic cloves and basil leaves, then pack them with beans, leaving ½ inch headspace. Fill the jars with the hot brine, leaving ½ inch. Wipe the jar rims and seal. Process 15 minutes in a boiling water bath (20 minutes for quarts). Wait about 4 weeks before opening to let the flavors blend and deepen.

Makes 8 pints or 4 quarts.

GREEN BEANS À L'ANGLAISE

This is how fine restaurants prepare fresh beans.

Take fresh-picked beans, a large pot of water, and 1 or 2 tablespoons of salt. (The salt sets the green color and you rinse it off in the cold running water.) Bring salted water to a rolling boil, put in fresh beans and cook until just tender-crisp. Drain beans into a colander and cool immediately under very cold running water. Drain on paper or kitchen towels. The beans will be a beautiful dark green. Use as is in salads, or reheat them thoroughly in some butter with fresh herbs just before serving.

Green Bean and Red Bell Pepper Vinaigrette

2 cups fresh green beans (cut and blanched)
2 red bell peppers (thinly sliced)
½ teaspoon chopped green onions
⅓ cup sherry wine vinegar
pinch sugar
2 tablespoons water
salt and pepper to taste
½ cup salad oil

Toss all the above ingredients together and chill one hour before serving to blend the flavors.

Serves 4.

Green Beans with Mushrooms

½ onion (finely chopped)
2 tablespoons butter
½ pound mushrooms, thickly sliced
1 pound green beans (washed and cut into 2-inch lengths)
1 cup chicken stock or bouillon
½ teaspoon paprika
¼ teaspoon dill
salt and pepper
½ cup sour cream

Brown the onions in the butter. Add the mushrooms and fry about 2 minutes, stirring occasionally. Remove from heat. Blanch the beans in salted water for about 30 seconds. Drain. Add the chicken stock to the mushrooms and onions. Bring to a boil. Add the paprika, dill, and salt and pepper to taste. Boil for 5 minutes. Add the green beans and sour cream. Simmer at a very low heat for 10 minutes and serve.

Serves 4.

Fresh Bean Salad Anglaise

1 cup each of yellow and green snap beans cooked à l'Anglaise (see page 15)
garnish: chopped parsley or chives

DRESSING:
6 small green onions, finely chopped
2 tablespoons tarragon vinegar (or your favorite herbed vinegar)
1 teaspoon salt
2 teaspoons dijon mustard
⅓ cup oil

Whisk together onions, vinegar, salt and mustard; add oil and whisk to blend well. Let dressing stand until ready to use. Put well-drained beans in a serving bowl. Just before serving the beans, stir dressing again and pour it over them. Toss lightly to blend. Sprinkle with chopped parsley or chives for a nice accent.

Serves 4.

Green Bean Pâté
with Basil

*This dish tastes sinfully rich, but it's not
in the least, so enjoy!*

**½ pound fresh green beans,
  trimmed
1 tablespoon vegetable oil
1 onion, coarsely chopped
3 hard-cooked eggs
3 tablespoons finely chopped
  fresh basil
1 teaspoon lemon rind
mayonnaise
seasoned salt and pepper
melba toast or crackers
garnish: nasturtium flowers**

Cook beans until tender by boiling
or steaming them. In a skillet, heat
oil; add onion and sauté until softened. Cool. In a food processor or
with a food chopper, process or
grind green beans, eggs, onions,
lemon rind and basil until roughly
puréed. Remove to a bowl; mix in
just enough mayonnaise to hold
mixture together. Stir in seasoned
salt and pepper to taste. Chill.
Garnish with whole nasturtium
blossoms. Serve with melba toast or
crackers.

Makes 2 cups.

Green Beans with Pecans

**1½ pounds snap beans, trimmed
1 tablespoon olive oil
2 tablespoons butter
¼ cup chopped scallions or
  shallots
¼ cup chopped fresh parsley
1 cup pecan pieces
salt
white pepper
optional: 1 or 2 teaspoons
  chopped fresh or ½ teaspoon
  dried summer savory**

Cook the beans until just tender.
Meanwhile, heat oil and butter in a
pan and sauté the shallots or scallions
until softened. Stir in the parsley
(and savory if used) and blend. Add
the beans and pecans, season with
salt and pepper—toss and serve.

Serves 6.

BEETS

DUTCH BEET SALAD

**6 large beets, peeled
1 bunch green onions, chopped
½ cup apple cider vinegar
2 tablespoons water
½ cup salad oil
pinch sugar
¼ teaspoon salt
¼ teaspoon black pepper**

Grate the fresh beets on the finest grater you have — preferably one used to grate lemon peel. If you are using a food processor, use the blade with the smallest holes. Place the grated beets in a bowl. Mix the remaining ingredients until blended and pour over the beets. Toss and marinate in refrigerator for several hours before serving. For an interesting variation substitute grated carrots and/or grated daikon radishes for one-third of the beets.

Serves 4 to 6.

BAKED BEETS

Once you have cooked red beets in this manner, you won't ever boil them again. In France they cook the beets before they come to market, and they are wonderful. Just pull up your beets, cut the tops back to about 3 inches, brush off most of the dirt and put the beets on aluminum foil on a cookie sheet. Bake in a 375° oven for approximately 1 hour — or until a fork pierces the beets easily. Remove from oven, cool, and remove the skins (and remaining tops). Now the beets can be prepared in any style — buttered, harvard, pickled, etc. We love them just simply buttered. The flavor after baking is intensified and delicious.

ROMANIAN SUMMER SOUP

For a hot summer day or evening. The soup is as flavorful as it is beautiful. For a change, try this with our golden beets. Serve chilled or at room temperature with thick slices of pumpernickel or fresh rye bread and butter.

- 6 medium-sized beets, including tops
- 2 medium-sized onions
- 8 cups chicken broth
- 1 cup sour cream
- 1 cup plain fresh yogurt
- 2 coarsely chopped, peeled cucumbers
- 1 bunch thinly sliced radishes
- 1 tablespoon lemon juice
- salt and pepper to taste
- 1 or 2 tablespoons fresh chopped dill leaf or 1 tablespoon dried

Peel the beets and cut into julienne strips. Wash and coarsely chop the beet greens and chop the onions. In a large pot, heat the chicken broth and add the beets, beet greens, and onions. Cook covered until the beets are tender, about 20 minutes. Remove from heat. Cool to room temperature, and then stir in the sour cream and yogurt. Add the chopped cucumber and radishes and the lemon juice. Correct seasoning, adding salt and pepper to taste. Serve in individual bowls with fresh dill leaf sprinkled on top.

Serves 8.

BEET BORSCHT

Refreshing, beautifully colored and especially good on a very hot day.

- 12 ounces cooked beets
- 12 ounces beef stock (or chicken)
- zest of 1 lemon (yellow part of lemon skin)
- juice of a lemon
- 3 or 4 tablespoons chopped fresh dill
- ½ teaspoon salt
- ¼ teaspoon black pepper
- 6 scallions, chopped
- 2 cups sour cream or one cup sour cream and one cup fresh plain yogurt
- garnish: chive blossoms, chopped chives

In blender or food processor combine beets with stock. Add lemon zest and juice, dill, salt, pepper and scallions. Mix until smooth, pour into a bowl and blend in the sour cream or sour cream and yogurt. Chill in the refrigerator until very cold. Taste for seasoning; it should be nice and lemony. Top each bowl with another spoonful of sour cream and the chopped chives, with their blossoms.

Serves 6.

BROCCOLI

BROCCOLI SALAD

2 heads of broccoli, cut into
   medium florets with 1-inch
   stems

DRESSING:
⅓ cup salad oil
2 tablespoons chopped sweet
   pickle or pickle relish
2 tablespoons fresh parsley
2 tablespoons chopped red or
   green pepper
2 tablespoons white wine vinegar
1 tablespoon chopped fresh
   chives
1 tablespoon fresh tarragon or
   1½ teaspoons dried
¾ teaspoon salt
¾ teaspoon sugar
½ clove garlic, crushed
pinch of cayenne pepper
garnishes: 1 chopped hard-boiled
   egg; nasturtium and/or calendula blossoms

Whisk together all the dressing
ingredients and set aside to let flavors
blend. Bring a pot of water to a boil
and boil or steam the broccoli until it
is tender-crisp—done but not over-
cooked! Immediately transfer to a
bowl of ice water to stop the cooking
process and keep the broccoli bright
green. Drain and cool in refrigerator
until well chilled. Arrange the chilled
broccoli on a serving platter and
pour over the blended dressing.
Garnish with chopped egg and calendula or nasturtium blossoms.

Serves 4 to 6.

GARLIC MARINATED BROCCOLI

*A fine dish that shows off the flavor of
fresh-picked broccoli. Great for icebox
raids.*

1 large head of broccoli cut into
   small 2- to 3-inch florets

MARINADE:
3 tablespoons olive oil
1 teaspoon finely minced garlic
2 tablespoons freshly chopped
   basil or 1 tablespoon dried
1 teaspoon fresh oregano or
   ½ teaspoon dried
2 teaspoons soy sauce
2 tablespoons vinegar
freshly ground pepper

Mix the marinade ingredients together. Steam or quickly boil broccoli florets until they are just tender-
crisp. Do not overcook! Drain immediately and chill broccoli in ice
water to set color and stop the cooking process. Toss the well-drained
broccoli with the marinade and let
flavors blend for at least ½ hour.
Serve at room temperature or chilled.

Serves 4.

BRUSSELS SPROUTS

BRUSSELS SPROUTS AND CARROTS WITH CREAMY LEMON-POPPYSEED SAUCE

A colorful and delicious fall dish.

>   5 tablespoons light olive oil
>   3 tablespoons fresh lemon juice
>   1½ teaspoons poppyseeds
>   1 teaspoon minced garlic
>   ½ teaspoon dijon mustard
>   ¼ teaspoon salt
>   pinch of cayenne pepper
>   1 egg, in shell
>   8 carrots cut into ½-inch slices
>   1 pound brussels sprouts,
>   trimmed
>   1 tablespoon chopped scallion—
>   green and white parts

Whisk oil, lemon juice, poppyseeds, garlic, mustard, salt, and cayenne pepper together until well blended. Heat a saucepan of water to boiling. Add the egg in shell; cook for one minute only. Break the egg into the sauce and whisk to blend. Steam the vegetables until tender-crisp; drain; pour sauce over vegetables and toss with vegetables to blend. Sprinkle the scallions over the top and serve. Can be served hot or at room temperature.

Serves 4 to 6.

MARINATED BRUSSELS SPROUTS

A piquant and tasty way to eat your sprouts.

>   1 pound brussels sprouts
>   2 tablespoons sweet pickle relish
>   2 tablespoons chopped pimiento
>   or red bell pepper
>   2 tablespoons finely chopped
>   scallions
>   ¼ cup dry white wine
>   1 tablespoon vinegar
>   1 teaspoon dijon mustard
>   2 tablespoons vegetable oil
>   1 clove garlic, finely chopped
>   ½ teaspoon salt
>   ¼ teaspoon pepper

Trim and clean brussels sprouts. Steam or boil them in a small amount of water until tender but firm; drain and cool quickly in ice water to stop the cooking process. In a medium bowl, combine the rest of the ingredients and mix together. Add the drained brussels sprouts and toss lightly. Cover and refrigerate for at least an hour to let the flavors blend. Serve chilled or at room temperature.

Serves 4 to 6.

CABBAGE

LEMON BUTTERED CABBAGE

¼ cup butter or margarine
½ teaspoon caraway or celery
  seed
1 medium head cabbage, coarsely
  chopped
juice and peel of ½ lemon
pepper

Melt the butter with the seed in a
large fry pan. Add the cabbage and
cook, stirring constantly, over high
heat, 3 to 4 minutes. Reduce the heat
and cover. Simmer 3 minutes only
until just tender. Stir in the lemon
juice and peel and add pepper to
taste. Serve right away.

Serves 4.

SWEET AND SOUR SAUTÉED CABBAGE

A new twist on an old favorite.

½ each small to medium-sized
  heads of red and green cabbage
  (or all of one color)
4 tablespoons butter
1 large or 2 smaller red apples,
  chopped into small ½-inch dice
3 tablespoons fresh lemon juice
2½ tablespoons firmly packed
  brown sugar
2 tablespoons cider vinegar
½ teaspoon salt
¼ teaspoon freshly ground
  pepper
¼ teaspoon ground cloves

Coarsely shred cabbage and set
aside. Melt butter in a heavy skillet.
Add apple(s) and cook them, stirring, for about 3 to 5 minutes, until
they begin to soften. Mix in the
lemon juice, brown sugar, vinegar,
salt, pepper and cloves. Add cabbage
and stir-fry until the cabbage is
tender but still crunchy—about 5 or
6 minutes. Serve right away.

Serves 4.

CALIFORNIA CABBAGE SALAD SUPPER

A complete meal when served with hot crusty french bread and a good full-bodied red wine.

**4 slices thick-sliced bacon
2 or 3 scallions, finely chopped
1 small head green or red cabbage, cored and shredded
3 tablespoons good wine vinegar
1 four-ounce package of garlic and herb "Alouette" cheese (or similar herb-flavored cream cheese)
freshly ground black pepper
chopped fresh parsley**

In a 12-inch skillet, fry the bacon crisp. Remove from pan and crumble it into fairly large bits. Pour out all but 2 tablespoons of the bacon drippings. Add the scallions to the drippings and fry until limp and translucent.

Add the shredded cabbage and cook over a high heat, stirring constantly until the cabbage begins to wilt. Add the crumbled bacon and the wine vinegar.

Divide the cabbage between two large dinner plates. Cut the Alouette cheese in half and top each plate of cabbage with one half of the cheese placed in the center of the hot cabbage portions.

Grind black pepper over all, and sprinkle with fresh parsley. Serve immediately, while still nicely hot. The cheese will begin to melt into the hot sautéed cabbage and each diner can enjoy the combination of flavors.

Serves 2.

ALSATIAN DILLED CABBAGE

A hearty filling dish for a cold fall evening. Excellent with pork, chicken, sausages or frankfurters.

**4 tablespoons butter
½ cup chopped onions
1 small firm cabbage head, about 2½ pounds, cut into small ½-inch dice
½ teaspoon salt
4 teaspoons chopped fresh dill or 3 teaspoons dried
1 tablespoon flour
1 cup sour cream (don't substitute)
1 tablespoon mild vinegar
1 teaspoon sugar**

Melt the butter in a large deep pan and sauté the chopped onions until softened and lightly golden in color. Add the diced cabbage, salt and dill, and stir to mix together. Cover the pan and cook over medium heat until the cabbage is *just* tender-crisp—don't overcook. Remove from heat briefly while you stir the flour into the sour cream. Put the cabbage back over medium heat, add the sour cream mixture and cook, stirring, until the cabbage is glazed and thickened, about 3 to 5 minutes. Add the vinegar and sugar. Stir to blend and serve immediately.

Serves 6.

CARROTS

CHOCOLATE CHIP CARROT CAKE

An irresistible cake; be prepared to share this recipe!

    1 cup butter
    2 cups sugar
    3 eggs
    2½ cups flour
    1 teaspoon baking soda
    1 teaspoon cinnamon
    ½ teaspoon nutmeg
    ½ teaspoon allspice
    2 tablespoons baking cocoa
    ½ cup water
    1 tablespoon vanilla
    2 cups shredded carrots
    ¾ cup chopped nuts
    ¾ cup chocolate chips

Preheat oven to 350°.

Cream butter and sugar until light and fluffy. Add eggs one at a time, beating well after each addition. Sift dry ingredients together; add to creamed mixture alternately with water and vanilla. Fold in carrots, nuts and chips. Turn into prepared 9 × 13-inch pan. Bake for 45 minutes. Cool and frost with:

    CREAM CHEESE FROSTING:
    ¼ cup butter at room tempera-
        ture
    6 to 8 ounces cream cheese at
        room temperature
    ½ teaspoon vanilla
    1 teaspoon grated orange peel
    2 cups powdered sugar, measured
        and then sifted
    2 to 3 tablespoons milk

Cream butter, cheese, vanilla, orange peel. Gradually mix in powdered sugar. Add milk gradually, thinning frosting to desired consistency.

CARROT SALAD DE SOL

A creative carrot salad with a gingery tang.

    4 cups shredded carrots
    2 tablespoons lemon juice
    pinch of salt
    ⅓ cup finely chopped candied
        grapefruit or orange rind
    ¼ finely chopped candied ginger
    ¾ cup chopped golden raisins or
        currants (your choice)
    optional: raw cashews or sun-
        flower seeds

Combine all the ingredients and let the flavors blend for a few hours.

Serves 4 to 6.

Cinnamon Glazed Baby Carrots

2 tablespoons butter
1½ pounds carrots, trimmed,
　scrubbed and left whole if
　young, quartered if mature
½ teaspoon salt
2 teaspoons sugar
water
½ teaspoon ground cinnamon

In a saucepan, melt the butter. Then add carrots, salt and sugar and enough water to barely cover the carrots. Cover and cook just until the carrots are tender. (Time will vary depending on age and size of carrots.) Remove the lid. Bring the pan to a boil and boil until the water has completely evaporated, leaving the carrots coated with a sticky, buttery glaze. Sprinkle with the cinnamon, mix and serve immediately.

Serves 4 to 6.

Fresh Carrots with Apricots

1 pound fresh carrots, shredded
6 dried apricots sliced into fine
　strips
2 tablespoons butter
2 tablespoons water
1 tablespoon sugar
1 tablespoon good wine vinegar

Heat butter and water in large skillet over medium–high heat. Add carrots and apricots. Sauté 2 to 3 minutes. Sprinkle the sugar over the top. Add vinegar. Stir and cook rapidly for 1 minute until nicely glazed and serve immediately.

Serves 4.

French Braised Carrots and Turnips

The sweet flavors and succulent textures of this dish will be enjoyed by carrot lovers who usually "hate turnips."

1 pound carrots, peeled and
　sliced ½ inch thick (baby
　carrots are delicious in this)
1 pound turnips, peeled, halved
　and sliced slightly thicker than
　the carrots
2 cups chicken broth
2 teaspoons sugar
2 tablespoons butter
salt and pepper to taste
fresh chives for garnish

Place the carrots and turnips in a large heavy saucepan with the chicken broth, sugar, butter, and salt and pepper to taste. Cook them, partially covered, over medium heat until they are tender, about 20 minutes (less if vegetables are quite fresh). Check the seasoning. Sprinkle with chopped chives and serve in a warmed serving dish.

Serves 4 to 6 as a side dish.

CAULIFLOWER

CHEESY CAULIFLOWER BAKE

Just as warm and comforting as rich mashed potatoes but without the heaviness. Garden fresh, sweet cauliflower makes all the difference in this recipe.

1 medium to large head of cauliflower cut into florets
2 tablespoons butter
2 tablespoons milk (or cream if you have it)
½ teaspoon salt
freshly ground white pepper to taste
½ cup grated Swiss cheese
¼ teaspoon grated nutmeg
3 tablespoons each bread crumbs and freshly grated Parmesan cheese

Cook cauliflower until very tender by steaming or cooking in boiling water. Drain. Thoroughly mash using a potato masher (or food processor) and add the butter, milk, salt, pepper and grated Swiss cheese, combining well. Put the cauliflower mixture into a well-buttered casserole dish and sprinkle with the nutmeg, bread crumbs and Parmesan. Bake until hot and bubbly—about 10 or 15 minutes at 350°. Serve immediately.

Serves 4.

WYN'S BROILED CAULIFLOWER

When our cauliflowers were cut in the trial garden this summer, everyone wanted to make a whole meal of this one dish.

Preheat the broiler. Break a head of white (or purple) cauliflower into florets and steam briefly until just tender. (Don't overcook.) Arrange the florets on a broiler pan and brush them generously with melted or softened butter, or top with a thick layer of grated Parmesan cheese and a very generous dusting of paprika. Broil until the cheese bubbles and begins to brown. Serve right away.

Serves 4.

CHARD

CALIFORNIA STUFFED CHARD

*Bright green chard leaves make perfect
wrappers for this handsome entrée,
which is halfway between stuffed grape
leaves and stuffed cabbage but lighter
than either dish. One of my all-time
favorite recipes.*

**15 large chard leaves with stems
   removed and reserved
2 medium onions, chopped
2 tablespoons butter
2 cups chicken stock or broth
2 tablespoons lemon juice
1 to 2 tablespoons good fruity
   olive oil
garnishes: lemon slices; fresh
   yogurt or sour cream**

**MEAT FILLING:
1¼ pounds ground veal or turkey
¼ pound lean ground pork
1 large clove garlic, chopped
¼ teaspoon nutmeg
½ teaspoon pepper
1 teaspoon salt
¼ cup parsley
1 teaspoon each fresh oregano
   and thyme (or ½ teaspoon
   each dried)
½ teaspoon Tabasco sauce
2 teaspoons Worcestershire sauce
1 egg, beaten
¼ cup milk**

Mix the meat filling ingredients
together until well combined and set
aside.

Immerse the chard leaves, 4 or 5 at
a time, in a pot of boiling water for 2
minutes or until limp. Remove with
a slotted spoon and drain well. Repeat with all the leaves and drain.
Discard the water.

Lay chard leaves out flat. Mound
several rounded tablespoons of the
reserved meat filling on the center of
each leaf. Fold sides of leaf over
center, then fold top and bottom
down. Roll each leaf into a compact
bundle. (Can be made ahead until
this point.)

Finely chop reserved chard stems.
In a large heavy pot, melt 2 tablespoons butter over medium heat.
Sauté the chopped onions and chard
stems for 5 minutes or until the
onion is soft. Lay chard bundles
on top of the sautéed vegetables, add
chicken stock and sprinkle with
lemon juice. Bring to a boil, then
reduce heat to a simmer. Drizzle 1 to
2 tablespoons olive oil over the
bundles. Simmer over low heat until
filling is done—about 35 minutes.
Garnish savory chard bundles with
fresh lemon slices and pass fresh
yogurt or sour cream to top the
bundles.

Serves 6 to 8.

BOUNTIFUL LASAGNE

A real crowd-pleaser, this dish will serve 16 people in a very satisfying manner, or the recipe can be halved to serve 6 or 8. Leftovers are delicious reheated in the microwave.

20 lasagne noodles
3 *large* bunches fresh chard or spinach
⅔ cup chopped onion
2 cloves minced garlic
2 tablespoons oil
2 cups grated raw carrots
3 cups sliced fresh mushrooms
two 15-ounce cans tomato sauce (or use thick homemade)
1 cup chopped pitted olives
2 teaspoons dried or 4 teaspoons fresh chopped oregano
3 cups ricotta or cream-style cottage cheese
¾ pound Monterey Jack or Mozzarella cheese, thinly sliced
¾ cup grated Parmesan cheese

Cook noodles in boiling salted water for 8 to 10 minutes. Drain. Wash spinach or chard well and cook very briefly in a small amount of boiling water—about 3 to 6 minutes. Drain very well and chop. In a large skillet, sauté the onion and garlic in the oil until soft. Add the carrots, mushrooms, tomato sauce, olives and oregano and heat thoroughly.

Preheat oven to 375°. Oil a large, deep casserole or pans. Layer in one-half each of the noodles, ricotta (or cottage cheese), drained chopped spinach or chard, sauce mixture, and cheese slices. Repeat, placing remaining one-half of the Monterey Jack slices on top. Sprinkle with the grated Parmesan cheese. Bake for 30 to 45 minutes, until hot and bubbly.

Serves 14 to 16.

BRODO DI BIETOLA E RISOTTO
Chicken, Chard and Rice Soup

This is a warm, rich-flavored soup that can be a whole meal in itself with hot crusty bread and butter.

2 bunches—about 1½ pounds—freshly-picked chard
¼ cup butter
¼ cup chopped onion
6 to 7 cups chicken broth
¾ cup Italian or short-grained white rice
½ cup freshly grated Parmesan cheese
1 tablespoon minced parsley
salt to taste
garnish: additional Parmesan cheese

Wash the chard well and cut both leaves and stalks into ½-inch-wide strips. In a 4- or 5-quart pot, melt the butter. Add the onion and sauté over medium heat until softened. Add the chard and stir to coat with butter. Cover the pot and heat for 4 or 5 minutes to wilt the chard.

Add 6 cups chicken broth; bring to a boil and add the rice. Cover and cook over medium heat until the rice is done, about 20 minutes. If the soup becomes too thick, add more broth. When the rice is done, add the fresh Parmesan and the parsley. Taste for seasoning. Serve piping hot sprinkled with more cheese.

Serves 6 to 8.

CORN

SOPA DE MAÍZ
Chili-Corn Soup

A very satisfying and rich-tasting soup that will make any meal seem festive.

4 cups fresh (8-12 ears) corn
1 cup chicken broth
2 tablespoons butter
2 cups milk (regular or low-fat)
¼ cup sugar
salt and white pepper
2 tablespoons roasted and peeled
    mild green chilis, diced (use
    Poblano or Anaheim)
tortilla chips
1 cup Monterey Jack cheese, cut
    in ½-inch cubes
garnish: fresh cilantro or parsley

Cut corn kernels off the cob; use a sharp knife or scraper. Put the corn and chicken broth in a blender or food processor. Blend just long enough to break up the kernels. *Do not purée.*

Put a fine sieve over a 4- or 5-quart saucepan and strain the corn and broth mixture, pressing with the back of a wooden spoon to extract as much liquid as possible. Discard the squeezed-out corn kernels. Add butter and simmer slowly 5 minutes, stirring to keep the corn bits from sticking. Add milk, sugar, salt and pepper to taste. Add the chilis and heat for another minute to blend flavors.

To serve: Place 3 or 4 broken tortilla chips in the bottom of individual soup bowls. Heat soup slowly. Add the cheese; when melted, serve immediately. Garnish with cilantro or parsley.

Serves 6.

LIGHT AND PUFFY
CORN PUDDING

A wonderful way to enjoy your harvest when fresh corn on the cob starts to lose its allure. Add 1 cup grated cheese to turn into a main-course meal.

4 eggs
2 cups fresh corn kernels cut
    from cobs
3 tablespoons flour
1 tablespoon sugar
1 cup milk or cream
salt and freshly ground pepper

Preheat oven to 325°. In a large bowl, beat the eggs thoroughly. Add corn, mixing well. Whisk the remaining ingredients slowly into the egg and corn mixture. Pour into a buttered 1½-quart casserole. Bake for 1 hour 20 minutes or until puffed and golden. A knife inserted into the center should come out clean. Serve hot.

Serves 4.

CRESSES

A Special Hint

For those who do not tolerate raw onions in salads and/or are cutting down on salt, the "bite" of cresses provides an excellent, satisfying alternative.

Cress Lover's Salad

Serve this appetizing salad on individual plates. It looks especially pretty paired with sliced red ripe tomatoes.

 2 cups cress (either watercress or curly cress), washed, dried and tough stems removed
 1 large clove garlic
 3 tablespoons good fruity olive oil
 1½ tablespoons wine vinegar
 ½ cup very finely grated Parmesan (don't use if too dried out—use only fresh sweet cheese)
 coarse salt to taste
 freshly ground pepper to taste

Put the prepared cress in a serving bowl. Combine the garlic, oil and vinegar in blender and process until the garlic is blended into the oil mixture. Toss the garlic dressing with the cress, then sprinkle on the Parmesan and toss well. Season to taste with salt and pepper.

Serves 2.

Creamy Cress Salad Dressing

 ⅔ cup olive oil (or other salad oil)
 2 cups tightly packed cress
 6 scallions, finely chopped
 ½ teaspoon salt
 1 teaspoon freshly ground pepper
 4 tablespoons sour cream or
    2 tablespoons sour cream and
    2 tablespoons very fresh plain yogurt

Combine all ingredients except sour cream in a food processor, blender or bowl and mix well. With machine running (or using whisk if preparing by hand), slowly add sour cream and yogurt, blending thoroughly. Refrigerate in airtight jar.

Makes about 1 cup.

CUCUMBERS

GINGER-LIME CUCUMBER PICKLES WITH CINNAMON BASIL

2 pounds pickling-size cucumbers, unpeeled
salt
1½ cups rice vinegar or plain white vinegar
1 cup sugar
5 tablespoons lime juice
1 cinnamon stick
6 whole cloves
2 tablespoons chopped fresh ginger
¼ cup chopped cinnamon basil

Halve cucumbers lengthwise; cut into 1-inch lengths. Put cucumbers in a colander. Sprinkle with salt. Allow to stand 30 minutes. Rinse off in cold water.

Combine remaining ingredients in a saucepan and bring to a boil, stirring until sugar is dissolved. Add cucumbers and simmer until they look glossy and transparent. With a slotted spoon, transfer cucumbers to sterilized jars. Boil down liquid until syrupy. Pour over cucumbers and allow to cool. Seal tightly, chill and store in refrigerator. Use within two weeks.

Makes about one quart.

BOBBIE'S GARDEN GAZPACHO

A perfect recipe for using the food processor, but be careful not to over-chop the vegetables.

1 cup finely chopped, peeled tomatoes
½ cup finely chopped green peppers
½ cup finely chopped cucumbers
¼ cup finely chopped scallions
1 tablespoon chopped parsley
3 cloves minced garlic
2 tablespoons minced chives
3 to 4 tablespoons tarragon vinegar
2 tablespoons olive oil (don't substitute unless you have to — olive oil tastes best here)
1 teaspoon salt
¼ teaspoon freshly ground pepper
1 teaspoon Worcestershire sauce
½ teaspoon Tabasco sauce (or more to taste)
3 cups tomato juice

Mix the above ingredients in a glass or stainless steel bowl and chill well.

Serves 4 to 8.

ROSAMUND'S FRENCH CORNICHONS

Best made in small batches as they are picked. These tiny pickles are traditionally served with pâté. They go especially well with savories such as cold cuts and rye bread or crackers and cheese.

> 1¾ cups tiny cornichon pickles, each no more than 1½ or 2 inches
> 1½ tablespoons canning or pickling salt
> 2 small peeled garlic cloves
> 2 three-inch sprigs of fresh tarragon or one generous teaspoon dried
> 1½ cups mild white wine vinegar
> 2 cups water
> 2 teaspoons sugar

Clean cucumbers under running water; remove all stems and blossoms, being careful not to cut the ends of the cukes. In a small china or glass bowl, combine cucumbers, salt, and just enough water to cover; let stand overnight at cool room temperature; drain.

Sterilize two half-pint canning jars; heat their caps and rings.

Put one garlic clove and a sprig of fresh tarragon in each drained hot jar. Pack with cucumbers.

In a small saucepan (not aluminum) heat the vinegar, the 2 cups of water and sugar to boiling over high heat. Cover cucumbers with this vinegar mixture and seal. Let flavors mature for two weeks before using them as an accompaniment to pâtés, cold cuts and savories of all kinds.

Makes 2 half-pint jars.

CUCUMBER GAZPACHO

This cool, refreshing, and surprisingly filling first course or high-summer lunch is easily made using the blender. An admirable use of the abundant mid-summer cuke harvest.

> 1 large tomato, peeled, and 1 chopped for garnish
> 1 large or 2 medium cucumbers, peeled, and 1 chopped for garnish
> ½ green pepper and ½ chopped for garnish
> ½ medium onion, chopped
> two 12-ounce cans of tomato juice
> ¼ cup olive oil
> ¼ cup red wine vinegar
> ½ clove garlic
> ¼ teaspoon Tabasco sauce
> ½ teaspoon salt
> ¼ teaspoon fresh pepper

Reserving the vegetable garnishes, put all the other ingredients in the blender with half of the tomato juice. Purée thoroughly and then add and blend the other half of the juice. Chill for several hours to blend flavors. Serve cold and pass bowls of the chopped garnishes.

Serves 4 to 6.

Eggplant

Crunchy Broiled Eggplant

This is a delicious and fast way to enjoy fresh eggplant and it doesn't use a lot of oil, as do so many eggplant recipes.

Slice an eggplant thin and spread each slice sparingly with mayonnaise. Then dip each slice in freshly grated Parmesan cheese, covering both sides. Arrange the slices on a non-stick or slightly oiled cookie sheet and broil them on each side just until they are golden brown and crunchy outside and soft and tender inside.

Serves 4.

Baked Garlic Eggplant

> **2 unpeeled eggplants or enough for 12 one-inch slices**
> **4 tablespoons good olive oil**
> **4 cloves garlic, each cut into six slivers**
> **salt and pepper**
> **parsley**

Preheat oven to 325°.
  Cut the eggplant into one-inch slices. Oil two 13½ × 8¾-inch baking dishes with 1 tablespoon of oil each. Insert 2 slivers of garlic into each slice of eggplant and arrange eggplant slices in a single layer on the pans. Pour remaining oil over the eggplant. Season with salt and pepper. Bake 25 minutes. Sprinkle with parsley.

Serves 4 to 6.

Sweet and Sour Eggplant

An easily prepared dish that really highlights the flavor of fresh-picked eggplants.

> **2 medium eggplants, sliced in ½-inch slices, then quartered**
> **salt**
> **2 tablespoons of olive or salad oil**
> **1 small finely minced clove of garlic (optional)**
> **2 tablespoons sugar**
> **2 tablespoons red wine vinegar**

Salt the eggplant slices and let them drain for 30 minutes, then rinse off and pat dry. Heat the oil in a large heavy skillet and add the eggplant (and garlic if used). Sauté until tender (8 to 10 minutes). Sprinkle with the sugar, turn over the slices and continue to cook briefly until they begin to caramelize. Add the vinegar and stir to blend. Serve immediately.

Serves 4.

ONIONS

GRILLED SCALLIONS OR BABY ONIONS

The sweet and mellow flavor of this dish is especially nice with our Red Beard scallions or Barletta baby onions. A fine accompaniment to grilled meats.

16 cleaned, whole scallions with the tops trimmed to 3 inches. Choose scallions about ½-inch thick or as they begin to get bulbous at the bottom. Or use baby onions.

MARINADE:
⅓ cup olive oil
1 large clove garlic, minced
1 teaspoon prepared mustard
½ teaspoon fresh ground pepper
salt to taste

Whisk together the marinade ingredients, and pour over onions in shallow pan. Marinate for several hours or as long as possible. Drain scallions. Grill over barbecue until soft and golden-light-brown. Transfer to platter and serve at room temperature with grilled meats, poultry or vegetables.

Serves 4.

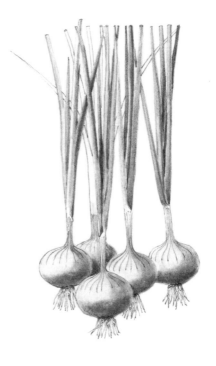

ROASTED ONIONS

Did you know that you can roast an onion like a potato? Don't peel the onions but put them to roast with whatever else is in the oven at 350° to 375°. The onions are done when they are soft and can be easily pierced (about 1½ hours). Split them in half and add butter and salt and pepper, or serve like baked potatoes, slicing off tops and adding butter and seasonings. This method of roasting is delicious using newly harvested onions.

PEAS

PEAS À LA FRANÇAISE
Peas braised with heads of lettuce

A traditional and succulent French dish for early peas and spring lettuce. In France this would be served as a separate course and eaten with a spoon as a special treat.

> 1½ firm heads of bibb lettuce
>   7 to 8 inches in diameter
> 5 tablespoons butter
> ½ cup water
> 1 tablespoon sugar
> ½ teaspoon salt
> 3 cups fresh petit pois
> 5 parsley sprigs, tied together
>   with white string
> optional addition: 10 baby onions

Wash the lettuce, remove any old leaves and cut into quarters. Wind several loops of kitchen string around each piece to hold it together when it cooks. In a heavy saucepan large enough to hold both lettuce and peas, heat 4 tablespoons of the butter, water, sugar and salt. Then add the peas and parsley. Place all the lettuce on top and with a baster dribble the liquid over it. Put a lid on the saucepan and bring to a boil. Turn heat to low and cook for about 10 minutes until the peas are tender, basting the lettuce from time to time. Discard the parsley and lettuce strings. Toss the peas and lettuce with the remaining 1 tablespoon of butter and serve at once.

Serves 4 as a first course or 6 as a vegetable dish.

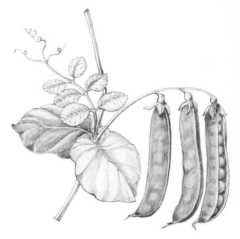

PETIT POIS SALAD

This is a colorful side dish or picnic take-along that will please everyone's palate.

> 3½ cups petit pois or very young
>   peas cooked in a little water
>   until tender, drained and chilled
> 1 cup sour cream
> 2 green onions, finely chopped
> 6 slices bacon, cooked crisp,
>   drained and crumbled
> ½ teaspoon salt
> freshly ground pepper

Toss the peas with the rest of the ingredients and serve.

Serves 6 to 8.

PEPPERS

BELL PEPPER BOUNTY

An aromatic and colorful salad to make in high pepper season.

3 tablespoons lemon juice
2 tablespoons minced fresh
parsley
½ teaspoon ground cumin
1 teaspoon sugar
1 small clove garlic, minced
(optional)
⅓ cup olive oil or your favorite
salad oil
2 red or purple bell peppers,
thinly sliced into lengthwise
strips (peel with a potato peeler
if desired)
2 green or yellow bell peppers,
thinly sliced into lengthwise
strips
salt and pepper to taste

In a small bowl, combine the lemon juice, parsley, cumin, sugar and garlic if used. Add oil gradually, whisking until thoroughly blended. Put the sliced peppers in a serving bowl and pour the dressing over them, mixing it well with the peppers. Add salt and pepper to taste. Chill, covered, for about 1 hour before serving to let flavors blend.

Makes 1½ to 2 cups.

SWEET RED BELL PEPPER SOUBICE WITH SAGE

Serve under baby vegetables, with roast chicken or over grilled fish. It's wonderful on pizza. Or simply spread on toast to serve as an appetizer.

½ cup butter
4 cups yellow onions cut into
chunks
2 tablespoons chopped fresh sage
4 roasted, seeded and chopped
sweet red bell peppers

Melt butter. Sauté the onions in the butter very, very slowly until they are very soft, aromatic and deep golden-brown color. Be patient and stir often, letting them cook down gently.

Purée the onions, sage and roasted peppers in a blender or food processor until very smooth. Cool. Add salt and pepper to taste.

If you want a thinner purée, thin with half and half and adjust seasoning.

Serves 4 to 6.

Salads

Mixed Fresh Greens with Curried Dressing

1½ pounds fresh assorted greens (enough for 6 to 8 people)

DRESSING:
2 tablespoons white wine vinegar
1 tablespoon vermouth
1 scant tablespoon dijon mustard
1 tablespoon soy sauce
¼ teaspoon ground cumin
½ teaspoon curry powder
1 teaspoon sugar
¼ teaspoon freshly ground pepper
⅓ cup salad oil

Wash, dry, and tear greens into bite-sized pieces. Combine all dressing ingredients in a jar and shake well. Pour into salad bowl. Place greens in salad bowl on top of dressing but do not toss. Cover bowl tightly with plastic wrap and refrigerate for an hour or so. Just before serving, toss after adding any or all of the following:

1 apple diced
⅓ cup dry roasted peanuts;
¼ cup golden raisins
4 scallions, chopped
1 tablespoon toasted sesame seeds

Serves 6 to 8.

California Citrus Salad

Light, crisp and very refreshing, the unusual combination of ingredients is a pure serendipity of colors and flavors.

¼ cup fresh grapefruit juice
½ teaspoon sugar
¼ teaspoon salt
⅓ cup oil
3 grapefruits, peeled and sectioned, white membrane removed
1 large bunch of red radishes, washed and thinly sliced
1 large head of crispy romaine, washed and torn into pieces; or enough lettuce for four people
⅓ cup toasted sunflower seeds

In a small bowl, whisk together the grapefruit juice, sugar and salt. Add oil slowly in a stream, whisking the dressing until it is blended. In the salad bowl, combine the grapefruit sections, sliced radishes and lettuce. Add dressing and toss. Sprinkle the sunflower seeds over salad and serve.

Serves 4.

Mixed Green Salad with "Hot Nuts and Bacon" Dressing

6 slices bacon, chopped
¼ cup chopped onion
2 tablespoons good-quality olive oil
1 large clove garlic, minced
¼ teaspoon freshly ground pepper
1 tablespoon mild vinegar
½ teaspoon freshly grated lemon zest (yellow part of lemon skin)
1 tablespoon lemon juice
1 tablespoon chopped parsley
½ teaspoon finely chopped fresh thyme or ¼ teaspoon dried
¼ teaspoon salt
2 teaspoons sugar
1½ quarts mixed salad greens: several lettuces, rocket salad, radicchio, a few leaves of sorrel, etc.
⅓ cup chopped toasted nuts— walnuts or pecans
1 tablespoon chopped parsley

Cook the bacon until crisp in a skillet or wok and then drain, reserving 1½ tablespoons of the bacon fat in the pan. Heat the skillet again and add crumbled, drained bacon, onion, olive oil, garlic and pepper. Sauté until the onion is slightly softened—several minutes. Add the vinegar, lemon zest, lemon juice, parsley, thyme, salt and sugar. Cook another minute or two or until the onion is translucent. Add the mixed greens all at once and toss quickly over the heat until the leaves are coated with dressing and warmed but not really wilted; about 15 seconds. Taste and add more salt if desired. Then toss in the chopped nuts and sprinkle with chopped parsley. Serve right away.

Serves 6.

Sweet & Sour Nutty Salad

The glazed crunchy nuts add something quite special and the other ingredients alternate between crispy and smooth, tart and sweet. We love it!

TOPPING:
½ cup sliced almonds
2 tablespoons sugar

DRESSING:
2 tablespoons wine vinegar
1 tablespoon lemon juice
¼ teaspoon salt
1 tablespoon sugar
⅓ cup salad oil
dash of Tabasco sauce

SALAD INGREDIENTS:
1 head romaine
½ head butterhead lettuce
½ cup thin-sliced celery
½ cup fresh bean sprouts
1 green onion, chopped fine
2 tablespoons chopped parsley
1 small can mandarin oranges, drained

Place sugar in a heavy skillet over medium heat. Stir well just until it turns honey color (don't let it brown). Remove from heat, add almonds, and stir until they are coated. Spoon onto a greased pan. Cool, break apart, and reserve. Combine all the dressing ingredients in a jar and blend.

Tear lettuce into bite-sized pieces. Combine in salad bowl with celery, bean sprouts, green onion and the mandarin orange slices. Toss with dressing and add parsley. Before serving, sprinkle on the glazed nuts.

Serves 6.

Garden Bouquet Salad with Lemon-Herb Vinaigrette

DRESSING:
1 small green onion, chopped fine
1 teaspoon dijon mustard
2 to 3 tablespoons lemon juice
1 tablespoon dry white wine
1 egg yolk
1 tablespoon minced parsley
1 tablespoon minced chive
blossom florets or chopped
chive leaves
¼ teaspoon salt
pinch of freshly ground pepper
¾ cup olive oil

With a whisk, combine all the ingredients except the oil. Slowly whisk in oil, beating continually until thoroughly blended. Taste for seasoning. Chill until ready to use.

SALAD INGREDIENTS:
2 heads radicchio (or red leaf
lettuce as a second choice)
2 heads mâche
3 or 4 fresh sorrel leaves
2 small heads bibb lettuce
12 to 14 leaves or 2 handfuls
young arugula (roquette) or
watercress
¾ cup fresh green and purple
basil leaves
½ cup calendula petals
¼ cup borage flowers

Wash and dry salad greens. Reserve 6 to 8 radicchio or red lettuce leaves. Tear remaining salad greens into bite-size pieces and combine with basil leaves in center of salad bowl. Line outer edge with reserved radicchio or red lettuce leaves. Sprinkle with flowers around the outside border. Whisk dressing and pour over the salad after presenting it at the table.

Serves 6.

Warm Shrimp Salad

An unusual and delicious first-course salad that tastes wonderfully extravagant.

DRESSING:
2 cloves garlic
2 shallots or 3 green onions,
chopped
2 tablespoons fresh or 2 teaspoons
dried tarragon
2 tablespoons chopped fresh
ginger
¼ cup lime juice
3 tablespoons red wine vinegar
1 tablespoon soy sauce
½ cup oil
1 tablespoon sesame oil
fresh pepper to taste

SALAD INGREDIENTS:
12 ounces medium-sized raw
shrimp, peeled and deveined
salad greens—two heads of
lettuce, one green, one red
leaf; one bunch of rocket salad
or other greens to taste, washed,
dried, and torn into bite-sized
pieces

Combine the dressing ingredients in a blender or food processor and mix until well blended. Marinate the shrimp in 2 tablespoons of the dressing for 30 minutes, reserving the remaining dressing.

Sauté the shrimp in their dressing marinade, stir-frying quickly, until they are no longer pink, about two minutes. Arrange salad greens in large salad bowl and scatter the hot shrimp on top. Pour the remaining dressing over the salad. Toss and serve.

Serves 4 to 6.

GREEK STYLE ENDIVE SALAD WITH LEMON DRESSING

Nice with garlic bread and a no-nonsense burgundy.

1 head of curly endive, washed
  and torn into bite-sized pieces
2 or 3 large tomatoes, cut up
1 green or red bell pepper, cored
  and cut into small pieces
1 cup of cucumber slices
1 small sweet onion, sliced and
  separated into rings
1/3 pound feta cheese, broken into
  1/2-inch pieces
18 Greek- or Italian-style olives

DRESSING:
1/4 cup fresh lemon juice
3/4 cup olive oil
3 teaspoons fresh or 1 1/2 teaspoons dry oregano

In a large salad bowl, layer the endive, tomatoes, pepper, cucumber, onion, cheese, and olives. Cover and refrigerate to chill well.

To serve, whip together the dressing ingredients and pour about 1/2 cup of the mixture over the salad. Toss lightly.

Serves 6.

MEMORABLE WILTED LETTUCE SALAD

2 leaf or butterhead lettuces
2 teaspoons sugar
8 slices very lean bacon, chopped
1/4 cup vinegar
2 teaspoons water
dash of salt and pepper
1 egg, beaten

Shred the lettuce into a large bowl. Fry the bacon crisp, but do not drain. Add the vinegar, water, sugar, salt and pepper and the beaten egg to the pan. Cook, stirring just until the mixture is thickened. Pour the dressing over the lettuce and toss until the salad is wilted. Serve right away and stand back for applause.

Serves 4 to 6.

PERFECT GREEN GODDESS DRESSING

1 clove garlic, chopped
1 tube anchovy paste
3 tablespoons chopped chives or
  scallions
1 tablespoon lemon juice
3 tablespoons tarragon wine
  vinegar
1/2 cup sour cream
1/2 cup mayonnaise
1/4 cup chopped parsley
fresh ground pepper to taste

Combine in blender and blend thoroughly. Outstanding on a salad of fresh romaine with thinly sliced fresh mushrooms.

Makes about 1 cup.

SPINACH

FLORENTINE BAKED EGGS

Wonderful for brunch or a light summer supper, with toasted English muffins.

**1 cup cooked and very well
    drained chopped spinach
⅛ teaspoon (a pinch) nutmeg
salt and pepper
½ cup heavy cream
3 tablespoons fresh basil, minced
8 drops Tabasco sauce
freshly ground white pepper
4 large eggs at room temperature
½ cup grated Swiss cheese
2 tablespoons freshly grated
    Parmesan cheese**

Preheat oven to 375°.

Mix spinach with nutmeg and salt and pepper to taste. Butter 4 large custard cups or individual ramekins. Line each with a nest of ¼ cup of spinach. Mix together the cream, basil and Tabasco. Pour 1 tablespoon of cream mixture into the center of each spinach nest. Break an egg into each ramekin and top with another tablespoon of cream mixture. Sprinkle with a grind of pepper and divide cheeses over the tops.

Place ramekins into a baking pan and pour boiling water into pan to come halfway up the side of the ramekins. Bake until eggs are set to your liking—about 10 to 12 minutes.

Option: Cooked chopped Canadian bacon can be added on top of spinach.

Serves 4.

FRESH SPINACH SALAD

Tender fresh spinach leaves, crispy sweet red apple and just a few bites of smoky bacon make this a salad to look forward to.

**1 very large bunch spinach (about
    1 pound), washed and dried
4 green onions, chopped
1 red-skinned apple, cored but
    not peeled, coarsely chopped
3 slices bacon, fried crisp, drained
    and patted dry, then crumbled**

**DRESSING (makes enough for
    several salads):
¼ cup honey
½ cup good red wine vinegar
1 cup olive or other salad oil
½ teaspoon salt
1 teaspoon ground black pepper
2 tablespoons Worcestershire sauce**

Whip the dressing ingredients together. Combine the salad ingredients, toss with desired amount of dressing, and serve immediately.

Serves 4.

Squash & Pumpkins

Fran's Blue-Ribbon Zucchini Relish

This relish uses up that overabundance of midsummer zucchini. A kitchen staple you'll use often, especially in barbecue season, it really appeals to "meat and potatoes" types who usually won't even contemplate zucchini.

    10 firm medium-sized zucchini
       (about 10 cups)
    1 tablespoon salt
    2 onions, coarsely chopped
    1 green pepper, diced
    1 red pepper or pimiento, diced
    2 stalks celery, sliced
    2½ cups cider vinegar
    2 cloves garlic, minced
    1½ cups sugar
    1 tablespoon mustard seed
    ½ teaspoon allspice
    1 teaspoon turmeric
    2 teaspoons celery seed
    ½ teaspoon black pepper

Wash zucchini well and remove ends; coarsely chop and mix with salt. Let stand 5 hours or overnight. Drain, rinse in cold water and drain once more.

Prepare other vegetables. Place in a saucepan with drained zucchini, vinegar, garlic, sugar and spices. Mix through, then bring to a boil, reduce heat and simmer for 30 minutes, stirring occasionally. Spoon at once into hot sterilized jars and store in the fridge to use with hot dogs, hamburgers, etc.

Makes 6 half-pint jars.

Zucchini with Walnuts

A great side dish with barbecue-grilled meats.

    4 cups zucchini cut in thin slices
    ⅓ cup sliced scallion tops
    2 tablespoons butter
    3 or 4 tablespoons dry sherry
    ½ teaspoon salt
    ⅓ cup coarsely chopped walnuts,
       toasted

In a large saucepan, combine zucchini, scallions and butter. Cook over low heat for 5 minutes. Stir in sherry and salt, cover and cook over low heat 3 to 5 minutes more until zucchini is tender. Stir in walnuts and serve.

Serves 4 to 6.

STUFFED HERBED ZUCCHINI

6 or 7 medium-sized zucchini
1 small onion, chopped
1 large clove garlic, chopped
3 tablespoons butter
1 cup seasoned bread crumbs
¾ cup freshly grated Parmesan
  cheese
4 teaspoons fresh sweet marjoram
¼ cup fresh parsley, chopped
salt and pepper
2 eggs, beaten

TOPPING:
¼ cup freshly grated Parmesan
  cheese

Wash zucchini, cut off ends, and steam until just tender. Cool. Split lengthwise, scoop out pulp, turn upside down and drain slightly. Mash pulp or spin in blender. Sauté the onion and garlic in butter until softened. Add squash pulp, crumbs, ½ cup of the cheese, herbs and seasonings. Add eggs and cook until mixture thickens. Stuff into zucchini shells, top with remaining cheese, and place in a buttered casserole. Bake at 375° until browned, about 25 minutes. Serve hot or at room temperature.

Serves 6 to 8.

ZUCCHINI AND BASIL PASTA SALAD

Excellent as a main dish or side dish with barbecued meats. Makes wonderful picnic fare.

4 medium zucchini very coarsely
  grated
1 teaspoon salt
2½ cups packed fresh basil leaves
½ cup olive oil
3 cloves garlic
¾ teaspoon fresh oregano or
  ½ teaspoon dried
6 cups chicken broth
¾ pound orzo (rice-shaped pasta)
¼ cup fresh lemon juice
¼ cup freshly grated Parmesan
  cheese, Asiago, or hard Monterey Jack cheese
3 tablespoons chopped parsley
salt and pepper

Sprinkle zucchini with salt in a colander and toss. Let stand 20 minutes, stirring once or twice. Squeeze zucchini dry. Transfer to large bowl. Blend basil, oil, garlic and oregano together well in food processor or blender. Add to zucchini; reserve.

Bring chicken broth to a boil in a large pot. Add orzo and reduce heat, cooking until orzo is just tender, about 10 to 12 minutes. Drain well. Stir the pasta into the zucchini. Add the lemon juice, grated cheese and parsley. Season to taste with salt and pepper.

Serve warm, at room temperature, or chilled.

Serves 8.

Yellow Squash with Basil, Pepperoni and Parmesan

For a light supper or lunch with french bread and red wine.

- 5 or 6 small yellow squash, chopped into chunks, enough to make 2 cups
- 1 tablespoon olive oil
- 1 tablespoon butter
- 1 small onion, chopped
- ¼ cup finely chopped pepperoni sausage
- ¼ cup freshly grated Parmesan cheese
- 1 tablespoon fresh basil, finely chopped

Heat the olive oil and butter together, then add the squash, cooking until they are just heated through. Remove the squash from the pan and reserve. Add the onion and pepperoni and cook until the pepperoni is crisp and the onion limp. Add the squash back into the pepperoni mixture, and cook until the squash is tender-crisp. Add the Parmesan and the fresh basil; stir and serve immediately.

Serves 2.

Stir-Fried Gingered Peas and Yellow Squash

The fresh flavors, colors, and crisp textures of the ingredients are kept intact in this perfumed dish.

- 3 tablespoons oil
- 3 tablespoons chopped fresh chives or scallions
- 2 teaspoons finely chopped fresh ginger
- 1 teaspoon finely chopped fresh garlic
- 1 pound sugar snap or snow peas, stems and tips removed (strings pulled from sugar snaps)
- ¾ pound yellow summer squash, thinly sliced
- 1 red bell pepper, chopped
- 2 tablespoons chopped fresh parsley or 1 tablespoon chopped fresh cilantro
- salt and pepper to taste

Heat oil in wok or deep skillet. Sauté chives or scallions, ginger and garlic until sweet smelling—about 1 minute. Add vegetables and stir-fry until tender-crisp—about 4 or 5 minutes. Sprinkle with parsley (or cilantro) and serve.

Serves 4 to 6.

PUMPKIN COBBLER

Everyone who tries this delicious dessert likes it better than pumpkin pie. The crust mixture rises to the top during baking to form a rich topping.

FILLING:
2 eggs, beaten
1 cup evaporated milk
3 cups cooked mashed pumpkin
(or butternut squash)
1 cup white sugar
½ cup dark brown sugar
1 tablespoon flour
1 teaspoon cinnamon
¼ teaspoon ginger
¼ teaspoon cloves
¼ teaspoon nutmeg
½ teaspoon salt

CRUST:
1 stick butter (½ cup)
1 cup flour
1 cup white sugar
4 teaspoons baking powder
½ teaspoon salt
1 cup regular or low-fat milk
1 teaspoon vanilla

TOPPING:
1 tablespoon butter
2 tablespoons white sugar

Preheat oven to 350°.

In a large bowl, combine eggs, milk and pumpkin; add the rest of the filling ingredients, mix well and set aside. Then prepare the crust: melt the stick of butter in a 9 × 11-inch baking pan. In another bowl, mix the remaining crust ingredients until just combined and pour into baking pan on top of the melted butter. Spoon or slowly pour the filling evenly over the crust batter in the pan. *Do not stir.* Dot the top with the remaining 1 tablespoon butter and sprinkle with the 2 tablespoons of sugar. Bake 1 hour.

Serves 8 to 10.

VICKI SEBASTIANI'S RICOTTA STUFFED SQUASH BLOSSOMS

A summer treat that shouldn't be missed.

12-15 squash blossoms; number used will vary depending on size, so have a few extra on hand.

FILLING:
1 pound ricotta cheese
1 medium onion, finely chopped
½ cup toasted almonds, finely chopped
½ cup freshly grated Italian Asiago (or Parmesan) cheese
½ teaspoon ground pepper
1 teaspoon seasoning salt
2 tablespoons fresh, minced basil (or 2 teaspoons dried)
2 tablespoons minced parsley
2 tablespoons melted butter

Preheat oven to 350°. Mix filling ingredients together. Stuff squash blossoms carefully; don't overfill. Drizzle the melted butter over blossoms and bake in 350° oven for 15 minutes.

Serves 4.

TOMATOES

PASTA WITH FRESH CHILI PEPPER AND TOMATO SAUCE

For the very best flavor use our Italian plum-type tomatoes if you've grown them; otherwise use small regular tomatoes.

8 ounces dried or 12 ounces fresh fettuccine or linguini
10 Italian plum tomatoes, quartered
⅓ cup good olive oil
2 or 3 cloves garlic, finely chopped
1 teaspoon oregano (dry) or 2 teaspoons fresh oregano
1 or 2 small fresh chili peppers, finely chopped (remove seeds if desired)
salt and pepper
freshly grated Parmesan cheese

Cook the pasta in boiling salted water, timing it so it will be done just before it is mixed with the sauce. Heat the olive oil in a large skillet, then add the tomatoes, garlic, oregano, chili peppers, salt and pepper. Sauté over medium heat about 5 minutes or until tomatoes are softened but still hold their shape. In a warm bowl, combine sauce with hot drained pasta and toss together. Serve right away. Pass the Parmesan cheese.

Serves 3 or 4.

TOMATO-LEMON CHUTNEY

An excellent chutney with a complex, not too sweet flavor. It makes a fine gift.

1 tablespoon oil
1 small whole fresh or dry chili pepper, crumbled
½ teaspoon cumin seed
¼ teaspoon nutmeg
¼ teaspoon mustard seed
4 large tomatoes, sliced very thin
½ fresh lemon
⅓ cup raisins or currants
½ cup sugar

Heat oil in a saucepan. Add the crumbled chili pepper, cumin seed, nutmeg, and mustard seed. When the seeds start to jump in the oil, add the tomatoes.

Quarter the lemon half, removing any seeds, and lay it on top of the other ingredients in the pan. Simmer, stirring as needed to keep from sticking, for 15 minutes. Stir in the raisins or currants, and the sugar. Continue to simmer, stirring frequently, until the mixture thickens, about 30 minutes. Cool and transfer to jars. Store chutney in the refrigerator.

Makes about 2 cups.

PASTA WITH FRESH TOMATOES, HERBS AND GARLIC SAUCE

Who wants to stand over a hot stove to enjoy fresh tomato-herb sauce? Try this recipe for a vividly colored, uncooked sauce that combines all the best summer flavors. Be sure to let the sauce stand for an hour before serving to blend all the flavors. A gardening cook's treasure.

> **8 ounces dried or 12 ounces fresh spaghetti or linguini**
> **5 large ripe tomatoes, peeled, seeded and coarsely chopped**
> **3 tablespoons chopped fresh sweet basil**
> **1 tablespoon chopped fresh chives**
> **3 tablespoons chopped Italian flat-leaf parsley**
> **3 garlic cloves, finely chopped**
> **½ cup fruity olive oil**
> **¾ cup finely grated Mozzarella or Fontina cheese**
> **¼ teaspoon each salt and freshly ground pepper**
> **lots of freshly grated Parmesan cheese**

Have all the ingredients at room temperature. Prepare the sauce by combining tomatoes, basil, chives, parsley, garlic, olive oil, Mozzarella cheese, salt and pepper. Let this sauce mixture stand at room temperature for about an hour to let the flavors blend. Cook and drain the pasta. In a warm bowl combine the hot drained pasta and the sauce. Toss together and serve right away. Pass the Parmesan cheese.

Serves 4.

TOMATO, OPAL BASIL AND MOZZARELLA SALAD

An alluring version of a very simple and traditional Italian dish.

> **1 teaspoon lemon juice**
> **2 tablespoons chopped purple basil**
> **1 tablespoon chopped parsley**
> **1 clove garlic, chopped**
> **2 tablespoons red wine vinegar**
> **5 tablespoons olive oil**
> **salt and freshly ground pepper**
> **fresh lettuce leaves**
> **4 large tomatoes, sliced ¼ inch thick**
> **8 ounces thinly sliced Mozzarella cheese**
> **1 red onion, peeled and thinly sliced into rings**
> **garnish: sprigs of purple opal basil**

In the container of a blender or food processor, combine lemon juice, basil, parsley, garlic, vinegar and olive oil. Blend or process until smooth. Season with salt and pepper to taste.

Line a large serving dish with the lettuce leaves. Arrange alternating slices of tomato and Mozzarella slices in rows, overlapping the slices a bit. Spoon the dressing over the salad. Sprinkle with black pepper; top with onion rings and garnish with sprigs of purple basil.

Serves 6.

SUN-DRIED HERB TOMATOES

Think of these as tomato "raisins" and use them anywhere you would like a strong, definitive tomato flavor: pastas, stews, etc. Also delicious as a colorful and savory addition to mixed green salads when first cut into thin strips.

> Italian plum-type tomatoes
> salt
> white vinegar
> good Italian olive oil
>
> **ADDITIONS FOR EACH JAR:**
> 2 garlic cloves
> 2 sprigs basil or rosemary

Cut the tomatoes in half and cut out the stems. Lay them cut side up in one layer on trays and lightly salt them. Put them out in the sun and allow them to slowly dehydrate until they become shriveled and with consistency like plump raisins. (Cover with cheesecloth or plastic screening to protect from insects.) Take the trays in at night if there is heavy dew. After dehydrating, dip each dried tomato half in white vinegar, shaking off the excess vinegar. Place the tomatoes in clean, sterilized pint jars with garlic and your choice of herbs and cover completely with the olive oil. For long shelf life, process jars in a boiling water bath for 15 minutes.

BAKED STUFFED TOMATOES

> 8 medium or 4 large ripe
>   tomatoes
> salt and pepper to taste
> 2 cups cooked rice
> 1 cup loosely packed fresh
>   parsley, chopped
> 1 cup loosely packed fresh basil,
>   chopped
> 3 garlic cloves, finely minced
> ½ cup olive oil
> ¼ cup anchovy fillets, drained
>   and mashed

Preheat oven to 375°.

Cut the tops off the tomatoes and scoop out the pulp, leaving a nice shell. Reserve tops and pulp. Sprinkle the shells with salt and let them drain upside down on paper towels.

In a large bowl, combine the cooked rice, parsley, basil, garlic, olive oil, and anchovies. Press the reserved tomato pulp through a strainer to get ½ cup tomato juice and discard the pulp. Add the tomato juice to the rice mixture, blend well, and season to taste.

Fill the tomatoes with stuffing, top them with the reserved tops, and put them in a well-oiled shallow baking pan. Bake for 30 minutes. Serve at room temperature.

Serves 4 to 8.

SPECIALTY COLLECTIONS

BABY VEGETABLES

Baby vegetables are either naturally tiny at maturity or they are varieties especially developed for their succulence and flavor when harvested at baby size. You'll find them well-suited for growing in the home garden, where their appealing small size, fragile nature and delicate flavor can be enjoyed at their fresh and tender best. In the kitchen, remember that baby vegetables are more tender with thinner, more delicate skins than mature vegetables. They will bruise easily and should be used quite promptly, as they don't hold as well as older vegetables. Babies just need a gentle washing rather than peeling or heavy processing before being prepared. The simplest and best ways of cooking them are to either steam or poach them in stock briefly, or (and this is the way most fine restaurant chefs prepare them) cook them until tender-crisp in a large pot of boiling salted water (the salt sets the colors). As soon as they are just tender, plunge the baby vegetables into ice-cube cold water to stop the cooking process and drain. To serve, heat them through by sautéing quickly in a bit of butter with herbs or other seasonings and/or serve with your favorite light sauce. The main thing to remember is not to overcook baby vegetables so that they hold their colors and shapes.

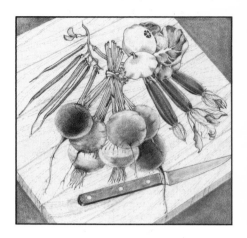

BAGNA CAUDA
Hot Dipping Sauce
for Baby Vegetables

On a platter or in a basket arrange assorted washed and trimmed baby vegetables of your choice, cleaned and at room temperature.

SAUCE:
¼ pound (1 stick) butter
¼ cup olive oil
4 cloves garlic, mashed
**1 two-oz. can anchovy filets,
   drained and chopped**

Heat the butter and olive oil in a small skillet and sauté the garlic and anchovies for five minutes over very low heat, stirring constantly. (The anchovies will melt into the sauce.) Transfer to a small warmed earthenware or enameled fondue or chafing dish which can be kept warm over a candle or on a hot tray.

Using fondue forks or long toothpicks, diners can enjoy dipping the vegetables in the piquant sauce. Stir sauce frequently.

Baby Squash, Nasturtium Blossoms and Herbs with Pasta

This herbed sauce is lovely on pasta with the bright colors of the petals and squashes.

fettucine noodles for two people
18 to 20 nasturtium flowers
1 teaspoon fresh thyme, very
   finely chopped
1 teaspoon fresh sweet marjoram,
   very finely chopped
2 teaspoons flat-leaf parsley, very
   finely chopped
2 scallions, very finely chopped
1 small clove garlic, mashed
4 tablespoons sweet butter,
   softened
6 baby yellow scallop squash
   with their blossoms
6 baby zucchini squash with their
   blossoms
½ cup chicken stock
salt and pepper
garnish: nasturtium and squash
   blossoms

Separate the nasturtium petals from their bases and chop them. Blend together the chopped petals, finely chopped herbs, scallion, garlic and butter and season with salt and pepper to taste. Allow the herb butter to stand for a half hour to let the flavors blend together. Cut the squashes into thin slices and the blossoms into strips. In a skillet melt 2 tablespoons of the herb butter and sauté the squash for 3 minutes. Add the chicken stock and squash blossoms and simmer over low heat for a few minutes. Heat salted water for the pasta and cook. Drain pasta well and add with the rest of the herb butter to the squash. Correct seasonings, mix well and serve immediately.

Serves 2.

Baby Carrots with Ginger and Sage Butter

2 pounds baby carrots, scrubbed
   clean
¼ pound unsalted butter (1 stick)
1½ tablespoons brown sugar
2 tablespoons freshly chopped
   ginger
juice of ½ lemon
¼ teaspoon salt
1 large clove garlic, mashed
1 tablespoon freshly chopped
   sage (or 2 teaspoons dried)

Poach carrots in water or chicken stock until just tender. Melt butter and add all other ingredients, then add the drained carrots and gently sauté 2 to 3 minutes to blend flavors. Serve.

Serves 6.

Herbed Dressing for Poached Baby Vegetables

½ cup olive oil
½ cup vegetable oil
¼ cup fresh dill leaf
2 tablespoons honey
⅓ cup chopped fresh basil
¼ teaspoon pepper
1 teaspoon salt
1 teaspoon dry mustard
1 tablespoon Worcestershire sauce
⅓ cup vinegar
2 cloves garlic, chopped

Combine and shake together well. Let flavors blend. Use to dress hot poached baby vegetables which can then be served either hot or at room temperature.

Makes about 2 cups.

SORREL AND SHALLOT BUTTER FOR BABY VEGETABLES

1 stick unsalted softened butter
½ cup sorrel leaves, chopped fine
3 tablespoons shallots, chopped fine
1 clove garlic, chopped
3 drops Tabasco sauce
salt to taste

Blend all the above together evenly. Put a small amount on top of each serving of your favorite cooked baby vegetables. Can also be used on top of steak or chicken breasts.

BABY CARROTS AND BEETS WITH TARRAGON YOGURT DIP

1 pound each poached or steamed baby carrots and beets, cooled and arranged on a platter.

Blend together the dip ingredients and taste for seasoning:

1½ cups yogurt
½ cup mayonnaise
2 large cloves garlic, mashed
2 tablespoons freshly chopped tarragon leaves (or 1 table-spoon dried)
¼ teaspoon salt
2 tablespoons wine vinegar
1 tablespoon sugar or honey

Allow dip to stand for ½ hour to blend flavors and serve with baby carrots and beets as a first course or appetizer. Leftover dip can also be used as a salad dressing.

Serves 6 as an appetizer.

BABY GREEN BEANS WITH ROASTED GARLIC, ANCHOVIES, OLIVE OIL AND ALMONDS

1 bulb roasted garlic*
2 pounds baby green beans
1 two-oz. can anchovies, drained and chopped
½ to ¾ cup almond halves
½ cup olive oil
2 tablespoons red wine vinegar
1 teaspoon Worcestershire sauce

Lightly blanch beans—cook just until tender-crisp. Cool quickly by plunging into cold water to stop cooking action. Drain and set aside.

Squeeze the roasted garlic pulp from the cloves. Combine the roasted garlic pulp with the anchovies, almonds, olive oil, vinegar and Worcestershire sauce and mix together. Toss with the drained beans and allow to sit at room temperature for an hour before serving to blend the flavors.

Serve on lettuce and garnish with red pepper strips.

To roast garlic: Cut off the top half-inch of the bulb with a serrated knife. Rub the outside of the bulb and the cut surfaces with olive oil. Bake at 375° for about 45 minutes. When garlic is soft, cool the bulb and then squeeze the roasted garlic pulp from the individual cloves.

BABY ONIONS IN BASIL CREAM

This luxurious dish is great served over grilled fish, especially salmon. Or use it over brown or wild rice as a side dish.

1 pound baby onions
boiling salted water
2 tablespoons butter
2 teaspoons shallots, finely
  chopped (scallions okay)
¼ cup fresh chopped basil
¼ cup dry vermouth
1 cup heavy cream

Cut the tops off the onions and discard. Put onions in boiling salted water for about 5 minutes. (If you have an abundance of chicken stock, poach them in it; they are tastier!)

Remove the onions. Cool. Take uncut end of onion and squeeze onion out the cut end. (You are removing the skins). Reserve the onions.

In a skillet or sauté pan, heat the butter and sauté the shallots and basil. *Deglaze with vermouth. Add cream. Simmer the sauce to reduce to desired consistency. Taste for salt. Add the onions and rewarm. Serve.

Serves 4 to 6.

* *To deglaze: Add and boil rapidly for one minute, scraping bits from pan.*

PICKLED BABY BEETS AND EGGS

The beautiful ruby colors of this traditional combination set off its flavor. A handsome appetizer, lunch dish or snack.

1 pound baby beets, trimmed
  and scrubbed
1 small onion, very finely sliced
4 to 6 shelled hard-boiled eggs
2 tablespoons brown sugar
2 to 3 tablespoons red wine
  vinegar
4 whole cloves
pinch of salt and pepper

Cook the beets in enough boiling water to cover them until they are just tender. Reserve the cooking water and skin the beets. Strain the cooking water to remove any residue, then add the sliced onion and the whole hard-boiled eggs, the brown sugar, vinegar, cloves and a pinch of salt and pepper. Taste and adjust the seasonings.

Marinate for one to four days in the refrigerator. The deep ruby color of the beet marinade will become more intense and color the eggs to a rosy hue. This pickled dish stores well in the fridge.

CHILI PEPPERS

Not all chili peppers are hot and there is much more to their flavor than most of us realize—until we try them! While there probably isn't a country in the world that doesn't grow some kind of pepper as a condiment, spice or vegetable, many of us are just discovering the diversity of their flavors and shapes. Each chili type has a distinctive taste, from mild and rich to spicy and piquant to fiery hot. Here are recipes for enjoying all their flavors.

CHILI-CHEESE PAN SOUFFLÉ

A light and satisfying one-dish meal. Try it with a simple salad and warm, crusty bread.

¼ cup butter, melted and cooled
5 eggs
¼ cup flour
½ teaspoon baking powder
¼ teaspoon salt
½ cup chopped poblano chilis that have been roasted and peeled
1 cup cottage cheese (small curd)
8 ounces Jack cheese (or half Cheddar, half Jack)

Preheat oven to 350°.

Melt the butter in an 8-inch square pan. In a bowl lightly beat the eggs. Add the flour, baking powder and salt and blend until well mixed. Add the melted butter from the baking pan, the chilis, cottage cheese and Jack cheese. Mix until just blended. Pour into the pan in which the butter was melted. Bake in a preheated 350° oven for 35 minutes or until puffed and golden brown. Serve immediately.

Serves 6 to 8.

CHILI-OLIVE DIP

2 cans sliced black olives
8 to 10 poblano chilis, roasted,* peeled and chopped, about 1 cup
3 scallions, cut into 1-inch lengths
1 small tomato, quartered and drained
2 tablespoons salad oil
2 tablespoons cider vinegar
1 tablespoon chopped fresh cilantro leaves

Combine all ingredients in a blender and process until barely blended. Serve as a dip with sliced jicama and/or tortilla chips.

Makes about 2 cups.

* To roast chilis: Put chilis on a baking sheet. Place under preheated broiler about 4 inches from heat; turn them until blistered and charred, about 10 or 12 minutes. Enclose the peppers in a paper bag and let them steam until they are cool to handle. Starting at the blossom end, peel the peppers under cold water, discarding the stems, ribs and seeds.

HOT PEPPER JELLY

Delicious with cream cheese or on dark breads. Also good with cold-cut sandwiches or with baked ham.

> 5 medium-sized jalapeño peppers
> 2 small green bell peppers and 1 small red bell pepper (or an additional green one)
> 6 cups sugar
> 2 cups cider vinegar
> 1 six-ounce bottle or 2 three-ounce pouches liquid pectin
> several drops of red or green food coloring (optional)
> 6 half-pint canning jars or jelly jars

Wear rubber gloves and split open the hot peppers; remove and discard seeds and coarsely chop peppers. Repeat with bell peppers. Place all the peppers in a blender or food processor and purée until liquefied. (Add a bit of the vinegar if needed to make blending easier.) You should have about 1 cup.

In a large (5-quart) pot combine the puréed pepper with the sugar and vinegar over high heat. Bring to a rolling boil, stirring constantly, add the pectin, and return to a rolling boil. Boil for exactly one minute.

Remove from heat, add coloring if desired, skim and immediately pour into half-pint canning jars; complete the seals by boiling water bath processing for 10 minutes or sealing with paraffin wax.

Makes about 6 cups.

SPICY MEXICAN FONDUE

This dish is easy to put together quickly for a special treat or unexpected company, and everyone will enjoy it.

> one 15½-ounce can refried beans
> ½ pound (2 cups) grated Cheddar cheese
> 2 tablespoons butter or margarine
> 2 tablespoons minced scallion
> 1 clove garlic, minced
> ½ teaspoon Worcestershire sauce
> 1 cayenne pepper, seeded and chopped
> 1 seeded and chopped Anaheim or poblano pepper
> ¾ cup beer at room temperature

Combine all the ingredients except the beer in a heavy saucepan. Heat, stirring, until mixture is heated through, 10 to 15 minutes. Add beer gradually, stirring. Transfer to a fondue pot.

Accompany with tortilla chips or fresh vegetables for dipping.

Makes about 3 cups dip.

FOUR-ALARM CAYENNE PEPPER CHICKEN

The peppers season this dish beautifully but they are very hot. Warn diners not to eat them!

1 large whole chicken breast, skinned and boned, cut into 2-inch-long strips (about 1¼ to 1½ pounds)
1 tablespoon each cornstarch and soy sauce
1 egg white, slightly beaten
1 clove garlic, minced
cooking oil
12 dried cayenne peppers, halved and seeded
garnish : ½ cup dry roasted peanuts

SEASONING SAUCE :
1 teaspoon cornstarch
½ teaspoon grated fresh ginger (or ¼ teaspoon dried)
1 tablespoon sherry
2 tablespoons soy sauce
1½ teaspoons sugar
2 teaspoons red wine vinegar
1 teaspoon chili paste with garlic
2 teaspoons hoisin sauce
3 tablespoons chicken stock
1 teaspoon sesame oil

Prepare seasoning sauce by mixing together ingredients. Set aside.

Place chicken in a small bowl with cornstarch, soy sauce, egg white and garlic. Mix well and refrigerate for ½ hour.

Heat 2 tablespoons of cooking oil in a wok or heavy skillet. Add peppers and cook until dark — about 15 seconds. Lower heat, add chicken and cook through — about 2 or 3 minutes. Add seasoning sauce and cook another minute until well combined and hot. Serve, sprinkling with the peanuts, over hot fluffy rice.

Serves 4.

TEX-MEX CASSEROLE

This savory vegetable casserole is also very good the next day and makes a great lunch "leftover" meal.

4 ears fresh corn
butter
3 medium onions, sliced thin
6 or 7 medium zucchinis, sliced thin
1 large seeded, chopped, *drained* tomato
8-ounce can of tomatillos, drained and diced, or 1 cup fresh
2 Anaheim chilis, seeded and chopped
1 small jalapeño chili, seeded and chopped
1½ teaspoons fresh oregano, or ¾ teaspoon dried
salt, pepper, butter
1 cup grated Jack or Cheddar cheese

Preheat oven to 350°.

Using a very sharp knife, cut the corn from the cobs and set aside. In a large skillet, heat a tablespoon of butter and sauté the onions and zucchini for 3 to 5 minutes over medium heat. Remove. Add another tablespoon or two of butter and sauté the tomato and tomatillos for 3 to 5 minutes. Lightly grease a large casserole. Combine all the vegetables together; season with oregano, salt and pepper. Sprinkle with the grated cheese and dot with a little butter.

Bake the casserole, covered with its lid or with foil, for 30 minutes. Then run it briefly under the broiler to brown the top before serving.

Serves 4 to 6.

Salsa de Tomatillo

For a mild but piquant alternative to red tomato-based salsa, try this authentic and handsome green salsa. It's delicious with cold chicken, enchiladas, chips, etc.

2 pounds fresh tomatillos
½ cup water
½ teaspoon salt
¼ cup scallion, cut into 1-inch lengths
¼ cup fresh cilantro leaves
3 or 4 fresh jalapeño peppers, trimmed, cored, seeded
1 teaspoon minced garlic
½ teaspoon sugar
1 teaspoon lemon juice

Peel husks off tomatillos: wash off sticky residue in cold water.

Bring water and salt to a boil in a medium saucepan. Add tomatillos and cook covered until softened, about 5 minutes. Remove from heat and transfer to a food processor or blender. Add remaining ingredients and process to a thick purée. Taste for seasoning.

Sauce can be stored tightly covered in refrigerator for up to 3 days.

Makes 3 to 4 cups.

Salsa Fresca

Perfect for dips or to spoon over barbecued chicken or hamburgers.

4 small tomatoes, finely chopped
9 scallions, white part only, chopped in 1-inch lengths
1 clove of garlic, puréed
2 or 3 fresh serrano or jalapeño peppers, seeded and finely chopped
3 or 4 mild green chilis roasted, peeled, seeded, finely chopped
1 tablespoon chopped fresh cilantro
½ teaspon salt
pinch of pepper and sugar
1 teaspoon red wine vinegar

Combine all ingredients in a small bowl.

Note: Salsa is always best served fresh but may be kept for up to 2 days in refrigerator. It may get watery after storage; pour off any excess liquid before serving.

Makes 3 to 4 cups.

Chili Pear Relish

2½ pounds fresh pears, peeled, cored and finely sliced
1 cup brown sugar, firmly packed
¾ cup cider vinegar
5 tablespoons water
3 tablespoons chopped onion
1 teaspoon salt
1 teaspoon chili powder
¼ teaspoon cumin
2 tablespoons chopped pimiento
4 tablespoons chopped green Anaheim chilis *and*
1 serrano or jalapeño chili, seeded and finely chopped

Place all ingredients in a heavy 4- or 5-quart saucepan; stir to blend. Cover and cook the mixture over low heat for 30 minutes. If liquid has evaporated, add an additional ¼ cup water. Uncover and continue cooking for about 25 minutes or just until the mixture is thickened, stirring frequently. Serve cold. Keeps well in the refrigerator.

Makes approximately 4 cups.

EDIBLE FLOWERS

For the last few years, we've been captivated by wonderful flower tastes and colors, and inspired by the discovery that traditions of flower cookery go back to Roman times. After many growing trials and even more enjoyable cooking sessions, we have assembled this collection of the most useful and pleasurable edible flower recipes. We invite you to enjoy these recipes as much as we did in creating them for both the eye and palate.

NASTURTIUMS

CENTERFOLD NASTURTIUM SALAD

Both the leaves and blossoms have a fine watercress-like flavor.

Arrange 15 rinsed nasturtium leaves around the outside edge of a large flat plate. Lay 15 clean nasturtium flowers on top of the leaves, with their stems pointing to the center of the dish.

Working toward the center of the plate, next add a layer of very finely sliced sweet onions, then a layer of three very thinly sliced tomatoes and a layer of 2 or 3 large stalks of celery, finely chopped. Continue the layers as above until the dish is full. Sprinkle ½ cup of vinaigrette dressing (page 87) over the salad and garnish by sprinkling with a finely chopped hard-boiled egg. Borage flowers also make a nice garnish.

Cover the salad and refrigerate for several hours to let the nasturtiums and other flavors blend before serving.

Serves 4.

NASTURTIUM SHRIMP APPETIZER SALAD

2 teaspoons fresh lemon juice
¼ cup olive oil
salt and freshly ground pepper
1 cup cooked, shelled shrimp, chopped coarsely
2 tablespoons finely chopped onion
1 small tomato, cubed
½ avocado, peeled and cubed
lettuce leaves
2 tablespoons chopped nasturtium leaves
nasturtium flowers

Place lemon juice in small bowl. Whisk in the oil and season to taste with salt and pepper. Add the shrimp and onion and toss lightly. Let stand for 15 minutes to let flavors blend.

Add in the tomato, avocado and chopped nasturtium leaves. Mound on lettuce leaves and surround with fresh whole nasturtium flowers.

Serves 2 to 4.

NASTURTIUM SANDWICH FILLINGS

Add chopped clean nasturtium flower petals to your favorite tuna, egg or chicken salad sandwich fillings. They will give them a colorful lift and tangy bit of flavor. Blend nasturtium petals with cream cheese or butter and spread on thin slices of dark bread for savory snacks or appetizers.

NASTURTIUM VINEGAR

Combine 12 rinsed and dried nasturtium flowers and 1 cup of white wine vinegar in a glass jar with a screw-on lid. (If the lid is metal, line it with plastic wrap.) Put on the lid and let the flowers steep for about 3 weeks to a month. Strain the jewel-colored vinegar through cheesecloth and rebottle in a pretty bottle. Use the vinegar with a fine oil for a really delicious vinaigrette dressing.

Makes 1 cup.

PICKLED NASTURTIUM SEEDS

Collect nasturtium seeds when they become small and green and soak them in brine to cover, made from 1 quart water mixed with ½ cup salt. Renew the brine every three days until enough seeds have been collected.

Drain the seeds and pack them in small jars. Pour over enough boiling white wine vinegar to cover, seal and store for about a week before using. Use as a piquant substitute for capers in any recipe.

BORAGE

BORAGE AND CUCUMBERS IN SOUR CREAM DRESSING

3 long cucumbers
salt
½ pint sour cream or plain yogurt
2 tablespoons rice vinegar
½ teaspoon celery seed
¼ cup chopped scallions
1 teaspoon sugar
salt and freshly ground pepper
¼ cup very young borage leaves, finely chopped
garnish: borage flowers or chive blossoms

Wash, score and very thinly slice the cucumbers. Salt lightly and let stand in a colander for 30 minutes to drain. Rinse off the salt and pat dry with paper towels.

In a bowl, mix remaining ingredients, adding salt and pepper to taste. Add cucumbers and toss lightly. Garnish with borage flowers or chive blossoms. Refrigerate 1 hour before serving.

Serves 6 to 8.

Vichyssoise with Borage Flowers

6 large leeks, cleaned, tops trimmed, leaving only white part
4 tablespoons butter
4 cups chicken broth
3 medium potatoes, peeled and diced
2 tablespoons chopped very young borage leaves
1 cup sour cream (or ½ cup plain yogurt and ½ cup sour cream)
salt and white pepper
nutmeg
garnish: borage flowers

Slice the leeks into thin slivers. Melt butter in a large saucepan; add leeks and sauté over moderate heat until softened. Add chicken broth, potatoes and chives. Bring to a boil and simmer covered for 35 minutes or until potatoes are tender. Strain the broth. Purée the vegetables in a food processor or blender. Combine broth and purée. Chill overnight.

Just before serving stir in 1 cup sour cream (or ½ cup yogurt and ½ cup sour cream). Add salt, pepper, and a dash of nutmeg. Serve in chilled soup bowls; garnish with borage flowers.

Serves 6 to 8.

Borage Garnishes

Lavender-blue borage blossoms make attractive edible garnishes. Try them on grapefruit halves or orange sections and in any fruit salad; in potato or green salad or with sliced hardboiled eggs. Use them as decorations on frosted cakes or frozen in ice cubes and added to herb teas.

Borage Tea

A very traditional herb tea.

In a warmed teapot put ½ cup finely chopped borage leaves and flowers. Pour in 2 cups of freshly made boiling water. Cover and let steep for 5 to 6 minutes. Strain and serve hot with honey and lemon if desired.

Borage tea is also refreshing as an iced tea; make it stronger and serve over ice cubes that have blue borage flowers frozen into their centers for an especially cooling drink.

Serves 2.

CALENDULAS

ORANGE-CALENDULA DROP COOKIES

6 to 8 fresh calendula blossoms
½ cup butter, room temperature
½ cup white sugar
grated rind of 2 oranges
2 tablespoons orange juice concentrate at room temperature
1 teaspoon vanilla
2 eggs, lightly beaten
2 cups flour
2½ teaspoons baking powder
¼ teaspoon salt
1 cup almond halves

Preheat oven to 350°. Lightly grease 2 cookie sheets.

Rinse calendulas. Pull off petals and set aside. In a bowl cream butter, sugar and orange rind until fluffy. Add orange juice concentrate and vanilla. Mix in eggs, stirring until blended.

Sift together flour, baking powder and salt. Blend calendula petals and dry ingredients into creamed mixture. Drop dough by teaspoonfuls onto cookie sheet. Press an almond half into each cookie. Bake 12 to 15 minutes until golden brown.

Makes 3 to 4 dozen.

CALENDULA CONFETTI EGGS
Scrambled Eggs with Calendula Petals

8 eggs
6 tablespoons milk
pinch of nutmeg
salt and pepper to taste
2 tablespoons butter
petals only from five good-sized calendula flowers, rinsed and chopped
4 slices of toast or muffins, buttered
optional topping: several tablespoons grated cheese

Beat the eggs with the milk and seasonings. Melt the butter in a skillet and scramble the eggs. Just before eggs are done, stir in the chopped petals. Pile the eggs on top of buttered toast or muffins and serve right away, topping with cheese if desired.

Serves 4.

CREAMY CALENDULA SOUFFLÉ

This blender soufflé goes together quickly and has a fine color and flavor. Good both fresh from the oven and cut into squares the next day.

- 1 tablespoon soft butter
- 2 tablespoons grated Parmesan cheese
- 6 eggs
- ½ cup half-and-half cream
- ¼ cup grated Parmesan cheese
- 1 teaspoon prepared mustard
- ½ teaspoon salt
- ⅛ teaspoon cayenne pepper
- dash of nutmeg
- ½ pound sharp Cheddar cheese, cut into small pieces
- 10 ounces cream cheese, cut into small pieces
- ½ cup calendula petals as well as whole flowers to use as garnishes

Preheat oven to 375°.

Spread butter inside a 5-cup soufflé dish or other deep baking dish or 5 or 6 individual baking dishes. Sprinkle with the 2 tablespoons Parmesan cheese.

In a blender or food processor, place eggs, remaining ¼ cup Parmesan cheese, the half and half, mustard, salt, pepper and nutmeg. Process or whirl until smooth.

Add Cheddar cheese piece by piece, while motor is running. Add cream cheese and process for 5 seconds. Stir in calendula petals. Pour soufflé mixture into prepared dish.

Bake for 45 to 50 minutes (bake individual soufflés 15 to 20 minutes). Tops should be golden brown and slightly cracked; don't overbake. Serve immediately, garnishing with whole calendula flowers.

Serves 5 or 6.

CURRY RISOTTO WITH CALENDULA PETALS

- 6 tablespoons butter or margarine
- 1½ onions, finely chopped
- 2 teaspoons curry powder
- 1 cup uncooked rice
- 1 rounded tablespoon tomato paste
- 2 cups chicken stock
- bouquet garni: 2 sprigs parsley, 1 bay leaf, 2 sprigs fresh thyme or ½ teaspoon dried leaf thyme; can be tied in cheesecloth or placed in a metal tea infuser
- ½ cup calendula petals
- salt and freshly ground pepper
- garnish: 1 cubed avocado, pimiento strips or diced red peppers, calendula petals

In a heavy-bottomed saucepan with lid, melt 4 tablespoons of the butter. Add onions and sauté until softened. Add curry powder and rice and stir over medium heat for 2 minutes. Add tomato paste, chicken stock and bouquet garni. Cover tightly and simmer until tender, about 20 minutes. Remove bouquet garni. Just before serving add remaining 2 tablespoons butter and the calendula petals. Season with salt and pepper to taste. Heat through and serve garnished with avocado cubes, pimiento or red pepper strips and a sprinkling of calendula petals.

Serves 6.

Tangerine Cole Slaw with Calendula Flower Garnish

2 cups chopped, unpeeled red apple
2 tablespoons freshly grated tangerine peel
3 cups fresh tangerine segments, seeded *
2 tablespoons chopped green bell pepper
5 cups finely shredded cabbage
12 calendula flowers, washed and dried

DRESSING:
⅓ cup sour cream
¼ cup mayonnaise
1 tablespoon each lemon juice and vinegar
2 tablespoons honey
½ teaspoon each mustard and celery seed
½ teaspoon salt
⅛ teaspoon freshly ground pepper
garnish: calendula blossoms

Combine apple, tangerine peel, tangerine segments and chopped green pepper with cabbage in a large bowl. Remove calendula petals from flowers and add the petals to the salad.

Blend together dressing ingredients and pour over cole slaw. Toss lightly to mix well. Taste for additional seasoning; i.e., lemon juice, salt and pepper. Chill thoroughly. Garnish with whole yellow and orange calendula blossoms.

Serves 6 to 8.

* *Canned, drained mandarin orange segments may also be used, with grated orange peel substituted for tangerine peel.*

Chive Blossoms

Potato Salad with Chive Blossom Mayonnaise

2 pounds small, thin-skinned boiling potatoes
⅓ cup white wine (or rice) vinegar
¼ teaspoon salt
pinch of pepper
¼ teaspoon dry mustard
¼ teaspoon sugar
1 tablespoon grated onion

DRESSING:
1 cup prepared mayonnaise (or use half mayonnaise and half fresh plain yogurt)
1 clove garlic, crushed
3 tablespoons chive blossom florets and chopped leaves
1 heaping teaspoon grated lemon rind
2 teaspoons lemon juice
1 tablespoon each finely chopped parsley, green pepper
salt and pepper to taste
garnish: whole chive blossoms

Boil or steam potatoes until tender when pierced. Let cool slightly, then peel and slice. Heat vinegar with salt, pepper, mustard and sugar and sprinkle over potatoes. Mix in grated onions. Toss well and cool. Combine the dressing ingredients. Mix with potatoes. Add salt and pepper to taste. Garnish with whole chive blossoms and serve.

Serves 6 to 8.

Cheesy Chive Blossom Omelet

4 eggs
1 teaspoon water
¼ teaspoon salt, or to taste
⅛ teaspoon white pepper
1 teaspoon chopped fresh parsley
1 tablespoon sweet butter
3 young chive blossoms, broken into individual florets
2 tablespoons grated Swiss cheese
garnish: whole chive blossoms

In a small bowl whisk together eggs, water, salt, pepper and parsley. Melt butter in a 10-inch omelet pan over high heat until butter sizzles but has not started to brown. Pour in egg mixture, shaking pan immediately. With the flat side of a fork stir eggs and move and tilt pan in a circular motion until eggs begin to set. Sprinkle chive florets and cheese down the center; allow cheese to melt slightly, then fold omelet over and serve. Garnish with whole chive blossoms.

Serves 2.

Chive Blossom Vinegar

Fill a clean glass or plastic jar half full of mature chive blossoms which have not started to fade in color. Fill the jar with white distilled vinegar (the mildest flavored) making sure all the blossoms are covered. Cap with a non-metal lid and set in the sun. In about 2 or 3 weeks the chive flowers will have transferred their lovely color and flavor to the liquid. Strain through cheesecloth and dilute with more vinegar if you find it too strong. Decant into any attractive glass jars or bottles and seal with corks or non-metal tops.

Anise Hyssop

Anise Hyssop-Honey Butter

½ cup honey
¾ cup butter, room temperature
2 tablespoons chopped anise hyssop flowers

Combine honey and butter, mixing until well creamed. Blend in flowers.

Serve in a crock to use on pancakes, waffles or muffins. Store in the refrigerator.

Anise Hyssop Flower Drop Cookies

1 bunch anise hyssop flowers
3 eggs
1 cup sugar
½ teaspoon vanilla
2 cups flour
1 teaspoon baking powder
½ teaspoon salt

Preheat oven to 325°. Line 2 to 3 cookie sheets with aluminum foil; lightly grease.

Strip petals off anise hyssop flowers to measure ⅓ cup. Chop fine. With an electric mixer, beat eggs until thick and lemon-colored. Add sugar and flower petals and beat for 5 minutes. Add vanilla.

Sift together flour, baking powder and salt and add to egg mixture. Continue beating for 5 minutes longer. Drop batter by teaspoonfuls onto lined cookie sheets, spacing well apart. Bake until they begin to color, about 12 to 15 minutes.

Makes about 3 dozen.

MARINATED ANISE HYSSOP BAKED CHICKEN

The flavors of ginger and anise hyssop add a fine perfume to this simple main dish.

> **1 cut-up frying chicken, 2½ to 3½ pounds**
>
> **MARINADE:**
> **1 tablespoon chopped fresh ginger**
> **1 cup finely chopped anise hyssop leaves and flowers**
> **1 teaspoon cinnamon**
> **3 cloves garlic, minced**
> **3 tablespoons oil**
> **3 tablespoons soy sauce**

Mix marinade ingredients together and spread evenly over the chicken pieces right in the baking pan. Let marinate for 2 to 4 hours. Bake at 375° for 45 minutes to an hour or until chicken is cooked and browned. Serve with fluffy rice.

Serves 3 or 4.

ANISE HYSSOP TEA

Harvest long sprigs of anise hyssop leaves. Rinse, shake off excess water and hang to dry in a cool dark place (or dry in a dehydrator). They make a naturally sweet-flavored and refreshing hot or iced tea with a licorice flavor.

BERRIES SERVED WITH ANISE HYSSOP CREAM

Rinse, drain and chill 1 box of blueberries or raspberries. Blend a little honey to taste with ½ cup of yogurt, sour cream, or slightly whipped cream and 1 tablespoon minced anise hyssop. Spoon sauce over berries and garnish with anise hyssop flowers.

Serves 2.

SPECIAL TREASURE CHINESE BEEF WITH ANISE HYSSOP

The anise hyssop adds a subtle flavor that enhances all the other ingredients in this simple and delicious dish. Serve with fluffy white rice.

> 1 pound flank steak, cut acoss the grain into strips 3 inches long and ½ inch wide.
> ½ cup chopped anise hyssop flowers and leaves
> ⅓ cup soy sauce
> 1 tablespoon brown sugar
> 2 tablespoons sherry
> 2 tablespoons vegetable oil
> ¼ cup chicken broth
> 2 teaspoons cornstarch dissolved in 2 teaspoons water

Combine flank steak with chopped anise hyssop, soy sauce, brown sugar, sherry. Marinate several hours.

Remove meat from marinade, reserving any remaining sauce. Heat wok or large skillet, add oil and stir-fry meat quickly over medium-high heat until brown. Add chicken broth and remaining marinade and heat through. Stir in cornstarch mixture and cook, stirring until thickened.

Serves 4 to 6.

LEMONY ANISE HYSSOP TEA BREAD

The delicate flavors of anise and lemon will please those who do not like things too sweet.

> 2 cups flour
> 1 tablespoon baking powder
> ½ teaspoon salt
> ½ cup butter at room temperature
> ½ cup sugar
> grated rind of one lemon
> ⅓ to ½ cup anise hyssop flowers, finely chopped
> 2 eggs, beaten
> ½ cup lemon juice
> ½ cup chopped walnuts

Preheat oven to 350°. Grease and flour an 8½ × 4½ × 2½-inch bread or loaf pan.

Sift together flour, baking powder and salt in a bowl. In another bowl, cream butter with sugar until fluffy, then add lemon rind, chopped flowers and the beaten eggs, and beat mixture just until thoroughly combined. Stir in the lemon juice. Gradually mix in the dry ingredients and nuts, mixing until blended. Spoon into prepared pan and bake 50 to 55 minutes. Cool on rack. Best-tasting when wrapped in foil and sliced the next day. Keeps well.

Makes one loaf.

Johnny Jump-Ups

Johnny Jump-Up Flowers as Edible Garnishes

These dainty, pretty flowers have a myriad of uses. Here is a list of some of our favorite ways of enjoying them as "edible art."

— Set off a simple dessert by combining fresh pineapple and kiwi slices with a small amount of kirsch and decorate with johnny jump-up blossoms. Also try this with bananas and oranges (or tangerines).

— Perk up everyday cottage cheese and fruit salads by garnishing with johnny jump-ups.

— For a romantic effect, decorate any frosted cake with fresh johnny jump-up flowers.

— Surround scoops of orange, pineapple or lemon sherbet with johnny jump-up flowers and mint leaves.

— Circle any pale-colored dip or spread, e.g., avocado, cream cheese, tuna, etc., with johnny jump-up flowers.

— Garnish plates of smoked or poached salmon with johnny jump-up flowers to set off its rosy color.

— Marinated vegetable salads, deviled eggs, and potato salads look appetizing when garnished with johnny jump-ups.

— Any green salad will be appetizing with an additional garnish of johnny jump-ups. Add them along with some mandarin orange slices for a particularly delicious effect.

Grapefruit Cups Cassis

This recipe is as attractive as it is appetizing and is especially nice for brunch. Have the grapefruits on the table when everyone sits down to whet appetites.

4 grapefruits
⅔ cup crème de cassis or any good fruit liqueur
2 oranges, sectioned
1 cup strawberries, sliced
garnish: johnny jump-up flowers, mint leaves

In a sawtooth fashion, cut the grapefruits in half. Carefully section out the fruit, reserving shells for serving. Cut out and discard white membrane. Peel oranges, removing membrane; cut into sections. Place grapefruit and orange sections in a bowl, pouring off excess juice. Pour crème de cassis (or other fruit liqueur) over fruit and chill for at least one hour.

At serving time add the berries to grapefruit and oranges. Spoon the fruit mixture into reserved grapefruit shells or use glass bowls. Garnish with johnny jump-ups and sprigs of mint leaves.

Serves 8.

HERB AND FLOWER CHEESE TERRINE

Lovely and special party fare. Decorate the top and sides of the terrine with extra flowers, then serve it in slices to show off the layered effect.

**1 pound very soft cream cheese
¾ pound very soft sweet butter, at room temperature
1 cup grated Asiago chese (or use very fresh Parmesan)
2 large cloves garlic, finely chopped
¾ cup fresh basil, finely chopped, or 6 tablespoons dried
¼ cup fresh oregano, finely chopped, or 2 tablespoons dried
2 teaspoons Worcestershire sauce
¾ teaspoon white pepper
¾ cup toasted pine nuts (or pecans can be used)
¾ cup finely chopped fresh parsley
salt to taste, as desired
1¾ to 2 pounds Italian Provolone cheese, thinly sliced
25 to 30 johnny jump-up flowers, more if you have them, and additional edible flowers if available.**

Cream together the softened cream cheese, Asiago or Parmesan cheese and butter. Add the garlic, basil, oregano, Worcestershire sauce, and pepper and combine thoroughly. Add the pine nuts and chopped parsley and mix again (we suggest using your hands and literally "squooshing" it together!). Salt mixture to taste, if desired.

Butter a bread or terrine pan. Line with waxed paper or parchment paper. Layer bottom of pan with Provolone cheese slices, then add a layer of the soft cheese mixture and a sprinkling of the johnny jump-up flowers. Continue to alternate layers of Provolone, soft cheese mixture and flowers. Try to get about 5 layers for a nice effect.

Refrigerate overnight. Remove from refrigerator and let stand about 15 minutes before turning out on serving platter. Remove paper and garnish with more johnny jump-ups (and other additional edible flowers if available). Serve in slices.

Serves 15 to 20.

CULINARY HERBS

Cooking with fresh herbs is a delight and having them in abundance is luxury. As every herb grower knows, it is a great pleasure simply having them in the kitchen and garden to taste and smell their varied flavors and fragrances.

There are really no "strict rules" you need to consider in using herbs in cooking; the best ones are those you make up yourself, reflecting your own preferences.

Remember that herbs should enhance rather than overpower a dish. Add in small amounts, tasting as you go. It is best to add the more delicate herbs in the last five to ten minutes of cooking a dish, so you don't cook away their volatile oils and flavors. A scissors is the best tool for snipping fresh-cut herbs into your dish. Dried herbs are generally about twice as strong as fresh ones, so measure accordingly in converting from one form to another. Frozen herbs can be easily crumbled into a dish with the fingers.

A good way to try an unfamiliar herb on your taste buds is to snip a small amount of it into a bit of butter or a little cottage cheese. Let the mixture sit for about an hour to absorb the flavor, then try it on a plain cracker.

In planning your kitchen garden, plant culinary herbs as close to the kitchen as possible so you'll find them convenient to use in everyday cooking.

AN HERBAL
SALT SUBSTITUTE

To use instead of salt.

> 2 tablespoons dried dill leaf, finely chopped
> 1 teaspoon dried oregano leaves, finely crumbled
> 2 tablespoons onion powder or finely ground onion flakes
> 1 teaspoon celery seed
> 2 tablespoons toasted sesame seeds
> ¼ teaspoon grated dried lemon peel
> pinch of freshly ground pepper
> ½ teaspoon paprika
> ½ teaspoon garlic powder

Combine all ingredients in a small bowl and blend well. Put into a shaker with large holes. Store in a cool, dark place. Serve on vegetables, salad, buttered bread, etc.

GOLDEN BROWN CHIVE ROAST POTATOES

These crispy browned potatoes end up in handsome accordion shapes.

6 large baking potatoes
cold water
¼ cup (½ stick) butter, melted
½ teaspoon salt
4 tablespoons freshly chopped chives
½ cup of your favorite shredded or grated cheese
3 tablespoons bread crumbs

Preheat oven to 350°.

Peel potatoes and place in a bowl of cold water until ready to use. Dry thoroughly and cut a thin slice off the long side of each potato so it can sit flat. With a sharp knife, cut vertical slits from the top *almost* to the bottom of each potato, being careful not to cut it through.

Dip the cut potatoes in melted butter and sprinkle with salt. Bake on a foil-covered baking sheet for 1½ hours, basting with the remaining butter. The potatoes will turn a crisp golden brown and the slits will open in accordion fashion as they bake. In the last 15 minutes, combine the chives, cheese and bread crumbs and stuff them into the slits in the potatoes, to form a delicious topping. Serve immediately and expect the diners to ignore everything else on their plates.

Serves 6.

BASIC HERBED SALAD DRESSING FOR SALAD LOVERS

If you are not in the habit of making your own dressing, try this and be converted!

¼ cup wine vinegar
1 to 2 tablespoons lemon juice (fresh squeezed is best)
½ teaspoon sugar
½ teaspoon mild prepared or dijon-style mustard
2 to 3 teaspoons freshly chopped herbs*
½ cup good light olive oil
1 garlic clove

Blend all ingredients, except the garlic, thoroughly with a whisk or fork. Let the flavors blend at room temperature. Rub the salad bowl with the freshly cut halves of the garlic clove. Add washed and dried assorted crispy greens. Pour over the whisked-up dressing, toss and serve promptly.

Dresses a salad for 4 to 6.

* Good combinations are: equal parts basil, parsley, thyme and oregano or equal parts basil, savory, thyme, or equal parts thyme, chives, basil.

Compound Herb Butters

Keep on hand to dress up any plain grilled meat, chicken or fish, as an emergency sauce for pasta, to swirl into soups and stews, or to serve on hot breads.

> 1 medium scallion, finely chopped
> ¼ cup packed fresh basil or parsley, or cilantro leaves, finely chopped
> 1 teaspoon fresh lemon juice
> ¼ teaspoon salt
> ¼ teaspoon freshly ground white pepper
> several drops hot pepper sauce
> ¼ teaspoon dry mustard
> ¼ pound (1 stick) unsalted butter, softened

Use a food processor to combine or mash together by hand the scallion and herbs. Add the lemon juice, salt and pepper, hot sauce, mustard and butter and mix together very thoroughly. Transfer to waxed paper or plastic wrap and roll into a log about 1 inch wide and 7 inches long. Freeze until ready to slice and use.

Makes ¼ pound.

Herbed Bread Sticks

These simple-to-make appetizers are really delicious; we usually double the recipe so we can satisfy everyone's desire for more.

> 1 small loaf extra-thin-sliced white bread
> ¼ teaspoon salt
> ⅛ teaspoon pepper
> 1 large clove garlic, chopped
> 2 tablespoons finely chopped fresh parsley
> 2 tablespoons finely chopped fresh chives
> 1 tablespoon fresh summer savory or sweet marjoram (or 1 teaspoon dried)
> ½ cup butter, softened
> 4 tablespoons freshly grated Parmesan cheese
> melted butter

Preheat oven to 350°.

Trim the crusts from bread slices. Roll the bread slices flat with a rolling pin. Mash together the garlic, salt and pepper. Add the herbs and blend in the butter. Add cheese. Spread each slice of bread with the herb-butter mixture and roll up tightly, securing with toothpicks. Place on a baking sheet seam side down. Brush lightly with melted butter.

Bake 12 to 15 minutes until lightly browned, turning them several times while baking. Serve hot.

Makes 20-24 depending on size of loaf of bread.

OLD-FASHIONED HERBED CHICKEN AND DUMPLINGS

A hearty one-dish meal that will please both gourmets and "just-plain-food" folks. The steaming, fluffy parsley dumplings make everyone happy!

1 large 3- to 4-pound chicken, cut into serving pieces
3 whole cloves
8 to 12 baby onions (or 2 large onions, peeled and cut into quarters)
4 to 6 carrots, peeled and cut into quarters
8 to 10 fresh mushrooms, cleaned
2 large cloves garlic, chopped
1 teaspoon fresh sweet marjoram, finely chopped
1 teaspoon fresh thyme, finely chopped
3 sprigs fresh parsley, chopped
2 teaspoons salt
1 teaspoon freshly ground pepper
1 cup dry white wine
1 cup sour cream (or ½ cup sour cream and ½ cup fresh plain yogurt)

DUMPLINGS:
1 cup biscuit mix
2 tablespoons freshly chopped parsley
6 tablespoons milk

Preheat oven to 375°.

Butter a deep, oven-proof casserole dish that can also be put on stove-top burner.

Remove excess skin and fat from chicken pieces and place in casserole. Stick the cloves into 4 of the onion pieces. Add all vegetables, herbs, and seasonings, and pour the wine over all. Cover the casserole and bake in oven until the chicken is just barely tender, about 35 to 45 minutes. *Do not overcook!*

Make dumplings: combine biscuit mix with chopped parsley. Stir in milk with fork until well moistened. Stir sour cream into the casserole, and remove it from the oven and place over medium heat on stove-top burner. When the chicken and vegetables are just bubbling, drop the dumplings from a teaspoon all around the edge of the casserole. Simmer 10 minutes uncovered and then 10 minutes covered.

Serve right away, giving each diner a generous portion of stew and several fluffy dumplings.

Serves 4 to 6.

HERBED FLOUR

2 cups flour
2 tablespoons minced dried herbs, a combination of several of the following: thyme, marjoram, savory, basil, dill, parsley
½ teaspoon salt
freshly ground pepper

Combine all the ingredients and keep the herbed flour in a glass jar to use for dusting chicken or fish and for using in biscuits, quiche or pizza crusts, crêpe batter or herb breads and muffins. For longer storage, keep the jar in the refrigerator.

Makes 2 cups.

HOMEMADE DILLED MUSTARD

This sweet and pungent homemade mustard is delicious with cold cuts, grilled sausages or cheese.

1 cup dry mustard
2 teaspoons salt
1 cup cider vinegar
¾ cup sugar
2 tablespoons finely chopped fresh dill leaf
¼ cup water
2 eggs, slightly beaten

Mix all of the ingredients except the eggs. Cover and let stand 4 to 6 hours. Pour into the top of a double boiler and heat gently. Add the eggs, stirring constantly. Cook over simmering water 10 minutes until thickened. Pour into containers, cover and chill. Keep refrigerated.

DILLED SUMMER VEGETABLES

A particularly fine combination of flavors and colors.

Steam together equal parts of fresh cut green beans, carrot chunks, and summer squash cut into chunks. Season the hot, tender vegetables with salt, pepper and butter to taste, then sprinkle very liberally with finely chopped fresh dill leaf. Mix and serve.

ROSY DILLED RADISH DIP

A rosy-pink all-purpose dip.

1 eight-ounce or large size package of cream cheese at room temperature
1 tablespoon lemon juice
1 tablespoon fresh dill or 1 teaspoon dried
1 clove garlic, minced
1 cup finely chopped radishes
garnish: nasturtium or calendula blossoms, or more sliced radishes

Combine all ingredients well. Refrigerate for several hours before serving with crackers, chips or vegetable strips. Garnish with nasturtium or calendula flowers, or sliced radishes.

Makes about 2 cups.

Noisettes d'Agneau Persillade
Parsleyed Lamb Chops

This dish is classic, elegant and easily prepared. It is especially good made with fresh single-leaf parsley.

8 lamb chops sliced 1½ inches thick
salt and pepper
3 tablespoons butter
3 tablespoons finely chopped shallots or scallions
⅓ cup dry white wine or dry vermouth

PERSILLADE TOPPING:
½ cup bread crumbs
6 tablespoons fresh parsley, minced
2 tablespoons minced scallions or shallots
1 clove garlic, minced
3 tablespoons melted butter (or margarine)
1 teaspoon grated lemon rind
garnish: lemon slices

Prepare *persillade* topping: Combine bread crumbs, parsley, scallion or shallot, garlic, melted butter and lemon rind. Set aside.

Carefully remove the bones from lamb chops. Leave all but a thin layer of fat on. Sprinkle with salt and pepper. Melt butter in a large heavy skillet. Stir in the shallots or scallions and sauté lightly. Add lamb chops and brown on all sides, then cook about 5 to 8 minutes or longer, depending on the doneness desired. Remove lamb chops to a baking dish.

Spoon off excess fat from skillet. Add wine and cook, scraping up all particles in bottom of pan. Simmer 3 to 4 minutes until wine is reduced to half. Pour mixture over lamb. Spread a portion of the *persillade* topping on each chop, pressing it down slightly. (May be prepared ahead to this point.)

Bake 5 minutes at 350° or until heated through. Garnish with lemon slices and serve.

Serves 4.

CREAMY PARSLEY SALAD DRESSING

½ cup salad oil
⅓ cup fresh parsley leaves, minced
3 scallions, finely chopped
½ teaspoon salt
½ teaspoon freshly ground black pepper
2 tablespoons sour cream or fresh plain yogurt.

Combine all ingredients except sour cream in food processor, blender or bowl and mix well. With machine running (or using whisk if preparing by hand), slowly add sour cream, blending thoroughly. Refrigerate in an airtight jar.

Makes about 1 cup.

GORGONZOLA AND FRESH THYME SAUCE FOR PASTA

1½ cups heavy cream
6 ounces top quality *aged* Gorgonzola cheese
1 teaspoon fresh thyme (or ½ teaspoon dried)
2 or 3 generous grates fresh nutmeg or ⅛ teaspoon ground nutmeg
Salt and white pepper

Combine cream and crumbled Gorgonzola, fresh thyme, nutmeg. Cook gently until it reduces by one-fourth. Add salt and white pepper to taste. Toss with steaming pasta.

You may add sliced, peeled apples and walnuts to the above. Offer extra nutmeg.

Serves 2.

CLAM COQUILLES OREGANO

An unusual and savory appetizer.

2 tablespoons olive oil
1 onion, finely minced
2 small cloves garlic, finely minced
2 eight-oz. cans minced clams (drain and reserve juice)
1 tablespoon fresh parsley, finely chopped
2 teaspoons fresh oregano, finely chopped
½ cup bread crumbs
⅛ teaspoon pepper
olive oil
6 slices bread, toasted and quartered

TOPPING:
2 tablespoons bread crumbs, mixed with
2 tablespoons freshly grated Parmesan cheese

Preheat oven to 375°.

In a small skillet heat oil, add onions and garlic and sauté until softened. Remove from heat. Add clams, herbs, crumbs and pepper. Add enough of the reserved clam juice to moisten.

Place a spoonful on toast squares. Arrange on a baking sheet. Sprinkle with topping mixture, then sprinkle with a few drops of olive oil. Bake 10 minutes, then place under broiler for several minutes to lightly brown.

May be prepared one day ahead or frozen up to the point of baking.

Makes 24.

ITALIAN GREEN BASILS

*A*romatic fresh basil leaves are one of the most indispensable summer flavors for both gardeners and cooks. Basil is an easy to grow and vigorous herb, producing abundant fragrant harvests of leaves. It is delicious fresh and easy to freeze or dry for later enjoyment. We were delighted to discover that the many regions of Italy have developed very fine-flavored but distinctly different strains of sweet green basil. Use them for these recipes or use any green basil fresh from your garden or greengrocer.

CLASSIC FRESH PESTO SAUCE

One of the best ways to keep an abundant basil harvest. Can be frozen for later use, too!

> 3 cups loosely packed fresh basil leaves, washed and drained
> ½ cup chopped fresh parsley
> 3 large cloves of garlic (more if you love it)
> ½ cup pine nuts (or pecan meats)
> 1 cup freshly grated Parmesan or Asiago cheese (use *fresh* cheese)
> 1 teaspoon fresh or ½ teaspoon dried oregano
> ½ teaspoon fresh ground pepper (or to taste)
> ½ to ⅔ cup fruity olive oil
> salt to taste

Combine all the ingredients in a food processor or blender, adding enough olive oil to make a thick smooth sauce. Add salt to taste. Add to fresh hot buttered pasta. Toss to combine and serve right away with fresh garlic bread and a crisp salad.

Serves 4.

CREAMY PESTO–TOPPED FISH

Simple, succulent and delicious!

> 6 slices or filets of firm white-fleshed fish
> 1 tablespoon lemon juice
> ¼ cup pesto sauce (see recipe at left)
> 3-ounce package cream cheese, softened
>
> TOPPING:
> ¼ cup each grated Parmesan cheese, bread crumbs

Preheat oven to 400°.
Butter a 9 × 13-inch baking pan. Sprinkle fish pieces with lemon juice and place in pan. Combine pesto sauce and cream cheese thoroughly and spread on top of the fish pieces evenly. Combine bread crumbs and Parmesan cheese and sprinkle over pesto. Bake 10 minutes or until the fish flakes easily with a fork.

Serves 6.

PESTO STUFFED TOMATOES

Cook one cup orzo or other rice-shaped pasta according to package directions. Stir in ⅓ cup pesto sauce (see recipe). Fill 4 hollowed-out, medium-sized tomatoes with mixture. Top with grated Parmesan cheese and bake at 375° for 15 minutes. Serve hot with barbecued steaks or chicken.

Serves 4.

BASIL BUTTER

Use on cooked vegetables or pasta, or on top of poached eggs or fish.

½ cup butter at room temperature
2 teaspoons lemon juice
1 tablespoon chopped fresh parsley
3 tablespoons chopped fresh basil
salt and pepper

Cream the butter and beat in the lemon juice, a little at a time. Beat in the parsley and basil and season with salt and pepper. Serve in a serving dish or place on wax paper and roll into a log. Chill overnight and slice to serve.

Makes ½ cup.

STUFFED BRANDIED MUSHROOMS

1 pound large fresh mushrooms
½ cup melted butter
2½ tablespoons butter
½ cup minced shallots or scallions
1 large mild Italian sausage
    (about 5 or 6 ounces)
3 ounces cream cheese, softened
⅓ cup bread crumbs
⅓ cup finely chopped fresh basil
3 tablespoons brandy
salt and pepper
garnish: fresh basil leaves

Preheat oven to 375°.

Wash the mushrooms, pat dry and remove stems. Finely chop stems. Squeeze in a towel to remove excess moisture; set aside. Dip each mushroom cap in the ½ cup melted butter, coating all sides and the cavity well. Place the buttered caps on a baking sheet and set aside.

In a skillet, melt the 2½ tablespoons butter. Add chopped mushroom stems and scallions and sauté until the moisture has evaporated. Transfer to a bowl.

Remove casing from sausage. Place in skillet over moderate heat. Crumble with a fork and sauté until browned. Drain off fat. Add to mushroom stems. Blend in cream cheese, bread crumbs, basil and brandy. Add salt and pepper to taste. Fill each mushroom cap with the mixture, mounding it.

Bake mushrooms for 10 minutes, watching them carefully to prevent scorching. Serve on a platter garnished with fresh basil leaves.

The filled, unbaked mushroom caps may be prepared one day ahead.

Makes 20 to 24 for appetizers; serves 4 as a main course.

BASIL PRESERVED
IN PARMESAN CHEESE

This mixture can be used to flavor vegetable soups, or, as a quick pasta sauce, just combine it with butter, garlic and fresh parsley. Delicious in anything that you want to have a taste of basil and as easy to use as peanut butter.

1 sterilized pint jar with lid
2 cups tightly packed, washed
 and dried basil leaves
1 cup *freshly* grated Parmesan or
 Asiago cheese
salt and pepper
olive oil

Very finely mince the basil leaves. Mix thoroughly in a bowl with the cheese.

Pour a fine sprinkle of salt and pepper in the bottom of the jar. Add a ½-inch layer of the basil-cheese mixture. Press down to ⅓ inch thick.

Add another thin sprinkle of salt and pepper and another layer of basil mixture. Continue packing the layers tightly until you have the jar full.

Top the jar with ¼ inch of olive oil. Seal and put in the refrigerator to use as needed. It will keep practically indefinitely.

Makes about 1½ cups.

ROMAN-STYLE
STUFFED ARTICHOKES

This simple recipe shows off the flavor of artichokes beautifully while making a handsome and elegant presentation at the table.

4 medium artichokes
juice of 1 large or 2 small lemons
½ cup boiling water
¼ cup olive oil
garnish: sprigs of fresh basil

STUFFING MIXTURE:
½ cup grated Parmesan cheese
½ cup fine bread crumbs
1 clove garlic, minced
2 tablespoons chopped fresh basil
2 tablespoons minced parsley
salt and pepper to taste

Preheat oven to 350°. Mix together the stuffing ingredients and set aside.

Discard the stem and outer leaves of the artichokes and trim the tops. Parboil in a large pot of salted water to cover for 15 minutes. Drain upside down; cool.

Spread the artichoke leaves apart. Using a small spoon or non-aluminum melon ball scoop, scrape out the fuzzy inedible (choke) part of the artichoke. Sprinkle inside with lemon juice. Spoon the stuffing into the center of each artichoke and between the leaves.

Pour the ½ cup boiling water into a baking dish that will be just large enough to hold artichokes close together. Arrange artichokes right side up, side by side in dish, and drizzle with the ¼ cup olive oil. Cover with foil. Bake artichokes for 1 hour, basting occasionally with additional olive oil.

Serve warm; garnish with sprigs of basil.

Serves 4.

THAI CHICKEN WITH BASIL

Quick, spicy, and delicious!

3 to 4 tablespoons finely chopped
   Anaheim or "California" green
   chilis, seeded
2 tablespoons soy sauce
1 teaspoon sugar
1 teaspoon vinegar
½ cup chopped fresh lettuce-leaf
   basil leaves
1 teaspoon chopped fresh mint
   leaves (or ½ teaspoon dried)
½ teaspoon cornstarch
3 tablespoons vegetable oil
2 whole chicken breasts (1 pound
   each), boned, skinned, cut into
   ¼-inch strips, 2 inches long
2 cloves garlic, minced
1 large onion, halved, then sliced
   ¼-inch thick

Mix together chilis, soy sauce, sugar,
vinegar, basil, mint and cornstarch;
set aside.

Heat 2 tablespoons of the oil in a
large frying pan or wok over high
heat. When oil is hot add chicken
and garlic. Cook, stirring constantly,
until meat loses its pinkness, about 4
minutes; turn out of pan and keep
warm.

Heat another tablespoon of oil in
pan, then add onion; cook stirring
for 2 minutes. Add chili mixture and
return chicken and juices to pan;
cook stirring until sauce thickens
slightly. Transfer to a serving platter
and keep warm. Serve with hot
fluffy rice.

Serves 4 to 6.

BUTTERFLIED BASIL SHRIMP

*Use as appetizers or for 4 luscious salad
servings.*

1 pound large raw shrimp, shelled
   and deveined, leaving tails on.
   Butterfly shrimp by cutting
   along the inner curve.
⅓ to ½ cup olive oil
1 large clove garlic, finely
   chopped
½ cup packed fresh basil, finely
   chopped
3 tablespoons dry vermouth
3 tablespoons lemon juice
salt and pepper to taste
garnish: fresh lemon slices,
   whole fresh basil leaves

Heat oil over medium heat. Add
garlic, chopped basil, vermouth and
lemon juice. Add shrimp and sauté,
stirring for 2 to 4 minutes—until
they all turn pink. Salt and pepper to
taste. Transfer to a bowl and chill to
let flavors blend for an hour or two.
Return to room temperature to
serve.

Skewer with garnishes to serve as
appetizers. Or, to serve as 4 salads:
line 4 salad plates with soft lettuce
leaves, arrange shrimp and sauce on
top and garnish with the lemon
slices and basil leaves.

SCENTED BASILS

Among our most popular specialty varieties are the rare and scented basils: lemon, opal, cinnamon and anise. All are true basil varieties with the different flavor characteristics their names describe. They are easily grown, handsome plants in the garden, and their intense scents make them quite irresistible in the kitchen.

SCENTED BASIL VINEGAR

This is our favorite way of enjoying the flavors of the scented basils year-round. If put up in fall at the end of the basil season, bottles make welcome holiday presents. Anise and cinnamon basil vinegars are a lovely soft pink color, opal basil is a deep rich garnet, and lemon basil makes a champagne-colored vinegar.

Pack large one-gallon plastic or glass jars half full with rinsed and air-dried leaves of any one of the scented basils. (Stems and flowers are okay; no need to separate leaves.) Fill up the jar with plain white vinegar heated almost to a boil (White vinegar is mildest and lets basil flavors come through.) Cover with plastic wrap and lid and allow to infuse for a month or two in a cool place. Strain vinegar through cheesecloth into small decorative jars or clean wine bottles and seal.

SCENTED BASIL VINEGAR CHICKEN

An easy-to-prepare dinner dish with a subtle taste and heavenly smell.

½ stick butter
1 large onion, finely chopped
4 skinned (and boned if desired) chicken breast portions
½ cup of any scented basil vinegar
¾ cup sour cream

Melt butter and sauté the onion until soft and translucent. Add the chicken breast pieces and sauté over low heat until the chicken is done—no pink shows when sliced. Remove the chicken pieces to a warm serving dish and keep warm. Add the basil vinegar to the pan and simmer, stirring in all the bits from the pan for about 5 minutes to reduce the sauce. Add the sour cream, mix and heat through but do not boil. Pour the sauce over the chicken breasts and serve over fluffy rice or noodles.

Serves 4.

SCENTED BASIL JELLIES

These delicate jellies are unusual, delicious and easily made. Their clear jewel-like colors of rose pink, deep garnet and champagne are quite beautiful. You'll find they are delicious with cream cheese and crackers or bagels and they make wonderful presents for others — and yourself!

> **1½ cups packed fresh anise, cinnamon, opal or lemon basil (choose one)**
> **2 cups water**
> **2 tablespoons rice vinegar**
> **pinch of salt**
> **3½ cups sugar**
> **3 ounces liquid pectin**

Wash and dry the basil in paper towels. Finely chop or process it in a food processor. Put the basil in a large saucepan, and crush the leaves, using the bottom of a glass. Add the water, bring slowly to a boil and boil for 10 seconds. Remove the saucepan from the heat; cover and let set for 15 minutes to steep.

Strain 1½ cups of liquid from the saucepan and pour through a fine strainer into another saucepan. Add the vinegar, salt and sugar and bring to a hard boil, stirring. When the boil can't be stirred down, add the pectin. Return to a hard boil that can't be stirred down and boil for exactly 1 minute, then remove saucepan from heat.

Skim off the foam and pour the hot jelly into hot, sterilized eight-ounce jelly jars. Leave ½-inch headspace and seal at once with sterilized two-piece lids, or melted paraffin.

Makes 4 eight-ounce jars.

SCENTED BASIL HONEY

Chop the fresh leaves of one of the scented basils and wrap in a cheesecloth pouch. Add to a jar of mild honey. Cover jar and place in gently boiling water for 45 minutes. Remove from water and cool. Store about 10 days to let the flavors blend. Remove herb; strain if desired.

ANISE BASIL

ANISE BASIL BAKED FISH

Before baking or poaching fish steaks, thick filets or whole fish, lay them on a bed of freshly picked anise basil. The herb will impart a subtle and delicious flavor in the cooking process. The anise basil can also be used when barbecuing fish; just tie a bunch together and use as a "brush" when basting the fish with butter or oil.

ANISE BASIL TOMATO SAUCE

Use anise basil in any tomato-sauce-based Italian dishes. You'll find it adds delicate flavors of both anise and fennel that enhance the tomato sauce in a particularly delicious way.

ANISE BASIL CHUTNEY

Good with pork and chicken or turkey.

one 28-oz. jar of mincemeat
1½ cups drained crushed pineapple (1 lb. 4 oz. size can)
1 teaspoon curry powder
2 tablespoons cider vinegar
1 cup tightly packed anise basil
  leaves; after measuring, finely
  chop

In a heavy saucepan, combine all
ingredients and bring to a boil.
Lower heat and simmer uncovered
for 20 minutes or until thickened.
Pour into clean glass jars and refrigerate to let flavors blend for several
hours. Store in refrigerator.

Makes about 6 cups.

MELAMBROSIA FRUIT

*A well-balanced and elegant combination
of flavors that is a refreshing and satisfying dessert after a rich meal.*

½ fresh pineapple cut into 1-inch
  cubes
1 cantaloupe cut into 1-inch
  cubes
1 teaspoon lemon juice
2 tablespoons honey
2 teaspoons Grand Marnier (or
  any good orange-flavored
  liqueur)
2 teaspoons finely minced fresh
  anise basil
1 teaspoon finely minced fresh
  mint

Combine fruits in an attractive serving bowl. In a separate bowl, whisk
together the lemon juice, honey,
orange liqueur, anise basil and mint.
Toss with the fruit and serve.

Serves 6.

CINNAMON BASIL

TIPSY CINNAMON BASIL CHUTNEY

*A delicious palette of flavors; makes
wonderful gifts too!*

2 cups fresh or frozen sliced
  peaches (mangos may be substituted, if desired)
½ cup canned "water packed"
  pineapple chunks (bite-size),
  drained
1 small unpeeled orange, quartered, seeded, sliced thin
2 tablespoons lemon juice
¾ cup sugar
2 tablespoons chopped cinnamon
  basil
2 tablespoons light rum

In a saucepan combine peaches (or
mangos), pineapple, orange, lemon
juice and sugar. Mix well. Bring to
boil, then simmer uncovered over
low heat until thick (approximately
30 to 40 minutes). During the last 5
minutes of cooking, add cinnamon
basil. Remove from heat and stir in
the rum. Spoon at once into hot
sterilized jars. Process the jars in a
boiling water bath for 15 minutes,
or store in refrigerator.

CINNAMON BASIL CHICKEN & NUT SPREAD

A wonderful spread for afternoon teas, receptions, or any time you want something special.

½ cup sweet butter, softened
1 tablespoon honey
⅔ cup very finely chopped cooked white meat of chicken
1 tablespoon washed, drained and finely chopped cinnamon basil leaves
6 tablespoons toasted almonds, finely chopped
salt to taste
very thin slices of bread

Blend softened butter and honey until smooth. Stir in chicken, cinnamon basil and almonds. Salt to taste, remove crusts from the bread and cut into shapes if desired. Spread with chicken mixture for open-face sandwiches. Recipe can be doubled.

Serves 4.

MULLED CINNAMON BASIL PUNCH

A very fragrant and satisfying punch served either hot or cold.

4 cups apple juice
¼ cup sugar
⅓ cup cinnamon basil leaves or to taste
1 cinnamon stick
½ teaspoon whole cloves
2 limes, thinly sliced

Heat apple juice, sugar, cinnamon basil, cinnamon stick and cloves, stirring until mixture comes to a boil. Reduce heat, stir in limes and simmer 5 minutes. Strain into mugs and serve hot, or cool and serve over ice for a cold drink.

APPLES BAKED WITH ORANGE JUICE & CINNAMON BASIL

4 large baking apples
½ lemon
½ cup chopped pitted dates
2 tablespoons raisins
1 tablespoon chopped cinnamon basil
peel of 1 large orange
juice of 4 or 5 oranges
additional fruit juice, if needed
sugar

Preheat oven to 350°.

Core apples almost through. Pare a 1-inch strip of skin from around the top. Rub cut surfaces with lemon, dropping a few drops into the core. Combine dates, raisins and cinnamon basil and fill center of apples with mixture. Arrange apples in a baking dish just large enough to hold them. With a vegetable peeler, carefully remove the orange part of the orange peel. Cut peel into very fine strips. Squeeze orange juice; pour around apples, using enough to make about ½-inch of juice in the dish. Drop cut strips of orange peel into juices.

Bake, basting with juices every 10 or 15 minutes, for 50 minutes or until apples are tender when pierced with a knife.

Sprinkle with a little sugar and broil with surface of fruit four inches below surface of heat. Baste with remaining syrup until glazed.

Best made ahead of time; serve at room temperature. A dollop of sour cream or *fresh* yogurt is a nice garnish.

Serves 4.

LEMON BASIL

LEMON BASIL HERBED RICE

2 tablespoons butter
3 tablespoons finely chopped
onions
1 cup uncooked rice
¼ cup chopped lemon basil
1 small bay leaf
1 tablespoon chopped parsley
several drops Tabasco sauce
2½ cups chicken stock
salt and white pepper to taste

Preheat oven to 400°.

Melt the butter in an ovenproof saucepan. Add the onion and cook until it is softened and translucent— about 5 minutes. Add the rice and cook, stirring, over medium heat for 3 minutes. Add lemon basil, the bay leaf, parsley, Tabasco and stock. Bring to boil, cover tightly and transfer to the oven. Bake 20 to 25 minutes or until rice is tender. Add salt and white pepper to taste. With a fork, fluff rice and serve.

Serves 3 or 4.

CHICKEN SCALLOPINI À LA LEMON BASIL

4 skinned and boned chicken or
turkey breast portions
salt and freshly ground pepper
butter or margarine
olive oil
½ cup dry wine
1 tablespoon lemon juice
½ cup heavy cream
⅓ cup lemon basil leaves, finely
chopped
½ teaspoon fresh thyme leaves
(or ¼ teaspoon dried)
2 teaspoons minced fresh parsley
garnish: lemon basil leaves and
fresh lemon slices

Place chicken pieces between sheets of plastic wrap and pound with the edge of a mug or a wooden mallet evenly and gently until they are ¼ inch thick. Dredge each piece with salt and pepper. In a large skillet, heat 1 tablespoon each butter and oil. When butter is melted, add as many chicken pieces as will fit without crowding and cook quickly for a minute or two on each side, or until the chicken loses its pinkness inside. Remove chicken pieces to a hot platter and keep warm. Cook rest of chicken pieces, adding more butter and oil as needed and remove to a warm platter. (May use 200° oven.)

Add the wine and lemon juice to the pan and cook over medium heat, stirring to blend in browned particles and juices. Boil until reduced by about half. Add the cream, lemon basil, thyme and parsley, boil until sauce thickens slightly. Pour any juices that collected on the chicken meat platter into the skillet. Taste sauce for seasoning, adding salt and pepper if needed. Pour sauce over the sautéed chicken and garnish with lemon basil leaves and lemon slices.

Serves 4.

LEMON BASIL MARINADE FOR GRILLED FISH OR CHICKEN

⅓ cup lemon juice
2 teaspoons dijon mustard
½ cup finely chopped fresh
  lemon basil
3 scallions, including some of the
  green tops, sliced thin
2 tablespoons dry white wine
½ teaspoon salt
¼ teaspoon freshly ground
  pepper
1 cup olive oil

In a bowl combine all ingredients except oil. Whisk in oil gradually until mixture is thoroughly blended. Marinate fish or chicken for 3 hours or overnight before grilling.

Wonderful with foods cooked over mesquite charcoal.

Makes 1½ cups.

FRESH FRUITS WITH LEMON BASIL DRESSING

This recipe is good for both the eyes and the appetite.

Assemble four servings of the following combination of fruits:

grapefruit sections
orange sections
strawberries
kiwis, peeled and sliced
avocado, peeled and sliced

DRESSING:
2 tablespoons fresh lemon basil
  leaves, chopped
juice of ½ orange
juice of ½ lemon
juice of ½ lime
1 cup yogurt or sour cream
2 tablespoons honey

Prepare fruits and arrange on individual plates or a platter. Refrigerate.

In a blender or food processor, combine the lemon basil leaves with the citrus juices. Process until puréed. Add yogurt or sour cream and honey and mix to blend. Taste and correct seasonings with more citrus juice or honey to suit your tastes. Spoon dressing over fruits and serve.

Serves 4.

PURPLE OPAL BASIL

CONFETTI RICE WITH TWO BASILS

A festive herbed rice dish that jazzes up any summer meal.

- 1 cup uncooked rice
- 2 large ears fresh corn (or use one 10-oz. package frozen corn, defrosted, when fresh corn isn't available)
- ½ cup finely chopped celery or fresh fennel
- ¼ cup chopped purple opal basil
- 1 red pepper or pimiento, finely chopped
- 2 tablespoons chopped parsley

VINAIGRETTE DRESSING:
- 2 scallions, finely chopped
- 3 tablespoons finely chopped lettuce-leaf green basil
- ¼ cup lemon juice
- ⅓ cup olive oil
- ½ teaspoon salt
- ¼ teaspoon pepper

Cook rice in salted boiling water according to package directions. Do not overcook. Drain. Cook the fresh corn until tender. (For frozen corn, cook for two minutes, drain.) Cut corn kernels off cob and combine with rice. Combine vinaigrette dressing mixture in a jar. Shake well and pour over rice/corn mixture. Gently mix in celery or fennel, purple basil, red pepper and parsley. Season with additional salt and pepper to taste. Serve at room temperature.

Serves 6.

CHEDDAR CRISPS

We haven't met anyone yet who didn't enjoy snacking on these. They make good appetizers, too.

- 8 ounces grated Cheddar cheese
- ½ cup butter at room temperature
- ½ teaspoon Tabasco sauce
- 1 teaspoon prepared mustard
- 1 cup flour
- 2 tablespoons chopped purple opal basil
- 1½ cups Rice Crispies cereal

Preheat oven to 350°.

In a large bowl mix cheese, butter, Tabasco and mustard. Blend in flour and chopped opal basil. When combined, stir in Rice Crispies. Blend carefully and shape into small balls. Place on a greased baking sheet and flatten with the bottom of a lightly floured glass. Bake 15 minutes. Serve hot.

The crisps may be made several days ahead and stored in an airtight container or frozen. Reheat 5 minutes when needed.

Makes 40.

Recipe Index

An Invitation to Our Readers

We'd like to send you a complimentary copy of our complete 104-page seed catalog. We feature over 350 varieties of fine vegetables, culinary herbs and specialty flower seeds as well as collections of seeds for different cuisines. The catalog includes helpful growing information and carefully chosen recipes for enjoying the garden's bounty.

Simply fill in your name and address on the back of this card and return it to us. We will mail your catalog promptly via first class mail.

Best Regards,

Renee Shepherd

An Invitation to Our Readers

We'd like to send you a complimentary copy of our complete 104-page seed catalog. We feature over 350 varieties of fine vegetables, culinary herbs and specialty flower seeds as well as collections of seeds for different cuisines. The catalog includes helpful growing information and carefully chosen recipes for enjoying the garden's bounty.

Simply fill in your name and address on the back of this card and return it to us. We will mail your catalog promptly via first class mail.

Best Regards,

Renee Shepherd

SHEPHERD'S
GARDEN SEEDS

Please send a complimentary copy of your catalog.

Name _____

Address _____

City _____ State _____ Zip _____

6116 Highway 9, Felton, California 95018, (408) 335-5400

SHEPHERD'S
GARDEN SEEDS

Please send a complimentary copy of your catalog.

Name _____

Address _____

City _____ State _____ Zip _____

6116 Highway 9, Felton, California 95018, (408) 335-5400